PSYCHOLOGY AND CONSUMER CULTURE

PSYCHOLOGY AND CONSUMER CULTURE

The Struggle for a Good Life in a Materialistic World

Edited by

Tim Kasser and Allen D. Kanner

AMERICAN PSYCHOLOGICAL ASSOCIATION • WASHINGTON, DC

Published by
American Psychological Association
750 First Street, NE
Washington, DC 20002
www.apa.org

To order   Tel: (800) 374-2721; Direct: (202) 336-5510
APA Order Department   Fax: (202) 336-5502; TDD/TTY: (202) 336-6123
P.O. Box 92984   On-line: www.apa.org/books/
Washington, DC 20090-2984   E-mail: order@apa.org

In the U.K., Europe, Africa, and the Middle East, copies may be ordered from
American Psychological Association
3 Henrietta Street
Covent Garden, London
WC2E 8LU England

Typeset in Goudy by MacAllister Publishing Services, Indianapolis, IN

Printer: Sheridan Books, Ann Arbor, MI
Cover Designer: Naylor Design, Washington, DC
Technical/Production Editor: Casey Ann Reever

The opinions and statements published are the responsibility of the authors, and such opinions and statements do not necessarily represent the policies of the American Psychological Association.

Library of Congress Cataloging-in-Publication Data
Psychology and consumer culture : the struggle for a good life in a
   materialistic world / edited by Tim Kasser and Allen Kanner.
      p. cm.
   ISBN 1-59147-046-3
      1. Consumption (Economics)—United States—Psychological aspects. 2.
   Materialism—Psychological aspects. 3. Acquisitiveness. 4. Identity
   (Psychology) 5. Consumers—Psychology. I. Kasser, Tim. II. Kanner,
   Allen.
   HC110.C6P76 2003
   306.3—dc21   2003004965

British Library Cataloguing-in-Publication Data
A CIP record is available from the British Library.

Printed in the United States of America on recycled paper
First Edition

To the memory of Erich Fromm, who pointed the way toward an understanding of psychology and consumer culture

CONTENTS

CONTRIBUTORS

Charles E. Couchman, Department of Clinical and Social Sciences in
     Psychology, University of Rochester, Rochester, NY

Mihaly Csikszentmihalyi, Peter F. Drucker Graduate School of
     Management, Claremont Graduate University, Claremont, CA

Edward Diener, Department of Psychology, University of Illinois,
     Urbana–Champaign

Joan DiFuria, Money, Meaning & Choices Institute, Kentfield, CA

Ronald J. Faber, School of Journalism and Mass Communications,
     University of Minnesota, Minneapolis

Stephen Goldbart, Money, Meaning & Choices Institute, Kentfield, CA

Jeffrey L. Greenberg, Department of Psychology, University of Arizona,
     Tucson

Priscilla J. Hambrick-Dixon, School of Education, Hunter College, City
     University of New York

Dennis T. Jaffe, Money, Meaning & Choices Institute, Kentfield, CA

Allen D. Kanner, private practice, Berkeley and Sebastopol, CA

Tim Kasser, Department of Psychology, Knox College, Galesburg, IL

Jean Kilbourne, Visiting Research Scholar, Wellesley Centers for Women,
     Wellesley, MA

Jeffrey Kottler, Department of Counseling, California State University,
     Fullerton

Velma D. LaPoint, Department of Human Development and
     Psychoeducational Studies, Howard University, Washington, DC

Diane E. Levin, Department of Education, Wheelock College, Boston, MA

Susan Linn, Judge Baker Children's Center, Boston, MA

Marilyn Montgomery, Department of Psychology, Florida International University, North Miami

Thomas A. Pyszczynski, Department of Psychology, University of Colorado at Colorado Springs

Michael D. Robinson, Department of Psychology, North Dakota State University, Fargo

Erika L. Rosenberg, Health Psychology Program, University of California, San Francisco

Richard M. Ryan, Department of Clinical and Social Sciences in Psychology, University of Rochester, Rochester, NY

Kennon M. Sheldon, Department of Psychology, University of Missouri, Columbia

David Shepard, Department of Counseling, California State University, Fullerton

Emily G. Solberg, Department of Psychology, University of Illinois, Urbana–Champaign, Champaign, IL

Sheldon Solomon, Department of Psychology, Skidmore College, Saratoga Springs, NY

Renée G. Soule, Berkeley, CA

Deborah Du Nann Winter, Department of Psychology, Whitman College, Walla Walla, WA

ACKNOWLEDGMENTS

Thanks to Russell Bahorsky, Lansing Hays, Ed Meidenbauer, Yelba Quinn, and Casey Reever at the American Psychological Association for their help and guidance. Thanks to Knox College for material support. Thanks to Gary Ruskin at Commercial Alert for introducing us to each other. Thanks to Mary Gomes, Larry Jaffe, and Virginia Kasser for their generosity.

PSYCHOLOGY AND CONSUMER CULTURE

1

WHERE IS THE PSYCHOLOGY OF CONSUMER CULTURE?

TIM KASSER AND ALLEN D. KANNER

Many economists agree that the growth of free-market economies rides in part on increasing profit and that increasing profit depends on rising consumption. It should therefore not be surprising that as the capitalistic economic system has continued its spread across the globe, consumerism, profit's younger twin, has followed close behind, entering more and more aspects of more and more people's lives. We are now continually exposed throughout our lifetimes to messages suggesting that we should work hard to earn money, which we can then spend on products and services, or which we can invest to make even more money. These messages have for years come from government agencies and educational systems, as well as cultural role models and myths; today, such messages are ever-present in the multiple media to which most of us are exposed. Advertising has even recently spread beyond its traditional media of television, radio, and print to unusual places like the computer, toilet stalls, and food packaging.

There is no escaping the fact that modern day humans live in a culture of consumption. This is true whether they reside in the largest metropolitan areas of North America or Southeast Asia or whether they are Amish or

Bhutanese people living on the global economy's figurative edges. To ignore the place of consumerism in people's lives would be tantamount to ignoring that humans are begotten through parents who raise them.

A STRANGE ABSENCE

Given that consumption is an integral part of human life, a casual observer might expect that the field of psychology would be replete with investigations and theories about how consumption and the material world relate to the human psyche. Other fields have certainly recognized and publicized some of the problems associated with consumer culture: The literatures in anthropology, sociology, and economics provide many excellent forays into the topic. In contrast, a PsychLIT search on related topics in psychology turns up very little that is relevant. Other professional organizations have taken activist stances on topics related to consumerism. For example, the American Academy of Pediatrics has recommended that children's exposure to the media be severely limited (American Academy of Pediatrics, 1999), and dental associations have opposed exclusive cola contracts between schools and soda companies ("Dental Association," 2000). In contrast, the American Psychological Association has only recently begun to consider the ethics of marketing to children (Clay, 2000).

Clearly, the discipline of psychology has been largely reticent about consumer culture. Although some consumer psychologists have conducted interesting research and devised intriguing theories about human consumption (Jacoby, Johar, & Morrin, 1998), issues of consumerism, commercialization, and materialism have generally not entered the science or practice of psychology as key variables to be understood. Why has consumer culture been generally ignored in psychology? We suggest three main reasons.

First, psychology has been relatively slow to focus on variables outside of the individual person. Instead, the field has traditionally been concerned with manipulating, measuring, and understanding intrapsychic processes or individuals' behavior. Historically, when psychologists do look outward, they tend to investigate relatively proximal variables, such as immediate environmental contingencies as they impinge on behavior or small groups such as families and parent–child dyads. Broader, more distal environmental factors such as socioeconomic status, qualities of neighborhoods, and individualism–collectivism have only recently entered the mainstream of academic psychology, having earlier been seen as the province of our colleagues in sociology, anthropology, economics, and cultural studies. Obviously, the culture of consumption is a very broad distal factor, one that psychologists, by temperament, training, and historical practice, have largely ignored.

A second reason why psychology has overlooked the culture of consumption can be attributed to its collusion with this very culture. Ever since early 20th-century psychologists such as H. L. Hollingworth, Walter Dill Scott, E. K. Strong, Jr., and John B. Watson used the discipline's methods and theories to invent a science of advertising and spread the consumerist mind-set (Buckley, 1982; Kuna, 1976, 1979), thousands of psychologists have followed in their footsteps, working for marketing and advertising companies and developing consulting firms to enhance and direct the consuming behavior of children and adults. Because much of the research conducted by these psychologists is privately funded by corporations, little of this knowledge base has made its way into the public domain of psychology, in no small part because the results are closely guarded as trade secrets. Furthermore, industry-based psychologists are unlikely to examine the problems associated with consumption, because doing so might be seen as "biting the hand that feeds me," a behavior oftentimes quickly extinguished, even in psychologists.

Psychology's ambivalent attitude toward social policy and social criticism is a third reason for its hesitance to explore the culture of consumption. Some thinkers hold that psychologists, and scientists more broadly, should limit their roles to investigation and forgo addressing the social policy implications of research (Kendler, 1999). Two anecdotes specific to the case of materialism are relevant here. First, one of us had an article on materialism rejected by a journal in part because a reviewer (and the journal editor) felt that (to paraphrase) the findings were clearly anti-capitalistic and the research was of the sort that the conservative Right frequently points to when it wants to cut funding. Second, one of our young colleagues in Europe, after presenting a poster about the problems associated with materialism, was told by one of his elders that he "should not be doing that kind of research." Although we have no data to back up our guess, we doubt that these types of comments are regularly made to psychologists who study depression, stereotyping, or cognitive development. To the extent that young psychologists are discouraged, censored, and even punished when they explore controversial issues related to capitalism and consumption, a disservice is done both to the field and to the people whose lives psychology is meant to improve.

THE PRESENT BOOK

The purpose of this book is to encourage psychologists to consider and investigate the manifold ways in which consumer culture influences our lives. To this end, we have brought together a group of excellent authors to write 13 chapters that touch on a range of topics spanning a variety of areas in psychology. Chapters in part I, Problems of Materialism, Capitalism, and Consumption, describe how these issues are important for understanding personal, social, and ecological well-being. In part II, Theoretical Approaches, contributors demonstrate that consumption-related issues can be fruitfully explored through extant psychological theories. The third part of the book,

Clinical Issues, describes the treatment of acquisitive desire and the problems of compulsive consumption and sudden wealth syndrome. The chapters in part IV, The Influence of Commercialism on Child Development, explore issues regarding childhood obesity and violence, children of color, and female adolescents.

At either the beginning or end of a volume such as this one, editors are typically expected to summarize or integrate the chapters; to reflect on and point out the underlying, common themes that run through many chapters; and to suggest important directions for future research and applications. Although we recognize the use and value of such an exercise for some books, we have resisted the temptation to follow this practice, as we believe that it would actually work against our primary purpose for the book. Pointing out common themes or arguing for particular directions to pursue is akin to pruning the branches of a young tree so as to give it a particular shape and to increase the probability that certain, particularly promising, branches bear fruit. Such pruning is useful for trees that have strong root systems but have not yet reached their full maturity, and thus for topics that have been fairly well-studied but are ready to move on to a next stage.

As we have pointed out, however, issues surrounding consumerism have yet to be widely recognized, studied, or even accepted by psychology; all we have at this point is a small bud with a nascent root system. For this reason, we believe that it would be premature to use our own limited and somewhat biased viewpoints to suggest particular themes or directions for the future; the ideal shape of this particular tree is not yet evident. Instead, we need to facilitate the expansion of roots and branches, because the plant is still young and in need of nurturing. By the same token, we need to increase the likelihood that the topic of consumerism becomes deeply rooted in the field of psychology so that it may bear bountiful fruit later. Indeed, we believe that the chapters in this book suggest many possibilities for future research as well as for changes in clinical practice and public policy.

We have therefore assembled these chapters in an attempt to reflect the diversity of disciplines, methodologies, theories, and topics present in the field of psychology, in the hope of showing that much of what psychologists do can be readily applied to issues concerning consumption. The chapters touch on many different subdisciplines of psychology, including clinical, developmental, social–personality, and cultural psychology, as well as religious, industrial–organizational, and other disciplines. The methods used include surveys, experiments, diary studies, phenomenological interviews, clinical cases, and the psychological analysis of cultural occurrences. The authors draw from a variety of theoretical perspectives, including those based in cognitive, dynamic, humanistic–existential, feminist, and sociocultural thought. The chapters touch on a wide range of topics, including personal well-being, interpersonal and family relationships, culture, consciousness, weight and appearance, violence, ecological behavior, death, self-control, identity, impulsive behavior, work stress, ethnicity, gender, personal expressiveness, and evolution. This diversity of discipline, methodology, perspective, and topic is very exciting to us, because it shows that psychologists of different orientations can approach topics regarding consumption and materialism and that issues related to consumerism do indeed connect with many other constructs in the "nomological network" of psychology. Furthermore, it supports our overall contention that consumerism is a vitally important issue for psychologists to study, because it touches on many aspects of what it means to be a human in the modern world.

In summary, we believe that the study of consumerism raises many important theoretical and practical issues for psychology, just as a psychological perspective has much to offer in understanding consumerism. We hope that this book suggests to many of our colleagues ways that they might bring their own particular theoretical, methodological, disciplinary, and topical expertise to bear on one of the most important challenges we face in the new millennium, a challenge psychology has thus far largely ignored. One of our main roles as psychologists is to help improve the quality of life of all humans; we believe that this book shows that attention to the culture of consumption, and to psychology's place within it, is necessary if we are to achieve this lofty goal.

REFERENCES

American Academy of Pediatrics. (1999). Policy statement on media education. *Pediatrics, 104,* 341–343.

Buckley, K. W. (1982). The selling of a psychologist: John Broadus Watson and the application of behavioral techniques to advertising. *Journal of the History of the Behavioral Sciences, 18,* 207–221.

Clay, R. A. (2000). Advertising to children: Is it ethical? *American Psychological Association Monitor on Psychology, 31,* 52–53.

Dental association blames tooth decay on too much soda pop. (April 15, 2000). *The Detroit News.*

Jacoby, J., Johar, G. V., & Morrin, M. (1998). Consumer behavior: A quadrennium. *Annual Review of Psychology, 49,* 319–344.

Kendler, H. H. (1999). The role of value in the world of psychology. *American Psychologist, 54,* 828–835.

Kuna, D. P. (1976). The concept of suggestion in the early history of advertising psychology. *Journal of the History of the Behavioral Sciences, 12,* 347–353.

Kuna, D. P. (1979). Early advertising applications of the Gale-Cattell order-of-merit method. *Journal of the History of the Behavioral Sciences, 15,* 38–46.

I

PROBLEMS OF MATERIALISM, CAPITALISM, AND CONSUMPTION

2

MATERIALISTIC VALUES: THEIR CAUSES AND CONSEQUENCES

TIM KASSER, RICHARD M. RYAN, CHARLES E. COUCHMAN, AND KENNON M. SHELDON

Homo sapiens have long distinguished themselves by their use of and desire for material objects, and human social environments have long worked to support these tendencies to consume. It seems safe to say, however, that never before in humankind's history has our drive toward materialism and consumption been afforded such opportunity for expression and satisfaction. Although this can be seen in the extravagance of wealthy individuals purchasing $6,000 shower curtains (Hales, 2002) and $20 million rocket excursions into outer space (Wines, 2002), more remarkable is the extent to which high levels of consumption are within reach of even the average person living in a Western society. Almost everyone in the United States owns a telephone, television set, and an automobile (U.S. Census Bureau, 2001), and the homes in which the lower middle class live have comforts like plumbing, heat, and air conditioning that far exceed those enjoyed by royalty 1,000 years ago. Consumption also plays an enormous role in most individuals' leisure activities, be it through watching commercial television, wandering the shopping malls, or surfing the Internet. And, wherever we go, our ears and eyes are bombarded with material messages encouraging us to purchase more and more.

Upon accepting the fact that most humans currently live in a culture of consumption, one might ask "Why? Why do we have this culture?" An economist might reply that a culture of consumption is a necessary outgrowth of the advanced capitalistic economic systems under which most Westerners live, because these systems require the production and purchase of ever-increasing amounts of goods. A historian might explain how consumer culture emerged from the industrial age or even earlier, how modern advertising developed and gained prominence, and how particular captains of capitalism changed society by the force of their wills. A political scientist might note the multiple ways in which governmental structures maintain and support the power and interest of businesses to earn money through the sale of goods and services, and how these same structures encourage consumption on the part of citizens.

Each of these explanations, as well as others which might be offered from other disciplines, meaningfully elucidates aspects of the culture of consumption. From a psychological perspective, however, they remain less than satisfying, for they do not consider the ways in which individual humans simultaneously create and are created by this culture. As recognized by most sociocultural and anthropological approaches (Barnard, 2000), in order for some dimension of a culture to exist, it must be supported by individual human beings who follow the beliefs and practices of that culture; at the same time, the individual humans who support that aspect of culture are themselves shaped by the beliefs and practices that they have internalized. Take, for example, the particular aspect of culture known as religion. In order for any religion to exist, a reasonably large number of individuals must believe in the tenets and engage in the practices it espouses. If everyone stopped going to its religious centers, practicing the way of life it encourages, and reading its texts, the religion would die out, as have many religions in the past. At the same time that a religion is created by its followers, its followers are shaped by the religion. When individuals believe in the ideas of the religion and engage in its practices, their identities, personalities, and behaviors are molded in particular and profound ways.

If we look at contemporary culture, we see that the media propagate messages to purchase items and experiences, that myths are passed on that say that America is the land of opportunity, that governments work to support capitalism, that business people make decisions on the basis of how to maximize profit, and that consumers amass debt to buy products such as sport utility vehicles and large-screen television sets. These actions can be viewed from many angles, but they must also be understood as reflecting the combined actions and beliefs of a large number of individuals who have internalized the capitalistic, consumeristic worldview. Thus, the culture of consumption is, in part, a shared worldview lodged within the psyches of the members of the culture. However, we must also recognize that living in a culture of consumption means that individuals are exposed to enormous pressures to conform to the beliefs and values of this culture. Accordingly, the worldview in a society shapes the identities and lives of its members, leading them to hold the goals and engage in the practices (e.g., watching commercial television, working for a paycheck, shopping at the mall, investing in the stock market) that support the culture.

In this chapter, we refer to the culture of consumption's constellation of aims, beliefs, goals, and behaviors as a *materialistic value orientation* (MVO). From our perspective, an MVO involves the belief that it is important to pursue the culturally sanctioned goals of attaining financial success, having nice possessions, having the right image (produced, in large part, through consumer goods), and having a high status (defined mostly by the size of one's pocketbook and the scope of one's possessions). We focus here on two questions: First, "What leads people to care about and 'buy into' materialistic values and consumption behavior?" And second, "What are the personal, social, and ecological consequences of having a strong MVO?"

We use as our point of reference a theory of materialistic values (Kasser, 2002) that is grounded in humanistic (Maslow, 1954; Rogers, 1964), existential (Fromm, 1976), and organismic (Ryan & Deci, 2000b) thought, as well as in substantial empirical data. We propose that an MVO develops through two main pathways: (a) from experiences that induce feelings of insecurity and (b) from exposure to social models that encourage materialistic values. We further show that when materialistic values become relatively central to a person's system of values, personal well-being declines because the likelihood of having experiences that satisfy important psychological needs decreases. Finally, we demonstrate that an MVO encourages behaviors that damage interpersonal and community relations, as well as the ecological health of the planet.

HOW DO PEOPLE BECOME MATERIALISTIC?

Research suggests two main pathways toward the development of an MVO. First, experiences that undermine the satisfaction of psychological needs can cause individuals to orient toward materialism as one type of compensatory strategy intended to countermand the distressing effects of feelings of insecurity. Second, materialistic models and values exert more direct influences on the development of an MVO through the processes of socialization, internalization, and modeling. In the next two sections, we review evidence supporting each of these propositions, and in the third section we show how interactions between the two pathways can explain the effectiveness of advertising and the spread of materialism in previously noncapitalistic societies.

Insecurity

According to our model, a strong MVO is one way in which people attempt to compensate for worries and doubts about their self-worth, their ability to cope effectively with challenges, and their safety in a relatively unpredictable world. For example, large salaries and the possession of material goods may be especially valued if they represent an attempt to gain approval and acceptance that is otherwise felt to be lacking. A strong MVO may also develop in situations where people feel that wealth, possessions, image, and status enhance their likelihood of meeting basic needs for safety and sustenance (i.e., when they are seen as necessary for continued survival).

One primary source of insecurity, in our view, involves exposure to environments and experiences that frustrate or block the fulfillment of people's basic psychological needs, such as those for autonomy, competence, and relatedness (Ryan & Deci, 2000b), as well as for safety (Maslow, 1954). A growing body of research suggests that individuals become more materialistic when they experience environmental circumstances that do not support such psychological needs. As reviewed below, both people's proximal interpersonal environments and their more distal socioeconomic and cultural environments are important to need fulfillment and, consequently, to the development of a strong MVO.

Several studies have explored the effects of family environments, showing that parental styles and practices that poorly satisfy children's needs are also associated with an increased MVO in children. For example, Kasser, Ryan, Zax, and Sameroff (1995) reported that late adolescents[1] focused on financial success aspirations (in comparison to self-acceptance, affiliation, or community feeling aspirations) were more likely to have mothers who made more negative and fewer positive emotional expressions about the adolescents and who described their own parenting styles as involving less warmth and democracy, along with greater control. Other studies have shown that children tend to be more materialistic when they have less frequent communication with their parents (Moore & Moschis, 1981), when their parents are over-involved, highly punitive, or quite lax in the structure they provide (Cohen & Cohen, 1996), and when they perceive their parents as less supportive of their desires for autonomy (Williams, Cox, Hedberg, & Deci, 2000). Each of these parental characteristics is likely to cause feelings of insecurity, which may be compensated for by the development of a strong MVO.

Divorce is another family experience that can interrupt the satisfaction of children's psychological needs, because it often leads to decreased stability, exposure to more hostility, and increased worries about being loved. Not surprisingly, then, Rindfleisch, Burroughs, and Denton (1997) found that

---

[1]Most were approximately age 18.

materialistic young adults are more likely to have divorced parents. The authors' investigation of mediational reasons for this finding led them to conclude that "it is the diminution of interpersonal resources such as love and affection, rather than financial resources, that links family disruption and materialism" (p. 321), a statement quite consistent with our framework. Of course, the high rate of divorce in the United States puts many children at risk of developing materialistic values.

Although characteristics of one's family environment bear consistent relationships with later material values, the broader institutional and cultural structures within which individuals live can also be more or less supportive of psychological needs. To take an obvious example, blatant political oppression clearly undermines the autonomy of those who are subject to it, just as constant warfare and dire poverty undermine feelings of safety and security. Research shows that certain characteristics of one's culture and society can foster insecurities and therefore influence the extent to which people espouse an MVO.

The relation between economic deprivation and materialism is currently the most well-researched of these social dimensions. Both Cohen and Cohen (1996) and Kasser et al. (1995) have shown that highly materialistic teens have experienced greater socioeconomic disadvantages, as measured by parental socioeconomic and educational status, as well as by neighborhood quality. From a broader perspective, the political scientist Inglehart has reviewed findings showing that national economic indicators can influence materialism. For example, poorer countries tend to be more materialistic than richer countries, generations raised in bad economic times are more materialistic than those raised in prosperous times, and national recessions generally increase people's materialism (Abramson & Inglehart, 1995). Like us, Inglehart has suggested that poor economic conditions cause feelings of deprivation or insecurity and that people may compensate for these feelings by focusing on materialistic goals. Poverty alone may not lead to the adoption of materialistic goals, as seen in the case of religious novitiates who give up their possessions; as described below, however, poverty may work in combination with social modeling to produce a strong MVO.

Although correlational studies relating MVO to characteristics of familial and social environments support our thesis, they cannot provide firm causal conclusions. Experimental evidence in favor of our viewpoint has been obtained by Kasser and Sheldon (2000), who manipulated feelings of insecurity by asking research participants to write essays about either death or music. Those whose mortality had been made more salient (i.e., whose insecurity had been raised) reported higher expectations for their salary and spending 15 years into the future (Study 1) and became greedier in a social-dilemma game (Study 2; see chap. 8 , this volume, for more on death and consumer society).

In summary, then, both correlational studies and experimental manipulations of insecurity point to the same conclusion: When people experience situations that do not support the satisfaction of their basic psychological needs, the resultant feelings of insecurity may lead them to adopt a more materialistic outlook on life as a way to compensate for these feelings. Perhaps materialistic pursuits have been evolutionarily ingrained within humans as a way to feel more secure and safe (e.g., Hungry? Get food. Being attacked? Grab a club.), and this tendency is especially heightened under the current clime of cultural consumerism.

Exposure to Materialistic Models and Values

A second pathway to the development of materialism involves exposure to materialistic models and values. From the time they are born, people receive implicit and explicit messages endorsing the importance of money and possessions. These endorsements take the form of parental values, the materialistic lifestyles of family members and peers, and the materialistic messages frequently found in popular culture, such as in the media. People often accept such messages, take on materialistic goals, and strive to attain them, as humans have a fundamental tendency to adopt ambient cultural and familial values and behavioral regulations, a process referred to as *internalization* (Ryan & Connell, 1989).

Evidence suggests that children do indeed take on the materialistic values of those in their social surroundings. Kasser et al.'s (1995) study of mothers and their adolescent children showed that when mothers thought it was highly important to pursue financial success, their children generally expressed the same value. Ahuvia and Wong (1998) assessed the extent to which people perceived their parents, peers, heroes, various other adult figures, and the local community as valuing materialist social values in comparison to values such as self-expression, belonging, aesthetic satisfaction, and quality of life. Individuals who reported growing up in a materialist social milieu were more likely to be materialistic themselves. Although additional research is required to expand on this work (especially through exploration of the influence of same-age peers), the results of these two studies do indeed suggest that people often internalize the materialistic orientations of the salient models around them.

Another extremely pervasive source of materialistic messages is popular culture and the media, epitomized by commercial television. Besides the sitcoms, dramas, and game shows with subtexts clearly extolling materialism (e.g., *The Price Is Right, Who Wants to Be a Millionaire?*), television is replete with advertisements painstakingly crafted to promote consumption (Richins, 1995). Advertisers have at their disposal many techniques designed to convince people to purchase their products. For example, they show products being used by people who are famous or extremely attractive (often both), or by someone who obtains some sort of social reward by using the product. The ads also display products amidst a level of wealth that is unattainable by the average consumer and often show idealized versions of life within the context of the advertisement. Such tactics create associations between the product and desirable outcomes and also teach consumptive behavior through modeling (Bandura, 1971).

Given the purpose of these techniques and the ubiquitousness of these messages, it is not surprising that studies consistently show a positive correlation between television watching and materialism. This has been reported across different age groups (Kasser & Ryan, 2001; Rahtz, Sirgy, & Meadow, 1988, 1989; Sheldon & Kasser, 1995) and in samples drawn from a number of different countries (Cheung & Chan, 1996; Khanna & Kasser, 2001). Notably, however, the causal pathway of these studies is ambiguous. Although it is certainly likely that television watching may increase an MVO, it is also possible that television may be more appealing to those with a high MVO because it may validate their worldview, present new ways to pursue materialistic goals, and help them escape from the anxiety associated with insecurity. Future research applying insights derived from the literature on television and aggression may help to untangle the relations between television and an MVO.

Effective Advertising and the Spread of Capitalism

Whereas the two pathways described above may each make independent contributions toward the development of an MVO, they may also interact. That is, people experiencing higher levels of insecurity may be more susceptible to the influence of environmental messages concerning the benefits of acquisitiveness, which may in turn make them feel increasingly insecure, and on and on in a vicious cycle. Below, we briefly describe how this interaction might explain the effectiveness of advertising and the spread of capitalistic ideology. (See part IV of this volume for discussions of similar dynamics in youth.)

Richins (1995) has noted that ads are often constructed to engender upward social comparisons that make viewers feel uncomfortably inferior. For example, women exposed to perfume ads with highly attractive models report less satisfaction with their own appearance (Richins, 1991). In our view, these comparisons heighten feelings of personal insecurity, which may then activate compensatory mechanisms designed to alleviate negative feelings. Although many compensatory methods may serve this purpose, the likelihood of choosing a materialistic or consumption-oriented method is increased by the fact that the ads themselves always present a very clear option for feeling better about oneself: buy the product! Moreover, compared to those who care little for materialistic pursuits, people with a strong MVO are more concerned with social comparison (Sirgy, 1998), are more likely to compare themselves with images of wealthy people (Richins, 1992), strongly endorse wanting to make money in order to prove that they are worthwhile people in comparison to others (Srivastava, Locke, & Bortol, 2001), and are more susceptible to normative influence, such that their buying habits are more influenced by wanting others to approve of their purchases (Schroeder & Dugal, 1995). Each of these factors not only makes materialistic individuals more likely to be attentive to and be influenced by materialistic messages but also might maintain and reinforce the feelings of insecurity that underlie an MVO. This makes such individuals even more susceptible to the craft of advertising.

The interaction of forces promoting insecurity and encouraging materialism can also partially explain how capitalistic, free-market economies have been spreading to formerly communist and socialist nations and to less economically developed nations (Ryan et al., 1999; Sen, 1999). Several factors relevant to our discussion thus far are at work here. First, as is clear from the anthropological literature, marketers intentionally attempt to foster consumeristic desires in developing countries (O'Barr, 1994). As television watching and advertising make their way into new markets, potential consumers are flooded with new models suggesting that a materialistic way of life brings happiness and with new messages suggesting that viewers have not "made it" unless they own the right products (Mander, 1991). Inevitably, these messages are internalized to some degree and have the net effect of promoting materialism.

Second, market capitalism strikes at the heart of family structure, decreasing resources that provide for quality caretaking and breaking apart a sense of relatedness with one's extended family and community (see Schwartz, 1994). As described above, less attention and nurturance provided to children produces greater insecurity, which in turn increases the likelihood that they will develop an MVO. Furthermore, the breakdown of the family may lead to increased materialism, as is shown in Rindfleisch et al.'s (1997) finding that children of divorced parents are likely to become more materialistic than children whose parents are not divorced.

Finally, free-market economies lead to the concentration of wealth in relatively few hands. The disparities that arise between subgroups within a culture or between different nations have become increasingly noticeable with the spread of modern media to more and more of the world's citizens. The salience of these disparities is likely to fuel increased social comparison, which, as we have noted above, is associated with increased materialism. Furthermore, such upward social comparison is likely to increase feelings of insecurity among the poor when combined with the dominant message that people are worthwhile to the extent that they own many prestigious goods and are financially successful. Thus, the poor, who already may be vulnerable to materialistic messages as a result of their relative lack of opportunities for need satisfaction, may be subject to yet another factor promoting an MVO.

MATERIALISM AND SUBJECTIVE WELL-BEING

Having specified some of the processes by which the values, goals, and beliefs of the culture of consumption become part of people's psyches, we now describe some of the consequences of holding an MVO. As we shall see, people who express a strong MVO report a number of experiences, feelings, and behaviors that are associated with a diminished quality of life.

A growing body of research demonstrates that people who strongly orient toward values such as money, possessions, image, and status report lower subjective well-being (see Kasser, 2002, for a fuller review). For example, Kasser and Ryan (1993, 1996, 2001) have shown that when people rate the relative importance of extrinsic, materialistic values as high in comparison to other pursuits (e.g., self-acceptance, affiliation, community feeling), lower quality of life is also reported. Late adolescents with a strong MVO report lower self-actualization and vitality, as well as more depression and anxiety. They also are rated by interviewers as lower in social productivity and general functioning and as higher in conduct disorders (Kasser & Ryan, 1993). Kasser and Ryan (1996) replicated this association between an MVO and lower well-being in a sample of adults, and Kasser and Ryan (1996, 2001) have demonstrated that an MVO in college students is positively associated with narcissism, physical symptoms, and drug use and negatively associated with self-esteem and quality of relationships. Sheldon and Kasser (1995, 1998, 2001) have presented similar results in college students and adults when using a mixed idiographic–nomothetic means of measuring value orientation, as well as measures of well-being including life satisfaction and affective experience.

Other researchers have reported similar results. Cohen and Cohen (1996) found that adolescents who admire others because of their possessions are at an increased risk for personality disorders. Indeed, placing a high priority on being rich was associated with virtually every Axis I and Axis II diagnosis assessed in their research. Materialism scales designed by Belk (1985) and Richins and Dawson (1992) have shown consistently negative associations with happiness and life satisfaction in several studies (see Sirgy's, 1998, review and Wright & Larsen's, 1993, meta-analysis). Finally, the negative associations between materialism and well-being have been replicated in samples of Australian (Saunders & Munro, 2000), English (Chan & Joseph, 2000), German (Schmuck, Kasser, & Ryan, 2000), Romanian (Frost, 1998), Russian (Ryan et al., 1999), South Korean (Kim, Kasser, & Lee, 2003), and Singaporian (Kasser & Ahuvia, 2002) students.

Although various explanations have been tendered for the negative associations between subjective well-being and an MVO (see, e.g., chap. 3, this volume), Kasser (2002) has presented an argument derived from needs-based theories. In brief, we posit that happiness and well-being, or *eudaimo-*

nia (Ryan & Deci, 2000a), derive largely from the satisfaction of psychological needs for security, competence, connection to others, and autonomy. As has already been shown above, people with a strong MVO have had experiences that poorly satisfied their needs for safety and security, and thus the lower well-being associated with an MVO is in part a consequence of the feelings of insecurity which led to the adoption of a materialistic lifestyle in the first place. However, an MVO is not just a "symptom" of unhappiness; it also leads people to engage in behaviors and have experiences that do a relatively poor job of satisfying their psychological needs. In this vein, we present a brief overview of research showing that the remaining three psychological needs are relatively poorly satisfied in people with a strong MVO. (See Kasser, 2002, for a fuller exposition.)

Competence

Evidence that people with a strong MVO have difficulty fulfilling their need for feeling competent comes from several sources. First, a strong MVO is associated with lower self-esteem (Kasser & Ryan, 2001) and greater narcissism (Kasser & Ryan, 1996), belying a contingent, unstable sense of self-esteem. Second, as mentioned above, people with a strong MVO are particularly concerned with social comparisons (Sirgy, 1998) and the opinions of others (Schroeder & Dugal, 1995), both of which can often lead them to feel badly about themselves. Third, successful pursuit of materialistic goals does little to improve people's happiness and well-being (Diener, Sandvik, Seidlitz, & Diener, 1993; Sheldon & Kasser, 1998). Thus, even when people are quite competent at attaining materialistic goals, we believe that this type of success rarely provides a deeply satisfying feeling of "true self-esteem" (Deci & Ryan, 1995).

Relatedness

The satisfaction of relatedness needs may also be substantially undermined by an MVO. For example, Kasser and Ryan (2001) have shown that the love relationships and the friendships of those with a strong MVO are relatively short and are characterized more by emotional extremes and conflict than by trust and happiness. Several factors probably contribute to this phenomenon. For one, people with a strong MVO tend to place less importance on values such as affiliation (Kasser & Ryan, 1993) and benevolence (Schwartz, 1996), thus decreasing the likelihood that they will seek out experiences of closeness with others. In addition, the attitudes expressed in an MVO can "bleed over" into one's relationships, leading others to be treated in an objectifying manner. Compared to those with a low MVO, people who are strongly focused on materialistic values report less empathy (Sheldon & Kasser, 1995), agree that they more often use their friends to get ahead in life

(Khanna & Kasser, 2001), score higher in Machiavellianism (McHoskey, 1999), and are more likely to compete than cooperate with their friends (Sheldon, Sheldon, & Osbaldiston, 2000). None of these styles of relating to others contribute to the close, interpersonally trusting, and warm relationships necessary for the deep satisfaction of relatedness needs.

Autonomy

The final need undermined by an MVO is autonomy—the feeling of choice, ownership, and deep engagement concerning one's activities. People with a strong MVO are less focused on having choices than they are on obtaining rewards (Kasser & Ryan, 1993). Furthermore, Sheldon and Kasser (1995, 1998, 2001) have demonstrated that an MVO is associated with pursuing one's goals because of feelings of internal guilt and external pressure rather than for reasons of fun or wholehearted identification. Srivastava et al. (2001) presented parallel results, showing that business students and entrepreneurs with a strong MVO report more concern with making money for reasons of internal and external pressure. Specifically, high materialistic values were associated with wanting to overcome self-doubt (e.g., "prove I am not a failure") and to appear positive in social comparisons (e.g., "to have a house and cars that are better than those of my neighbors"). Such poor self-regulation works against the satisfaction of the need for autonomy (Ryan, 1995).

A final problem concerning autonomy is that a strong MVO often leads people to focus more on rewards than on the inherent fun of the activities in which they are engaged, which in turn can undermine feelings of intrinsic motivation (Deci, 1971). Indeed, focusing on money is associated with less engagement and more alienation in one's leisure, work, and relationship activities (Khanna & Kasser, 2001; see also chap. 6, this volume).

MATERIALISTIC VALUES AND THE WELFARE OF SOCIETY

Although it is disconcerting to know that the ideology encouraged by our culture of consumption undermines the personal well-being and need satisfaction of those who accept its values, a strong MVO also leads people to engage in behaviors and hold attitudes damaging to our communities and to the world's ecological health (see chaps. 4 & 5, this volume).

A healthy community is based on people helping one another, on cooperation, and on mutual trust. Several pieces of evidence suggest, however, that a strong MVO is associated with less "civil" behavior. For example, an MVO tends to conflict with the desire to help the world be a better place and to take care of others (Cohen & Cohen, 1996; Kasser & Ryan, 1993, 1996, 2001; Schwartz, 1996), decreasing the likelihood that people oriented toward materialism will behave pro-socially. Indeed, research shows that people strongly focused on materialistic values are also lower in social interest, pro-social behavior, and social productivity and are more likely to engage in anti-social acts (Kasser & Ryan, 1993; McHoskey, 1999). That they have more manipulative tendencies (McHoskey, 1999) and compete more than cooperate (Sheldon & McGregor, 2000; Sheldon et al., 2000) provides further evidence that an MVO undermines what is best for the whole community.

An MVO can also lead people to care less about environmental issues and to engage in more environmentally destructive behaviors and attitudes. Materialistic values conflict with values to protect the environment (Abramson & Inglehart, 1995; Schwartz, 1996) and are associated with more negative attitudes toward the environment and fewer environmentally friendly behaviors (Richins & Dawson, 1992; Saunders & Munro, 2000). An MVO has also been associated with increased greed and heightened consumption in simulated social dilemmas involving ecological issues (Sheldon & McGregor, 2000).

In summary, the culture of consumption, as represented by an MVO, not only degrades psychological health, but spreads seeds that may lead to its own destruction. Materialistic values not only heighten our vulnerability to serious social and environmental problems, but also undermine our ability to work cooperatively in finding solutions to these problems.

CONCLUSION: IMPLICATIONS AND DIRECTIONS

Our ideas about how materialistic values are inculcated into individuals, and the data showing how an MVO diminishes personal, social, and ecological well-being, have a number of implications for theoretical, clinical, and social change issues.

Theory

In psychology, the dominant theory behind much empirical research and clinical work is a behavioral or cognitive viewpoint, which suggests that striving for important social rewards, obtaining one's goals (whatever they may be) and integrating into society (whatever its values) are key features of psychological well-being. The evidence presented here, in contrast, shows that when people focus on obtaining rewards, when they concern themselves with materialistic goals, and when they espouse the values of the dominant consumer culture, the result is lower well-being. From the needs-based theory we use, influenced by humanistic and organismic assumptions, these results make sense; an MVO reflects and exacerbates people's alienation from their natural strivings to grow, actualize, and connect with others. Because behavioral and cognitive perspectives typically do not contain such theoretical constructs as basic psychological needs and organismic actualization and integration, the results reviewed above are seemingly at odds with such viewpoints on humans and their well-being. Furthermore, behavioral and cognitive perspectives have few theoretical constructs to explain how feelings of insecurity might lead to the internalization of an MVO, because their viewpoints typically only acknowledge the direct roles of learning and imitation in the internalization of values, not more "dynamic" pathways.

We raise these theoretical points in the hope of demonstrating how the study of the culture of consumption can address academic problems of concern to theorists and researchers. That is, the literature reviewed above, inspired by humanistic, organismic, and existential viewpoints, suggests the need for some important revisions to mainstream psychology's dominant paradigm concerning human motivation and well-being.

Increasing Personal Well-Being

Psychologists have long played an important role in helping people make changes in their personal lives to improve their well-being. All too often, however, the focus has been on a client's symptoms, with the broader scope of the person's problems, indeed, the person's whole lifestyle, being ignored (see chap. 9, this volume). The research we have presented shows that a number of problems that clinicians encounter (e.g., narcissism, anxiety, depression, conduct disorder, drug and alcohol problems) may be involved with a strong MVO. Thus, clinical work may benefit from the exploration of clients' value orientations to determine whether they are indeed focused on money, possessions, image, and status. If so, this MVO may signal poor past need satisfaction and may be leading clients into experiences that undermine the satisfaction of basic needs in the present.

The chapters in part III of this volume discuss in more detail how therapists might deal with clinical issues related to the culture of consumption, but here we briefly suggest the following. First, clients may benefit from exploring how past insecurities may have led them to develop an MVO and from discussing how other value orientations may be more satisfying. Second, helping clients clarify what is important to them and what guides their decisions may help them to see how they have been seduced by cultural consumption messages. Third, it may be useful to point out to clients how they continue to maintain an MVO, believing they will finally be happy when they have more money or higher status, even though the evidence from their personal lives (and from scientific studies) suggests the emptiness of this pursuit. By helping clients to see the stresses and dissatisfactions inherent in their acceptance of these cultural messages, they may be able to break the vicious cycles of materialism.

If clinicians succeed in helping clients disengage from their MVO, different values must take their place. Research shows that when people are focused on intrinsic values such as self-acceptance, personal growth, affiliation, and helping others, better well-being is typically evidenced (Kasser & Ryan, 1993, 1996; Ryan & Deci, 2000b). Effective clinical strategies from various theoretical perspectives could be developed to help shift people's value orientations from unsatisfying, materialistic ones to values and goals that may increase the likelihood of satisfying patients' needs and, thereby, their well-being.

Psychology and Social Change

The empirical skills and strengths of psychology might also be applied to counteract some of the problems inherent in the culture of consumption and in an MVO (see chap. 5, this volume). One might even argue that psychology bears a special responsibility to do so, given that our discipline's findings have often been used to support and encourage the culture of consumption. Many theoretical ideas from psychology have been "profitably" applied to business, advertising, and education to focus people more heavily on rewards and praise and to more efficiently direct workers, students, and consumers into the channels of action desired by consumer culture.

Psychology must begin, therefore, by acknowledging how it has helped spread the culture of consumption and now use these same skills to slow (and, may we hope, reverse) materialism. So, rather than studying how to convince children, adolescents, and adults to purchase products and hinge their self-worth on what they own, psychologists might turn to developing media literacy programs and other types of interventions that would increase individuals' resilience in the face of advertising. Rather than focusing on the use of rewards (supposedly) to improve student creativity and worker productivity, psychologists could give more attention to understanding how grades and paychecks can actually detract from people's intrinsic interest and performance in certain activities (Deci, Koestner, & Ryan, 1999). Rather than ignoring the detrimental impact of people's values on the environment, psychologists might begin to study how to help individuals leave smaller "ecological footprints" and live materially simpler lifestyles. And rather than supporting the dominant cultural belief that happiness and well-being are the result of increasing personal and national economic growth, psychologists might begin to educate more broadly the public that increases in GNP and even one's own salary do not equate with increases in happiness (Diener et al., 1993; Myers, 2000) and that materialistic values actually undermine well-being.

Through such efforts, we may be able to weaken the hold that the capitalistic, consumeristic worldview has on both people's psyches and on the culture, and thereby improve the quality of life for humans, as well as the many other species inhabiting our planet.

REFERENCES

Abramson, P. R., & Inglehart, R. (1995). *Value change in global perspective*. Ann Arbor: University of Michigan Press.

Ahuvia, A. C., & Wong, N. (1998). *Three types of materialism: Their relationship and origins*. Manuscript submitted for publication.

Bandura, A. (1971). *Social learning theory*. Morristown, NJ: General Learning Press.

Barnard, A. (2000). *History and theory in anthropology*. Cambridge, England: Cambridge University Press.

Belk, R. W. (1985). Materialism: Trait aspects of living in the material world. *Journal of Consumer Research, 12,* 265–280.

Chan, R., & Joseph, S. (2000). Dimensions of personality, domains of aspiration, and subjective well-being. *Personality and Individual Differences, 28,* 347–354.

Cheung, C., & Chan, C. (1996). Television viewing and mean world value in Hong Kong's adolescents. *Social Behavior and Personality, 24,* 351–364.

Cohen, P., & Cohen, J. (1996). *Life values and adolescent mental health*. Mahwah, NJ: Erlbaum.

Deci, E. L. (1971). Effects of externally mediated rewards on intrinsic motivation. *Journal of Personality and Social Psychology, 18,* 105–115.

Deci, E. L., Koestner, R., & Ryan, R. M. (1999). A meta-analytic review of experiments examining the effects of extrinsic rewards on intrinsic motivation. *Psychological Bulletin, 125,* 627–668.

Deci, E. L., & Ryan, R. M. (1995). Human autonomy: The basis for true self-esteem. In M. Kernis (Ed.), *Efficacy, agency, and self-esteem* (pp. 31–49). New York: Plenum Press.

Diener, E., Sandvik, E., Seidlitz, L., & Diener, M. (1993). The relationship between income and subjective well-being: Relative or absolute? *Social Indicators Research, 28,* 195–223.

Fromm, E. (1976). *To have or to be?* New York: Harper and Row.

Frost, K. M. (1998). *A cross-cultural study of major life aspirations and psychological well-being*. Unpublished doctoral dissertation, University of Texas at Austin.

Hales, L. (2002, October 19). The splashiest shower curtain; No silver lining in ousted CEO's $6,000 extravagance. *Washington Post,* p. C2.

Kasser, T. (2002). *The high price of materialism*. Cambridge, MA: MIT Press.

Kasser, T., & Ahuvia, A. C. (2002). Materialistic values and well-being in business students. *European Journal of Social Psychology, 32,* 137–146.

Kasser, T., & Ryan, R. M. (1993). A dark side of the American dream: Correlates of financial success as a central life aspiration. *Journal of Personality and Social Psychology, 65,* 410–422.

Kasser, T., & Ryan, R. M. (1996). Further examining the American dream: Differential correlates of intrinsic and extrinsic goals. *Personality and Social Psychology Bulletin, 22,* 280–287.

Kasser, T., & Ryan, R. M. (2001). Be careful what you wish for: Optimal functioning and the relative attainment of intrinsic and extrinsic goals. In P. Schmuck & K. M. Sheldon (Eds.), *Life goals and well-being: Towards a positive psychology of human striving* (pp. 116–131). Goettingen, Germany: Hogrefe & Huber.

Kasser, T., Ryan, R. M., Zax, M., & Sameroff, A. J. (1995). The relations of maternal and social environments to late adolescents' materialistic and prosocial values. *Developmental Psychology, 31,* 907–914.

Kasser, T., & Sheldon, K. M. (2000). Of wealth and death: Materialism, mortality salience, and consumption behavior. *Psychological Science, 11,* 352–355.

Khanna, S., & Kasser, T. (2001). *Materialism, objectification, and alienation from a cross-cultural perspective.* Manuscript in preparation.

Kim, Y., Kasser, T., & Lee, H. (in press). Self-concept, aspirations, and well-being in South Korea and the United States. *Journal of Social Psychology, 143,* 277–290.

Mander, J. (1991). *In the absence of the sacred: The failure of technology and the survival of the Indian nations.* San Francisco: Sierra Club Books.

Maslow, A. H. (1954). *Motivation and personality.* New York: Harper and Row.

McHoskey, J. W. (1999). Machiavellianism, intrinsic versus extrinsic goals, and social interest: A self-determination theory analysis. *Motivation and Emotion, 23,* 267–283.

Moore, R. L., & Moschis, G. P. (1981). The effects of family communication and mass media use on adolescent consumer learning. *Journal of Communication, 31,* 42–51.

Myers, D. G. (2000). The funds, friends, and faith of happy people. *American Psychologist, 55,* 56–67.

O'Barr, W. M. (1994). *Culture and the ad.* Boulder, CO: Westview Press.

Rahtz, D. R., Sirgy, M. J., & Meadow, H. L. (1988). Elderly life satisfaction and television viewership: Replication and extension. In S. Shapiro & H. H. Walle (Eds.), *1988 AMA winter educators' conference—Marketing: A return to broader dimensions* (pp. 409–413). Chicago: American Marketing Association.

Rahtz, D. R., Sirgy, M. J., & Meadow, H. L. (1989). The elderly audience: Correlates of television orientation. *Journal of Advertising, 18,* 9–20.

Richins, M. L. (1991). Social comparison and the idealized images of advertising. *Journal of Consumer Research, 18,* 71–83.

Richins, M. L. (1992). Media images, materialism, and what ought to be: The role of social comparison. In F. Rudmin & M. L. Richins (Eds.), *Materialism: Meaning, measure, and morality* (pp. 202–206). Provo, UT: Association for Consumer Research.

Richins, M. L. (1995). Social comparison, advertising, and consumer discontent. *American Behavioral Scientist, 38,* 593–607.

Richins, M. L., & Dawson, S. (1992). A consumer values orientation for materialism and its measurement: Scale development and validation. *Journal of Consumer Research, 19,* 303–316.

Rindfleisch, A., Burroughs, J. E., & Denton, F. (1997). Family structure, materialism, and compulsive consumption. *Journal of Consumer Research, 23,* 312–325.

Rogers, C. R. (1964). Toward a modern approach to values: The valuing process in the mature person. *Journal of Abnormal and Social Psychology, 68,* 160–167.

Ryan, R. M. (1995). Psychological needs and the facilitation of integrative processes. *Journal of Personality, 63,* 397–427.

Ryan, R. M., Chirkov, V. I., Little, T. D., Sheldon, K. M., Timoshina, E., & Deci, E. L. (1999). The American dream in Russia: Extrinsic aspirations and well-being in two cultures. *Personality and Social Psychology Bulletin, 25,* 1509–1524.

Ryan, R. M., & Connell, J. P. (1989). Perceived locus of causality and internalization: Examining reasons for acting in two domains. *Journal of Personality and Social Psychology, 57,* 749–761.

Ryan, R. M., & Deci, E. L. (2000a). On happiness and human potentials: A review of research on hedonic and eudaimonic well-being. *Annual Review of Psychology, 52,* 141–166.

Ryan, R. M., & Deci, E. L. (2000b). Self-determination theory and the facilitation of intrinsic motivation, social development, and well-being. *American Psychologist, 55,* 68–78.

Saunders, S., & Munro, D. (2000). The construction and validation of a consumer orientation questionnaire (SCOI) designed to measure Fromm's (1955) "marketing character" in Australia. *Social Behavior and Personality, 28,* 219–240.

Schmuck, P., Kasser, T., & Ryan, R. M. (2000). Intrinsic and extrinsic goals: Their structure and relationship to well-being in German and U.S. college students. *Social Indicators Research, 50,* 225–241.

Schroeder, J. E., & Dugal, S. S. (1995). Psychological correlates of the materialism construct. *Journal of Social Behavior and Personality, 10,* 243–253.

Schwartz, B. (1994). *The costs of living: How market freedom erodes the best things in life.* New York: W. W. Norton.

Schwartz, S. H. (1996). Values priorities and behavior: Applying of theory of integrated value systems. In C. Seligman, J. M. Olson, & M. P. Zanna (Eds.), *The psychology of values: The Ontario symposium* (Vol. 8, pp. 1–24). Hillsdale, NJ: Erlbaum.

Sen, A. (1999). *Development as freedom.* New York: Knopf.

Sheldon, K. M., & Kasser, T. (1995). Coherence and congruence: Two aspects of personality integration. *Journal of Personality and Social Psychology, 68,* 531–543.

Sheldon, K. M., & Kasser, T. (1998). Pursuing personal goals: Skills enable progress, but not all progress is beneficial. *Personality and Social Psychology Bulletin, 24,* 1319–1331.

Sheldon, K. M., & Kasser, T. (2001). "Getting older, getting better": Personal strivings and psychological maturity across the life span. *Developmental Psychology, 37,* 491–501.

Sheldon, K. M., & McGregor, H. (2000). Extrinsic value orientation and the tragedy of the commons. *Journal of Personality, 68,* 383–411.

Sheldon, K. M., Sheldon, M. S., & Osbaldiston, R. (2000). Prosocial values and group assortation in an N-person prisoner's dilemma. *Human Nature, 11,* 387–404.

Sirgy, M. J. (1998). Materialism and quality of life. *Social Indicators Research, 43,* 227–260.

Srivastava, A., Locke, E. A., & Bortol, K. M. (2001). Money and subjective well-being: It's not the money, it's the motives. *Journal of Personality and Social Psychology, 80,* 959–971.

U.S. Census Bureau. (2001). *Statistical abstract of the United States: 2001 (121st ed.).* Washington, DC: U.S. Government Printing Office.

Williams, G. C., Cox, E. M., Hedberg, V. A., & Deci, E. L. (2000). Extrinsic life goals and health risk behaviors in adolescents. *Journal of Applied Social Psychology, 30,* 1756–1771.

Wines, M. (2002, September 4). Russia scraps space plans of pop star. *The New York Times,* p. E1.

Wright, N. D., & Larsen, V. (1993). Materialism and life satisfaction: A meta-analysis. *Journal of Consumer Satisfaction, Dissatisfaction, and Complaining Behavior, 6,* 158–165.

3

WHY ARE MATERIALISTS
LESS SATISFIED?

EMILY G. SOLBERG, EDWARD DIENER, AND MICHAEL D. ROBINSON

A substantial research literature reviewed elsewhere in this book indicates a negative relation between materialism and subjective well-being (SWB). Given the clear inverse correlation between reports of well-being and materialism, the next question is why this is the case. A number of possible explanations have been suggested; however, not all of them have been fully examined. In this chapter we investigate several explanations for the relation between materialism and SWB, and we report new evidence from our laboratory testing these explanations. Altogether, we report on the data from 13 studies.

First, we test whether the inverse correlation between materialism and SWB is partly due to how materialism is measured. For example, the Belk (1985) Materialism Scale has items that appear to contain a large neuroticism component (e.g., "I am bothered when I see people who buy anything they want"). One of the three subscales of the Belk Materialism Scale is designed specifically to measure envy, clearly a negative emotional state. Although the Material Values Survey (among other scales; Richins & Dawson, 1992) does not appear to overlap with the construct of neuroticism, it, like the Belk scale, is correlated with neuroticism and disagreeableness (Sharpe, 2000). To the extent that measures of materialism correlate with neuroticism, neuroticism would seem to be a potential confounding factor that might actually explain the negative associations with well-being (e.g., McCrae, 1990).

A second possible reason for the inverse relation between materialism and SWB may have to do with whether people think they are more distant from their material goals than from their other goals. In other words, there may be a larger gap between their actual and ideal states in the material domain than in other domains of life. In part because of the rather impossible ideals of wealth and consumption propagated by television, advertising, and popular culture, people may seek standards of wealth that lie well beyond their present means (Richins, 1995). Such a gap between actual possessions and desired possessions could well contribute to dissatisfaction among materialistic persons. In this chapter, we examine whether materialistic goals per se lower SWB or, alternatively, whether perceived discrepancies between current and desired states (which are plausibly higher for materialistic goals) account for the lower SWB of materialists.

Another possible explanation for the negative relation between materialism and SWB is that unhappy people may seek material possessions in order to feel better. Such a compensatory reaction would clearly be stronger among those who are relatively low in SWB compared with those who are high. Related to this explanation, Kasser and Sheldon (2000) found that a manipulation related to existential insecurity (e.g., writing about one's own death) caused participants to endorse goals that were more materialistic. However, research on terror management theory indicates that there is something special about mortality salience relative to other manipulations of unhappiness or insecurity (chap. 8, this volume). Thus, it is possible that manipulations based on mortality salience are fundamentally different from manipulations of happiness or insecurity. To investigate the relation between insecurity and materialistic values, we manipulated feelings of inadequacy in ways other than mortality salience to see whether low SWB might be a cause of adopting materialistic values. This seemed a plausible hypothesis because of the relatively concrete and visible nature of materialistic goals relative to non-materialistic ones. That is, because of the concrete nature of materialistic goals, progress may be more apparent in materialistic domains relative to nonmaterialistic ones, providing distressed individuals an obvious (and publicly verifiable) way to make apparent progress.

Any correlational finding invites speculation that the direction of causality may flow from A to B or from B to A (or both). In the previous paragraph, we indicated our belief that it is plausible that the relation between materialism and SWB flows from insecurity (i.e., low SWB) to the adoption of materialistic values. It also seems important to investigate the reverse causal direction. Of interest is whether the temporary activation of thoughts related to materialism leads to lower SWB, here defined as mood states, which are more transitory than life satisfaction (Robinson, 2000).

Another explanation for the inverse relation between materialistic goals and SWB relates to the incompatibility of adopting materialistic versus other goals. That is, people may pursue materialistic goals at the expense of nonmaterialistic goals (e.g., goals related to intimacy or achievement) that might ultimately be more satisfying (McClelland, 1987). For example, the pursuit of wealth may leave less time for family and friends, arguably critical ingredients of happiness (Myers, 1999). Diener and Seligman (2002) found that happy people, without exception, had social relationships that were marked by closeness and quality. It is reasonable to think that materialistic goals may interfere with the establishment and maintenance of such relationships, because time spent on one set of goals would seem to leave less time to spend on others.

Finally, it may be that some goals and values are more fun to work toward than others. Related to this explanation, McClelland (1987) has argued that intrinsic rewards attach to the pursuit of goals that are satisfying *for their own sake*. Materialistic goals may not fall into this category because they are relatively recent within our evolutionary history (chap. 8, this volume). If this is the case, then the pursuit of money and possessions may be a cause for distress relative to the pursuit of goals that are pertinent to our evolutionary needs (Myers, 1999; chap. 8, this volume).

HYPOTHESIS 1: THE SCALE CAUSES THE RESULTS

Materialism can be measured in a number of ways, ranging from asking people to rate their agreement with different items, to having people rank order their values, to having people complete implicit computer tasks. It is possible that the way in which materialism is measured has a profound effect on whether the construct correlates negatively with SWB. For example, the Belk (1985) Materialism Scale consists of items that, at face value, seem to assess a person's propensity to worry and to be unhappy. People who tend to worry or are generally unhappy may agree with these statements not because they are materialistic, but because they agree with the negative emotional tone of the statements. The high correlation between such materialism scales and neuroticism is a problem because neuroticism and SWB are typically negatively related (Lucas, Diener, & Suh, 1996). Studies 1 through 4 examine the role of neuroticism in explaining the materialism–SWB relation.

Other measures of materialism are less correlated with neuroticism, which may increase our confidence that the relation between SWB and materialism is true and not artifactual. For example, simply rating the degree to which one values different goals (e.g., money, love) does not seem on the surface to be related to neuroticism; if so, such a value preference measure of materialism may offer a better assessment of the materialism–SWB relation. We examine relevant data in Study 3. Potentially, an even less face-valid assessment of the materialism–SWB relation would rely on an implicit measure of materialism. If, using an implicit measure of materialism, the negative relation with SWB is still obtained, one would be hard pressed to argue that self-report confounds or demand characteristics were responsible (Greenwald & Banaji, 1995). Study 4 examines this possibility.

Study 1

The Belk Materialism Scale (Belk, 1985), the Satisfaction With Life Scale (SWLS; Diener, Emmons, Larsen, & Griffin, 1985), and a 10-item Neuroticism Scale were administered to 219 undergraduate students. We found the correlation between the Materialism Scale and the SWLS to be significant ($r = -.21, p = .01$). We also found the correlation between the Materialism Scale and neuroticism to be significant ($r = .39, p = .01$). We next computed a partial correlation between the Belk Materialism Scale and the SWLS while holding neuroticism constant, and we found that the correlation between materialism and satisfaction was nonsignificant ($r = -.09$, $p = .20$). These results suggest that at least this measure of materialism is confounded with neuroticism and that neuroticism may sometimes represent a confounding factor in evaluating the relationship between materialism and SWB.

Study 2

The Belk Materialism Scale, the SWLS, and a measure of neuroticism were administered to a sample of 156 adult participants through a mail survey. The correlation between scores on the Belk Materialism Scale and the SWLS was again significant ($r = -.27, p = .00$), and scale scores and neuroticism were again found to be substantially related ($r = .41, p = .01$). When neuroticism was controlled for, the relation between Belk Materialism and SWLS dropped to $-.10$ ($p = .22$). These results again suggest that the relation between materialism and SWB may be artifactual, at least when the measure of materialism correlates moderately with neuroticism.

In light of the findings from Studies 1 and 2, it seemed important to investigate the materialism–SWB relation using measures of materialism that were less confounded with neuroticism. In Study 3, we took our lead from Kasser and Ryan (1993, 1996), who found that results involving the prioritization of (materialistic vs. nonmaterialistic) values was associated with differences in SWB. A strength of Study 3 is that it drew on an international sample involving several thousand participants. The international nature of the sample is important because research has suggested that people from different countries tend to adopt different values (Triandis & Suh, 2002). In this respect, our data base allowed us to make generalizations across cultures that point to the universal consequences of adopting certain values.

Study 3

Data from 7,150 students from around the world were collected in the international college student sample (see Suh, Diener, Oishi, & Triandis, 1998, for a more complete description of the sample). The students were asked in a straightforward manner to rate how important different domains (e.g., money, love, health) were to them. The correlation between the degree to which participants valued money and their scores on the SWLS was $-.14$ ($p = .01$). In contrast, the correlation between the degree to which students valued love and satisfaction with life was $.15$ ($p = .01$). When frequency of negative affect (NA; which is virtually the same as neuroticism) was controlled, we found similar correlations between valuing money and satisfaction with life ($r = -.13, p = .001$). Study 3, unlike Studies 1 and 2, suggested that the materialism–SWB relation was not artifactual (i.e., that it was not due to the common variance involving neuroticism). Obviously, Study 3 was also important in suggesting that the (negative) relation between materialism and SWB is universal across cultures.

Although Study 3 gives us reason to trust the negative relation between materialism and SWB, we have recently suggested that self-reports of constructs, no matter how carefully designed, are ultimately fallible (e.g., Robinson, Vargas, & Crawford, 2003). This is because certain thoughts, values, and beliefs are ultimately unavailable to the person making the self-reports (Boring, 1953; Greenwald & Banaji, 1995). Considering the construct of SWB, we have generally been impressed by the idea that people have conscious access to their subjective experiences (Robinson, 2000; Robinson et al., 2003). However, we have been less impressed by the ability of the average person to report on his or her motivations and values (McClelland, 1985; Robinson et al., 2003).

Recently, Schmuck (2001) examined whether an implicit measure of materialism (a priming task) was related to well-being. He primed participants with intrinsic, extrinsic, or neutral words and used positive and negative words as targets to determine the speed with which different people associated intrinsic or extrinsic words with positive and negative words. This priming measure correlated with two of the six well-being measures (but not with the composite well-being measure) in that study. In Study 4 we used an implicit measure of materialism in order to extend our understanding of the relation between materialistic values and SWB.

Study 4

The Implicit Association Task (IAT; Greenwald, McGhee, & Schwartz, 1998) was modified to measure the speed with which people identify themselves with expensive material objects, compared to the speed with which they identify themselves with inexpensive (but equally pleasant) objects. The

IAT procedure had participants quickly classify words on a computer screen. The first trials involved participants hitting one key if they saw words relating to themselves (e.g., me, I) and another key if they saw words related to others (e.g., them, you). Next they were told to hit one key if they saw words relating to expensive objects (e.g., diamonds), and another key if they saw words relating to inexpensive objects (e.g., flower). After they grew accustomed to the meaning of these keys, participants were asked to simultaneously categorize words denoting expensive and inexpensive objects along with words relating to themselves or to others with the same fingers. For example, participants were shown a word and instructed to hit the left key if the word was either expensive or related to them and to hit the right key if the word was either inexpensive or related to others. Then the key assignments were switched so that the "inexpensive" words were paired with the "me" words and vice versa. To compute a measure of implicit materialism, we computed how much faster the participant was at categorizing expensive words when they were paired with the "me" key than when they were when paired with the "not me" key. Using this difference score, we measured implicit levels of materialism (i.e., the extent to which they associated the self-concept with material goods). Previous research suggests that such an IAT measure should be valid (Greenwald et al., 1998; Greenwald & Farnham, 2000; Greenwald et al., 2002).

Thirty-eight students completed this implicit measure of materialism. These students also were instructed to carry a Palm Pilot for 1 week and answer a brief survey about their moods five times a day when paged. Participants were paged seven times a day and were instructed to answer at least five of these pages. We combined nine items (afraid, anxious, nervous, angry, irritable, guilty, ashamed, sad, and downhearted) to form a measure of NA and eight items (happy, cheerful, calm, relaxed, proud, confident, excited, and enthusiastic) to form a measure of positive affect (PA).

The IAT measure of materialism was correlated with the Palm Pilot measures of mood. The faster participants were able to identify themselves within the context of expensive objects, the lower were their Palm Pilot ratings of pleasant mood ($r = -.37$, $p = .02$); they also showed marginally higher Palm Pilot ratings of sad emotions ($r = .31$, $p = .06$). We conducted a final analysis to determine whether this implicit measure of materialism correlated with neuroticism; we found no relation between them.

An important reason for using the IAT-adapted measure of materialism is that it is difficult to fake and therefore self-presentational issues are minimized. Kim (2001), for example, showed that participants are not able to "fake good" on the IAT even when instructed to do so. Participants, in fact, do not even know how to respond in such a way as to present a positive self-image. Therefore, our findings of a relation between implicit materialism and mood states in daily life are all the more remarkable. The findings suggest that materialism, even when measured implicitly, is detrimental to SWB.

Conclusions

These studies shed light on how the measurement of materialism may influence the strength of the materialism–SWB relation. It seems clear that the Belk (1985) Materialism Scale is so highly correlated with neuroticism that, when neuroticism is controlled, the relation between materialism and satisfaction with life drops substantially. Correlating the Belk Materialism Scale with well-being thus may inflate estimates of the relation between materialism and well-being, compared to when materialism is measured in a way that does not automatically involve worry. Studies 3 and 4, however, show that a significant correlation with SWB is still evident using other measures of materialism. Study 3 shows that self-reports of the importance of money, a more straightforward operationalization of materialism than the Belk scale, correlate negatively with happiness. Study 4 shows that even implicit measures of materialism, such as those based on the IAT (Greenwald & Farnham, 2000), predict lower levels of happiness in daily life. Thus, whereas confounds related to neuroticism can explain the results of Studies 1 and 2, they cannot explain the results of Studies 3 and 4. Given that these multiple operationalizations of materialism all indicate an inverse relation between materialism and SWB, we conclude that the relationship is likely real rather than an artifact of measurement confounds.

HYPOTHESIS 2: PEOPLE ARE MOST DISTANT FROM THEIR MATERIAL GOALS

Another possible explanation for the relation between materialism and well-being is that people generally are more distant from their material goals than from most other goals. Material standards may be higher as a result of television and advertising constantly bombarding us with images of desirable material possessions that we do not have (Richins, 1995). Furthermore, money is a fetishistic object and absolute wealth can never be fully attained (Marx, 1887). Because there is no limit to how much money or how many possessions someone might have, people who highly value material goals may feel that they are distant from their aims. This discrepancy, in turn, can lead to lower levels of satisfaction (Michalos, 1985). This may be particularly true of most students because of their scant income while in school. It is also likely that college students have higher aspirations for material success in the future, because a college education makes them more marketable in the future. It is therefore possible that students who value the financial domain will be particularly vulnerable to lower levels of satisfaction than other populations as a result of the especially greater discrepancy between what they have and what they want. Given that a large number of materialism studies are conducted on student samples, this is an important hypothesis to test. We use three different samples to examine this hypothesis.

Study 5

We examined data collected by Michalos (1985) involving 13,500 student respondents from 31 countries around the world. Participants were asked to rate their satisfaction (on a 9-point scale) in a number of domains, including finances, health, family, employment, friends, housing, partner, recreation, religion, self-esteem, transportation, and education. It was found that of the domains presented, the students were least satisfied with the financial domain. For example, finances and transportation were rated the lowest of the domains (4.14 and 4.20 respectively), whereas family and friends were rated the highest (5.31 and 5.30 respectively). A paired samples t test found a significant difference between finances and transportation (which was the second lowest rated domain; $t = 4.26, p < .001$).

We examined more detailed data from a sample of 1,630 Canadians. Participants were asked to compare 13 different domains (finances, relationship, etc.) to various comparison standards—the past, other people, the desired level, and the needed level. For example, respondents were asked to rate the degree to which other people have more resources than they do in each of the domains (other standard), as well as the degree to which they themselves had more resources now than in the past (past standard). We omitted the job domain from the analysis because most students did not have jobs. The largest discrepancies between current standing and multiple standards (e.g., ideal, past, other) always occurred in the financial domain. Thus, for example, people felt that their current status in terms of financial resources was quite a bit lower than their desired standing, as well as their needs in this area. The fact that such discrepancies were more notable in the financial domain than in other domains indicates that students in general are the least satisfied with their finances. Therefore, students who are materialistic may be less happy because they value a domain that is different from their comparison standards. Nonmaterialistic people, in contrast, may value other domains that are associated with smaller discrepancies between current status and comparison standards, thus promoting happiness.

Study 6

We attempted to replicate this pattern of findings in a different manner. Data were taken from the same sample (7,147 college students from 41 countries) examined in Study 3. Students reported (using a 7-point scale) the least satisfaction with their finances (4.11) in comparison to 21 other broad domains such as religion (4.79), family (5.38), education (4.89), recreation (4.61), nation (4.40), freedom (5.08), friends (5.45), romance (4.35), self (4.83), transportation (4.27), and travel and textbooks (tied for second lowest at 4.20).

A second, similar set of data was collected from students around the world (9,849 respondents in 47 countries), and similar results were found.

Students were instructed to rate 21 domains on a 9-point scale. Out of 21 domains, finances were rated the lowest (5.09), followed by textbooks (5.18) and study habits (5.27). The three highest domains were family (7.07), friends (6.93), and morality (7.10).

The results from Studies 5 and 6 are interesting because they indicate that the financial domain is the one that people are generally least satisfied with, even though most of our respondents, including the Canadians, came from very affluent societies. It might be that material success is such an open-ended goal, with models of very high consumption available, that people rarely feel that they have achieved it. There is always the next raise, the faster car, the bigger home, or the more extravagant vacation tantalizing the materialist (see chap. 8, this volume). With respect to nonmaterial domains, the same open-endedness may not apply. For example, people rarely seek more than one spouse at a time. Additionally, whereas money can be quantified very precisely, intimacy and friendship cannot. One wants to be healthy and happy, but not "extravagantly" so. These considerations allow us to understand why discrepancies (between actual and desired states) tend to be higher in the financial domain than in other domains.

Study 7

In the previous studies, we demonstrated with two rather large samples that the largest gap between where people are and where they want to be is in the financial domain. It is likely that people who place a high value on the financial domain are further from their goals and therefore are less satisfied than people who place a higher value on nonmaterial goals. We examined this hypothesis directly in Study 7.

Sixty-nine undergraduate students were asked to consider different goal areas, including financial and material success; self-acceptance and personal growth; intimacy and friendship; societal contribution; popularity; physical attractiveness; and achievement. These domains were based on those assessed by Kasser and Ryan's (1996) Aspiration Index. Participants were asked to rate the following: (a) how important success in this area is to you, (b) where you currently are in each area, (c) where the average person your age is in each area, (d) where you want to be currently in each area, and (e) where you would ideally want to be in the future in each area.

Our first hypothesis, that the largest gap between current and ideal standing would occur in the financial domain, was strongly supported. The difference between the financial goal gap and the societal goal gap (the next largest gap) was statistically significant ($t = 2.03$, $p = .018$). However, when examining the gaps between where one is and wants to be currently, the financial gap was no longer the largest gap. The new largest gap size was in the area of helping society and others, followed by self-acceptance, then by achievement, and finally by financial goals. A plausible interpretation may be that students value money but see their chances for accumulating it as more relevant to future goals than current ones. After all, these students are in college, where the primary purpose is to learn rather than to make money. After graduating from college, financial goals are likely to be more important to their current concerns.

Can the greater discrepancy related to material (vs. nonmaterial) goals explain why materialists tend to be less happy? To determine whether this was the case, we examined whether the degree to which people place importance on their financial goals interacted with financial gap size in predicting SWLS scores. Because we found that the material gap was the largest for people, we reasoned that the people who place high importance on this domain were likely to have low satisfaction because of the large gap size in general. Z-scores were computed for ratings of the importance of finances, as well as for the gap size between (a) current standing and current desires and (b) currant standing and ideal desires. These two z-scores (both gaps and importance) were multiplied to create an interaction term (i.e., Gap × Importance), and all three terms (gap, importance, and interaction) were entered into a regression equation with the SWLS (Diener et al., 1985) as the dependent measure. When the gap between current standing and current desires was used, the interaction term was significant ($b = -.28, p = .03$), indicating that people who place a higher value on the material domain had lower levels of life satisfaction when their gap size was large. None of the other terms in the regression were significant. We repeated this procedure with the other financial gap, namely, the discrepancy between current financial status and ideal financial status in the future. Again, the interaction between gap size and importance ratings (for the financial domain) was significant ($b = -.29, p = 02$). By contrast, the main effects (for financial gap size and the importance of the financial domain) were not significant.

In summary, the results suggest that having materialistic goals per se is not a cause of unhappiness, provided that the person is satisfied with his or her current status in this area. Relatedly, having a large gap in the financial domain (between current and desired status) is not a cause of unhappiness, provided that the person places little value in this gap. However, the combination of (a) valuing the financial domain and (b) having a large gap in this area may be a cause of unhappiness. Materialists may be generally less happy because they do place importance on material goals and because material goals are associated with a larger discrepancy between current and desired status.

Conclusions

The results of these three studies indicate support for the gap hypothesis. In each sample, the largest gap between current and ideal status pertained to the financial domain. To the extent that participants valued this domain, they tended to have lower SWB. The results suggest that it is possible to be a happy materialist, but only if one is happy with what one has (rather than preoccupied with what one aspires to have). The problem with materialism, however, may be that this is rarely the case. It is always possible to have newer, better, and more goods, rendering material pursuits ultimately unsatisfying (see also chaps. 2 & 8, this volume).

HYPOTHESIS 3: UNHAPPY PEOPLE BECOME MATERIALISTIC

Thus far, we have primarily concerned ourselves with correlational moderators of the materialism–SWB relation. Although such results are informative concerning the relation, they do not address the potential causal connections flowing from materialism to unhappiness or the converse. In this section, we consider whether materialistic values follow from emotional distress. In this connection, people may seek material objects when they are unhappy in order to draw attention away from the self. Or, people may seek material objects when unhappy because material objects are highly visible signs of success. It is worth noting that this hypothesis is somewhat related to Hypothesis 1, which posits that neuroticism accounts for the association between materialism (particularly as measured by the Belk, 1985, scale) and well-being. The two hypotheses are similar because of the high correlation between neuroticism and unhappiness. If unhappiness does in fact lead to materialistic values, then perhaps it would not be so detrimental to use items that include components of neuroticism when measuring materialism. Research conducted by Kasser and Sheldon (2000) does indeed suggest that materialism may serve a defensive function when the person is distressed. In this study, insecurity was manipulated by having participants write about death. Although thoughts about death have been shown to give rise to distress, they have also been shown to give rise to a variety of seemingly defensive behaviors that may be specific to managing the terror of one's own mortality (see chap. 8, this volume).

Because of these highly specialized effects involving mortality salience, it is an open question whether other causes of distress also give rise to materialistic values. To investigate this possibility, we manipulated distress by asking participants to think of deficiencies in their lives. We then had them rate the importance of materialistic (vs. nonmaterialistic) domains. Study 8 used a within-subject design, whereas Study 9 used a between-subjects design.

Study 8

Forty undergraduate students completed a number of ostensibly unrelated questionnaires in a 1-hour session. At the beginning of the session they rated the importance of different goals (popularity, achievement, financial–

material, intimacy–friendship, attractiveness, helping society–others, and self-acceptance). Toward the end of the session they were asked to write for 5 minutes about the areas of their lives that are disappointing or inadequate and then to rate the importance of the same list of goals. We examined the change in ratings for different types of goals and found that after writing about their inadequacies, participants rated financial goals as significantly more important than they had at the beginning of the session ($t = 4.12, p = .001$). They also rated achievement goals as more important ($t = 2.85, p = .007$); however, the ratings for the other goals did not change. These results suggest that distress does lead to a materialistic value orientation, at least temporarily. However, because there was no control group in this study, it is possible that people simply make higher ratings only in the material domain when they are given a second chance to rate the importance of domains. Therefore, we sought to replicate this result using a proper control group.

Study 9

In this study, we attempted to replicate the previous findings using a between-subjects design. Students were randomly assigned to one of two groups. They were either asked to write for 5 minutes about areas in their life in which they felt inadequate or areas in their lives where they were doing well. Following this manipulation, the students were asked to rate the importance of different goals (listed in the previous study) such as finances, intimacy, and so on. There were no significant differences between the two groups in this study.

Conclusion

Study 9, which used a between-subjects manipulation of distress, did · not replicate Study 8. Thus, we are left to conclude that there may be something to the idea that distress makes people materialistic but that our results are inconclusive. However, adding the results of Study 8 to the studies reported by Kasser and Sheldon (2000), it would seem that this hypothesis warrants further study. In this respect, we are left with some important questions. Is there something specific to thoughts about death that motivates materialistic values? Or does any form of distress lead to materialism? Why do distressed people turn to materialistic concerns? Perhaps people (unconsciously) think that material goods can distract them from aversive forms of self-awareness (Baumeister & Boden, 1994), or perhaps people seek material goods because they think such goods will make them feel better (Tice & Bratlavsky, 2000). We are impressed with the idea that materialism serves a defensive function (chap. 8, this volume), but we believe that further research is necessary to pin it down.

HYPOTHESIS 4: THINKING ABOUT MATERIALISTIC CONCERNS LEADS TO UNHAPPINESS

The previous studies addressed the influence of low levels of SWB on materialistic values. In Studies 10 and 11 we briefly considered the opposite causal direction, from materialistic values to SWB. Although getting people to adopt materialistic goals that they did not previously have did not seem feasible for our manipulations, it certainly is feasible to alter the accessibility to consciousness of having materialistic goals. Indeed, some theorists have argued that such manipulations can have transitory influences on goal-directed activity (Carver & Scheier, 1990; Ortony, Clore, & Collins, 1988). In Study 10, we asked people to think about their goals in the area of material goods as opposed to relationships. Such a manipulation should alter the accessibility of materialistic goals, potentially influencing mood states as a consequence. In Study 11, we attempted a more subtle manipulation of goal-directed activity. Based on the idea that goals become activated by relevant stimuli in the environment (Ortony et al., 1988), we asked people to determine whether objects presented on the computer screen were expensive or not expensive. Categorization activity should alter the accessibility of the dimension used to differentiate stimuli, in this case their material value (Bruner, 1957). We sought to determine whether such a materialistic orientation, altered on a temporary basis, could affect mood states.

Study 10

Fifty-nine participants were randomly assigned to one of two conditions. Half were instructed to write about their financial goals, whereas the other half wrote about their relationship goals. After 5 minutes of writing, the participants were asked to rate to what degree they were currently feeling the following emotions: pleasant, good mood, elated, unpleasant, bad mood, depressed, ashamed, guilty, anxious, uneasy, proud, and confident. These items were grouped into the categories of positive emotions, negative emotions, guilt, anxiety, and pride. The manipulation did not alter any of the mood scales.

Study 11

Seventy-two participants rated their moods on the same scale as in Study 10 and then completed a computer task in which they categorized words quickly into two categories (expensive and inexpensive) for about 5 minutes. By doing this we hoped to increase the accessibility of a materialistic way of evaluating objects. We then measured moods after this induction but found no mood changes.

Conclusion

Both manipulations sought to alter the accessibility of materialistic goals, either somewhat directly (Study 10) or somewhat indirectly (Study 11). If the accessibility of materialistic goals is an important determinant of SWB, we might expect the manipulations to alter mood states. Furthermore, if materialistic goals are relatively open-ended and difficult to satisfy (see the preceding studies), we might have expected a manipulation of their accessibility to have a negative influence on mood states. In essence, such manipulations should have made participants somewhat aware of the material goods that they do not possess but desire.

However, we found no significant priming effects. Admittedly, these null results do not rule out a causal flow from materialistic goals to SWB, particularly because it would seem to be impossible to get people to adopt materialistic goals that they do not have. It may still be the case that "living" the materialistic values rather than simply thinking about them leads to unhappiness. Nevertheless, the results of Studies 10 and 11 do at least provide some relevant evidence on the influence of accessible materialistic goals on SWB. We are left to conclude that the evidence for unhappy feelings leading to materialistic goals is a bit stronger than the evidence for materialistic goals leading to unhappy feelings. However, we are cautious in making this statement. It is thus an open question whether potentially stronger manipulations of materialistic goals could alter SWB. One idea for potential study is to have participants classify material objects (e.g., new car) as personally desirable. Such a manipulation might be more successful in altering mood states if it targeted latent, but unmet, materialistic desires.

HYPOTHESIS 5: FOCUSING ON MATERIAL GOALS CONFLICTS WITH OTHER GOALS

It is possible that materialistic goals, in and of themselves, are not a detriment to SWB but that having materialistic goals tends to interfere with the achievement of other, nonmaterialistic goals. The detriments in the area of nonmaterialistic goals, in turn, may be responsible for the lower SWB of materialists. Indeed, such an explanation for the materialism–SWB relation was suggested by Kasser et al. (chap. 2, this volume). Such an explanation is based on the idea that inevitable trade-offs occur when one pursues certain goals (e.g., materialistic ones) rather than others (e.g., nonmaterialistic goals). More specifically, to the extent that a person's energies and efforts are directed toward acquiring money and goods, the person may have less energy and effort to direct toward personal relationships.

The negative relation that likely exists between the pursuit of materialistic as opposed to nonmaterialistic goals must be viewed as a relative tendency rather than an absolute one. If so, it should be possible to isolate materialistic individuals who continue to invest time and energy in their relationships, thereby preserving a relatively high level of SWB. In Study 12, we sought to verify the idea that the effects of materialism on SWB are indirect, through detriments in the area of personal relationships.

Study 12

To examine the association between relationship quality, materialism, and SWB, we asked 95 participants to complete a number of measures. Materialism was measured using 18 items taken from the Material Values Survey (Richins & Dawson, 1992). Students also completed the SWLS (Diener et al. 1985), and the Positive and Negative Affect Scale (PANAS; Watson, Tellegen, & Clark, 1988). In addition, participants carried a personal digital assistant (PDA) for 1 week and answered a brief survey about their moods five times a day when paged. We combined nine items (afraid, anxious, nervous, angry, irritable, guilty, ashamed, sad, and downhearted) to form a measure of NA, and eight items (happy, cheerful, calm, relaxed, proud, confident, excited, and enthusiastic) to form a measure of PA. We next had three friends or family members of each participant complete a short questionnaire, which included a 10-item measure of relationship quality (sample item: This person appreciates me for who I am; Cronbach's ∂ = .83). People who scored high on materialism had family and friends who rated their relationship quality as lower than people low in materialism ($r = -.38$, $p = .001$). This suggests that normally there is a trade-off between having materialistic goals and having high-quality relationships. Materialism was marginally related to the SWLS score ($r = -.20$, $p = .06$), and global PANAS PA ($r = .17$, $p = .10$), and significantly related to PANAS NA ($r = .23$, $p = .03$), PDA PA ($r = -.23$, $p = .03$), and PDA NA ($r = .32$, $p = .002$). Next we examined whether the inverse relation between materialism and well-being was attributable to the negative impact of materialism on relationship quality. When the relationship quality rated by family and friends was controlled, correlations between materialism on the one hand and SWLS ($r = -.09$, $p = .42$), global NA ($r = .17$, $p = .12$), and PA PDA ($r = .17$, $p = .11$) on the other were no longer significant. However, the relation involving NA PDA ratings remained significant ($r = .24$, $p = .03$).

Conclusion

In summary, the results confirm that the effects of materialism on SWB are at least partly mediated by relationship quality. Materialists tended to have relationships of lower quality (as assessed by their family and friends). Furthermore, with relationship quality controlled, the relations between materialism and SWB decline. These results suggest that a materialist can be happy if he or she is able to preserve the quality of his or her relationships. However, the inverse relationship between materialism and relationship quality suggests that there are built-in trade-offs that tend to undermine the quality of materialists' relationships.

HYPOTHESIS 6: MATERIAL GOALS ARE LESS ENJOYABLE TO WORK TOWARD

A final hypothesis is that material goals may simply be less enjoyable to work toward. It may be that when pursuing relationship goals, people have a more enjoyable experience (e.g., socializing with friends). Conversely, when people are pursuing material goals, they may be working hard to make money or stressing out about saving money. Alternatively, they may also be shopping, which to some is an enjoyable experience. In the next study we use Palm Pilot data in order to determine whether people do in fact have a less enjoyable time while they are working toward financial goals than toward other types of goals.

Study 13

We asked 112 participants to carry a Palm Pilot for 1 week and record their moods, as well as what their goals were when they were paged (approximately five times per day). We first conducted an analysis of variance to determine whether people have different levels of PA and NA when working toward six different types of goals (financial, achievement, self-acceptance, popularity, helping society, and intimacy). We found significant differences in participants' PA ($F = 12.30, p < .001$) and NA ($F = 2.87, p = .014$) while working toward the different goals. The means indicated that people experienced the least PA while working toward financial goals in comparison with the other five goals. This was not found for NA, however. We next used t tests to compare the financial domain with the other domains. We found that participants reported significantly less PA when they were working toward financial goals than when they were working toward all of the other goals except achievement-related ones. For example, the pursuit of intimacy was related to much higher levels of PA than was the pursuit of financial goals ($t = 6.13, p < .001$). Expressed in terms of this relation, there was a $-.23$ correlation ($p = .001$) between PA and the pursuit of financial (positively keyed) as opposed to intimacy (negatively keyed) goals.

Conclusion

It is likely that people tend to pursue financial goals while at work and intimacy goals while socializing. An interesting question is whether the inverse relation between the pursuit of financial goals and PA is due to the setting involved (i.e., work vs. socializing) or the intrinsic nature of the type of goal pursuit (i.e., financial vs. intimacy). Fortunately, in addition to asking participants whether they were pursuing financial goals at the time of the page, we also asked them to indicate whether they were at work or not, as well as whether they were socializing or not. Controlling whether people were working or not, the inverse relation between the pursuit of financial (vs. intimacy) goals was still significant, $B = -.21$, $p = .001$. Additionally, the relation was still significant when controlling for whether they were socializing or not, $B = -.20$, $p = .001$. Finally, the relationship was significant when both working and socializing activities were controlled, $B = -.18$, $p = .001$. Thus, the pursuit of financial goals was associated with lower PA, regardless of the setting, suggesting that something inherent to the pursuit of financial goals is detrimental to happiness.

GENERAL CONCLUSIONS

The results of our studies suggest that materialism appears to be toxic to SWB and that this relation is multidetermined. Specifically, we examined six hypotheses for why materialism is associated with lower SWB. We found support for three of these hypotheses. Materialists' poorer social lives were related to lower levels of SWB. However, it could be the case that people with few friends or bad social skills tend to focus on material things to compensate. We also found evidence that working toward material goals is less rewarding in the moment than working toward other goals. We found support for the hypothesis that the gap between what people have and what they want in the material domain is larger than in other domains; therefore, valuing this domain highly is detrimental to well-being. In three studies, the largest gap between where people are and where they want to be was in the financial domain. We found that the degree to which people valued the financial domain moderated the relation between the financial gap size and satisfaction with life. We found partial support for the hypothesis that unhappiness leads to the adoption of material values. The within-subject design showed support for this hypothesis, but this was not replicated using a between-subjects design. Finally, we found little support for the hypotheses that simply thinking about financial goals and material objects leads to lower SWB, or that the materialism–SWB relation is spurious because of the relationship between materialism and neuroticism.

Our results have implications at the national level for policies related to economic development. Living in a wealthy country is related to higher SWB, and wealthier nations have greater freedom, human rights, and equality (Diener, Diener, & Diener, 1995). Along with other benefits of living in wealthy countries, financial success appears to confer emotional benefits, even when the variations in financial success pertain to higher levels of income (see Diener & Oishi, 2000). This suggests that nations, especially poor ones, might not totally want to eschew economic growth. Nations are likely to grow economically if people in them are very concerned about gaining wealth, but such concerns are related to lower SWB. At the same time, people in nations that achieve economic development are, on average, happier. Thus, there is an unresolved paradox involving economic growth and happiness: Whereas national wealth predicts positive SWB, relatively materialistic people within any given culture tend to be less happy. It may be that economic success cannot simply be equated with materialistic values (although see chap. 8, this volume, for a different interpretation). In this respect, we provided plenty of evidence for the idea that the personal (rather than cultural) adoption of materialistic goals is associated with lower SWB.

Research on the reasons behind the relation between materialism and SWB has only just begun. Further studies should be conducted to examine the hypotheses above with broader samples. New hypotheses are also likely to be developed and tested. Future studies should also focus on materialism cross-culturally to see whether the relation holds in other societies and contexts. Perhaps in other countries there is a smaller, or even a positive, relation between materialism and SWB. This might be particularly true in poor countries in which the struggle for financial wealth is related more closely to the struggle for survival. Data from other nations might lead to the refinement of plausible hypotheses of why materialists are less happy.

In summary, materialism appears to work against people's attainment of a sense of well-being. A question then is how a modern nation can continue to experience the benefits of economic development, such as high levels of health care and advances in science, and yet dampen the excessive materialism that seems to be toxic to SWB. It is not sufficient to criticize the material lifestyle; alternative value systems must be developed. Perhaps if people knew the costs of materialism, particularly with respect to personal relationships and SWB, they would be more likely to balance their materialistic and nonmaterialistic goals (Myers, 1999). It may be possible to have one's cake and enjoy it too, although there appear to be forces, some of which we have illuminated, that render the pursuit of one's cake less enjoyable.

REFERENCES

Baumeister, R. F., & Boden, J. M. (1994). Shrinking the self. In T. M. Brinthaupt & R. P. Lipka (Eds.), Changing the self: Philosophies, techniques, and experiences. SUNY Series, Studying the Self (pp. 143–173). Albany: State University of New York Press.

Belk, R. W. (1985). Materialism: Trait aspects of living in the material world. Journal of Consumer Research, 12, 265–280.

Boring, E. G. (1953). A history of introspection. *Psychological Bulletin, 50,* 169–186.

Bruner, J. S. (1957). On perceptual readiness. *Psychological Review, 64,* 123–152.

Carver, C. S., & Scheier, M. F. (1990). Origins and functions of positive and negative affect: A control-process view. *Psychological Review, 97,* 19–35.

Diener, E., Diener, M., & Diener, C. (1995). Factors predicting the subjective well-being of nations. *Journal of Personality and Social Psychology, 69,* 851–864.

Diener, E., Emmons, R. A., Larsen, R. J., & Griffin, S. (1985). The Satisfaction With Life Scale. *Journal of Personality Assessment, 49,* 71–75.

Diener, E., & Oishi, S. (2000). Money and happiness: Income and subjective well-being across nations. In E. Diener & E. M. Suh (Eds.), *Culture and subjective well-being* (pp. 185–218). Cambridge, MA: MIT Press.

Diener, E., & Seligman, M. E. P. (2002). Very happy people. *Psychological Science, 13,* 80–83.

Greenwald, A. G., & Banaji, M. R. (1995). Implicit social cognition: Attitudes, self-esteem, and stereotypes. *Psychological Review, 102,* 4–27.

Greenwald, A. G., Banaji, M. R., Rudman, L. A., Farnham, S. D., Nosek, B. A., & Mellott, D. S. (2002). A unified theory of implicit attitudes, stereotypes, self-esteem, and self-concept. *Psychological Review, 109,* 3–25.

Greenwald, A. G., & Farnham, S. D. (2000). Using the Implicit Association Test to measure self-esteem and self-concept. *Journal of Personality and Social Psychology, 79,* 1022–1038.

Greenwald, A. G., McGhee, D. E., & Schwartz, J. L. K. (1998). Measuring individual differences in implicit cognition: The implicit association test. *Journal of Personality and Social Psychology, 74,* 1464–1480.

Kasser, T., & Ryan, R. M. (1993). A dark side of the American dream: Correlates of financial success as a central life aspiration. *Journal of Personality and Social Psychology, 65,* 410–422.

Kasser, T., & Ryan, R. M. (1996). Further examining the American dream: Differential correlates of intrinsic and extrinsic goals. *Personality and Social Psychology Bulletin, 22,* 280–287.

Kasser, T., & Sheldon, K. M. (2000). Of wealth and death: Materialism, mortality salience, and consumption behavior. *Psychological Science, 11,* 348–351.

Kim, D.-Y. (2001). *Voluntary controllability of the Implicit Association Test (IAT).* Manuscript submitted for publication.

Lucas, R. E., Diener, E., & Suh, E. (1996). Discriminant validity of well-being measures. *Journal of Personality and Social Psychology, 71,* 616–628.

Marx, K. (1887). *Das kapital.* Moscow: Progress Publishers.

McClelland, D. C. (1987). *Human motivation.* New York: Cambridge University Press.

McClelland, D. C. (1985). How motives, skills, and values determine what people do. *American Psychologist, 40*(7), 812–825.

McCrae, R. R. (1990). Controlling neuroticism in the measurement of stress. *Stress Medicine, 6,* 237–241.

Michalos, A. C. (1985). Multiple discrepancy theory. *Social Indicators Research, 16,* 347–413.

Myers, D. G. (1999). Close relationships and quality of life. In D. Kahneman, E. Diener, & N. Schwarz (Eds.), *Well-being: The foundations of hedonic psychology* (pp. 374–391). New York: Russell Sage Foundation.

Ortony, A., Clore, G. L., & Collins, A. (1988). *The cognitive structure of emotions.* New York: Cambridge University Press.

Richins, M. L. (1995). Social comparison, advertising, and consumer discontent. *American Behavioral Scientist, 38,* 593–607.

Richins, M. L., & Dawson, S. (1992). A consumer values orientation for materialism and its measurement: Scale development and validation. *Journal of Consumer Research, 19,* 303–316.

Robinson, M. D. (2000). The reactive and prospective functions of mood: Its role in linking daily experiences and cognitive well-being. *Cognition and Emotion, 14,* 145–176.

Robinson, M. D., Vargas, P., & Crawford, E. G. (2003). Putting process into personality, appraisal, and emotion: Evaluative processing as a missing link. In J. Musch & K. C. Klaner (Eds.), *The psychology of evaluation: Affective processes in cognition and emotion* (pp. 275–306). Mahwah, NJ: Erlbaum.

Schmuck, P. (2001). Life goal preferences measured by inventories, subliminal and supraliminal priming and their relation to well-being. In P. Schmuck & K. M. Sheldon (Eds.), *Life goals and well-being: Towards a positive psychology of human striving* (pp. 132–147). Goettingen, Germany: Hogrefe & Huber.

Sharpe, J. P. (2000). A construct validation study of the Belk Materialism Scale and the Material Values Scale. *Dissertation Abstracts International, 60* (8-B), 4287B.

Suh, E., Diener, E., Oishi, S., & Triandis, H. C. (1998). The shifting basis of life satisfaction judgments across cultures: Emotions versus norms. *Journal of Personality and Social Psychology, 74,* 482–493.

Tice, D. M., & Bratlavsky, E. (2000). Giving in to feel good: The place of emotion regulation in the context of general self-control. *Psychological Inquiry, 11,* 149–159.

Triandis, H. C., & Suh, E. M. (2002). Cultural influences on personality. *Annual Review of Psychology, 53,* 133–160.

Watson, D., Tellegen, A., & Clark, L. (1988). Development and validation of brief measures of positive and negative affect: The PANAS scales. *Journal of Personality and Social Psychology, 54,* 1063–1070.

4

GLOBALIZATION, CORPORATE CULTURE, AND FREEDOM

ALLEN D. KANNER AND RENÉE G. SOULE

Materialistic values and practices have been around since time imme-morial. However, modern consumerism is unique in that it is driven by pow-erful corporations whose very survival depends on people purchasing more products (Korten, 1995; Mander, 1991). Through their vast influence on the media, government, and the millions of workers they employ, corporations are reshaping American culture by fostering the belief that happiness is attained through the satisfaction of material needs (Herman & Chomsky, 1988; Jacobson & Mazur, 1995; Klein, 1999; Lee & Solomon, 1990). In recent years, the reach of corporations has become global, and their message has infiltrated even the most remote human societies (Mander & Goldsmith, 1996; Norberg-Hodge, 1991). Without considering this larger context, any study of consumerism is bound to be incomplete.

We believe that consumerism is one of the most important issues for psychologists to address at this point in history. However, to do so without an understanding of corporations and the culture they create would be to miss the boat. Such an unbalanced approach would be not only inaccurate but also unfair, because it tends to "blame the victim" and absolve corporations

49

of their role in creating and advancing the problem. Furthermore, when social reality is ignored and the personal is overemphasized, efforts to mitigate the harmful effects of consumerism are likely to fail.

The power and influence of corporations are undeniable. Of the world's largest 100 economies, 52 of them are not countries, but corporations (Mander, Barker, & Korten, 2001). Through extensive lobbying and campaign contributions, these multinational corporations have enormous influence on governments and laws. Through their ownership of the media (Herman & Chomsky, 1988; Jacobson & Mazur, 1995; Kanner & Gomes, 1995; Klein, 1999; Lee & Solomon, 1990; McChesney, 1997) and public relations firms (Larson, 1992; Stauber & Rampton, 1995), they control or influence an astounding amount of information and mold the way Americans think and feel about a great range of topics. Oddly enough, since the late 1800s corporations have had the legal status of persons (Grossman & Adams, 1993; Korten, 1995). However, they have far more resources available to them than any real individual and, at least in theory, are immortal (Korten, 1995). It is curious that, of all our society's institutions, including those of government, religion, and education, only corporations are afforded this special status.

In this chapter we make the link between corporate culture and many issues of interest to psychologists, including work stress, family conflict, education, creativity and imagination, the negative effects of advertising, and, potentially, the direction of psychology itself. In order to do so, we briefly describe the ongoing expansion of corporate culture, including its most recent expression through economic globalization. Although these large political and social considerations may at first seem far removed from the everyday concerns of psychologists, our intention is to show that globalization and corporate efforts to commercialize and commodify American society lie at the heart of modern consumerism.

Another purpose of this chapter is to examine the way freedom is eroded by corporate culture. Ironically, although American corporations have arisen from a society that cherishes freedom, their single-minded pursuit of profit frequently stands in direct opposition to democratic values and practices. Corporate policy and actions often compromise both outer and inner freedom, with dire psychological consequences. These threats to freedom range from corporate designed international treaties that weaken national sovereignty to the emotional constriction that arises when people constantly defend themselves from the onslaught of commercials.

At present, the vanguard of corporate expansion is globalization. The rash of corporate mergers and acquisitions in recent years is the direct result of multinational corporations jockeying for position in the international marketplace (Danaher, 1996; Korten, 1995). Beyond economic competitiveness, however, globalization has also meant that corporate culture is being exported worldwide. As we shall see, this extension of corporate culture is also reshaping people's lives in the United States.

GLOBALIZATION

Before they were shut down by protests and the objections of third world countries, the 1999 World Trade Organization (WTO) meetings held in Seattle were set to address, among other things, barriers to trade in the international education "industry" (Education International/Public Services International, 1999; Shadwick, 2000). For example, currently most countries do not recognize each other's advanced academic degrees. The WTO is considering whether this practice is a barrier to trade. Proponents of free trade in higher education would like to see degree programs "harmonized" across nations. Were this to happen, educational institutions could create standardized, and highly profitable, online degree programs, which could then be marketed internationally.

There are several implications in this scenario for psychology. The first is that the United States, like all other nations, would have to recognize psychology degrees granted by foreign universities. The second is that multinational educational corporations could create standardized, online degree programs that would also have to be internationally recognized. The harmonization of graduate coursework in psychology could severely hamper the ability of different countries to develop their own theories and approaches. Psychologists in the United States could also potentially face a huge influx of foreign-trained psychologists who would be willing to work for lower pay than their U.S. colleagues.

Psychologists, like most people in America, are generally unaware of the secret workings of the WTO or the more general processes underlying globalization, despite the many ramifications they have for their lives. For this reason, we briefly describe the organizations and treaties that are giving shape to the global economy.

Global Economy: "A Rising Tide Raises All Boats"

Economic globalization is the extension of export-centered, free-market capitalism from the developed countries, led by the United States, to the developing nations (Friedman, 1999; Stiglitz, 2002). It is based on several deeply held principles that include the primacy of growth; the need for free trade to stimulate growth; the removal of governmental laws that inhibit the international movement of goods, services, and money; and the belief that every country should produce only those products that it can competitively market in the global economy, while importing everything else, a philosophy called *comparative advantage* (Cavanagh & Mander, 2002; Mander, 1996). Globalists claim that when followed, these principles will lead to unprecedented global wealth, the end of poverty, the improvement of living conditions everywhere, the spread of freedom and democracy, and the protection of the environment (Cavanagh & Mander, 2002; Friedman, 1999; Stiglitz,

2002). They believe globalization is the natural and inevitable outcome of historical processes that are furthering human progress and unleashing unparalleled creativity and productivity. Globalists celebrate international corporations as innovative and efficient institutions that are ideally suited to build the integrated world economy (Cavanagh & Mander, 2002). We would add that implicit in this system is a psychological model of human motivation and behavior that assumes that people are most creative and productive under conditions of fierce but fair competition (see also Friedman, 1999).

Supporters of globalization claim much success over the last few decades, including an increase in length of life and standards of living that are enjoyed by millions around the world. They point to vast improvements in the economies of such diverse countries as Chile, Poland, and China (Friedman, 1999; Stiglitz, 2002).

The global economy is being molded by a number of international trade and economic institutions, such as the WTO, International Monetary Fund (IMF), and World Bank, as well as by international trade agreements such as the General Agreement on Tariffs and Trade (GATT), North American Free Trade Agreement (NAFTA), the European Union's Maastricht Agreement, and the proposed Free Trade Area of the Americas (FTAA). These institutions and treaties serve both to bring developing countries into the global marketplace and to monitor and regulate international trade (Stiglitz, 2002). The WTO, which evolved from the GATT, determines the rules and regulations governing international trade and settles trade disputes, whereas the IMF and World Bank provide loans to countries for development or during economic crises. The various trade agreements increase free trade among regions of neighboring countries (Stiglitz, 2002). As such, these institutions and agreements are responsible for many of the benefits attributed to globalization (Friedman, 1999; Stiglitz, 2002).

Critics of globalization, however, point out that this world-altering system poses a major threat to the environment, the economic well-being of the vast majority of the world's population, and to democracy (Cavanagh & Mander, 2002; Danaher & Burbach, 2000; Korten, 1995; Mander, 1996; Mander & Goldsmith, 1996; Norberg-Hodge, 1991). They note that on a planet with finite resources, a global economy based on continuous growth is fundamentally unsustainable, as is an international marketplace that is heavily dependent on exportation (Mander, 1991; Norberg-Hodge, 1991). The global transportation of goods by sea shipping, air cargo, and trucking is a major source of environmental degradation (Cavanagh & Mander, 2002). Moreover, rather than helping the poor, in recent decades the policies of the IMF and World Bank have led to an increase in poverty worldwide and to economic crises in East Asia, Russia, Mexico, and Argentina (Cavanagh, Welch, & Retallack, 2001; Mander et al., 2001; Stiglitz, 2002). Critics also observe that globalization is creating a worldwide monoculture steeped in materialistic values (Mander, 1991; Norberg-Hodge, 1991). They further note that by centralizing power in the hands of multinational corporations, which are run in a highly undemocratic manner, and by elevating economic trade above national sovereignty (more on this below), the global economy is a threat to democracy itself (Danaher & Burbach, 2000; McChesney, 1997; Nader &Wallach, 1996).

Finally, opponents of globalization are concerned that its promotion of corporate ownership of public assets (privatization) is destroying the commons. The *commons* is the communal heritage of people from time immemorial that includes, among other things, natural resources such as air and water, scientific knowledge, public health and education, and the human genome (Bollier, 2002; Rowe, 2001). By privatizing and commodifying the commons, corporations make these resources available only to those who can afford them. In general, critics of globalization believe it is fatally flawed and should be replaced by more humane and sustainable economic systems (Cavanagh & Mander, 2002).

Structure of Globalization

To understand the strong negative reactions globalization engenders, it is worth examining more closely some of the policies and practices of its major institutions and the trade agreements on which it is based. For example, one of the main functions of the WTO is to settle trade disputes between countries, especially when one nation claims that another nation's laws constitute an unfair barrier to trade (Danaher & Burbach, 2000; Rademacher, 2000). These disputes, which take the form of one country suing another through the WTO, are typically driven by the corporate interests of the aggrieved nation. Moreover, for the three nations included in NAFTA, a corporation from one country can directly sue another country through the WTO. If a WTO suit is successful, the losing nation has a choice of either compensating the corporation for its projected economic losses, which can run into the billions of dollars, or removing the offending law. These suits are decided by a WTO dispute panel, which meets in secret and whose decisions are final—there is no appeal (Beck & Danaher, 2000; Stiglitz, 2002). For example, the U.S. chemical company, Ethyl Corporation, sued the Canadian government in 1998 for $250 million for banning MMT, a gas additive that has been shown to cause brain damage in laboratory animals. Canada settled the suit by paying Ethyl Corporation $13 million for losses already incurred and rescinded the law. In June 1999, the Canadian company, Methanex, sued California for nearly $1 billion for beginning to phase out another gas additive, MTBE, that is suspected of being carcinogenic and of having contaminated groundwater across the state. The case is pending (Bottari, 2001; Public Citizen's Global Trade Watch & Friends of the Earth, 2001; Rademacher, 2000).

Globalization further compromises national sovereignty through the loan policies of the IMF and World Bank (Cavanagh et al., 2001; Mander et al., 2001). These institutions provide loans to developing countries that frequently include conditions called Structural Adjustment Programs (SAPs). For instance, some SAPs have stipulated that countries drastically reduce public spending, lower wages, weaken or eliminate environmental laws, and remove tariffs and other obstacles that restrict foreign investment and otherwise make it difficult for multinational corporations to do business (Bello, 1995; Heredia & Purcell, 1995). Ostensibly SAPs, by reducing wages and lowering environmental protections, enable a country to lower the costs of production, increase profits, and therefore repay its loans. What in fact happens is that multinational corporations reap most of the profits whereas loan recipient nations become poorer and are unable to repay their debts (Bello, 2000; Cavanagh et al., 2001; Mander et al., 2001).

International trade agreements, such as the GATT, NAFTA, and FTAA, greatly expand corporate investment rights and protections, often to the detriment of local industry (Barlow, 2001; Economic Policy Institute, 2001; Nader & Wallach, 1996; Public Citizen's Global Trade Watch & Friends of the Earth, 2001). Under these treaties governments must grant companies from other member nations treatment as favorable as that given to their own companies. This allows multinational corporations to move freely into another country and out-compete smaller, local industries (Nader & Wallach, 1996; Public Citizen's Global Trade Watch & Friends of the Earth, 1996). The FTAA, which would expand NAFTA to all Central and South American countries except Cuba, would extend and even increase the rights guaranteed by NAFTA to corporations (Barlow, 2001). Like most global trade agreements, the FTAA is being negotiated in secret by government officials and their corporate advisors (Barlow, 2001).

With treaties and international monetary institutions paving the way, multinational corporations bring not only their goods and services but also their massive advertising campaigns to foreign lands (Mander, 1991; Norberg-Hodge, 1991). For many poor countries globalization has meant the importation of corporate culture, with its materialistic values, fast-paced competition, and slick glamor. For example, after living in the small Himalayan country of Ladakh for 16 years when the forces of globalization were first taking hold, linguist Helena Norberg-Hodge (1991) reported having seen people "proudly wear[ing] wrist watches they cannot read and for which they have no use" (p. 140) and apologizing for serving their far healthier traditional food instead of instant noodles. She observed that when developing countries are brought into the global economy, "As their desire to appear modern grows, people are rejecting their own culture" (p. 140). The loss of national sovereignty and cultural diversity are unintended but nevertheless tragic outcomes of globalization (Mander, 1991, 1996; Norberg-Hodge, 1991, 1996; Shiva & Holla-Bhar, 1996).

CORPORATE CULTURE

Few aspects of American life are untouched by corporate culture. In this section, we explore the undesirable influence of corporations on work and family life, academia, and psychology itself. We also address the role of corporate advertising in the commercialization and commodification of American society.

Work and Family

As American corporations seek to expand in a fiercely competitive global marketplace, the pressure for greater employee commitment mounts. In her book, *Time Bind*, sociologist Arlie Hochschild (1997) described the development in corporate America of escalating demands that employees work longer hours and make their jobs the centers of their lives (see also Schor, 1991, 1998). Parents are forced to neglect their children and each other in order to clock enough hours at their jobs. As Hochschild found in her interviews at "Amerco," a Fortune 500 company, parents no longer have time to care for their sick children.

> In [one] case, the son of a single mother needed surgery, but because she had already used up her sick days and her vacation days, she chose to wait six months to schedule the surgery so she could arrange a day off. In response to this delay, her son's doctor threatened to press charges of child abuse. In another instance, the coworkers of a single father at Amerco covered for him each night during fifteen-minute extensions of his thirty-minute break so that he could drive to his house and put his ten-year-old daughter, home alone, to bed. On discovering this arrangement, his supervisor stopped the practice. The supervisor in a third case threatened to fire a mother who left work to care for a daughter with a dangerously high fever. (pp. 169–170)

Through the use of such concepts as "company loyalty" and "team spirit," corporations have become quite skilled at convincing workers that these time demands are necessary and even desirable. Corporations encourage people to spend more time at work by creating far more inviting workplaces, offering everything from child-care to gymnasiums to better food at the cafeterias. Hochschild observed that as the corporate environment becomes more livable and people spend more time on the job, work replaces the family and neighborhood as the center of community life. Ironically, for many people, returning to their neglected homes means having to deal with resentful and needy spouses and children. This pattern has become so extreme that many people come to experience work as a blessed escape from an impossible home situation.

To cope with insufficient time with their families, many Amerco employees who were parents "corporatized" their home-life, running it on a tight, efficient schedule and, when they could afford to, "outsourcing" family duties to paid professionals. In doing so, they had less time together as a family for talking, having fun, or simply relaxing. According to Hochschild, these parents used three strategies to justify to themselves such a stringent, no-frills approach to raising their children. The first was simply to deny that their families needed much time from them. As Hochschild stated, "[T]hey emotionally downsized life" (p. 221). Second, those who outsourced family duties "detached their own identities from acts they might previously have defined as part of being 'a good parent' or a 'good spouse'" (p. 221). Third, "many parents divided themselves into a real and a potential self, into the person each of them was and the person each of them would be 'if only I had time.' Often the real self had little time for care at home while the potential one was boundlessly available" (p. 221). Additionally, although they realized it was a poor substitute, some parents would attempt to compensate for their absence by buying their children large quantities of toys, clothes, and other desired products.

As psychologists, we are familiar with conflicts between work and family obligations and with stress arising from the unrelenting pace of modern life. Rarely, however, do we frame these issues as stemming from a dehumanizing corporate system that is attempting to remain competitive in the global marketplace. This larger context is traditionally considered outside the purview of our field. Instead, psychologists support the view that conflicts between work and family life are primarily individual issues.

Along with the time bind, other corporate sources of stress for workers include now standard business practices such as mergers, acquisitions, and companies relocating out-of-state or overseas in search of cheap labor, tax breaks, and so on (Kivimaki, Vahtera, Penetti, & Ferrie, 2000). Such occurrences contribute to a rise in job insecurity that has reached beyond the average worker into the upper levels of management: Following an acquisition or merger, even CEOs no longer feel safe (Mander, 1991). The expendability of workers is part of a larger trend in which corporations themselves are commodified. Today companies are purchasing one another as pure investments, irrespective of what the acquired company might produce or provide. This practice increases the likelihood of mergers and acquisitions, thus making corporate jobs even less secure. Employees become but tiny pawns in this rapidly accelerating monopoly game. Yet each small move disrupts lives, destroys communities, and fractures careers.

Advertising

Beyond the workplace, the most obvious influence of corporate culture on the American psyche is through advertising. Commercials manipulate people's strongest desires and greatest fears to convince them to buy the proffered products. Corporations spend tens of billions of dollars annually on their marketing efforts, including hiring actors, producing commercials, and paying for media time. Even if only a small fraction of these huge sums are devoted to marketing research, then the effectiveness of advertising would likely be one of the most studied psychological topics of our time (Kanner & Gomes, 1995).

Ads do far more than sell products. Commercials are having a substantial negative influence on child development and adult identity (Kilbourne, 1999; see also, chaps. 12, 13, & 14, this volume), a phenomenon that has barely been explored by the psychology profession.

The negative impact of advertising is evident in several ways. The first is that commercials often promote harmful products. We see this in the enormous number of ads that promote junk food, which contributes to obesity and other health problems (see chaps. 12 & 14, this volume). Second, advertising frequently upholds stereotypes regarding gender, race, class, and sexual orientation (see chaps. 13 & 14, this volume).

A third problem emerges from the cumulative impact of advertising. People are exposed to thousands of commercials a day, practically every day of their lives. One meta-message that cuts across most, if not all, commercials is the idea that happiness is to be found primarily in material goods and services (see chaps. 2 & 3, this volume). Thus, the sheer volume of commercial messages promotes materialism, irrespective of the content of what is being advertised (Kanner & Gomes, 1995).

Finally, when people are advertised to, they are objectified in a very specific manner. Their value and worth as a human being is reduced to that of a consumer. As a result, people's identity becomes increasingly based on their ability to buy things. They also judge others by the same criterion.

It is useful here to draw from work on objectification by feminist psychologists (Fredrickson & Roberts, 1997; Kaschak, 1992) who have analyzed the objectification of women in patriarchal societies. Ellen Kaschak (1992), in *Engendered Lives*, wrote about the "male gaze," which occurs when men look at women primarily as sex objects rather than as whole, complex human beings. The objectifying male gaze is often experienced as demeaning and humiliating. In a similar fashion we could speak of the "commercial gaze" that corporations turn onto people as they reduce them to "consumer objects." This is most explicit in advertising trade journals, where different forms of media, such as television, radio, and magazines, solicit advertising from corporations by promising to deliver large numbers of customers to them. By the time an advertisement appears, the potential consumer has already been sold to the marketer.

Just as early feminists helped women identify their feelings of violation under the objectifying male gaze, so too could psychologists help people become aware of their constant objectification under the commercial gaze. When individuals become aware that they are being objectified, a whole series of reactions ensues, including feelings of anger, shame, and moral indignation, as well as resolve to resist the commercial gaze and take action to reduce its occurrence.

The impact of the commercial gaze is growing through the intrusion of advertising into areas of our lives that were previously commercial-free, a process we call *commercial encroachment*. A recent example of such encroachment is when the Internet company IUMA held a contest in which 10 winners were each awarded $5,000 to name their newborn child IUMA (It's an IUMA, 2001). Another example comes from the *San Francisco Chronicle*, which recently reported, "Two years ago, Halfway, Ore. changed its name (unofficially) to Half.com after an Internet startup firm ponied up $75,000" (Gordon, 2002). Commercial encroachment takes advantage of the shock value of breaking social barriers. Many people are initially disturbed, if not outraged, by these new advertising techniques, yet they quickly acclimate to them.

Although people might adjust to commercial encroachment, they nevertheless become defended against it. For example, they may try to ignore advertising (avoidance) or tell themselves they are unaffected by commercials (denial). These defenses are at best only partially successful; corporations would not spend tens of billions of dollars annually on marketing if their research and, most important (for them), their profits did not confirm its effectiveness. However, as people defend themselves against commercial encroachment, they unknowingly lose the ability to be open and receptive in their social environment. For example, in *No Logo*, Naomi Klein (1999) described how the sponsors at rock concerts have become so prominent that they are displacing the musicians as stars of the show. The concertgoers are no longer free to relax and enjoy the music without commercial messages pouring in.

The first cousin to commercial encroachment is "creeping commodification." *Commodification* involves replacing the intrinsic worth of an object or activity with its external monetary value. As we illustrate below in the case of higher education, it is advantageous for corporations both to create more commodities and to commodify what was previously outside the monetary system (Bollier, 2002). The more commodities the more opportunities for profit.

Higher Education

One area of American life that is increasingly subject to commercial encroachment and creeping commodification is higher education (Shadwick, 2000; White, 2000). As David Nobel (2000) observed, corporate influence on higher education starts from the top down:

> Over the last two decades, the upper managements of academia and corporate America have become inextricably bound through a thickening web of interlocking directorates. Corporate executives have long dominated university boards; now top academic administrators routinely sit

on Fortune 500 boards, sometimes earning more in fees and retainers associated with these directorships than they do from their academic positions. In addition to serious conflicts of interest, this network of relationships generates a corporate ethos and managerialist regime in academia indistinguishable from that of private industry. Most important, it encourages academic administrators to view higher education in much the same way as do their boardroom brethren; namely, as a site of employee training, commodity production, and capital accumulation. (pp. 52–53)

As universities come to be run as if they were big businesses, many familiar corporate practices are taking root. For example, in the business world, the practice of "outsourcing" involves replacing full-time employees with part-time workers. In academia, outsourcing occurs when the teaching load of full-time professors is shouldered by part-time faculty, who are paid less and receive few or no benefits. The logical extension of this trend would be the abandonment of tenure altogether (Bray & Bray, 2000), as corporations do not grant their employees, even CEOs, a permanent job. The demise of tenure would, of course, greatly reduce academic freedom.

Students, too, are being entered into the business equation. Administrators have recast them as both consumers of education and products created by universities. Students themselves have adopted this corporate perspective by evaluating their education primarily in terms of how marketable it has made them (Huber, 2000).

Corporate culture has also made great inroads into research and development. The 1980 Bayh–Dole law gave universities the patent rights to all inventions, discoveries, and other productions of their employees. Universities, in turn, sell these patents to the commercial sector, a privatization process that is called "technology transfer" (Minsky, 2000, p. 95; Slaughter & Leslie, 2000). The result of Bayh–Dole is that the government, in essence, subsidizes corporate research and development, because corporations do not pay for failed (government-sponsored) university research but only for successful results. Another outcome is that corporations have successfully suppressed the publication of unfavorable findings about their products (Kniffin, 2000; Lustig, 2000). Other companies have delayed publication of research for years pending not only the development of a product, but also its marketing strategy. These profit-driven practices disrupt the free-flow of information and the exchange of ideas that are the lifeblood of academia and that constitute the academic commons.

In response to corporate funding, many universities are providing increasing support to areas of study most likely to yield products or research findings useful to corporations (Slaughter & Leslie, 2000). At the same time, less profitable disciplines find the size of their faculty and university sponsorship shrinking. As this trend gains momentum, we can only speculate how psychology departments might gear their research and clinical efforts towards serving the marketplace. It is doubtful, for example, that corporations would provide subsidies to study the types of problems outlined in this book.

Classes themselves are also being commodified. Universities are competing with each other to develop and market large numbers of online courses to be sold to distance-learning students and to the public at large. Universities can pay a faculty member a set fee to develop an online class and then sell it in perpetuity (Nobel, 2000; Slaughter & Leslie, 2000). Because of its profitability, the massive effort to develop online courses is going forward without adequate research and debate on the quality of traditional classroom teaching versus online learning (Price, 2000).

Even the climate of campus life is being commercialized. Corporate advertising routinely appears on campus grounds. Universities are signing exclusive contracts with private companies for food, janitorial services, and bookstores (Nobel, 2000; Ruben, 2000). When corporations succeed in placing their products and services on campus, beyond immediate sales they also garner the implicit endorsement of the university.

The many inroads that corporations are making into higher education are not so much due to a "corporate conspiracy" but to the idea that has taken hold in the business world that American universities are fair game for the marketplace. This reflects a belief within corporate culture that anything that can be commercialized and commodified ought to be, a belief that is also gaining greater acceptance in American society.

Clinical Psychology

Another area that has been permeated by the values and practices of corporate culture is health care. Clinical psychologists, in particular, have experienced the commodification of their work with the advent of managed care, which has decimated private practice (Miller, 1996). Under the pretext of streamlining health services, managed care organizations, such as HMOs and PPOs, were created by large insurance companies as a way to reduce business expenditures and increase profits. Psychologists who participate in these systems have had to accept reduced fees, a substantial increase in paperwork, and a lower standard of care, including clinically contraindicated limits on the length of treatment they can offer (Miller, 1996).

For financial reasons, managed care companies favor short-term therapies, such as cognitive–behavioral, over longer term forms of treatment. Their endorsement of these approaches has had a major impact on the growing popularity of short-term therapy. Although this trend may have occurred partially in response to client feedback and new developments in theory and research, what we wish to emphasize is that the demands of corporate interests have played a major role in the direction that clinical psychology is currently taking.

FREEDOM

Corporate culture's influence is growing on many fronts, from its enormous claim on employees' time to advertising that is spreading like wildfire to the commodification of public services such as education and health care. In the process, many forms of freedom are being compromised, from national sovereignty to academic freedom, to the freedom to participate in public life without being exposed to the commercial gaze. Given the cultural dominance of corporations, it is not clear to us how Americans will react when they finally come to understand the full extent of corporate influence, from the personal to the global. Will they be outraged and moved to action, or will they simply acquiesce to what seems natural and familiar?

As we have indicated throughout this chapter, corporate culture suppresses both inner and outer freedom. What is the remedy to this situation? To generate alternatives to corporate control, people must engage in an ongoing public discourse in which our society is free to imagine a wide range of possibilities outside the corporate frame. We believe psychologists could make a significant contribution to this dialogue. For instance, psychologists can help legitimize people's ambivalence and concerns about corporate culture as a healthy response to a crazy situation. Many people feel angry, fearful, sad, or demoralized by the increasing power of corporations over their lives. At the same time they feel confused, for don't corporations provide the material wealth necessary to realize the American Dream?

Multicultural psychology provides a helpful model for psychologists to understand the effects of corporate culture, because it is a field of study that directly deals with the interface of freedom (both inner and outer), oppression, and individual experience (Creighton & Kivel, 1992; Vasquez & Femi, 1993; see also West, 1993). Many of its key ideas, such as institutionalized and internalized oppression, are applicable to the concerns of this chapter. *Institutionalized oppression*, such as institutionalized sexism and racism, refers to the systemic, pervasive, and routine forms of oppression that are supported subtly and overtly by social norms and practices. One example of institutionalized sexism is women receiving less pay than men for comparable work. *Internalized oppression* comes about when members of an oppressed group adopt the same distorted view of themselves that is held by the culture of the dominant group and further believe that the power of the dominant culture cannot be effectively challenged. Examples of internalized oppression include people of color coming falsely to believe that Euro-Americans are inherently smarter than they are or that resisting racism is futile.

Similarly, *institutionalized corporate culture* refers to systemic and pervasive corporate oppression that is supported by American society's norms and practices. The power of corporations to subvert democratic processes internationally and in the United States, to coerce people into untenable work and family conflicts, and to saturate our environment with commercial messages are examples of institutionalized corporate culture.

Internalized corporate culture comes about when people adopt the same view of themselves that is promoted by corporate culture, namely, that their primary roles in life are as consumers and workers, with the emphasis on being a consumer. The corporate ideal of success becomes the model for personal success.

Internalized corporate culture is further characterized by the belief that corporate power cannot be effectively challenged. Believing anything else is deemed highly unrealistic and even utopian. A crucial step in countering the perceived futility of changing corporate culture is to free people's imagination to explore alternatives. This would mean removing the stigma and the sense of hopelessness that make it unsafe to step outside a corporate vision of the future. One role that psychologists can play in this regard is to help people realize that internalized corporate culture exists and that the initial steps to overcoming it involve facing fears of ridicule and a sense of futility. Only by grappling with internalized corporate culture can people be free to imagine other possibilities, both for themselves and for society.

Perhaps America is currently at a similar point in history regarding corporate culture as it was in the 1950s in relation to sexism and racism. At that time it seemed absurd to assume that within a few decades we would see two White women and an African American man on the Supreme Court and the acceptance in many circles of stay-at-home fathers and mixed-race adoptions. Individuals who envisioned these changes had to wrestle with their own internalized sexism and racism, as well as with tremendous social opposition, whereas the majority of people accepted the status quo. In a parallel fashion, there are groups and individuals presently generating alternatives to corporate culture (for a review, see Cavanagh & Mander, 2002), but it is our impression that most people currently are resigned to the inevitability of corporate power.

However unlikely it seems now, within decades Americans could be actively reforming or even dismantling corporations. Other forms of business that do not depend on escalating consumerism, but instead are structured around the well-being of employees, the local community, and the environment, could be taking hold (Cavanagh & Mander, 2002). To get to this point, however, people must free themselves from both institutionalized and internalized corporate culture.

CONCLUSION: GREED VERSUS GENEROSITY

When considering alternatives to corporate culture, we believe it is useful to contrast the psychology of greed with the psychology of generosity. Corporate greed is a cliché, but it is worth noting that corporate culture also sanctions individual greed. In the corporate world, rich people are expected to devote much of their time and energy to getting richer. Such behavior is admired rather than viewed as a sign of emotional immaturity and developmental arrest. The drive among the wealthy to keep acquiring is compulsive and therefore ultimately unsatisfying (Hyde, 1983; Kasser, 2002).

Greed is characterized by emotional constriction and paranoia. People in the grip of greed develop a scarcity mentality. They feel that they can never accrue enough wealth to have their needs fully met, and believe they must constantly compete with others for scant resources. Moreover, greedy individuals reduce others, and the world in general, to potential sources for greater wealth.

Contrast the qualities of greed with those of generosity. The experience of generosity is expansive and flowing and includes an implicit trust in the world's abundance (Hyde, 1983). The generous person is more caring than competitive and gives of herself or himself freely. Furthermore, although the details are beyond the scope of this chapter, we have found great wisdom and complex psychological insight embedded in the gift-giving and gift-exchange practices of some traditional societies, where generosity is far more valued than material wealth (Hyde, 1983). Perhaps the promotion of generosity is one of the best antidotes to greed and, by extension, to consumerism.

In a more generous world, globalization would shift from its current emphasis on commerce to the international sharing of ideas, knowledge, art, cultural wisdom, and other noncommercial treasures. Because of its traditional emphasis on nonmaterialistic concerns such as interpersonal relationships, intrapsychic processes, and life-span development, psychology would flourish in such an exchange. In the meantime, our field has much to offer by documenting and publicizing the great harm of escalating consumerism. To do so fully requires addressing the threat to inner and outer freedom posed by corporate culture. Focusing on this greater context takes vision and courage.

REFERENCES

Barlow, M. (2001). *The free trade area of the Americas: The threat to social programs, environmental sustainability and social justice* (Vol. 1). San Francisco: International Forum of Globalization.

Beck, J., & Danaher, K. (2000). Top ten reasons to oppose the World Trade Organization. In K. Danaher & R. Burbach (Eds.), *Globalize this! The battle against the World Trade Organization and corporate rule* (pp. 98–102). Monroe, ME: Common Courage Press.

Bello, W. (1995). Structural adjustment programs: "Success" for whom? In J. Mander & E. Goldsmith (Eds.), *The case against the global economy: And for a turn toward the local* (pp. 285–293). San Francisco: Sierra Club Books.

Bello, W. (2000). Reforming the WTO is the wrong agenda. In K. Danaher & R. Burbach (Eds.), *Globalize this! The battle against the World Trade Organization and corporate rule* (pp. 103–119). Monroe, ME: Common Courage Press.

Bollier, D. (2002). *Silent theft: The private plunder of our common wealth.* London: Routledge.

Bottari, M. (2001). NAFTA's investor "rights." *Multinational Monitor, 22,* 9–16.

Bray, D. W., & Bray, M. W. (2000). Succeed with caution: Rethinking academic culture at RPI, PSU, and CSU. In G. D. White (Ed.), *Campus, Inc.: Corporate power in the ivory tower* (pp. 55–60). Amherst, NY: Prometheus Books.

Cavanagh, J., & Mander, J. (Co-Chairs). (2002). *Alternatives to economic globalization (a better world is possible): International Forum on Globalization.* San Francisco: Berrett-Koehler.

Cavanagh, J., Welch, C., & Retallack, S. (2001). The IMF formula: Prescription for poverty. *International Forum on Globalization: Special Poverty Report, 1*(3), 8–10.

Creighton, A., & Kivel, P. (1992). *Helping teens stop violence: A practical guide for counselors, educators, and parents.* Alameda, CA: Hunter House.

Danaher, K. (Ed.). (1996). *Corporations are gonna get your mama: Globalization and the downsizing of the American dream.* Monroe, ME: Common Courage Press.

Danaher, K., & Burbach, R. (Eds.). (2000). *Globalize this! The battle against the World Trade Organization and corporate rule.* Monroe, ME: Common Courage Press.

Economic Policy Institute. (2001, April). *NAFTA at seven: Its impact on workers in all three nations* (Briefing Paper). Washington, DC: Author.

Education International/Public Services International. (1999, November). *The WTO and the millennium round: What is at stake for public education? Common concerns for workers in education and the public sector.* Ferney-Voltaire Cedex, France: EI/PSI Joint Publication.

Fredrickson, B. L., & Roberts, P. (1997). Objectification theory: Toward understanding women's lived experiences and mental health risks. *Psychology of Women Quarterly, 21,* 178–206.

Friedman, T. (1999). *The lexus and the olive tree.* New York: Farrar, Straus and Giroux.

Gordon, R. (2002, July 31). Coit carpet cleaning tower? S. F.'s name game. *San Francisco Chronicle,* pp. A15–A16.

Grossman, R. L., & Adams, F. T. (1993). *Taking care of business: Citizenship and the charter of incorporation.* Cambridge, MA: Charter.

Heredia, C., & Purcell, M. (1995). Structural adjustment and the polarization of Mexican society. In J. Mander & E. Goldsmith (Eds.), *The case against the global economy: And for a turn toward the local* (pp. 273–284). San Francisco: Sierra Club Books.

Herman, E. S., & Chomsky, N. (1988). *Manufacturing consent: The political economy of mass media.* New York: Pantheon Books.

Hochschild, A. R. (1997). *The time bind: When work becomes home and home becomes work.* New York: Metropolitan Books.

Huber, S. (2000). Faculty workers: Tenure on the corporate assembly line. In G. D. White (Ed.), *Campus, Inc.: Corporate power in the ivory tower* (pp. 119–139). Amherst, NY: Prometheus Books.

Hyde, L. (1983). *The gift*. New York: Random House.

It's an IUMA. (2001, March/April). *Adbusters, 9*(24), 18.

Jacobson, M. F., & Mazur, L. A. (1995). *Marketing madness: A survival guide for a consumer society*. San Francisco: Westview Press.

Kanner, A. D., & Gomes, M. E. (1995). The all-consuming self. In T. Roszak, M. E. Gomes, & A. D. Kanner (Eds.), *Ecopsychology: Restoring the Earth, healing the mind* (pp. 77–91). San Francisco: Sierra Club Books.

Kaschak, E. (1992). *Engendered lives: A new psychology of women's experience*. New York: HarperCollins.

Kasser, T. (2002). *The high price of materialism*. Cambridge, MA: MIT Press.

Kilbourne, J. (1999). *Deadly persuasion: Why women and girls must fight the addictive power of advertising*. New York: Free Press.

Kivimaki, M., Vahtera, J., Penetti, J., & Ferrie, J. E. (2000). Factors underlying the effect of organizational downsizing on health of employees: Longitudinal cohort study. *British Medical Journal, 320,* 971–975.

Klein, N. (1999). *No logo: Money, marketing, and the growing anti-corporate movement*. New York: Picador and St. Martin's Press.

Kniffin, K. (2000). The goods at their worst: Campus procurement in the global pillage. In G. D. White (Ed.), *Campus, Inc.: Corporate power in the ivory tower* (pp. 36–50). Amherst, NY: Prometheus Books.

Korten, D. C. (1995). *When corporations rule the world*. West Hartford, CT: Berrett-Koehler.

Larson, E. (1992). *The naked consumer: How our private lives become public commodities*. New York: Penguin Press.

Lee, M. A., & Solomon, N. (1990). *Unreliable sources: A guide to detecting bias in news media*. New York: Carol Publishing.

Lustig, J. (2000). Perils of the knowledge industry: How a faculty union blocked an unfriendly takeover. In G. D. White (Ed.), *Campus, Inc.: Corporate power in the ivory tower* (pp. 319–341). Amherst, NY: Prometheus Books.

Mander, J. (1991). *In the absence of the sacred: The failure of technology and the survival of the Indian Nations*. San Francisco: Sierra Club Books.

Mander, J. (1996). Facing the rising tide. In J. Mander & E. Goldsmith (Eds.), *The case against the global economy: And for a turn toward the local* (pp. 3–19). San Francisco: Sierra Club Books.

Mander, J., Barker, D., & Korten, D. C. (2001). Does globalization help the poor? *International Forum on Globalization (IFG): Special Poverty Report, 1*(3), 2–5.

Mander, J., & Goldsmith, E. (Eds.). (1996). *The case against the global economy: And for a turn toward the local*. San Francisco: Sierra Club Books.

McChesney, R. W. (1997). *Corporate media and the threat to democracy*. New York: Seven Stories Press.

Miller, I. G. (1996). Managed care is harmful to outpatient mental health services: A call for accountability. *Professional Psychology: Research and Practice, 27*, 349–363.

Minsky, L. (2000). Dead souls: The aftermath of Bayh–Dole. In G. D. White (Ed.), *Campus, Inc.: Corporate power in the ivory tower* (pp. 95–105). Amherst, NY: Prometheus Books.

Nader, R., & Wallach, L. (1996). GATT, NAFTA, and the subversion of the democratic process. In J. Mander & E. Goldsmith (Eds.), *The case against the global economy: And for a turn toward the local* (pp. 92–107). San Francisco: Sierra Club Books.

Nobel, D. F. (2000). Money changers in the temple. In G. D. White (Ed.), *Campus, Inc.: Corporate power in the ivory tower* (pp. 51–54). Amherst, NY: Prometheus Books.

Norberg-Hodge, H. (1991). *Ancient futures: Learning from Ladakh.* San Francisco: Sierra Club Books.

Norberg-Hodge, H. (1996). The pressure to modernize and globalize. In J. Mander & E. Goldsmith (Eds.), *The case against the global economy: And for a turn toward the local* (pp. 33–46). San Francisco: Sierra Club Books.

Price, R. (2000). Wiring the world: Ameritech's monopoly on the virtual classroom. In G. D. White (Ed.), *Campus, Inc.: Corporate power in the ivory tower* (pp. 218–236). Amherst, NY: Prometheus Books.

Public Citizen's Global Trade Watch & Friends of the Earth. (1996). NAFTA's broken promises: Evidence of NAFTA's failure. In K. Danaher (Ed.), *Corporations are gonna get your mama: Globalization and the downsizing of the American dream* (pp. 115–120). Monroe, ME: Common Courage Press.

Public Citizen's Global Trade Watch & Friends of the Earth. (2001). *NAFTA chapter 11 investor-to-state cases; Bankrupting democracy.* Washington, DC: Author.

Rademacher, D. (2000, Spring). WTO: After Seattle, the story is coming out. *Terrain,* pp. 23–27.

Rowe, J. (2001). The hidden commons. *Yes! A Journal of Positive Futures, 18,* 12–17.

Ruben, M. (2000). Penn and Inc.: Incorporating the University of Pennsylvania. In G. D. White (Ed.), *Campus, Inc.: Corporate power in the ivory tower* (pp. 194–217). Amherst, NY: Prometheus Books.

Schor, J. B. (1991). *The overworked American: The unexpected decline of leisure time.* New York: Basic Books.

Schor, J. B. (1998). *The overspent American: Upscaling, downshifting and the new consumer.* New York: Basic Books.

Shadwick, V. (February, 2000). Global issues on higher education. *NEA Higher Education Advocate, 17*(4), 12.

Shiva, V., & Holla-Bhar, R. (1996). Piracy by patent: The case of the Neem tree. In J. Mander & E. Goldsmith (Eds.), *The case against the global economy: And for a turn toward the local* (pp. 146–159). San Francisco: Sierra Club Books.

Slaughter, S., & Leslie, L. (2000). Professors going pro: The commercialization of teaching, research, and service. In G. D. White (Ed.), *Campus, Inc.: Corporate power in the ivory tower* (pp. 140–156). Amherst, NY: Prometheus Books.

Stauber, J., & Rampton, S. (1995). *Toxic sludge is good for you.* Monroe, ME: Common Courage Press.

Stiglitz, J. (2002). *Globalization and its discontents.* New York: W. W. Norton.

Vasquez, H., & Femi, I. (1993). *A manual for unlearning oppression and building multicultural alliances.* Oakland, CA: Todos, Sherover Simms Alliance Building Institute.

West, C. (1993). *Race matters.* New York: Vintage Books.

White, G. D. (Ed.). (2000). *Campus, Inc.: Corporate power in the ivory tower.* Amherst, NY: Prometheus Books.

5

SHOPPING FOR SUSTAINABILITY: PSYCHOLOGICAL SOLUTIONS TO OVERCONSUMPTION

DEBORAH DU NANN WINTER

In the wake of the September 11 terrorist attacks on the World Trade Center and the Pentagon, the world economy faltered. Nervous about the future, consumers and investors across the globe skittishly curtailed their spending, and the United States's Dow Jones industrial average wobbled and sagged. During the months that followed, daily news reports about economic indicators looked for hopeful signs of economic recovery—resumption of travel, consumer purchasing, and holiday extravagance—with newscasters and journalists clearly implying that a return to conspicuous consumption would indicate a resumption of emotional well-being.

Considering that the industrial world is characterized by its overconsumption of resources, I was surprised that not a single report that I read during the fall of 2001 mentioned the possibility that reduced spending might be a blessing in disguise for the sustainability of our planetary home. Not one report noted that our current levels of overconsumption jeopardize our future security. Yet even a cursory glance at the world's environmental predicament clearly shows that the continued existence of our species requires that we find ways to lower our impact on the world's resources.

Depletion of the earth's resources is driven by conspicuous consumption. In 1966, less than a quarter of U.S. homes had an area exceeding 2,000 square feet; by 1994, 47% did (Myers, 2002). Although global averages of consumption have increased in the last 50 years, people in the industrialized world, particularly the United States, drive consumption dangerously beyond the planet's resource base. Since 1950, the world's richest 20% have doubled their consumption of meat and timber. The richest 20% now consume 85% of all paper. Between 1960 and 1997, the percentage of Americans who own dishwashers increased from 7 to 50; the percentage of people who own clothes dryers rose from 20 to 71; and the percentage of people who have air conditioning increased from 15 to 73 (Bureau of the Census, 1979, 1998, as cited by Myers, 2002).

In the industrialized world, we consume far more than our fair share of the planet's resources. We use 3 times as much freshwater, 10 times as much energy, and 19 times as much aluminum as people in industrializing countries, evidence that those of us in the richest countries have the greatest responsibility to find ways to convert our consumer economy to a sustainable one. We must convert because our current consumption levels are clearly unsustainable. Either we find ways to change our abuse of the planet's resources, or weather catastrophes, disease, war, and starvation will do it for us.

In this chapter, I describe important examples of our unsustainable resource use, focusing on some examples of everyday overconsumption behaviors that drive our environmental crisis. I then go on to suggest some ways that psychologists might promote changes in consumption behavior. My major claim is that reducing consumption is necessary for long-term sustainability. Psychology offers an array of concepts and tools for changing consumption behaviors, which will be a key task for psychologists of the 21st century (Oskamp, 2000).

WORLD INDICATORS OF UNSUSTAINABLE HUMAN CONSUMPTION

Human beings are currently on a crash course. Our present levels of consumption, pollution, and population growth are quickly eating up the Earth's carrying capacity (the maximum number of individuals that a given environment can support long-term), making our future existence problematic, if not improbable. To live on the planet, humans depend on a stable climate, protection from lethal solar radiation, clean air and water, and a continuous supply of natural resources, including soil, water, minerals, and organic materials. A large body of evidence suggests that modern human behavior threatens each of these life-sustaining resources. Industrialization, and the daily human behaviors that come with it, have already seriously affected climate change, deforestation, water supplies, and land use.

Climate Change

When I sit in my car tomorrow morning and drive to work, I will contribute to global warming by depositing excess carbon emissions into the atmosphere. Global warming is already well underway. The average temperature of the Earth's surface rose from 13.27°C in 1866, to 13.84°C in 1950, to 14.35°C in 1999 (Dunn, 2000b). The burning of fossil fuels, which contributes to global warming, has soared from 1.6 billion tons in 1950 to 6.3 billion tons in 1998 (Dunn, 2000a). Meanwhile, atmospheric concentration of carbon dioxide has grown steadily since 1958, especially from the burning of fossil fuels.

The warmest 23 years on record have occurred since 1975. Global warming will continue to cause sea levels to rise because of thermal expansion and glacial melting. These rises threaten coastal regions, make cropland unusable, and could displace millions of people (Flavin & Dunn, 1999). Floods, hurricanes, and storms will increase, as will droughts and desertification. Overspending the planet's fossil fuels on increased production of consumer goods will also lower production in the future (Flavin & Dunn). Already fish harvests went down sharply in 1998 as a result of unusual weather patterns and over-fishing (Gardner, 2000).

Our everyday behaviors cause dangerous patterns of pollution, resource depletion, and climate change. In addition to driving a car almost every day, I recently took three airline trips to professional meetings. Airline transportation is the most fuel-inefficient way to travel. Transportation choices contribute greatly to pollution, global warming, and resource depletion because 95% of it is fueled by oil and its various derivatives (gasoline, including diesel fuel, jet fuel, and so on). Globally, transportation is the fastest growing source of carbon emissions (Sheehan, 2001). Citizens of the United States travel twice as far as Europeans, using 18 barrels of oil per person per year in comparison to Canadians, who use 13, and Japanese, Australians, and New Zealanders, who use an average of 6. With the increasing motorization of the world, per capita car use continues to rise. In 2001, we drove 10 times as many cars as we did in 1950. Car ownership is already very high in the industrialized world, but it will grow more rapidly in the developing world, where it is seen as one of the first signs of emerging prosperity. Per capita motorization is expected to more than double between 1997 and 2020 (Sheehan). Of particular concern is the surging demand in developing areas of Asia and Latin America, where rapid industrialization will increase the demand for oil at 2 to 3 times the rate of industrialized countries. The rate of fuel consumption in China and India is expected to rise by 3.8% each year

(Sheehan). However, the United States alone uses more than one third of the world's transport energy (Sheehan).

Meanwhile, globally we use well over 20 times the energy per year that we used in 1900. We have gone from using 911 million tons of oil equivalent per year to well over 9,600 million tons (Klare, 1999). Perhaps a blessing in terms of carbon emissions and global warming, at current rates of consumption, the world's oil supply is diminishing rapidly; the last 20% of it will be the most expensive to extract and process. International tensions and military actions are likely to increase as limited supplies are exhausted (Homer-Dixon, 1991). Indeed, U.S. military intervention in Afghanistan and Iraq are not irrelevant to the world's largest untapped deposits of oil located near the Caspian Sea; in the late 1990s the U.S. State Department supported the Taliban, along with plans by Unical Oil Co., to build a pipeline through Afghanistan and Pakistan (Rashid, 2000), and as the United States threatened Iraq with military invasion in the fall of 2002, oil companies were lining up to design installations on the oil fields between Iraq and Kuwait (Morgan & Ottaway, 2002).

Deforestation

Consumer activities are killing the world's forests. Harvesting, development, and fuel gathering have already destroyed approximately four fifths of the world's original forest cover. Globally, the destruction of forests increased dramatically between 1960 and 1990, particularly in the tropics, where forests were cleared to provide land for agriculture, livestock, and human communities. Large-scale logging for both timber and paper pose a major threat to the world's forests (Abramovitz, 1998).

Deforestation is particularly dangerous to the planet's ecosystem because forests produce oxygen while absorbing harmful CO_2 emissions. Deforestation interacts with global warming to generate changed weather patterns, flooding, landslides, and clogging of waterways (Abramovitz & Mattoon, 1999). In addition, forests house important biodiversity, sheltering a majority of the Earth's plant and animal species; deforestation causes great loss of the world's genetic endowment. The relative consequences of commercial logging, fuel wood gathering, agriculture, and development on deforestation remain unknown. However, the impact of logging is often underestimated because of its secondary effect on road building, flooding, and damage to other parts of the ecosystem.

Contrary to the digital revolution's promise of a paperless society, paper use has increased more than sixfold since 1950. In general, richer countries use more paper. With close to 22% of the world's population, the United States, Japan, and now China use more than 71% of the world's paper (Mattoon, 2000). Only about 10% of paper goes into making long-lasting products like books; as of 1997, almost half of the world's paper has been used for packaging. Virgin wood fiber made up 55% of the world's fiber supply, one fifth of the world's total wood harvest. In addition, paper made up a large proportion of municipal solid waste, about 40% in industrial countries (Mattoon).

Like transportation, daily human behaviors drive deforestation. To write this chapter, I depended on paper for manuscript drafts as well as the newspapers, journals, and books on which it is based. Most people use paper only once. Although recycling has increased dramatically in the last decade, recycled paper contributes less than 40% to total fiber supply (Mattoon, 2000). Meanwhile, excessive paper use continues to grow. The average U.S. household receives 553 pieces of junk mail each year, a figure that is expected to triple by the year 2010. In the United States, nearly 10 billion mail-order catalogs are discarded each year (Abramovitz & Mattoon, 1999).

Our gluttonous use of paper stems partly from inappropriate pricing mechanisms. Paper is often cheaper than its real cost because the supply of paper often outpaces demand. When new mills get financed, owners must run them constantly to pay off debt; this oversupply of paper causes prices to fall and encourages people to use paper for trivial matters (Abramovitz & Mattoon, 1999). Consequently, those of us in the industrialized world become increasingly annoyed by mounting piles of paper while our forests continue to be depleted.

Clean Water

Although water covers most of the Earth's surface, only 3% of it is usable—the rest is frozen, salty, or inaccessible. Unfortunately, the small amount of usable water is deteriorating quickly as pollution from industrialization accelerates. The capacity of groundwater to sustain people and ecosystems is under grave threat, as massive quantities of chemicals are sent into the earth, poisoning the aquifers and causing irreversible damage. The major culprits are pesticides and fertilizers that run off from farms and lawns, petrochemicals that leak from faulty storage tanks, chlorinated solvents and heavy metals from industrial trash, and nuclear contaminants from energy and weapons production. Although most of the pollution is unintentional, 60% of the hazardous waste in the United States is disposed of by injecting it into deep underground wells, and evidence of waste seepage into drinking water supplies has been documented in parts of Florida, Ohio, Oklahoma, and Texas (Sampat, 2000). Chemical pollution of aquifers is long lasting—1,400 years—compared to 16 days for river water (Sampat, 2000); in the Columbia basin of Washington state the radioactive waste that has leaked into the Central Columbia Plateau Aquifer has a half-life of 250,000 years (Sampat, 2001). By the mid-1990s nearly 60% of wells sampled in agricultural areas of the United States contained pesticides (Sampat, 2001).

In the last 50 years, demand for groundwater expanded dramatically and the world's use of water tripled (Brown, 2000). Two thirds of the freshwater used goes to irrigation to grow about 40% of our food. However, because water use in industry produces about 70 times as much profit as that used for agriculture, industrial use of water is expected to continue growing quickly beyond its current 22% (Sampat, 2001). Between industrial and agricultural uses, freshwater aquifers are being depleted quickly, resulting in a current worldwide water deficit of an estimated 200 billion cubic meters a year. In other words, 200 billion cubic meters are currently being withdrawn from aquifers without being restored (Sampat, 2001). Over-pumping of aquifers in China, the United States, North Africa, India, and Saudi Arabia exceeds 160 billion tons of water per year (Brown). Between population growth and increased consumption, the number of people living in water deficit countries will jump from 505 million in 2001 to over 2.4 billion in the next 25 years (Flavin, 2001).

Although household use accounts for only 12% of freshwater depletion, daily behaviors of people in industrialized countries indirectly threaten the world's freshwater supply through overconsumption of industry-produced products, packaging, and irrigated food. Thus consumers bear responsibility for major depletion of water levels through their product choices. Meat consumption takes a particularly large toll on the world's water supply: Each calorie from meat consumed takes 7 times the energy required to produce one calorie from grain. Moreover, because grain is irrigated to grow cattle feed, water is essentially wasted and contaminated to produce meat (Riebel & Jacobsen, 2002).

Loss of Soil and Agricultural Land

As water tables fall, so does the amount of land available for agricultural production. The amount of arable land peaked in 1981 and has since decreased 6% (Oskamp, 2000). The major culprits are degradation from erosion and salinization, as well as development of human settlements. Worldwide, grain harvest area fell by 647 million hectares in 1999, leaving us with the smallest area since 1972 (Gardner, 2000). As global population continues to climb, harvest area per person continues to fall: As of 2000, the planet had only .11 hectare per person, one third less than that of 1972. Land degradation decreases agricultural productivity in many parts of the world. For instance, in China soil erosion and desertification has ruined as much cropland as has urbanization and rural construction. Over-irrigation has salinized and desertified parts of the United States, particularly Oklahoma.

Consumers contribute to loss of agricultural land in at least two ways: (a) by supporting nonsustainable farming practices when they purchase food grown in nonsustainable ways and (b) by not participating in community decision-making about how agricultural lands should be designated. When citizens who care about sustainable agriculture are not involved in local planning, decisions get made by real estate developers, local contractors, and others who stand to gain financially from excessive sprawl.

Summary

Unsustainable human behaviors destroy water, land, forests, and energy reserves throughout the world. Similar pictures of ecological decline could be drawn for air pollution, mineral depletion, and loss of biodiversity. By now the global predicament should be clear: In the words of the World Scientists' Warning to Humanity, signed by 1,600 eminent scientists across the globe in 1992:

> A great change in our stewardship of the Earth and the life on it is required, if vast human misery is to be avoided and our global home on this planet is not to be irretrievably mutilated. (Union of Concerned Scientists, 1992)

Although the intersecting problems of diminishing water, land and forests, combined with overpopulation and global warming, seem overwhelming, Brown (2000) reminded us of the need for, and plausibility of, sudden social change. Just as scientific thought has undergone sudden shifts of paradigms (Kuhn, 1962), so has the modern social world seen abrupt shifts in attitude and practice. For example, the political systems of eastern Europe underwent rapid and massive changes in the 1990s. Political scientists did not anticipate the unprecedented change in practice and thinking that enabled most countries to reorganize their economies and political structures through bloodless revolutions. Settlements of tobacco lawsuits provide another example. After decades of denying the health impacts of cigarettes, U.S. tobacco companies agreed to massive financial settlements with 46 states. This sudden and radical change in policy has had both environmental and health benefits.

Other evidence suggests that the world community may be ready to change its consumption levels. For example, Shell Oil and DaimlerChrysler are leading a consortium of corporations that will enable Iceland to become the world's first hydrogen-based economy. In the United States, forest practices swiftly changed in the late 1990s to emphasize selective rather than clear cutting; road building for logging was put suddenly on moratorium. Brown (2000) argued that pulling ourselves out of our ecological predicament would require that we stabilize both population and climate change and that we use taxes to reorganize the world economy to promote these two key aspects of environmental sustainability. Although I agree that taxes are crucial, I doubt that government leaders currently have the wisdom and fortitude to enact appropriate tax structures without massive public appreciation for them. Thus, economists have an important role to play in building a sustainable society, but so do psychologists.

CAN PSYCHOLOGY HELP SAVE THE WORLD?

Most people think that environmental problems lie outside the domain of psychology; pollution, resource depletion, and overconsumption are usually seen as engineering issues to be addressed by environmental biologists, chemists, geologists, physicists, or economists. Although psychology is rarely thought to be relevant, I argue that it is crucial for our survival because our environmental crisis has been brought on largely by the thoughts, feelings, attitudes, values, and behaviors of human beings. Clearly, technological solutions will not help unless they change human behavior. Sooner or later, psychologists must play an integral role in designing sustainable cultures (see chaps. 2, 4, 6, & 8, this volume), and I hope that this book encourages more psychologists to accept this important challenge. Below I discuss a handful of the ways in which insights from psychology might be used to help reverse our dangerous levels of consumption.

There are many different psychological approaches to the question of how to foster sustainability (Gardner & Stern, 1996; Howard, 2000; McKenzie-Mohr, 2000). My own approach is to examine big theories in psychology for insights into our environmentally destructive behavior. I like the theoretical approach because I hope it stimulates the imaginations of many people, recruiting them (you?) to work on these problems. The following ideas are in no way exhaustive, and I offer them to begin a conversation about how psychology might contribute to the crucial task of curbing consumption and cultivating environmentally responsible behavior. (For expanded versions of much of the following discussion, see Winter, 1996; Winter & Koger, 2004; for a more condensed version, see Winter, 2000.)

Neo-Analytic (Depth) Approaches

Neo-analytic theory derives from Freud's ideas about psychoanalysis. Although these approaches tend to receive less quantitative empirical attention than others, I find the insights they provide provocative for helping us think about how to change overconsumption behavior.

In neo-analytic terms, our environmental crisis results from our inherited alienation from nature. Freud was pessimistic about our ability to transcend our struggle with the natural world, whose forces he saw as evil. Written in the throes of the industrial revolution, his *Future of an Illusion* (1927) claimed that civilization is primarily a strategy to defend against nature. Later, Freud went on to propose that civilization can even be defined by the degree to which humans find ways to exploit and transform our natural environment.

From this perspective, our instinctive urges lead us unconsciously toward destruction. Eros, the sexual instinct, spurs us toward dangerous levels of overpopulation, and our aggressive urges (from the instinct Thanatos) lead us to militarization, war, and other forms of violent destruction.

Industrialization and urbanization exacerbate these instinctually based behaviors. Thus, uncontrolled instincts cause our species to reproduce and foul its nest with little conscious awareness of the consequences of our self-destructive behaviors.

We could not continue to exercise these environmentally damaging behaviors without a variety of defense mechanisms. Facing our perilous planetary predicament would bring us so much anxiety that we use defenses to remain unconscious about the possibility of our own extinction. So we continue to operate as if our dangerous behaviors are trivial, even though they are treacherous. For example, although most of us know something about the connection between global warming and fossil fuel use, we rationalize our inappropriate behaviors, supplying good-sounding but problematic explanations—driving alone to the office because "carpooling is inconvenient" or buying unneeded consumer goods because "they are on sale." We exercise denial and displacement to keep our anxiety about our environmental predicament at bay: We busy ourselves with daily chores of work and family and quickly turn our attention away from disturbing environmental reports in the news as soon as we sense that doing something about them requires change in our behavior. We use emotional distancing techniques when we learn about environmental problems; for example, we believe that toxic waste is a problem for that community, not for ourselves individually; water depletion is a problem for those farmers, not for me; species extinction is trouble for other species, not for ours. Emotional distancing can also be observed by the commonly used phrase "radical environmentalist," as if someone who takes environmental problems seriously is radical and cannot possibly use a reasoned approach, or as if those who are sensible would not rattle on about environmental problems. Thus, with the aid of defense mechanisms, we focus on short-term outcomes at the expense of future generations, because the anxiety we would experience otherwise would be overwhelming.

Unfortunately, governments and corporations collude with our individual defenses. For example, the U.S. government helps us suppress disturbing information about nuclear waste by intentionally hiding it (Gerber, 1992). Corporations use advertising to stimulate our consumer appetites without mentioning environmental costs (Durning, 1992); even colleges and universities support our emotional defenses by designing curricula that focus on the magnificent creations of human civilization without examining the diminishing physical resources that have been spent to produce them (Orr, 1992).

Our short-sighted and ineffectual relationship to nature might also result from damaged object relations (Buckley, 1986; Greenberg & Mitchell, 1983). From the neo-analytic perspective, our inability to consider the impact of our actions on our environmental home stems from a damaged relationship with our primary caretaker. We narcissistically think that "Mother Earth" will take care of us forever, or we do not address our relationship with the planet because we too easily feel despair or overwhelmed.

From the neo-analytic perspective, our salvation lies in transforming unconscious motivations into conscious awareness and action. Whereas Freud posited that libidinal impulses are the substance of the unconscious, ecopsychologists suggest that part of our deeply buried unconscious is the "ecological self," that part of us that realizes our profound connection with the ecological world (Bragg, 1996), but has been repressed by urban–industrial culture (Roszak, 1992). E. O. Wilson conceptualized the ecological self as biophilia, which he defined as "the innate tendency to focus on life and lifelike processes" (Wilson, 1984, p. 1). In other words, we have lost touch with this positive bond because of life in industrialized societies.

Some ecopsychologists have argued that advertising is most likely to seduce us into overconsumption when we do not connect with our ecological self, because our incomplete self craves definition and identity. By purchasing material objects we try to address this craving, but satisfaction of the deeper spiritual needs is fleeting (Kanner & Gomes, 1995). Indeed, recent empirical work shows that consumerism is correlated with anxiety and depression (Saunders & Munro, 2000; see also chaps. 2 & 3, this volume).

From this perspective, solving our environmental problems will require that we re-awaken the ecological unconscious through such techniques as practicing mindfulness (Sewell, 1995; see also chap. 7, this volume) and experiencing wilderness (Harper, 1995; Swanson, 2001), in addition to other forms of ecotherapy (Clinebell, 1996). Ecotherapy teaches people to be "nurtured by nature" by experiencing their profound love and connection with the natural world, as well as to "nurture nature" by realizing their commitments to behaviors that contribute to sustainability. Both the nurturing of and the nurturing by nature are reciprocal processes that can be used therapeutically to heal the split between the individual ego and the ecological world.

Because the neo-analytic and ecopsychological approaches attribute overconsumption to our emotional and spiritual difficulties, psychologists can contribute to building a sustainable world by encouraging people to face their feelings about our environmental crisis, by helping them to reconnect with their ecological selves, and by empowering them to take action on specific individual and political dimensions. As long as people refuse to feel their anxiety, despair, shame, or ecological connection, they remain unable to muster the psychic energy required to make necessary change; instead, their energy is exhausted defending against their feelings, thus robbing them of their full intelligence for finding creative solutions. The same defenses that keep us disconnected from the environment also keep us separated from ourselves and other people. When people are allowed to experience their feelings in safe settings, they are empowered to take positive actions on what otherwise would be overwhelming problems (Macy, 1983).

Behavioral Approaches

Finding the ecological self and becoming aware of unconscious feelings may be valuable experiences, but sooner or later we need to translate our feelings of profound connection with the natural world into environmentally responsible behaviors. B. F. Skinner put it this way over a quarter of a century ago:

> what we need is a technology of behavior. . . . Better contraceptives will control population only if people use them. . . . Overcrowding can be corrected only by inducing people not to crowd, and the environment will continue to deteriorate until polluting practices are abandoned. (Skinner, 1971, pp. 4–5)

From a behavioral perspective, a technology of behavior consists of identifying the situational stimuli that both accompany and reinforce environmentally relevant behavior. Geller (1987) outlined two main approaches: (a) stimulus control management, that is, changing the cues, models, requests, and instructions that precede behavior; and (b) contingency management, that is, changing the rewards and costs that follow behaviors. Much empirical research demonstrates the power of both of these strategies.

For example, using stimulus control management, Aronson and O'Leary (1982/83) had live models in a shower room demonstrate water conservation by turning off the water while soaping up; others in the same shower room followed. Requests to reduce litter are effective when they are posted (Geller, 1980); videotaped instructions have reduced energy consumption (Winett et al., 1982); and even clean garages have reduced littering (Cialdini, Kallgren, & Reno, 1991).

Many more studies have used reinforcement to change environmentally relevant behaviors. Monetary rebates, raffle tickets, and cookies have been used to change behaviors such as riding buses (Everett, Hayward, & Meyers, 1974), cleaning up litter (Powers, Osborne, & Anderson, 1973), and setting thermostats for lower energy use (Walker, 1979). Evidence also suggests that feedback about behavior is a valuable reinforcer; behaviors changed in appropriate directions when researchers posted the speed limit for drivers (Van Houten, Nau, & Marini, 1980) and gave readouts of electricity use to users (Winett et al., 1982).

Changing overconsumption behaviors is difficult in environments with frequent cues and models that encourage overconsumption, such as clearance sales, so-called "free miles" on airlines, and other programs designed to reduce the apparent costs of unnecessary consumption. Whenever so-called short-term reinforcers are more salient than long-term costs, the situation is ripe for what Hardin (1968) called the "tragedy of the commons" (p. 1244). Individuals continue to consume until a resource they share is exhausted, unless additional information, regulations, or moral exhortations are provided. Laboratory games (Bell, Petersen, & Hautaluoma, 1989) have shown the difficulty people have in changing their behaviors for long-term sustainability when short-term contingencies support environmentally destructive behavior.

A behavioral approach would suggest that regulations and taxes would discourage overconsumption by appropriately rewarding and penalizing environmentally relevant purchasing behaviors. For example, the state of Oregon achieved 90% recycling of glass bottles after instituting a 5-cent refund on returns. The designation of a carpool lane reserved for automobiles with two or more passengers has successfully reduced automobile use. One intriguing suggestion is a progressive consumption tax that would tax not what people earn, but what they spend—that is, the difference between their earnings and their savings (Frank, 1999). Of course, the reinforcements for lawmakers have to be addressed before we can hope that such a sensible consumption tax policy might be adopted. As long as campaign finance is based on corporate donations, it is unlikely that lawmakers will be willing to enact tax laws that might hurt the short-term economic growth of industry, even though they would help the long-term health of society. From this perspective, the best way to insure public policies that address long-term environmental health is to change reinforcement contingencies of the lawmakers by changing the way campaigns are financed.

Social Psychological Approaches

A couple of decades ago, one study found that the best predictor of whether people purchased solar equipment is the number of acquaintances they had who currently owned such equipment (Leonard-Barton, 1981). Environmental behavior is socially influenced. It is based on how people define a situation in socially meaningful terms. Other people's behaviors provide important information for appropriate action, and people frequently change their environmentally relevant behavior as a result of social diffusion—they do as others around them do (Leonard-Barton, 1981).

One of the greatest obstacles to changing consumption patterns is that overconsumption is normalized through observation of others. Excessive Christmas shopping, amassing credit card debt, and purchasing luxury vacations and products are commonly observed behaviors throughout the industrialized world that communicate to others that acting in these ways is "the way things are" and that such behavior is a product of human nature. Yet given the short clip of industrialized culture (100 years) in the longer span of human presence on the planet (1 million years), a moment's reflection shows that overconsumption is anything but a product of human nature.

One of the socially mediated reasons for overconsumption is probably social comparison (Festinger, 1954). Whether people feel good or bad depends on whom they are comparing themselves to (Marsh, Kong, & Hau,

2000; Smith et al., 1996). Although most people in industrialized cultures ought to know their lives are endowed with extravagant wealth compared to earlier epochs of human existence, most people compare themselves with a small set of immediate peers and find something to make them feel less well-endowed. Consequently, most people mistakenly believe that they would be happier with a 20% increase in their income (Myers, 1993).

From a social psychological perspective then, reducing overconsumption depends on providing social environments in which overconsumption is viewed as silly, unethical, or obscene. During the 1960s, the middle-class American lifestyle (which included a home in the suburbs, car, swimming pool, etc.) appeared empty and immoral to many of the country's college students, who participated in a "counterculture" which denigrated materialism and instead celebrated emotional connection and expression. Today many of those college students, now middle-aged, own their own suburban homes, not to mention second homes and SUVs. The consumer culture has eclipsed the antimaterialist counterculture.

In the face of the dominant culture, an important strategy for helping people decrease their consumption is thus to provide comparison groups who value reduced consumption. The small but growing "voluntary simplicity" movement (Cairns, 1998; Elgin, 1993) offers cultural support for nonmaterialist choices and a lifestyle associated with more environmentally responsible behaviors, such as resisting impulse buying (Iwata, 1999). Web sites such as http://www.simpleliving.net and http://www.newdream.org are excellent resources for reducing consumption and connecting with others who share similar goals. The norm for what is environmentally acceptable may also be changing, as research on attitudes about environmental problems shows an increasingly widespread endorsement of pro-environmental values across age groups, socioeconomic classes, cultures, and countries (Dunlap & Mertig, 1995). Dunlap and Mertig demonstrated that public citizens, in both industrialized as well as industrializing nations, express increasing concern about damaged environments and their effects on health and increasingly endorse environmental protection. Perhaps we can hope that the ground is being prepared for a massive shift in public opinion, and eventually public policy, toward ecological, rather than economic, optimization.

Cognitive Approaches

The cognitive approach stresses the importance of information and how it is framed or communicated. From this standpoint, changing our overconsumption behavior depends on changing people's perceptions and thoughts about environmental problems, because much of our overconsumption is driven by mindlessness (see chap. 7, this volume).

Although it might seem logical that education, from this perspective, is the key, many researchers have shown that information campaigns have limited effects on environmentally relevant behavior (Howard, 2000; McKenzie-Mohr, 2000; Stern & Oskamp, 1987). Education campaigns fail more often when alternative behaviors are not apparent, are inconvenient, or are costly. Abstract knowledge about environmental problems does little to change behavior in any substantial way.

Nevertheless, recognition of environmental problems clearly depends on the way information is presented. Visibility is an important factor that governments and corporations clearly consider. For example, the U.S. Forest Service formally designed what they called *viewsheds*, that is, "area[s] with high visual sensitivity as seen from selected travel routes [which] are managed to attain and perpetuate an attractive, natural-appearing landscape" (1990, p. S29). In other words, they leave intact cosmetic strips of trees along highways in order to hide ugly clear-cuts stretching just beyond view. Similarly, visually compelling images like the Exxon-Valdez oil spill galvanized public opinion about environmental hazards in 1988, as did the phrase "[a] hole the size of a football in your living room wall," which provided people with a strong enough visual image to sign up for a home energy audit (Gonzales, Aronson, & Costanzo, 1988). If information is presented in visually compelling ways, we cognitively respond appropriately.

Some important roles to be played by cognitive psychologists in addressing overconsumption include studying public perception of consumption behaviors and finding ways to increase public recognition of the environmental crises brought on by these behaviors. For example, perhaps cognitive psychologists could work with companies to provide "green labels," whereby units of energy, freshwater, or forest fiber consumed would be listed for consumers, just as calories, fat grams, and fiber are now listed. Companies could promote their products with environmentally responsible statistics, and consumers would have a way of understanding the environmental implications of their consumer choices. Similarly, cognitive psychologists who have already been involved with risk assessment might help consumers understand the risks of manufacturing a product by providing risk information. Writing articles for *Consumer Reports* and other consumer guides could greatly enhance public awareness of the environmental damage that shopping promotes.

CONCLUSION

Psychologists can play an important role in helping consumers become more informed and sophisticated about their environmentally destructive behaviors, in designing situations that support alternative behaviors, and in finding ways to support more responsible choices. Doing so requires psychologists to become better educated about the dangerous course of our present consumerist culture and to come to see the future of civilization on the planet as a key psychological problem to be solved. Although clinicians and scientists need more technical information about specific environmental problems, they are already especially well-equipped to pose questions, make interventions, and work to modify environmentally relevant behaviors—in therapy sessions, in schools, in communities, and in consumer settings like shopping malls and grocery aisles. Moreover, because business, agriculture, and government institutions (including the military; Renner, 1991) use vastly more resources than do individual households (Stern, 2000), psychologists should also address the behavior of key decision-makers in larger social groups and agencies. Whether we begin by addressing feelings (from a neo-analytic perspective), environmental stimuli and contingencies (from a behavioral perspective), norms (from a social perspective), or information (from a cognitive perspective), it is important that we begin, and begin very soon.

From a psychological perspective, consumerism will never make a life more worthwhile than it otherwise would be. Research shows that personal happiness correlates not with income and material possessions, but with healthy relationships, with friends and family, with meaningful work, and with enough leisure time to enjoy them (Argyle, 1987; see also chaps. 2 & 3, this volume). In the words of global analyst Alan Durning, "[T]he very things that make life worth living, that give depth and bounty to human existence, are infinitely sustainable" (1991, p. 169). As we heal ourselves and the planet by finding ways to live less destructively on the Earth, by slowing down the mad rush for material consumption, and by participating in building a sustainable society, we will be improving the mental health of all of us. I can think of no other goal more worthy or more imperative.

REFERENCES

Abramovitz, J. N. (1998). Forest decline continues. In L. R. Brown, M. Renner, & C. Flavin (Eds.), *Vital signs, 1998: The environmental trends that are shaping our future* (pp. 124–125). New York: Worldwatch Institute.

Abramovitz, J. N., & Mattoon, A. T. (1999). Reorienting the forest products economy. In L. R. Brown, C. Flavin, H. F. French, & L. Starke (Eds.), *State of the world, 1999: A Worldwatch Institute report on progress toward a sustainable society* (pp. 60–77). New York: Worldwatch Institute.

Argyle, M. (1987). *The psychology of happiness.* London: Routledge.

Aronson, E., & O'Leary, M. (1982/83). The relative effectiveness of models and prompts on energy conservation: A field experiment in a shower room. *Journal of Environmental Systems, 12,* 219–224.

Bell, P. A., Petersen, T. R., & Hautaluoma, J. E. (1989). The effect of punishment probability on overconsumption and stealing in a simulated commons. *Journal of Applied Social Psychology, 19,* 1483–1495.

Bragg, E. A. (1996). Towards an ecological self: Deep ecology meets constructionist self-theory. *Journal of Environmental Psychology, 16,* 93–108.

Brown, L. R. (2000). Challenges of the new century. In L. R. Brown, C. Flavin, H. French, S. Postel, & L. Starke (Eds.), *State of the world, 2000: A Worldwatch Institute report on progress toward a sustainable society* (pp. 3–21). New York: Norton.

Buckley, P. (1986). *Essential papers on object relations*. New York: New York University Press.

Cairns, J. (1998). The Zen of sustainable use of the planet: Steps on the path to enlightenment. *Population and Environment, 20*(2), 109–123.

Cialdini, R. B., Kallgren, C. A., & Reno, R. R. (1991). A focus theory of normative conduct: A theoretical refinement and reevaluation of the role of norms in human behavior. *Advances in Experimental Social Psychology, 24,* 201–234.

Clinebell, H. (1996). *Ecotherapy: Healing ourselves, healing the earth*. New York: Haworth.

Dunlap, R. E., & Mertig, A. G. (1995). Global concern for the environment: Is affluence a prerequisite? *Journal of Social Issues, 51*(4), 121–138.

Dunn, S. (2000a). Carbon emissions fall again. In L. R. Brown, M. Renner, & B. Halweil (Eds.), *Vital signs, 2000: The environmental trends that are shaping our future* (pp. 66–67). New York: Norton.

Dunn, S. (2000b). Global temperature drops. In L. R. Brown, M. Renner, & B. Halweil (Eds.), *Vital signs, 2000: The environmental trends that are shaping our future* (pp. 64–65). New York: Norton.

Durning, A. T. (1991). Asking how much is enough? In L. Brown, C. Flavin, & S. Postel (Eds.), *State of the world, 1991* (pp. 153–169). New York: Norton.

Durning, A. T. (1992). *How much is enough? The consumer society and the future of the earth*. New York: Norton.

Elgin, D. (1993). *Voluntary simplicity: Toward a way of life that is outwardly simple, inwardly rich* (Rev. ed.). New York: Quill.

Everett, P. B., Hayward, S. C., & Meyers, A. W. (1974). The effects of a token reinforcement procedure on bus ridership. *Journal of Applied Behavior Analysis, 7,* 1–9.

Festinger, L. (1954). A theory of social comparison processes. *Human Relations, 7,* 117–140.

Flavin, C. (2001). Rich planet, poor planet. In L. R. Brown, C. Flavin, & H. French (Eds.), *State of the world, 2001: A Worldwatch Institute report on progress toward a sustainable society* (pp. 3–20). New York: Norton.

Flavin, C., & Dunn, S. (1999). Responding to the threat of climate change. In L. R. Brown, C. Flavin, & H. F. French (Eds.), *State of the world, 1999: A Worldwatch Institute report on progress toward a sustainable society* (pp. 113–130). New York: Norton.

Frank, R. H. (1999). *Luxury fever: Why money fails to satisfy in an era of excess*. New York: Free Press.

Freud, S. (1927). *The future of an illusion*. New York: Norton.

Gardner, G. T. (2000). Fish harvest down. In L. R. Brown, M. Renner, & B. Halweil (Eds.), *Vital signs, 2000: The environmental trends that are shaping our future* (pp. 40–41). New York: Norton.

Gardner, G. T., & Stern, P. C. (1996). *Environmental problems and human behavior*. Boston: Allyn & Bacon.

Geller, E. S. (1980). Applications of behavioral analysis for litter control. In D. Glenwick & L. Jason (Eds.), *Behavioral community psychology: Progress and prospects* (pp. 254–283). New York: Praeger.

Geller, E. S. (1987). Applied behavior analysis and environmental psychology. From strange bedfellows to a productive marriage. In D. Stokols & I. Altman (Eds.), *Handbook of environmental psychology* (Vol. 1, pp. 361–388). New York: Wiley.

Gerber, M. S. (1992). *On the home front: The cold war legacy of the Hanford nuclear site*. Lincoln: University of Nebraska Press.

Gonzales, M. H., Aronson, E., & Costanzo, M. A. (1988). Using social cognition and persuasion to promote energy conservation: A quasi-experiment. *Journal of Applied Social Psychology, 18*, 1049–1066.

Greenberg, J. R., & Mitchell, S. A. (1983). *Object relations in psychoanalytic theory*. Cambridge, MA: Harvard University Press.

Hardin, G. (1968, Dec. 13). The tragedy of the commons. *Science, 162*, 1243–1248.

Harper, S. (1995). The way of wilderness. In T. Roszak, M. E. Gomes, & A. D. Kanner (Eds.), *Ecopsychology: Restoring the earth, healing the mind* (pp. 183–200). San Francisco, CA: Sierra Club Books.

Homer-Dixon, T. F. (1991). On the threshold: Environmental changes as causes of acute conflict. *International Security, 16*, 76–116.

Howard, G. S. (2000). Adapting human lifestyles for the 21st century. *American Psychologist, 55*, 509–515.

Iwata, O. (1999). Perceptual and behavioral correlates of voluntary simplicity lifestyles. *Social Behavior and Personality, 27*, 379–386.

Kanner, A. D., & Gomes, M. E. (1995). The all-consuming self. In T. Roszak, M. E. Gomes, & A. D. Kanner (Eds.), *Ecopsychology: Restoring the earth, healing the mind* (pp. 77–91). San Francisco: Sierra Club Books.

Klare, M. T. (1999). *Resource wars: The new landscape of global conflict*. New York: Holt.

Kuhn, T. (1962). *The structure of scientific revolutions* (3rd ed.). Chicago: University of Chicago Press.

Leonard-Barton, D. (1981). The diffusion of active-residential solar energy equipment in California. In A. Shama (Ed.), *Marketing solar energy innovations* (pp. 243–257). New York: Praeger.

Macy, J. R. (1983). *Despair and personal power in the nuclear age*. Philadelphia: New Society.

Marsh, H. W., Kong, C.-K., & Hau, K. T. (2000). Longitudinal multilevel models of the big-fish-little-pond effect on academic self concept: Counterbalancing contrast and reflected-glory effects in Hong Kong schools. *Journal of Personality and Social Psychology, 78,* 337–349.

Mattoon, A. T. (2000). Paper piles up. In L. R. Brown, M. Renner, & B. Halweil (Eds.), *Vital signs, 2000: The environmental trends that are shaping our future* (pp. 78–79). New York: Norton.

McKenzie-Mohr, D. (2000). Fostering sustainable behavior through community-based social marketing. *American Psychologist, 55,* 531–537.

Morgan, D., & Ottaway, D. B. (2002, September 15). In Iraqi war scenario, oil is key issue. *The Washington Post,* pp. A01.

Myers, D. G. (1993). *The pursuit of happiness: Who is happy and why.* New York: Morrow.

Myers, D. G. (2002). *Social psychology* (7th ed.). Boston: McGraw-Hill.

Orr, D. W. (1992). *Ecological literacy: Education and the transition to a postmodern world.* Albany: State University of New York Press.

Oskamp, S. (2000). A sustainable future for humanity? How can psychology help? *American Psychologist, 55,* 496–508.

Powers, R. B., Osborne, J. G., & Anderson, E. G. (1973). Positive reinforcement of litter removal in the natural environment. *Journal of Applied Behavior Analysis, 6,* 579–586.

Rashid, A. (2000). *Taliban: Militant Islam, oil, and fundamentalism in central Asia.* New Haven, CT: Yale University Press.

Renner, M. (1991). Assessing the military's war on the environment. In L. R. Brown, C. Flavin, & S. Postel (Eds.), *State of the world, 1991* (pp. 132–152). New York: Norton.

Riebel, L., & Jacobsen, K. (2002). *Eating to save the earth: Food choices for a healthy planet.* Berkeley, CA: Ten Speed Press.

Roszak, T. (1992). *The voice of the Earth.* New York: Simon & Schuster.

Sampat, P. (2000). Groundwater quality deteriorating. In L. R. Brown, M. Renner, & B. Halweil (Eds.), *Vital signs, 2000: The environmental trends that are shaping our future* (pp. 124–125). New York: Norton.

Sampat, P. (2001). Uncovering groundwater pollution. In L. R. Brown, C. Flavin, & H. F. French (Eds.), *State of the world, 2001: A Worldwatch Institute report on progress toward a sustainable society* (pp. 21–42). New York: Norton.

Saunders, S., & Munro, D. (2000). The construction and validation of a consumer orientation questionnaire (SCOI) designed to measure Fromm's (1955) "marketing character" in Australia. *Social Behavior and Personality, 28,* 219–240.

Sewell, L. (1995). The skill of ecological perception. In T. Roszak, M. E. Gomes, & A. D. Kanner (Eds.), *Ecopsychology: Restoring the earth, healing the mind* (pp. 201–215). San Francisco, CA: Sierra Club Books.

Sheehan, M. O. (2001). Making better transportation choices. In L. R. Brown, C. Flavin, & H. French (Eds.), *State of the world, 2001: A Worldwatch Institute report on progress toward a sustainable society* (pp. 103–122). New York: Norton.

Skinner, B. F. (1971). *Beyond freedom and dignity*. Englewood Cliffs, NJ: Prentice-Hall.

Smith, R. H., Turner, T. J., Garonzik, R., Leach, C. W., Urch-Druskat, V., & Weston, C. M. (1996). Envy and schadenfreude. *Personality and Social Psychology Bulletin*, *22*, 158–168.

Stern, P. C. (2000). Psychology and the science of human–environment interactions. *American Psychologist*, *55*, 523–530.

Stern, P. C., & Oskamp, S. (1987). Managing scarce environmental resources. In D. Stokols & I. Altman (Eds.), *Handbook of environmental psychology* (Vol. 2, pp. 1043–1088). New York: Wiley.

Swanson, J. (2001). *Communing with nature*. Corvallis, OR: Illahee Press.

Union of Concerned Scientists (1992). *World scientist's warning to humanity* [Pamphlet]. Available from Union of Concerned Scientists, 2 Brattle Square, Cambridge, MA 02238, (617) 547-5552, Fax (617) 864-9405.

U.S. Forest Service. (1990). *Summary: Final environmental impact statement. Umatilla National Forest*. Portland, OR: Author.

Van Houten, R., Nau, P., & Marini, Z. (1980). An analysis of public posting in reducing speeding behavior on an urban highway. *Journal of Applied Behavior Analysis*, *13*, 383–395.

Walker, J. M. (1979). Energy demand behavior in a master-meter apartment complex: An experimental analysis. *Journal of Applied Psychology*, *64*, 190–196.

Wilson, E. O. (1984). *Biophilia: The human bond with other species*. Cambridge, MA: Harvard University Press.

Winett, R. A., Hatcher, J. W., Fort, T. R., Leckliter, I. N., Love, S. A., Riley, A. W., et al. (1982). The effects of videotape modeling and daily feedback on residential electricity conservation, home temperature and humidity, perceived comfort, and clothing worn: Winter and summer. *Journal of Applied Behavior Analysis*, *15*, 381–402.

Winter, D. D. (1996). *Ecological psychology: Healing the split between planet and self*. New York: HarperCollins.

Winter, D. D. (2000). Some big ideas for some big problems. *American Psychologist*, *55*, 516–522.

Winter, D. D., & Koger, S. (2004). *The psychology of environmental problems* (2nd ed.). Hillsdale, NJ: Erlbaum.

II

THEORETICAL
PERSPECTIVES

6

MATERIALISM AND THE EVOLUTION OF CONSCIOUSNESS

MIHALY CSIKSZENTMIHALYI

The other chapters in this volume are by authors who have studied the topic of materialism for a long time and have good data to support their arguments. My interest in the subject is recent and so far rather tangential. Nevertheless, the work on optimal human functioning I have been pursuing for the past 35 years is relevant to the topic and may help to provide a different perspective on it. In this chapter I plan to start by describing a holistic model for understanding the psychology of materialism, then I examine the motivation underlying it, and suggest ways to overcome excessive reliance on it. To illustrate the argument, I draw on a set of interviews with exceptional business leaders who had been nominated by peers as having been both successful financially and socially responsible. These interviews, collected in the course of a study funded by the Templeton Foundation as part of the Good Work project jointly directed by Howard Gardner, William Damon, and myself, are described in greater detail in Csikszentmihalyi (2003).

CONTEXT OF MATERIALISM

To provide a context for the understanding of materialism, it is useful to agree on a conceptual framework broad enough to illuminate all the facets of the issue. For this purpose let me introduce what I call—with only a whiff of grandiosity—a theory of life. It is a theory based on three simple axioms that are themselves self-evident:

1. What we call life is a sequence of events in consciousness— that is, *experiences* (thoughts, emotions, sensations, etc.)— that take place over the life-span.
2. In order to appear in consciousness, experiences require the allocation of psychic energy, that is, *attention*. Psychic energy, however, is limited by the information-processing capacity of the brain.
3. Therefore, the quality and content of a person's life depend on what he or she has paid attention to over time.

Arguments justifying these assumptions have been presented in earlier works (e.g., Csikszentmihalyi, 1978, 1990, 1993), so I will not rehearse them here. They are an extension of the insights developed more than 100 years ago by William James (1890), in chapter 11 of his *Principles of Psychology*.

On the basis of these axioms, we may define *materialism* as the tendency to allocate excessive attention to goals that involve material objects: wanting to own them, consume them, or flaunt possession of them. What is "excessive" is relative to the total amount of attention at the disposal of the person. We all must invest attention in material goals in order to survive, but there is a threshold along the continuum after which any further investment detracts from the ability to experience other aspects of life—such as relationships, aesthetic experiences, or the development of the body and the mind. There is no precise way to assess where that threshold lies, but in recent years useful measures have been developed to assess the relative salience of materialism in the psychic economy (Kasser & Ryan, 1993; Schmuck & Sheldon, 2001; Sheldon & McGregor, 2000). It follows that a materialist is a person whose psychic energy is disproportionately invested in things and their symbolic derivatives—wealth, status, and power based on possessions—and therefore whose life consists mainly of experiences with the material dimension of life.

Why should anyone invest psychic energy in things? To answer that question, we should further distinguish a *material experience* from one that is social, aesthetic, cognitive, or spiritual in character. In other words, just because I am paying attention to a thing, it does not mean that I am attending to its *thingness*. For instance, in a study of how people relate to meaningful objects in their homes, we found that such objects are cherished because they remind the owner of family members, ancestors, important life events, personal accomplishments, and values. Such experiences are clearly not primarily material in character (Csikszentmihalyi & Rochberg-Halton, 1981). In fact, arguably it is almost impossible to have a purely material experience. Objects are generally tools; we attend to them in order to achieve some goal or experience beyond the thing itself. So it would seem that materialism is not primarily a function of the materiality of the objects one attends to, but rather of the goals pursued through the interaction with the objects.

Although the need to increase control over material objects, or greed, is an ancient human tendency decried as a sin by most world religions, in the past its impact on the nonhuman environment has been slight because people could own at best a few livestock and a few tools. As the anthropologist Marshall Sahlins (1972) has argued, possessions were seen as life-threatening hindrances by hunter-gatherers who needed to move lightly over the landscape in search of nutrition. Even in the relatively prosperous France of the Middle Ages, most people lacked manufactured products such as furniture (LeRoy Ladurie, 1979), and not even kings had access to petroleum or electricity. The human "footprint" on the ecology was therefore light, and the desire for material goods was an understandable and almost benign motivation. As technology has made the mass production of innumerable artifacts possible, and as people learned how to extract energy from everything from water turbines to nuclear reactors, the unbridled need for material possessions is posing a severe threat to our physical survival, as well as to our psychological well-being.

More generally, we may call *material goals* those that aim at the preservation of the organism in its present state—those that satisfy the homeostatic needs of survival and safety, or the "lower order" needs in the Maslovian hierarchy (Csikszentmihalyi, 2000). In contrast, we may speak of *transcendent goals* when persons use some of their psychic energy to reach outside their own needs and goals and invest in another system, thus becoming a stakeholder in an entity larger than their previous selves. Curiosity, empathy, generosity, responsibility, and charity are some ways that transcendent goals are manifested. The most familiar example is when a person devotes attention not just to selfish interests, or to material goals in general, but to the needs of others, or to the cosmic forces that we assume must rule the universe. Religions cannot exist unless men and women invest some of their psychic energy into transcendent goals; hence most of them warn against attending only to material goals (Belk, 1983; Massimini & Delle Fave, 1991).

This ability to transcend self-interest is presumably a recent capacity of consciousness, which itself is the result of the human nervous system having reached a complex level of material organization. However, this explanation is not reductive: On the contrary, the fact that somehow a material system has become able to reach out to other beings, and to see itself as part of a cosmic pattern, is an extraordinary step in evolution. Obviously we are not acting like transcendent beings all of the time or even very often. The centripetal forces of selfishness are still too strong. Given all the threats from the environment and from other humans, we could not survive long if we did not devote most of our attention to self-preservation. However, if we devoted all our energies only to take care of Number One we would stop growing. The evolution of consciousness requires that we turn psychic energy away from present needs to create ideas, feelings, relationships, and objects that did not exist before.

Whether one is being materialistic cannot be established by simply observing overt behavior. It is possible to approach anything in a materialist way: For example, televangelists stress the cash returns of spirituality, and many people go to the symphony or the museum in order to be seen and admired rather than to be transported to a new level of experience. Conversely it is possible to be involved in an ostensibly materialist activity such as business, and yet pursue primarily transcendent aims. In a recent study of business leaders, we found many whose psychic energy was not absorbed by the making of profits, but instead was focused on goals that benefit larger systems (Csikszentmihalyi, 2003). For instance, the founder of the outdoors equipment-maker Patagonia, Yvon Chouinard, described the goals of his company as follows:

> Our mission statement is to use business to find solutions to the environmental crisis. I'm constantly pushing everyone in the company to realize that's why we are in business. That is the reason. We are not in the business to make a profit. We're not in the business to make a product. We're in the business to really change the way other companies operate. (Csikszentmihalyi, 2003, p. 150)

Don Williams, CEO of Trammell-Crow, the commercial real-estate company, had involved his organization in philanthropic activities for years. Recently he decided to leave the leadership position to work part time and remain on the Board while devoting more of his psychic energies directly to transcendent goals:

> For me, today, work is a platform for social involvement. . . . My passion today is focused on the comprehensive renewal of our lowest income neighborhoods in Dallas . . . it is unjust in America for so many of our people to not receive a good education, not to have access to a decent job, and not to have access to a decent home. That is an injustice. By the way, if you don't have an educated workforce coming up, if we have a society that is eroded overwhelmingly with drugs and crime, that's not good for business. Now that's not the model under which I do that, but I think there's a case there that's very good for business to take home. (Csikszentmihalyi, 2003, p. 150)

When a person pursues business in this way, it ceases to be primarily materialistic; whereas a preacher who promises that prayer will make you healthy or rich is using religion for material aims. What counts is the outcome of the psychic energy invested: Is it exhausted within the system as presently constituted, or is it directed to the growth of the system and to the enhancement of the goals of other systems as well? In the latter case, one would not consider the experience to be materialistic.

FORMATION OF PSYCHOLOGICAL CAPITAL

The content of life is limited by the amount of information we can process through attention. In this sense attention, or psychic energy, is our most scarce resource. Like all resources, it can be used for different purposes. It can be "invested" in activities that provide immediate gratification or provide future benefits, or it can be "wasted" doing things that are neither enjoyable nor conducive to personal growth.

It is useful to borrow the concept of capital to illustrate a basic distinction in the use of attention. In economics, *capital* has been defined as "resources withheld from current consumption and allocated instead to future expectations" (Drucker, 1986, p. 27). One may want to restrict the notion of capital to economic resources invested in the expectation of financial profit, but this traditional definition applies only to a small set of a much larger phenomenon.

Consider the kind of choice most of us confront every day upon coming home from work: Do I sit down to read a stimulating book (or take a bike ride, play the guitar, volunteer at the hospital), or do I sit down in front of the TV? Most people would agree that watching television would be the more pleasant choice. It would be easier, more relaxing, more hassle-free. Which choice would contribute more to my well-being in the long run? Again, most people would probably say, the first one.

However, what is the resource being "consumed" while watching television and "withdrawn from consumption" when involved in the second set of activities? If at the psychological level the most basic resource is attention, we would conclude that it is attention that is being consumed. The state of the organism changes very little while watching television. There is little increase in the complexity of the mind: Few new affective, conative, or cognitive skills are built as a result of viewing (Kubey & Csikszentmihalyi, 2002). By contrast, engaging in hobbies; sports; or artistic, volunteer, and social activities tends to build the complexity of skills in these areas.

Although pleasurable activities are easier and more attractive, the attention consumed by them does not provide "greater future returns"—in fact, the returns tend to decrease over time (i.e., we tend to get bored and listless). On the other hand, the effort spent in learning to play a guitar, in learning a new language, in playing a sport, or in helping others does tend to bring greater returns in the future—that is, we get more enjoyment from life as a result of learning new skills and perceiving new opportunities.

It is easier to develop psychological capital if others have invested some of their psychic energy in our well-being. Parenting that builds the children's psychological complexity through the simultaneous presence of support and challenge is one venue (Csikszentmihalyi & Rathunde, 1997; Rathunde, 1996). Another is the "cultural capital" and "social capital" that sociologists emphasize—namely, the resources in knowledge and social support that children inherit from their families (Bourdieu, 1993; Coleman, 1988). The attentional resources invested in parenting become the children's social capital, which makes it easier for them to build their own psychological capital and, in turn, pass it on as social capital to *their* children.

Other obvious sources of social capital are education and work. Unfortunately, many schools and many workplaces do not promote the growth of complexity. But there are exceptions. For instance, Gerald Greenwald, CEO of United Airlines, answered a question about what gave meaning to his work by stressing the rewards of helping his employees build their psychological capital:

> For me, it has been clearly the whole process of the development of the person. That is what has brought meaning to my work. As I've seen people grow as individuals, grow in who they're becoming as well as what they're doing, grow as parents, grow as contributors in their community or contributors in their churches or places of worship, grow as healthy citizens, all those things are fulfilling to me and bring meaning to the fact that work results in that. What other activity could I be involved in where I could be involved with as many people where they had an opportunity to produce something, to achieve a result, and in all that, to also develop as a person? (Personal communication, September 29, 1999)

Expressions such as these are by no means just nice words uttered in order to look good. Greenwald, like the other businesspeople included in our study, had been nominated because he did actually "walk the walk" on his job. Psychological complexity would advance much more quickly if more business leaders did the same.

CONFLICT BETWEEN PLEASURE AND ENJOYMENT

One might ask, if the production of psychological capital improves the quality of life so much, why do we spend so little time on it in relation to the time we spend in activities that consume psychic energy without leaving any real benefits? To answer this question, we must keep in mind that the programs contained in our brains are not harmoniously ordered according to a single plan or design. The Cartesian view of the mind was that of a machine designed for logical reasoning. By contrast, Freud believed that the mind was simply a tool manipulated by libidinal instincts for the purpose of experiencing pleasure. Both views are wrong; first of all, there is no single logic or purpose that accounts for how the mind works (see, e.g., Barkow, Cosmides, & Tooby, 1992; Damasio, 1994). A more accurate metaphor would be that of a broker who each day conducts hundreds of transactions at the request of clients who want to buy or sell a stock on the market. In this view, the "clients" are the various instructions coded in our brains in the course of evolution, instructions that have facilitated the survival of our ancestors in the past. These instructions are usually independent of each other, and often they tell us to do contradictory things. There is a program that makes us want to be with other people where it is safe, but there is also a program for wanting to be alone where we can be free. We have instructions for sexual promiscuity together with instructions for fidelity. And so on.

All of the instructions we carry in our genes, and learn from the rules of the culture in which we are born, fall into two broad categories. The first contains programs for hoarding energy: to relax, lay in supplies against all future contingencies, impress our neighbors with our possessions, and be comfortable. The second includes injunctions to expend energy: to explore, to be adventurous, and to be of service to others. Both are necessary for the survival of the species: Without the first, we would exhaust ourselves; without the second, we would stagnate and stop evolving. It would be preferable, perhaps, if these contradictory impulses were better coordinated, or subservient to an overarching logical mind that could activate either one set of programs or the other, as needed. However, that is not the case; usually we act according to one or the other set of instructions "unthinkingly," now listening to the brain we inherited from lizards, now listening to the rules laid down by Moses.

Thus, evolution has built two contradictory motivations into our nervous system: *pleasure*, which is the well-being we feel when eating, resting, and procreating; and *enjoyment*, which is the exhilarating sensation we feel when going beyond the requirements of survival (Csikszentmihalyi, 1993; Ryan & Deci, 2000; Waterman, 1993). Pleasure is a powerful source of motivation, but it does not produce change; it is a conservative force that makes us want to satisfy existing needs and to achieve comfort and relaxation. It is the motivation that makes us look for material resources to improve the quality of life —after all, these are scarce and everyone wants them, so they must be valuable. The concreteness of material goals also makes them seem more real than more complex goals. However, the improvement that money, power, and comfort produce is often simply that of removing momentarily the anxiety we all experience when confronting mortality and finitude (see also chap. 8, this volume). "More stuff" promises security and comfort, even when the benefits are short-lived and we need ever more stuff to regain equanimity in the face of the slings and arrows inherent in living. There is nothing wrong with seeking pleasure in material goals, but individuals for whom it becomes the main reason for living are not going to grow beyond what the genes have programmed them to desire.

Enjoyment, on the other hand, is not always pleasant, and it can be very stressful at times. A mountain climber may be close to freezing, utterly exhausted, in danger of falling into a bottomless crevasse, yet she would not want to be anywhere else. Sipping a cocktail under a palm tree at the edge of the turquoise ocean is nice, but it just does not compare to the exhilaration she feels on that freezing ridge. At the moment it is experienced, enjoyment may be physically painful and mentally taxing; but because it involves a triumph over the forces of entropy and decay, it nourishes the spirit. Enjoyment builds memories that enrich lives in retrospect, and it gives confidence for facing the future.

Because enjoyable activities usually require more effort than those that provide pleasure, and their rewards are often delayed, all too often the short-term logic is to choose pleasure over enjoyment. For instance, in our studies using the experiential sampling method (Csikszentmihalyi & Larson, 1984; Csikszentmihalyi & Schneider, 2000), we often show individuals the results of the week during which they reported what they were doing and how they felt about it, and we ask: "Look, this is how happy you reported being when the pager signaled while you were watching television. And here is how much more happy you reported being while playing basketball or playing the piano. Can you tell me then why you spent 15 times as many hours last week watching TV than doing active leisure?"

Confronted with such questions, most people hem and haw, and admit that yes, it's much more enjoyable to do some active form of leisure, but it also requires more energy to get organized for it. Turning on a TV set, by contrast, is very easy and therefore attractive when one feels tired.

However, it would be a mistake to assume that opting for enjoyment over pleasure is tantamount to delaying gratification. What we find in our studies is that growth-producing, complex activities not only build the ability to enjoy a richer life later, but they are actually enjoyed more in the present compared with more glamorous and heavily advertised pleasurable activities.

For instance, many entrepreneurs and professionals find that their work provides a sense of adventurous growth that produces enjoyment greater than any money could buy. One of the business leaders we interviewed describes his attitude toward work:

> It's an enormous responsibility and it's an enormous challenge. And it's the most fun job in the world! I love coming to work every morning. I can't wait to get here. I can't wait, because everyday something else is going to happen.

One finds the same enthusiasm for work—although less often—among salaried and even assembly-line workers. Again, the issue is not so much *what* one does but *how* one does it. As Studs Terkel (1974) and many others who study work have noted, if one is proud of one's job and tries to do one's best at it, it can become as fun and interesting as that of any executive.

FLOW: THE EXPERIENCE OF ENJOYMENT

Among successful scientists, artists, physicians, lawyers, and business leaders, one finds that they express the same sort of enthusiasm about their work. Unfortunately, most jobs do not have enough challenges or enough variety to provide that level of enjoyment. There are also many wealthy and well-known professionals or business persons whose work has become routine. Such people then look for enjoyment outside work or to the pleasures provided by material experiences. The more boring and routine everyday life becomes, the more likely that the number of those seeking substitutes for enjoyment will increase. But what does it mean that a person enjoys something?

In the last few decades, studies conducted around the world have shown that whenever people feel a deep sense of enjoyment they describe their experience in very similar terms. Regardless of age, gender, or education, they report very similar mental states. What they actually do at the time is wildly different—they may be meditating, running a race, playing chess, or doing a surgical operation, but what they feel when they really enjoy what they are doing sounds remarkably the same. I have given the name of *flow* to this common experience, because so many of the people used the analogy of being carried away by an outside force, of moving effortlessly with a current of energy, at the moments of highest enjoyment (Csikszentmihalyi, 1975, 1990, 1996).

Here are three quotes from among the close to 8,000 interviews collected over the years in our laboratory, as well as by colleagues around the world, providing some glimpses of how the flow experience feels. The first is from an expert rock-climber who describes his mental state when climbing:

> The task at hand is so demanding and rich in its complexity and pull . . . one tends to get immersed in what is going on around him, in the rock, in the moves that are involved . . . search for handholds . . . proper position of the body—so involved he might lose consciousness of his own identity and melt into the rock.

Compare his quote with that from an inner-city African American teenager who plays basketball after school:

> The court—that's all that matters . . . sometimes on court I think of a problem, like fighting with my steady girl, and I think that's nothing compared to the game. You can think about a problem all day but as soon as you get in the game, the hell with it! . . . When you are playing basketball, that's all there is on your mind.

Or with the account from a surgeon describing why his job is so enjoyable:

> In good surgery everything you do is essential, every move is excellent and necessary; there is elegance, little blood loss, and a minimum of trauma. . . . This is very pleasant, particularly when the group works together in a smooth and efficient manner.

These individuals describe some of the basic elements of flow: The task at hand draws people in with its complexity to such an extent that they become completely involved in it. There is no distinction between thought and action, between self and environment. The important thing is to do each move as well as possible, because even lives may depend on it. Other elements of the experience are a sense of control, a loss of the sense of time, and a good fit between what a person can do and what the opportunities of the situation are. When these conditions are present, we feel a sense of exhilaration that is rare in life.

However, flow does not require a life-and-death setting to be enjoyable. The most widely reported flow activity the world over is reading a good book, when one gets immersed in the characters and the vicissitudes of their fictional lives to the point of forgetting oneself. Remarkably often flow is experienced when at work, as told by this 76-year-old woman who still farms in the Italian Alps:

> It gives me a great satisfaction to be outdoors, to talk with people, to be with my animals. . . . I talk to everybody—plants, birds, flowers, and animals. Everything in nature keeps you company, you see nature progress each day. You feel clean and happy: Too bad you get tired and have to go home. . . . Even when you have to work a lot it is very beautiful.

This woman describes her work as though it were a romantic idyll. In fact, she gave this account after walking several miles down mountain meadows carrying on her back a bale of hay twice as tall as she is. Nevertheless, by paying attention to the complexity of the natural world around her, she was able to become at one with it and to enjoy the experience. Often the experience is the result of spending time with others in a close interaction. Here is a mother describing her most precious moments:

> When I'm working with my daughter, when she is discovering something new. A new cookie recipe that she has accomplished, that she has made herself, an artistic work that she has done that she's proud of. Her reading is one thing that she's really into, and we read together. She reads to me, and I read to her, and that's a time when I sort of lose touch with the rest of the world, I'm totally absorbed in what I am doing.

Paying attention to one's daughter, watching her grow and discover new things, and appropriately responding to her changing self requires as much psychic energy as it takes to be a good rock-climber, farmer, or surgeon. By getting immersed in such a complex activity, one's own self becomes more complex and stronger.

MATERIALISM AS A SUBSTITUTE FOR ENJOYMENT

I propose that when a person cannot build a self based on flow, he or she tries to build a self with the help of material goals and material experiences. These include competitive striving for wealth and power and seeking pleasure in its various forms, such as passive leisure and consumer behavior. The saying that "nature abhors a vacuum" is true of the human psyche as well: During waking hours, we need a constant stream of experiences to keep the mind working properly. In everyday life, people often find themselves in an existential vacuum where no clear need suggesting a specific goal presents itself to consciousness. Normal American teenagers, for instance, when paged at random moments of the day, report 30% of the time that what they are doing is not what they want to do but that they can't think of anything else they would rather be doing instead. Although this pattern is strongest when teenagers are in school, it is also typical of responses at home (Csikszentmihalyi & Schneider, 2000). We have less data from adults, but what there is suggests that they also spend quite a large part of their days in a state where, as far as they are concerned, "there is nothing to do."

This pattern is significant because when a person feels that there is nothing to do, the quality of experience tends to decline. One feels less alert, active, strong, happy, and creative. Self-esteem declines. Contrary to what one might expect, such a negative experiential state is more likely to occur at home during free time than at work, where goals are usually clear and attention is more readily engaged (Csikszentmihalyi & LeFevre, 1989).

This suggests that, in addition to the existential needs described by Maslow (e.g. Maslow, 1968) and others, we also have an *experiential* need—perhaps peculiar to human beings—to keep consciousness in an organized state, focused on some activity that requires attention. When there is nothing to do, attention starts to turn inward, we begin to ruminate, and, frequently, get depressed. By and large, when we start thinking about ourselves rather than about what we need to accomplish, attention turns to deficits: We are getting old and fat, we are losing our hair, our children are getting in trouble, we have not accomplished much in life. As a result, our mood begins to turn sour (Csikszentmihalyi, 1993, 1996; Csikszentmihalyi & Figurski, 1982). The downward spiral of rumination is interrupted only when attention is again engaged by some need that suggests a goal: preparing dinner, taking the dog for a walk, or if all else fails, watching a show on TV. Yet trying to fill unstructured time with passive entertainment does not work well; the quality of experience while watching TV is barely more positive than that of the slough of despond that awaits the unfocused mind (Kubey & Csikszentmihalyi, 1990).

The experiential need to keep entropy from overwhelming consciousness is responsible for a great deal of material values and consumer behavior. It could be said of shopping, as McLuhan (1964) said of television, that "the medium is the message." In other words, it often does not matter what we are shopping *for*—the point is to shop for anything, whatever. Shopping is a goal-directed activity and thus fills the experiential vacuum that leads to depression and despair. (See also chaps. 7 & 10, this volume.) That we have to pay, that is, expend the equivalent of psychic energy, for what we acquire lends an additional importance to the activity. If we spend money, it must be worthwhile. As Linder (1970) pointed out, the value of the goods we consume in leisure becomes a measure of the value of our time: If in one hour's time I drink $20 worth of a single-malt Scotch, while listening to a stereo that depreciates at the rate of $5 an hour, in an apartment whose rent prorates at $10 an hour, then it means that my time is worth at least $35 an hour —even without counting the cost of clothing, furniture, girlfriend, and so forth that may also be contributing to the value of my time.

Thus, consuming is one of the ways we respond to the void that pervades consciousness when there is nothing else to do. Shopping and surrounding ourselves with possessions is a relatively easy way to forestall the dread of nonbeing, even though this does not improve the quality of our lives because no psychological capital is accumulated in the process. Of course, reliance on materialist coping mechanisms is encouraged by the huge economic apparatus of advertising and merchandising, which has become so ingrained in our society. A particularly egregious example of such dependence on purchasing as a pabulum for terror was the reaction of so many political leaders after the September 11 attack. The advice one heard most often in the aftermath of that tragedy was to go out and shop. Buying an extra car or refrigerator was supposed to be an act of patriotic defiance against the enemies, an act that confirmed the meaningfulness of our lives.

Material resources beyond a rather low threshold contribute little to a positive experience, a fact that is by now fairly well established. The first line of evidence concerning the futility of expecting material well-being to produce happiness is based on a variety of surveys conducted over several decades (Csikszentmihalyi, 1999; Diener, 2000; Myers, 2000; see chap. 11, this volume). For instance, although the average income for Americans measured in constant dollars has doubled in the last 40 years, the level of happiness they report has not changed. Winning the lottery creates a small blip of happiness that lasts a few months, after which the lucky winner's happiness returns to what it was before (Brickman, Coates, & Janoff-Bulman, 1978). In a current longitudinal study tracking more than 800 American teenagers through high school and beyond, we find that teenagers from the most affluent suburbs tend to be less happy and have lower self-esteem than those from middle-class communities and even than those living in inner city slums (Csikszentmihalyi & Schneider, 2000). Several researchers have shown that excessive concern with financial success and material values is associated with lower levels of life satisfaction and self-esteem, presumably because such concerns reflect a sense of "contingent worth" predicated on *having* rather than *being* (Kasser & Ryan, 1993; Richins & Dawson, 1992; see also chaps. 2 & 3, this volume).

Another source of evidence bearing on the effects of material experiences is through a study in which we correlated the happiness that American adults reported experiencing in their free time with the amount of fossil and electrical energy consumed by the activity they were doing at the time (Graef, Gianinno, & Csikszentmihalyi, 1981). If a person was reading a magazine when the pager signaled, for example, more energy was expended than if he or she had been reading a book, because producing a magazine (in terms of manufacturing paper, printing, sales, distribution, etc.) requires more BTUs of energy per unit of reading time than it takes to produce a book. Thus, if there was a direct relationship between energy consumption and quality of experience, a person should be happier when reading a magazine than when reading a book. Instead, we found the opposite: a slight but significant negative relationship between the average BTU load of activities and the happiness people experienced while doing them. There was an interesting gender difference: For men, BTUs did not relate to happiness at all, whereas for women the relationship was quite strong in the negative direction. According to the Department of Energy (Graef et al.,1981), about 7% of all the energy consumed in the United States is spent on discretionary leisure activities, from traveling to snowmobiling, from skiing to TV watching. It is important to realize, therefore, that a substantial amount of this energy could be saved without impairing the quality of life, and that quality of life could perhaps be improved by simply choosing "green" leisure activities to fill one's free time.

Why is there a negative relationship between energy consumed and happiness? The reason activities with low external physical energy requirements result in greater happiness is that they usually require greater inputs of psychic energy. Having a good conversation makes very little demands on environmental energy, but it demands concentrated attention and mental activity and can be very enjoyable. So in flow-producing activities like reading, gardening, painting, working on crafts, writing poetry, or doing mathematics, people report being happier than when they are passively consuming goods or entertainment (Csikszentmihalyi, 1996, 1999).

CONCLUSION: ENJOYMENT AS AN ALTERNATIVE TO MATERIALISM

Almost half a century ago, the social philosopher Hannah Arendt warned that advances in technology and the increase in free time were providing us with the opportunity to consume the whole world.

> That . . . consumption is no longer restricted to the necessities but, on the contrary, mainly concentrates on the superfluities of life . . . harbors the grave danger that eventually no object of the world will be safe from consumption and annihilation through consumption. (Arendt, 1956, p. 133)

This outcome is made even more likely by people's increasing reliance on material experiences to construct their lives. To the extent that flow in everyday life is rare and that material success has achieved a hegemony relative to other forms of success, an increasing amount of psychic energy is likely to be devoted to the pursuit of material goals. This then would accelerate the "annihilation through consumption" of the world Arendt (1956) foresaw half a century ago.

Looking at the impact of humankind on the planet, one of three scenarios is likely to play out in the coming decades. One is a coming to pass of the danger Arendt and many others have warned us about: a quick deterioration of the planetary environment, an exhaustion of such basic resources as water and fossil fuels, followed by warfare and civil discord for the possession of the dwindling resources. The second possibility is that technology saves us despite our greed. Practical use of renewable energy, new agricultural practices, and desalinization of seawater could do the trick. It would be nice if this came to pass, but it would not be wise to bet the farm on it.

Finally, there is the possibility of a steady transformation of our lifestyles from one built around material experiences to one rich in transcendent experiences. This may be the hardest and least likely scenario, but in the long run it would be the most promising. If instead of pleasure and the false security of material goals we built our lives around investments of psychic energy in complex activities that provide flow, we would be happier as well as more likely to survive on a planet freed from the threat of terminal depletion.

To achieve such a goal, many habits engrained in our lifestyles have to change and many of the institutions that have arisen to supply our habits and then exploit them have to be regulated or transformed (see chaps. 4 & 5, this volume). Parents have to learn that buying a car as a graduation present is not the best way to express love for their children—teaching them to enjoy life is a far better gift. Schools have to realize that learning without joy is useless in the long run. Politics have to focus on the goal held foremost by the Declaration of Independence—the pursuit of happiness—not just by facilitating material goals, but by striving to support the evolution of psychological complexity in its various forms. To achieve all this, however, we need to agree on a new covenant—a set of nonmaterial goals that in the past religions have taught and which science has been unable to formulate thus far.

Such changes are not easy for two simple reasons: The genetic instructions we carry are still set to a survival mode in an environment of material scarcity, and the social institutions that have developed over time depend in large part on being able to exploit our material goals. When 2,000 years ago the Christians introduced a new lifestyle into the Roman Empire, one that dispensed with pomp and power, the stakeholders in the old regime realized the danger this posed to the institutions that protected their privileges. Thus, Christians were fed to lions and burned at the stake. How would the World Bank, the Enrons, Savings-and-Loans, and their political allies react if a new worldview based on voluntary simplicity really gained ground? Human nature has not had a chance to change that much in two millennia, and technology can be more potent than lions and stakes.

REFERENCES

Arendt, H. (1956). *The human condition*. Chicago: University of Chicago Press.

Barkow, J., Cosmides, L., & Tooby, J. (Eds.). (1992). *The adapted mind: Evolutionary psychology and the generation of culture*. Oxford: Oxford University Press.

Belk, R. (1983). Worldly possessions: Issues and criticisms. In R. Bagozzi & A. M. Tybout (Eds.), *Advances in consumer research* (Vol. 10, pp. 514–519). Ann Arbor, MI: Association for Consumer Research.

Bourdieu, P. (1993). *The field of cultural production*. New York: Columbia University Press.

Brickman, P., Coates, D., & Janoff-Bulman, R. (1978). Lottery winners and accident victims: Is happiness relative? *Journal of Personality and Social Psychology, 36,* 917–927.

Coleman, J. S. (1988). Social capital in the creation of human capital. *American Journal of Sociology, 94,* 95–120.

Csikszentmihalyi, M. (1975). *Beyond boredom and anxiety*. San Francisco: Jossey-Bass.

Csikszentmihalyi, M. (1978). Attention and the wholistic approach to behavior. In K. S. Pope & J. L. Singer (Eds.), *The stream of consciousness* (pp. 335–358). New York: Plenum.

Csikszentmihalyi, M. (1990). *Flow: The psychology of optimal experience*. New York: HarperCollins.

Csikszentmihalyi, M. (1993). *The evolving self*. New York: HarperCollins.

Csikszentmihalyi, M. (1996). *Finding flow: The psychology of engagement with everyday life*. New York: Basic Books.

Csikszentmihalyi, M. (1999). If we are so rich, why aren't we happy? *American Psychologist, 54,* 821–827.

Csikszentmihalyi, M. (2000). The costs and benefits of consuming. *Journal of Consumer Research, 27,* 267–272.

Csikszentmihalyi, M. (2003). *Good business leadership, flow, and the making of meaning*. New York: Viking.

Csikszentmihalyi, M., & Figurski, T. (1982). Self-awareness and aversive experience in everyday life. *Journal of Personality, 50,* 15–28.

Csikszentmihalyi, M., & Larson, R. (1984). *Being adolescent: Conflict and growth in the teenage years*. New York: Basic Books.

Csikszentmihalyi, M., & LeFevre, J. (1989). Optimal experience in work and leisure. *Journal of Personality and Social Psychology, 56,* 15–22.

Csikszentmihalyi, M., & Rathunde, K. (1997). The development of the person: An experiential perspective on the ontogenesis of psychological complexity. In W. Damon (Series Ed.) & R. M. Lerner (Vol. Ed.), *Handbook of child psychology: Vol 1. Theoretical models of human development* (pp. 635–685). New York: Wiley.

Csikszentmihalyi, M., & Rochberg-Halton, E. (1981). *The meaning of things: Domestic symbols and the self*. New York: Cambridge University Press.

Csikszentmihalyi, M., & Schneider, B. (2000). *Becoming adult: How teenagers prepare for the world of work*. New York: Basic Books.

Damasio, A. (1994). *Descartes' error*. New York: Putnam.

Diener, E. (2000). Subjective well-being: The science of happiness and a proposal for a national index. *American Psychologist, 55*, 34–43.

Drucker, P. F. (1986). *Innovation and entrepreneurship*. New York: HarperBusiness.

Graef, R., Gianinno, S., & Csikszentmihalyi, M. (1981). Energy consumption in leisure and perceived happiness. In J. D. Claxton, C. D. Anderson, J. R. Brent & G. H. G. McDougall (Eds.), *Consumers and energy conservation* (pp. 47–55). New York: Praeger.

James, W. (1890). *Principles of psychology*. New York: Henry Holt.

Kasser, T., & Ryan, R. M. (1993). A dark side of the American dream: Correlates of financial success as a central life aspiration. *Journal of Personality and Social Psychology, 65*, 410–422.

Kubey, R., & Csikszentmihalyi, M. (1990). *Television and the quality of life*. Hillsdale, NJ: Erlbaum.

Kubey, R., & Csikszentmihalyi, M. (2002). Television addiction. *Scientific American, 286*, 74–81.

Le Roy Ladurie, E. (1979). *Montaillou*. New York: Vintage Press.

Linder, S. (1970). *The harried leisure class*. New York: Columbia University Press.

Maslow, A. (1968). *Toward a psychology of being*. New York: Van Nostrand.

Massimini, F., & Delle Fave, A. (1991). Religion and cultural evolution. *Zygon, 16*, 27–48.

McLuhan, M. (1964). *Understanding media*. New York: Signet.

Myers, D. G. (2000). The funds, friends, and faith of happy people. *American Psychologist, 55*, 56–67.

Rathunde, K. (1996). Family context and adolescents' optimal experience in school-related activities. *Journal of Research on Adolescence, 6*, 603–616.

Richins, M. L., & Dawson, S. (1992). A consumer values orientation for materialism and its measurement: Scale development and validation. *Journal of Consumer Research, 19*, 303–316.

Ryan, R. M., & Deci, E. L. (2000). On happiness and human potentials: A review of hedonic and eudaimonic well-being. *Annual Review of Psychology, 52*, 141–166.

Sahlins, M. (1972). *Stone age economics*. Chicago: Aldine Press.

Schmuck, P., & Sheldon, K. M. (Eds.). (2001). *Life-goals and well-being*. Göttingen, Germany: Hogrefe & Huber.

Sheldon, K. M., & McGregor, H. (2000). Extrinsic value orientation and the tragedy of the commons. *Journal of Personality, 68*, 383–411.

Terkel, S. (1974). *Working*. New York: Pantheon.

Waterman, A. S. (1993). The conception of happiness: Contrasts of personal expressiveness (eudaimonia) and hedonic enjoyment. *Journal of Personality and Social Psychology, 64*, 678–691.

7

MINDFULNESS AND CONSUMERISM

ERIKA L. ROSENBERG

Many Americans pride themselves on being informed consumers, that is, on making careful assessments of the items they purchase and how much they need them, and on comparison shopping for the best bargains. Indeed, the American marketplace is brimming with options for the ready consumer, so much so that even when deciding to buy a box of cereal, there are enough choices to fill an entire aisle at the local supermarket. Some brands are selected more frequently than others, reflecting better value, better quality, or better marketing. We have lots of choices.

Or do we? My argument is that much of modern American consumer behavior consists of automatic and unexamined actions. What and how much we consume stems more from unconscious choices than from mindful deliberation. Advertising capitalizes on this automaticity to exploit the insatiable need for fulfillment that burdens many modern humans in industrialized countries (Cushman, 1990; Fromm, 1955). How do we remedy this problem? Educating people about the consequences of consumerism is helpful, but people are not likely to act on that new knowledge unless they are ready to hear it and use it.

In this chapter I explain how the cultivation of mindfulness may serve as an antidote to consumerism. This argument hinges on two key points.

First, advertisers and corporations capitalize on powerful psychological processes to strengthen automaticity in consumer behavior. Mindfulness may enhance one's awareness of potentially accessible cognitive–behavioral processes underlying consumption that have become relatively automatic. It can make consumption more a matter of choice than of impulse clouded by the illusion of choice. Second, these nonconscious choices about consumption are driven by a need for fulfillment. Mindfulness might remedy the need for fulfillment that is endemic in modern society (Tulku, 1978), not only by enhancing awareness but also by increasing interrelatedness among people. Thus, the cultivation of mindfulness is offered as a prescription for reducing the destructive effects of consumerism in our society because it can alert us to how we are manipulated to buy particular products, increase our awareness of the implications of consumerism for the world, and facilitate connection among people. I conclude the chapter by outlining an empirical agenda for exploring this largely unresearched area.

MINDFULNESS DEFINED

On the most essential level, mindfulness is awareness and the ability to see the happenings of one's inner and outer worlds. Mindfulness can be viewed as an ongoing process of expanding one's awareness to include stimuli that might otherwise be filtered out or not attended to, of becoming aware of the kinds of biases to which one's mind might typically be vulnerable, and of maintaining a nonjudgmental stance toward what arises in one's own mind (including emotions as well as sensations provided from one's own body and the outside world).

The notion of mindfulness has recently gained visibility in academic psychology through the writings of Ellen Langer (1989), but its roots lie in the ancient contemplative traditions of the East. Although mindfulness is cultivated by most meditative practices, the term *mindfulness meditation* typically is applied to a wide variety of techniques that derive from the Theravada Buddhist meditation practice of *Vipassana*, which is also known as *insight meditation*. Vipassana training is aimed at the cultivation of awareness and the application of sustained attention to understanding both the ways in which one's mind works and the impermanent nature of the phenomenal world. The training develops present awareness, nonjudgmental observation, nonconceptual awareness (experiencing without identifying or labeling the experience), and awareness of changes in conscious experience (cf. Gunaratana, 1991; Kabat-Zinn, 1990; Nhat Hahn, 1987; Wallace, 1999). Mindfulness meditation practices do not directly encourage quieting of the mind; rather, they encourage the awareness that everything that may arise in one's mind—be it a thought, an emotion, or a sensation—eventually dissipates. The meditator is trained simply to note experiences as they occur, without clinging to or ascribing value to them. These skills allow one to keep thoughts and emotions in perspective. For example, when one is sitting in meditation and a pain arises, one can simply observe and experience the sensation of pain, note its textures and qualities, and then carry on with awareness, rather than becoming overwhelmed by the pain, identifying with the pain, or catastrophizing it. Such observation frees mental space and allows one to see that feelings—such as pain—need not dominate one's consciousness or be self-defining. "In mindfulness, one is an unbiased observer whose sole job is to keep track of the constantly passing show of the universe within" (Gunaratana, 1991, p. 153). Mindfulness is inquisitive and curious or, as Pema Chödrön wrote, "mindfulness is an open-ended inquiry into our experience" (2001, p. 94).

People who are mindful are more aware of their thought processes, more deliberate in the choices they make for action, and less susceptible to the persuasive influence of others. Actions that originate from a foundation of mindfulness are more likely to be a result of conscious choice, that is, to be carefully contemplated behavior. Mindful behavior, then, is the polar opposite of reflexive or impulsive action.

In addition to the centuries of experiential evidence that mindfulness meditation is psychologically beneficial, recent empirical research has demonstrated the psychological and physical health benefits of such mind training. Forms of mindfulness meditation training offered in health care and other therapeutic settings have been shown to be very effective for the treatment of stress disorders (Kabat-Zinn et al., 1992), chronic pain (Kabat-Zinn, Lipworth, & Burney, 1985), psoriasis (Kabat-Zinn et al., 1998), depression (Teasdale et al., 2000), obsessive–compulsive disorder (OCD, Schwartz, 1997), and borderline personality disorder (Linehan, Armstrong, Suarez, Allmon, & Heard, 1991; Linehan, Heard, & Armstrong, 1993). Furthermore, after people learn these techniques, they tend to stick with them in the long-term (Kabat-Zinn & Chapman-Waldrop, 1988; Miller, Fletcher, & Kabat-Zinn, 1995; Shapiro, Schwartz, & Bonner, 1998). These totally secular training programs work by teaching people how to relate to their mental experiences differently, by not clinging to destructive thought patterns, unpleasant emotions, or pain. Schwartz (1999) has even demonstrated that the application of mindfulness techniques to the treatment of OCD produces changes in brain circuits thought to be responsible for the disorder.

My argument is that the qualities of mind developed by mindfulness training can help people see how they are subtly induced to engage in consumerist behaviors. Specifically, mindfulness training can address at least two problems of consumerism: (a) the nonconscious psychological processes that are exploited by corporations and advertisers to shape consumer preferences, and (b) the underlying life dissatisfaction and the need for fulfillment that might be temporarily satisfied by consumption activities.

Psychological Processes Support Nonconscious Consumer Choices

Most consumer behavior is automatic. In general, people do not realize how much they consume or how they have come to rely on consumption as a means of recreation or temporary fulfillment, because they examine neither their actions nor the underlying needs that are temporarily satiated by buying things. Advertising, in particular, uses nonconscious processes to make us want to consume by capitalizing on our tendency to be automatic rather than mindful buyers, by using the mere exposure principle, and by conditioning us.

Mindlessness

Ellen Langer popularized the concept of mindfulness in her 1989 book, which was a layperson's guide to de-automatizing behavior and enhancing one's flexibility of thinking. In that book and in her writings since then, Langer has drawn on her social psychological research on mindless behavior, or behavior that has previously been accessible to consciousness but has become nonconscious over time. She has shown that people often do things automatically without examining the instructions or even their options for action. For example, in a classic study in social psychology, Langer, Blank, and Chanowitz (1978) had confederates ask office workers who were waiting to make copies whether they could cut in front of them to use the copier. She manipulated the length of the paper to be copied (5 or 20 pages), the structure of the request, and the nature of the justification for the request. In one condition, the request was unjustified: "Excuse me, I have 5 (or 20) pages. May I use the Xerox machine?" In contrast, the justified requests either were based on real information ("Excuse me, I have 5 [20] pages. May I use the Xerox machine, because I am in a rush?") or based on placebic information: ("Excuse me, I have 5 [20] pages. May I use the Xerox machine, because I have to make copies?"). Note that the placebic request had the same "justified" structure as the request based on a real excuse, but the justification was meaningless. Langer et al. found that for the requests to make a small number of copies (5), people were more likely to comply with the confederate's request if it was justified than if it was not, but that there was no difference in compliance rates between the real and placebic justified conditions. This indicates that people responded automatically when presented with a "reason," but they did not mindfully attend to the reason. When the request was to make 20 copies, however, only the "real" information condition yielded compliance rates higher than the other conditions. Thus, when moderate effort is required of the people, they are less likely to respond mindlessly (i.e., when they have a stake in a situation and they are forced to think). These findings and others (e.g., Langer & Imber, 1979) substantiate Langer's (1989) claim that actions performed mindlessly are potentially accessible to consciousness, given the appropriate conditions.

Other situations that tend to lead to mindless responses are tasks that are overlearned. Shifting a well-learned task from conscious to nonconscious status certainly has its advantages. For example, if we always deliberately thought about all the movements required to drive a car, we would probably have more accidents. It serves us well to make some things automatic, as excessive attention impairs performance of both motoric (Innes & Gordon, 1985; Singer, Lidor, & Cauraugh, 1993) and cognitive tasks (Langer & Weinman, 1981). Langer (1989) argued, however, that people fall into the tendency to automatize too readily. Only when given a reason to direct attention to their abilities (e.g., through the use of labels that denote particular skill levels) do people attend to task components, whether they are experts or novices (Langer & Imber, 1979). Often it is not in our best interest to behave automatically, and our tendencies to automatize make us susceptible to the effects of priming and other cognitive biases simply because we do not consciously attend to those sources of bias (Langer, 1989).

One can extend this logic to the study of consumption—the persuasive messages that compel us to buy particular products or convince us that we need rather than want certain products capitalize on our habit of processing information automatically or mindlessly. In this context, mindlessness might best be conceptualized as a mental set that predisposes us to manipulation by advertisers.

Marketing and advertising prey on mindless processing by both encouraging it and exploiting it. The enormously successful enterprise of cable shopping networks, for example, depends on people not thinking very much about whether they really need something before they buy it. Tune into a cable shopping channel at any given moment, and you may see two women explaining the urgency that you buy a "rare" porcelain figurine of Little Bo Peep right away, because there are only 56 left and look how many people are purchasing it right now as we speak (the screen displays in the upper left corner the countdown of the number of figurines being sold). Viewers who have watched the channel long enough to hear the pitch do not have time to consider whether they need this item or not, because if they take the time to think, all of the figurines might be gone. This technique exploits the less thoughtful viewer and encourages mindless purchasing. Later in the chapter (see section on "Mindfulness and the Problem of Automaticity") I discuss research that shows that susceptibility to such marketing gimmicks can be reduced when people are more mindful (cf. Pollock, Smith, Knowles, & Bruce, 1998).

Mere Exposure

In a series of clever social psychological experiments, Zajonc (1968) demonstrated that people prefer familiar objects. Zajonc presented abstract shapes to observers very quickly—at near subliminal presentation speeds. Over numerous trials some shapes were repeated and others were not, but so many shapes were shown that participants did not recall seeing the "familiar" objects. Therefore, there was no conscious processing of these shapes being familiar. Nevertheless, if observers had been exposed to them previously, their ratings of how much they liked these shapes were greater than their ratings of totally novel shapes.

Mere exposure is one of many nonconscious processes by which advertisers convince people that they need to buy particular products. Using supraliminal overexposure (and perhaps some subliminal techniques, although this is a highly debated topic), advertisers capitalize on familiarity effects, that is, they capitalize on mindlessness. How often are we bombarded with images of a particular product over and over again? Why must we see the same detergent ad three times during a 30-minute program? Basic exposure is the easiest, least creative way that advertisers attempt to form our preferences. This may take the form of a brief television commercial simply presenting a succession of images of the product (with little or no verbal content), repeated commercials in a brief period of time on the same network, or more subtle, sophisticated techniques such as product insertions in major television shows or motion pictures.[1] Marketing of children's movies or summer action "blockbusters" takes the exposure approach to an extreme: We are bombarded with action-packed trailers both on television and in theatres, commercials about movie-related products (e.g., the McDonald's Spider-man Happy Meal), and endorsements of other products by movie characters (e.g., Spider-man eating Doritos). Consumer research shows that we prefer products or styles that we have seen more often, regardless of whether we have prior practical experience with the product (Baker, 1999; Schindler & Holbrook, 1993).

Conditioning

It is through conditioning that we learn to think that we need to acquire particular products in order to be happy. Classical conditioning pairs the presentation of an object to buy (presumably a neutral stimulus) with pleasant or desirable "unconditioned" stimuli to create an association between the product and something pleasant. We eventually begin to associate the pleasantness with the product alone and our desire to have it becomes a conditioned response. An example of this is the typical advertisement in which a beautiful woman strokes and admires a new car while she sits next to the man who owns it. The desirable woman and the car appear together repeatedly, thereby creating an association between the two. Such processes clearly play a role in product preferences (Baker, 1999).

---

[1]Product insertion also draws on other powerful techniques such as modeling and reinforcement.

It is perhaps more obvious how operant conditioning can be applied to the same situation, whereby the behavior of buying the car is reinforced with the reward of a beautiful woman. Buy the car, get the babe. Anything desirable and potentially relevant to fulfillment can be seen as an associate or consequence of procuring a particular product: companionship, social status, popularity, money, or a beautiful home, to name but a few examples. Operant conditioning is prevalent in advertising and remains a very effective marketing tool (Peter & Nord, 1982; Winters & Wallace, 1970).

Mere exposure and the various forms of conditioning constitute processes of which we are typically unaware; that is, we do not always realize when we are being conditioned or when mere exposure effects may be building up. With both education (about how our minds can be manipulated) and increased mindfulness, however, such nonconscious processes may become available to conscious awareness, as described later in the chapter.

Consumption and the Need for Fulfillment

The second major problem of consumerism that can be addressed by mindfulness involves the motivations behind consumption. Although there are many reasons why people consume, I am particularly concerned with the idea that the consumption of goods quickly but temporarily satisfies an underlying need for fulfillment. Although this is primarily a psychological thesis, the idea that a consumer economy creates a void to be filled is rooted in various social and economic theories that have appeared over the past century. For instance, Marx (1867/1909) argued that capitalism creates a false sense of individualism, one that exploits workers and leaves the populace susceptible to manipulation by manufacturers. Much later Simmel (1990) implied that money perpetuates this problem—the inherent flexibility of currency threatens the moral order by removing the personal element from trade. Money objectifies trade relations and contributes to the isolation of the individual. In psychology, Fromm (1947) proposed a personality type that can emerge from an isolated self in a consumer economy: the marketing character. People of this type have so lost a sense of inherent worth and connection to others that they have come to see themselves as a commodity. Seeing oneself as a commodity comes from a sense of isolation, which ultimately stems from the fundamental human need of interrelatedness that is not being met (Fromm, 1955).

These ideas that capitalism, a market economy, and consumerism contribute to a false sense of individualism receive an incisive hermeneutic analysis in the writings of Philip Cushman (1990). Cushman's psychological thesis is that the modern (post-World War II), Western self is empty. Over the centuries humans have moved from a more communal to a more autonomous existence, characterized by a lack of shared experience and meaning. Cushman attributed the movement toward this isolated sense of autonomy to numerous historical influences, such as Europe's movement toward capitalism, the objective empiricism of enlightenment (which decontextualized the individual), Victorianism, and the industrial revolution (which brought us out of the farm and into the factory). Many of the ills of modern Western society may be linked to inner emptiness, such as low self-esteem, conspicuous consumption, absence of personal convictions, drug abuse, and eating disorders. Furthermore, emptiness makes people more vulnerable to the influences of cult leaders, charismatic political leaders, unethical psychotherapists, and the advertising industry.

Cushman's argument is most relevant to consumerism in terms of his discussion of attempts to compensate for inner emptiness. The empty self needs filling, so it is easy to influence and control. This is a major mechanism encouraging consumerism. Advertisers and major corporations seek to reassure or soothe us with products. Yet, advertising offers an illusory cure. Advertising cannot create a web of meaning like a rich communal, shared culture can, and so it substitutes what Cushman describes as "life style" solutions:

> One prominent type of ad offers the fantasy that the consumer's life can be transformed into a glorious, problem-free life—the "life" of the model who is featured in this ad. This can be accomplished by purchasing and "ingesting" the product, which will magically transfer the life-style of the model to the consumer. By surrounding themselves with the accoutrements of the model, by ingesting the proper liquid while wearing the proper clothing, all the while exhibiting the proper shape, customers seek to "become" the model. The customer's problems will simply disappear when the magical transfer takes place. (Cushman, 1990, p. 605)

I would argue that the hunger of the self to find quick remedies for inner emptiness also fosters the illusion of choice in our buying behaviors. As illustrated earlier, a good deal of what underlies our choices about which brands to buy is a function of mindless cognitive processing. Indeed, what Cushman described as a "magical transfer" likely is fueled by such nonconscious processes as classical and operant conditioning. If people could wake up to the sources of emptiness, as well as to the ways in which their minds are being manipulated, the problem of overconsumption (and its destructive consequences). Mindfulness could also address the problem of inner emptiness by halting the feeding of emptiness with momentary fixes of new products and people turn to more enriching forms of fulfillment.

Cushman's (1990) argument that consumption and the ownership of things do not lead to real satisfaction in life is echoed by other writers (e.g., Durning, 1995) and is empirically substantiated. Although consumption may temporarily induce a sense of satisfaction with life (Oropesa, 1995), it offers little in terms of long-term life fulfillment. People from wealthier nations report higher levels of subjective well-being than people from poorer nations (Argyle, 1987; Veenhoven, 1984, as cited in Csiksentmihalyi, 1990), but these differences may be linked with higher levels of equality and human rights in wealthier nations, rather than possessions per se (Diener, Diener, & Diener, 1996; Diener & Suh, 1999). Studies of less affluent nations show no relationship between happiness and ownership (Fuentes & Rojas, 2001; chaps. 2 & 3, this volume, discuss similar ideas).

American Buddhist educator Joseph Goldstein (2002) has made an argument similar to mine. He said that much of consumer behavior is compulsive and seems to be an attempt to compensate for something deeper that is missing. He also argued that consumer society preys on our need for more things, often "co-opting spiritual values to do so":

> A recent automobile advertisement shows a handsome young couple standing in front of a new car, surrounded by all the latest consumer delights. The caption reads, "To become one with everything you *need* one of everything." (Goldstein, 2002, pp. 34–35)

Again, a lifestyle solution is being offered for a deeper problem, and it is doomed to fail.

MINDFULNESS AS AN ANTIDOTE TO CONSUMERISM

Mindfulness provides an antidote to the problems of automaticity and the need for fulfillment. I explain how this works as well as suggest interventions promoting mindfulness and an empirical agenda for studying these proposals.

Mindfulness and the Problem of Automaticity

Mindfulness is a powerful antidote to the human tendency toward automatic responding, which corporations and advertisers exploit in the service of consumerism. People can become more aware of psychological processes that previously may have been automatic, such as conditioning (Spielberger, Berger, & Howard, 1963), and less susceptible to advertising gimmicks that prey on mindless processing of information (Pollock et al., 1998).

Pollock and her colleagues studied the "That's-Not-All" technique (TNA), a popular trick of advertising that relies on a form of mindless, automatic processing. They found that when people are put in a situation that lends itself to more mindful thinking, they are less susceptible to the TNA. The experiment involved the "reduced cost" version of the TNA technique, wherein an item of an initial price is suddenly offered at a reduced price, as a function of a last minute change in circumstances; for example, "This cupcake is normally $1, but I can let you have it today for 75 cents" (Pollock et al., 1998, p. 1153).[2] In the guise of a psychology club chocolate sale, Pollock et al. manip-

---

[2]The other popular form of TNA is the *added value form*, in which an initial offer is expanded to include extra items. For a comparison of the effectiveness of various forms of TNA, see Burger (1986).

ulated three variables: the size, and thus cost, of the box of chocolate (large or small), the influence condition (control or TNA), and whether participants were given a reason for buying the chocolates: no reason; the placebic reason that "this candy is made of chocolate and sold in this box"; or a real reason, namely, "These Sweet Shop chocolates are fudge hand-dipped in chocolate with pecans. Also, Sweet Shop has been in business over 20 years" (p. 1155). For the small (lower priced chocolates) box only, the TNA exerted a powerful effect on compliance, dramatically increasing sales compared to the control condition. Consistent with the findings of Langer et al. (1978), the placebic reason was as effective as the real reason in increasing sales compared to the no reason condition, but only for the smaller box. That is, this difference did not occur in the large (more costly) box condition. The authors reasoned that individuals relied on peripheral processing (à la Petty & Cacioppo, 1986) in the small box condition: When they do not have a large investment at stake, people are more likely to process information peripherally, and peripheral processing is more likely to be automatic or mindless. In the large box condition, the participants were forced to use central route processing, which requires more conscious deliberation and rational thought, or more mindful thinking. Under mindful conditions people were less susceptible to the TNA manipulation. One can reason that as mindfulness increases, people are less likely to engage in mindless thinking more generally.

The problem with the Pollock study (and many of Langer's) is that it is hard to know whether the people in the mindful conditions are really all that mindful per se. What degree of attentional focus makes something a mindful state versus just a conscious state? How does this mindful state compare with the type of mindfulness developed through a contemplative practice? Is it categorically different or just lesser in degree? The answers to these questions guide the interventions that are needed to prevent people from relying on the type of mindless action on which advertisers capitalize.

At any rate, it seems reasonable (and somewhat empirically substantiated) to assume that if one is less inclined toward mindless processing, then one is less susceptible to the manipulation of advertisers. Furthermore, if people are more attentive to their own experiences, to input from their environment, and to how they respond to that input, then they would be able to choose more carefully what to buy and when to buy it. This means understanding one's true needs (i.e., we really don't need everything that is marketed to us) and taking care to choose products that are better for us and for the planet. We can choose more socially conscious products, instead of those that are more convenient or whose names are more familiar simply because we have been exposed to them. We can take the time to discover which companies use methods of manufacturing that are less environmentally disruptive and which donate a percentage of profits to worthwhile causes. Or we might choose to find out how certain products are made and where they are made, so that we can avoid buying garments that were produced in sweatshops of developing countries or exotic rugs that are the product of child labor. With more mindfulness might come more attention to the negative effects of consumerism, and we might choose not to buy certain products at all, to buy less generally, or to recycle and reuse more in an effort to create a less disposable economy.

Mindfulness and the Need for Fulfillment

Increased awareness improves one's chances of seeing the ways in which one is unfulfilled and how one's actions affect well-being. By learning to savor conscious experience as it happens, people can learn to appreciate the wonder of life and find a deeper sense of fulfillment with their daily lives, one that external pleasures—such as possessions, drugs, or sex—cannot provide. As Pema Chödrön wrote: "Mindfulness is loving all the details of our lives, and awareness is the natural thing that happens: life begins to open up, and you realize that you're always standing at the center of the world" (1991, p. 28). People can achieve greater relaxation, as well as experience an aliveness that enhances their appreciation of all they encounter.

According to Csiksentmihalyi (1990; see also chap. 6, this volume), failure to find enjoyment is a function of failure to "restructure consciousness," to transform ordinary experience into potentially optimal experience. That is, the internal conditions of the mind are at least as important as external conditions such as income, the number of goodies one possesses, or health. Although Csiksentmihalyi uses the term *flow* to describe this state of optimal experience, he could easily be referring to mindfulness: "Some people enjoy themselves wherever they are, while others stay bored even when confronted with the most dazzling prospects" (1990, p. 83). Something can be done to enhance people's appreciation of daily experience, to heighten their awareness of their lives, and to make them less vulnerable to manipulation and false sources of satisfaction. People who engage in activities that are characterized by flow states experience greater satisfaction with their tasks (Csiksentmihalyi, 1989). People who are mindful, I would argue, experience greater satisfaction with everything. Although this assertion remains empirically untested, thousands of years of contemplative practice suggests it is true.

Mindfulness may also be related to fulfillment in terms of how it can facilitate connectedness with others. When mindful, people are more open to experience (Rosenberg, 2001), and this openness of mind serves as a foundation for opening one's heart (Chödrön, 1991, 2001). When we are more aware of our thoughts, feelings, and actions, it becomes more difficult for us to ignore the feelings and circumstances of others. In this way, increased mindfulness lays the foundation for increased compassion. Practices that enhance connectedness with others address the problem of isolation that underlies the empty self, as described in Cushman's (1990) critique. The cultivation of such skills should also reduce the magnitude of consumerism in our society. In fact, several theorists have argued that increasing community and a sense of connection with others may be the best remedy for the sense of emptiness that supports the consumer mentality (Durning, 1995; Fromm, 1955; Kanner & Gomes, 1995; see also chap. 2, this volume).

In the *Mahayana* tradition of Buddhism, which is the tradition from which Zen and all schools of Tibetan Buddhism emerged, the cultivation of compassion goes hand in hand with the development of awareness (Wallace, 1993). It is not enough to be awake to the sources of suffering—one must also feel compassion for oneself and others and use that compassion to fuel actions that are beneficial to all beings. Compassionate action can counteract the destructive intrapsychic and planetary effects of consumerism by facilitating connection between people. When people are more connected, more a part of a greater community of human beings, then many of the problems of consumerism become more solvable. For one, people can realize that they are not alone in the sense of isolation that supports wasteful consumption. Moreover, such connection can help increase awareness of the predicament of our human condition on this planet and of the consequences of wasteful consumption for the Earth (cf. Macy, 1995). Mindfulness and compassion work together here: When we are truly awake and open our hearts to the condition of others, we cannot ignore the effects of mass consumption. At that point it is hard not to act.

CONCLUSION: FUTURE DIRECTIONS

Educational Intervention

Ultimately these ideas must be brought into the educational setting. Children can be taught methods for enhancing mindful thinking (in general terms), and schools can offer specific programs geared toward raising awareness of consumerism. Parker Palmer (1998), Linda Lantieri (2001), and Rachael Kessler (1998) train teachers and develop innovative classroom curricula for the cultivation of mindful learning, compassion, and connection. These educational innovators are attempting to show that children become happier, healthier, and more empathic adults if these principles are encouraged when they are young (cf. Glazer, 1999). Their goals dovetail with those of the socio-emotional learning (SEL) movement,[3] because they also aim to teach empathy and better emotional functioning to teachers and children.

---

[3]The SEL movement grew from the publication of Daniel Goleman's (1995) book, *Emotional Intelligence*, but was really an area of applied developmental psychology research for at least a decade before that. SEL research has produced school curricula that teach socio-emotional skills and tools for social judgment (cf. Greenberg, Kusche, Cook, & Quamma, 1995).

Education theorist and innovator Parker Palmer runs the Courage to Teach program, which begins with developing the "identity and integrity" of the teachers (Palmer, 1998). Palmer's program incorporates contemplative and other practices to help teachers learn specific skills related to great teaching, such as good listening, open-mindedness, trust, and connective capacity. Linda Lantieri (2001), a veteran of the SEL movement, developed classroom curricula for teachers and students, in which she aims to bring the "sacred" into secular classrooms. Lantieri drew on rituals from numerous spiritual traditions, ranging from Buddhism to Native American spiritual practice, to cultivate emotional competence, moral development, and interconnectedness. Similarly, Rachael Kessler taught attentional exercises to increase what she calls the "teaching presence" (Kessler, 1998). *Teaching presence* refers to the capacity of the teacher to be present in the moment, which Kessler argued can foster connection with the students. The work of these educational innovators offers great promise for teaching our children to be more mindful of their actions; to date, little has been done to empirically evaluate the effectiveness of these programs, but some research is currently underway.

Cultivation of general contemplative skills in teachers and students should help people raise their children to be less susceptible to the mindless behaviors that support consumerism. However, we can also offer programs specifically designed to educate children about the hazards of consumerism and how mindful thinking can help us be more thoughtful about how we act in a consumer society.

When I was in 6th grade in California in the 1970s, I participated in a program on propaganda. We learned about the methods advertisers use to try to manipulate our minds and became familiar with various propaganda techniques that are used to convince potential buyers to purchase products or services. Those lessons had an impact on me—the exercises were fun and the messages powerful. Currently there are no such mandated programs in the California public school system. Nevertheless, it should be possible to develop specific exercises for children that not only cultivate a mindful stance, but also teach them to recognize attempts to draw them toward particular products. Furthermore, parents and teachers can educate children to adopt behaviors that discourage mindless consumerism by viewing less commercial television, practicing mindful purchasing habits, and turning children's innate curiosity toward the natural world and away from possessions and television. A radical approach is to adopt the philosophy of Waldorf schools, which requires all students and their families to abstain from watching television and to avoid contact with many forms of media. Parental co-viewing with children when they do watch TV—to mute commercials or explain why commercials are unpleasant and manipulative—may be more tenable for most families than banning TV viewing altogether, and it can be particularly instructive in helping children realize what advertising is all about. Even doing this in the classroom with older kids (5th grade and higher) could be very instructive and would likely make a lasting impression. These ideas all merit further study as possible means of reducing blatant consumerism and heightening awareness of the hidden forces that support consumer behavior in our society.

Ways to Enhance Mindfulness

Typically, mindfulness training involves extended contemplative practice. People often enter into such types of practices through various forms of Buddhist meditation. Contemplative development of mindfulness need not be a spiritual undertaking, however. A secularized version of mindfulness meditation training, Jon Kabat-Zinn's Mindfulness Based Stress Reduction (MBSR), is a unique package of sitting meditation (which emphasizes breath awareness; nonattachment to thoughts, emotions, and sensations; and regular bringing of one's attention back to one's breath), body scan (moving one's attention down the body, from head to toe, attending to the various sensations), and Hatha yoga (stretches and postures designed for enhancing awareness and strengthening muscles and improving balance). MBSR has gained attention worldwide for its effectiveness in managing anxiety, stress, and chronic pain (Kabat-Zinn et al., 1992; Kabat-Zinn et al., 1998). In fact, a major health maintenance organization now offers MBSR training programs to its clients as part of a wellness program.

A different and considerably less time-consuming approach to enhancing "mindfulness" is that taken by Langer. She has shown that giving people simple instructions on how to become more engaged with tasks and to have more control over one's environment (which she labels a type of mindfulness training, although it differs considerably from the contemplative sort) can enhance longevity and lead to more successful aging (Alexander, Langer, Newman, Chandler, & Davies, 1989; Langer, Beck, Janoff-Bulman, & Timko, 1984). It is not clear whether the type of mindfulness Langer manipulated in her studies is at all comparable to that developed by more extensive meditation training. Are Langer and others who have taken a social psychological approach to mindfulness (e.g., Pollock et al., 1998) really developing mindfulness, or are they just subtly manipulating the allocation of attentional resources? Whatever the case, both ways of increasing awareness offer promise for reducing human susceptibility to the coercion and manipulation that underlie much of consumer culture. Specifically, people can be taught to recognize how they are manipulated by advertising, how they can make more choices about whether to consume, and how they can better understand motives underlying consumer behavior.

An Empirical Agenda

Researchers have shown that mindfulness training improves a variety of physical and mental health problems (Kabat-Zinn et al., 1992; Kabat-Zinn et al., 1998; Teasdale et al., 2000), and, more recently, that it leads to significant reduction in stress in normal adults (Williams, Kolar, Reger, & Pearson, 2001). However, much work remains to be done to show the benefits of mindfulness training in terms of improving life satisfaction. Furthermore, with the exception of a single study on how mindfulness affects susceptibility to a popular advertising technique (Pollock et al., 1998), no work to date has explored the relationship between mindfulness and consumer attitudes or behavior. Yet several ideas raised in this chapter offer many possibilities for empirical study. One important question is whether mindfulness training reduces consumption—through increasing awareness both of how advertising manipulates our consumer behavior and of how we learn to turn to consumption as a means of temporary fulfillment in life. More generally, how are life satisfaction and well-being related to mindfulness and the development of awareness and compassion skills? Does teaching people these skills foster a sense of connectedness? One could direct these questions specifically to issues of consumerism to determine whether teaching people mindfulness skills changes their consumer behavior. What about offering special instructions to heighten awareness of consumer manipulation, either through in-depth mindfulness training or shorter mindfulness interventions? Might the additional attentional resources available with the enhancement of mindfulness help people become more resistant to the persuasive techniques used by advertisers? For example, it would be particularly interesting to see whether mindfulness helps mitigate against the automaticity involved in influential communications (Cialdini, 2001) and decreases the likelihood that individuals are influenced by peripheral routes of persuasion (Petty & Cacioppo, 1986). Questions about mindfulness could also be applied to special problems or contexts of consumerism; for example, does Internet buying (or any type of impulse buying for that matter) rely on mindless processing, and can it be reduced by mindfulness training? After research has established whether mindfulness training is helpful, programs can be implemented to disseminate this training widely.

Given the improbability of our culture moving away from a consumerist orientation, it is vitally important that we uncover methods for dealing with the harmful effects of consumption. We need not only to heal the wounds to our minds and our planet that are caused by massive consumption, but also to cultivate ways to consume more mindfully. Researching the problem of consumerism offers good opportunity to recommend the psychological benefits of mindfulness training and may help serve as a rationale for including this type of training in a broad range of educational programs. One can envision mindfulness training moving into the public schools the way the SEL movement has begun to permeate elementary and secondary school curricula. Many teachers of Buddhist meditation in the West have argued that the development of mindfulness can be helpful to everyone, regardless of spiritual persuasion, and it need not require any type of religious commitment. It simply requires a sincere desire to open one's eyes.

REFERENCES

Alexander, C. N., Langer, E. J., Newman, R. I., Chandler, H. M., & Davies, J. L. (1989). Transcendental meditation, mindfulness, and longevity: An experimental study with the elderly. *Journal of Personality and Social Psychology, 57*, 950–964.

Argyle, M. (1987). *The psychology of happiness*. London: Methuen.

Baker, W. E. (1999). When can affective conditioning and mere exposure directly influence brand choice? *Journal of Advertising, 28*, 31–46.

Burger, J. M. (1986). Increasing compliance by improving the deal: The that's-not-all technique. *Journal of Personality and Social Psychology, 51*, 277–283.

Chödrön, P. (1991). *The wisdom of no escape*. Boston: Shambala Publications.

Chödrön, P. (2001). *The places that scare you*. Boston: Shambala Publications.

Cialdini, R. B. (2001). *Influence: Science and practice* (4th ed.). Boston: Allyn & Bacon.

Csiksentmihalyi, M. (1989). Optimal experience in work and leisure. *Journal of Personality and Social Psychology, 56*, 815–822.

Csikszentmihalyi, M. (1990). *Flow: The psychology of optimal experience*. New York: HarperCollins.

Cushman, P. (1990). Why the self is empty: Toward a historically situated psychology. *American Psychologist, 45*, 599–611.

Diener, E., Diener, M., & Diener, C. (1996). Factors predicting the subjective well-being of nations. *Journal of Personality and Social Psychology, 69*, 851–864.

Diener, E., & Suh, E. M. (1999). National differences in subjective well-being. In D. Kahneman, E. Diener, & N. Schwartz (Eds.), *Well-being: The foundations of hedonic psychology* (pp. 434–450). New York: Russell Sage.

Durning, A. T. (1995). Are we happy yet? In T. Roszak, M. E. Gomes, & A. D. Kanner (Eds.), *Ecopsychology* (pp. 68–76). San Francisco: Sierra Club Books.

Fromm, E. (1947). *Man for himself: An inquiry into the psychology of ethics*. New York: Holt, Rinehart, & Winston.

Fromm, E. (1955). *The sane society*. Greenwich, CT: Fawcett Books.

Fuentes, N., & Rojas, M. (2001). Economic theory and subjective well-being: Mexico. *Social Indicators Research, 53*, 289–314.

Glazer, S. (Ed.). (1999). *The heart of learning*. New York: Tarcher/Putnam.

Goldstein, J. (2002). *One dharma*. San Francisco: Harper San Francisco.

Goleman, D. (1995). *Emotional intelligence*. New York: Bantam Books.

Greenberg, M. T., Kusche, C. A., Cook, E. T., & Quamma, J. P. (1995). Promoting emotional competence in school-aged children: The effects of the PATHS curriculum. *Development and Psychopathology, 7*, 117–136.

Gunaratana, H. (1991). *Mindfulness in plain English*. Somerville, MA: Wisdom Publications.

Innes, J. M., & Gordon, M. J. (1985). The effects of mere presence and a mirror on performance of motor tasks. *Journal of Social Psychology, 125*, 479–484.

Kabat-Zinn, J. (1990). *Full catastrophe living.* New York: Delacourt Press.

Kabat-Zinn, J., & Chapman-Waldrop, A. (1988). Compliance with an outpatient stress reduction program: Rates and predictors of program completion. *Journal of Behavioral Medicine, 11*, 333–352.

Kabat-Zinn, J., Lipworth, L., & Burney, R. (1985). The clinical use of mindfulness meditation for the self-regulation of chronic pain. *Journal of Behavioral Medicine, 8*, 163–190.

Kabat-Zinn, J., Massion, A. O., Kristeller, J., Peterson, L. G., Fletcher, K. E., Pbert, L., et al. (1992). Effectiveness of a meditation-based stress reduction program in the treatment of anxiety disorders. *American Journal of Psychiatry, 149*, 936–943.

Kabat-Zinn, J., Wheeler, E., Light, T., Skillings, A., Scharf, M. J., Cropley, T. G., et al. (1998). Influence of a mindfulness meditation-based stress reduction intervention on rates of clearing in patients with moderate to severe psoriasis undergoing phototherapy (UVB) and photochemotherapy (PUVA). *Psychosomatic Medicine, 60*, 625–632.

Kanner, A. D., & Gomes, M. E. (1995). The all-consuming self. In T. Roszak, M. E. Gomes, & A. D. Kanner (Eds.), *Ecopsychology* (pp. 77–91). San Francisco: Sierra Club Books.

Kessler, R. (1998, June). The teaching presence. *The Forum, 35*. Retrieved April 21, 2003, from http://ncip.org/articles/Presence.html

Langer, E. J. (1989). *Mindfulness.* Reading, MA: Addison-Wesley.

Langer, E. J., Beck, P., Janoff-Bulman, R., & Timko, C. (1984). An exploration of the relationships among mindfulness, longevity, and senility. *Academic Psychology Bulletin, 6*, 211–226.

Langer, E. J., Blank, A., & Chanowitz, B. (1978). The mindlessness of ostensibly thoughtful action: The role of "placebic" information in interpersonal interaction. *Journal of Personality and Social Psychology, 36*, 635–642.

Langer, E. J., & Imber, L. G. (1979). When practice makes imperfect: Debilitating effects of overlearning. *Journal of Personality and Social Psychology, 37*, 2014–2024.

Langer, E. J., & Weinman, C. (1981). When thinking disrupts intellectual performance: Mindfulness on an overlearned task. *Personality and Social Psychology Bulletin, 7*, 241–243.

Lantieri, L. (Ed.). (2001). *Schools with spirit: Nurturing the inner lives of children and teachers.* Boston: Beacon Press.

Linehan, M. M., Armstrong, H. E., Suarez, A., Allmon, D., & Heard, H. L. (1991). Cognitive–behavioral treatment of chronically parasuicidal borderline patients. *Archives of General Psychiatry, 48*, 1060–1064.

Linehan, M. M., Heard, H. L., & Armstrong, H. E. (1993). Naturalistic follow-up of a behavioral treatment for chronically parasuicidal borderline patients. *Archives of General Psychiatry, 50*, 971–974.

Macy, J. R. (1995). Working through environmental despair. In T. Roszak, M. E. Gomes, & A. D. Kanner (Eds.), *Ecopsychology* (pp. 240–262). San Francisco: Sierra Club Books.

Marx, K. (1909). *Capital* (E. Unterman, Trans.). Chicago: C. H. Kerr. (Original work published 1867)

Miller, J. J., Fletcher, K. E. , & Kabat-Zinn, J. (1995). Three-year follow-up and clinical implications of a mindfulness meditation-based stress reduction intervention in the treatment of anxiety disorders. *General Hospital Psychiatry, 17,* 192–200.

Nhat Hahn, T. (1987). *The miracle of mindfulness.* Boston: Beacon Press.

Oropesa, R. S. (1995). Consumer possessions, consumer passions, and subjective well-being. *Sociological Forum, 10,* 215–244.

Palmer, P. J. (1998) *The courage to teach: Exploring the inner landscape of a teacher's life.* San Francisco: Jossey-Bass.

Peter, J. P., & Nord, W. R. (1982). A clarification and extension of operant conditioning principles in marketing. *Journal of Marketing, 46,* 102–107.

Petty, R. E., & Cacioppo, J. T. (1986). *Communication and persuasion: Central and peripheral routes to attitude change.* New York: Springer-Verlag.

Pollock, C. L., Smith, S. D., Knowles, E. S., & Bruce, H. J. (1998). Mindfulness limits compliance with the "that's-not-all" technique. *Personality and Social Psychology Bulletin, 24,* 1153–1157.

Rosenberg, E. L. (2001). *The development of the mindfulness inventory.* Unpublished manuscript, College of William & Mary.

Schindler, R. M., & Holbrook, M. B. (1993). Critical periods in the development of men's and women's tastes in personal appearance. *Psychology and Marketing, 10,* 549–564.

Schwartz, J. (1997). *Brain lock: Free yourself from obsessive–compulsive behavior.* New York: Harper.

Schwartz, J. M. (1999). First steps toward a theory of mental force: PET imaging of systematic cerebral changes after psychological treatment of obsessive–compulsive disorder. In S. R. Hameroff, A. W. Kaszniak, & D. J. Chalmers (Eds.), *Toward a science of consciousness III: The third Tucson discussions and debates.* Cambridge, MA: MIT Press.

Shapiro, S. L., Schwartz, G. E., & Bonner, G. (1998). Effects of mindfulness-based stress reduction on medical and premedical students. *Journal of Behavioral Medicine, 21,* 581–599.

Simmel, G. (1990). *The philosophy of money.* London: Routledge.

Singer, R. N., Lidor, R., & Cauraugh, J. H. (1993). To be aware or not aware? What to think about while learning and performing a motor skill. *Sports Psychologist, 7,* 19–30.

Spielberger, C. D., Berger, A., & Howard, K. (1963). Conditioning of verbal behavior as a function of awareness, need for social approval, and motivation to receive reinforcement. *Journal of Abnormal and Social Psychology, 67,* 241–248.

Teasdale, J. D., Segal, Z., Williams, M. G., Ridgeway, V. A., Soulsby, J. M., & Lau, M. A. (2000). Prevention of relapse/recurrence in major depression by mindfulness-based cognitive therapy. *Journal of Consulting and Clinical Psychology, 68,* 615–623.

Tulku, T. (1978). *Openness mind.* Berkeley, CA: Dharma Publishing.

Wallace, B. A. (1993). *Tibetan Buddhism from the ground up.* Boston: Wisdom Publications.

Wallace, B. A. (1999). *Boundless heart: The cultivation of the four immeasurables.* Ithaca, NY: Snow Lion.

Williams, K. A., Kolar, M. M., Reger, B. E., & Pearson, J. C. (2001). Evaluation of a wellness-based mindfulness stress reduction intervention: A controlled trial. *American Journal of Health Promotion, 15,* 422–432.

Winters, L. C., & Wallace, W. H. (1970). On operant conditioning techniques. *Journal of Advertising Research, 10,* 39–45.

Zajonc, R. B. (1968). Attitudinal effects of mere exposure. *Journal of Personality and Social Psychology, 9,* 1–27.

8

LETHAL CONSUMPTION: DEATH-DENYING MATERIALISM

SHELDON SOLOMON, JEFFREY L. GREENBERG, AND THOMAS A. PYSZCZYNSKI

Modern man is drinking and drugging himself out of awareness, or he spends his time shopping, which is the same thing.

—Ernest Becker, *The Denial of Death*

Humans are by nature consumers. This book, although published on recycled paper, is a product of the consumption of trees; it is up to you—the reader—to decide whether the tome in its entirety, or this chapter in particular, is worth the timber or the energy used to recycle it. Yet, before we burden ourselves with too much lumbering guilt about that, we should recognize that all living organisms are consumers. Plants "consume" nutrients from the soil and photosynthesize solar energy; herbivores derive their sustenance by consuming the plants; carnivores and omnivores in turn consume the herbivores and other carnivores. Humans are thus of necessity consumers; this is natural and should be seen as such. However, from the birth of "civilization" 10,000 or so years ago, as we moved from small groups of semi-nomadic hunter-gatherers to permanent town dwellers primarily dependent on agriculture and domesticated animals for our livelihood, humans have been obsessively preoccupied with conspicuous possession and consumption, relentlessly striving to accumulate money and lavish materials in vast excess of what is physically necessary to survive and prosper. As Ivan Boesky, the American investment banker, put it, "What good is the moon if you can't buy or sell it?" (Morris, 1986).

The purpose of this chapter is to explain the psychological underpinnings of conspicuous consumption from the perspective of terror management theory (Greenberg, Pyszczynski, & Solomon, 1986; Solomon, Greenberg, & Pyszczynski, 1991). Our basic thesis is that conspicuous consumption is a direct result of the uniquely human awareness of mortality and the pursuit of self-worth and death transcendence that this awareness engenders. For Mary Poppins, "Enough is as good as a feast," but this nominally sensible approach to life has never been embraced or practiced by the human race. For humans, enough has never been enough; and avaricious acquisitiveness has rendered human history a giant plundering shopping spree, one that predates the first suburban shopping mall by thousands of years. For example, Native American tribes of the Pacific coast from Oregon to Alaska held potlatches on special occasions to display their wealth and emphasize their superiority over their peers:

> Each individual according to his means, constantly vied with all others to outdistance them in distributions of property. The boy who had just received the first gift of property selected another youth to receive a gift from him. The youth he chose could not refuse without admitting defeat at the outset, and he was compelled to cap the gift with an equal amount of property. When the time came for repayment if he had not doubled the original gift to return as interest he was shamed and demoted and his rival's prestige correspondingly enhanced. (Benedict, 1935, as quoted by Roheim, 1943, p. 12)

During the Gilded Age before World War I, the term *conspicuous consumption* was coined by Veblen (1902) to describe the lavish spending habits of money-besotted families such as the Rockefellers and Vanderbilts. We have been hyper-conspicuously consuming ever since. For example, a report in London's *The Independent* (Moreton, 1997) described three businesspeople having dinner for a whopping £13,000 (well over $20,000 at the exchange rate at the time), including a £5,000 bottle of burgundy from which each businessperson drank one glass before giving the rest to the waiter! The Neiman-Marcus Christmas catalogue for 2001 continued in this tradition of prolific excess: Featured items included a $6,700,000 Limited Edition Bell Helicopter for dad; a $70,000 "Silver Belle" custom Lexus for the wife; a $25,000 "Seussian Grinch Roadster" model car; and a $4,000 gingerbread house (a custom-made replica of one's own domicile, of course) for the kids.

But so what? "The business of America is" after all, "business."

Shouldn't people be encouraged to spend and consume wantonly, if for no other reason than it is their inalienable right to do so in pursuit of the life, liberty, and happiness as asserted in the Declaration of Independence, the document that inspired the formation of the United States of America? We think not, for three reasons.

First, money, to borrow a phrase from the Beatles, cannot buy you love, and money apparently cannot buy happiness either. People with often enormous amounts of money are, contrary to commonsense folk wisdom, actually no happier than their less wealthy counterparts, and they are statistically more prone to depression and other forms of psychopathology (see, e.g., Frank, 1999; Kasser & Ryan, 1993; D. G. Myers, 1993; D. G. Myers & Diener, 1995; see also chaps. 2, 3, 6, & 11, this volume).

Second, obsessive superfluous consumption now permeates all levels of American society, creating a culture of mindless greedy acquisitiveness (e.g., The Prayer of Jabez, based on a passage in the Old Testament interpreted by Evangelical Christians suggesting that greed is Godly, has sold four million copies in America; A. Brown, 2001), to the economic detriment of many middle and lower class citizens. Greed and consumption rule in America, and no one even bothers to hide these proclivities. When an American company experiences an economic downturn, who absorbs the blow? Do the Board members forgo their raises, stop purchasing their new yachts, or, heaven forbid, take a pay cut and sell their luxury vehicles or seasonal homes? Or are the livelihoods of thousands of workers diminished or eliminated instead? Driving to work one day, one of us heard a business report on the car radio that went something like this: "Worker productivity rose last month, while wage inflation was reduced; this is good news because it means we're getting more out of American workers while paying them less." We wonder whether this really was good news for the majority of people listening to that broadcast. It is as if workers were an unlimited supply of a disposable resource to be exploited, rather than humans with families, lives, consumption needs, and fiscal aspirations, however modest, of their own.

This brings us to our final reason for why wanton consumption is not a good idea. Human beings' insatiable lust for money and consumption leads to a massively inequitable distribution of the world's wealth and natural assets, fostering economic and political instability, and at present, the very real danger of self-imposed extinction of the human race by fatal depletion of natural resources (see, e.g., chap. 5, this volume). According to a United Nations report issued in 1999 (as described in "Rise and Rise of the Super-rich," published in London's The Guardian on July 14, 1999), the world's three richest people are worth more than the combined resources of 36 countries. The richest 200 people in the world have a combined income equivalent to 41% of the world's population. According to the UN, an annual contribution of 1% of the wealth of these 200 people would be enough to give free access to primary education to every child on the planet. Americans belched one-fifth more carbon into the atmosphere than China (with 4.5 times as many citizens) in 1996; the average American uses 115 times more paper and 227 times as much gasoline as the average citizen of India (N. Myers, 1997). This level of consumption is beyond the carrying capacity of the earth and threatens the integrity of "strategic resource stocks such as topsoil, forests, grasslands, fisheries, biodiversity, climate, and the atmosphere" (N. Myers, 1997, p. 54).

Although it is easy (and fun) to critique contemporary American examples of greed and extravagance, given the long and extensive human history of gratuitous consumption, we cannot just chalk it up to the influence of modern capitalism or corporate culture; rather, it is a consequence of basic universal human needs. Indeed, we argue that if contemporary humans are more extravagantly wasteful, it is primarily because of modern technology rather than because of any new social or psychological developments. We present historical and empirical evidence in support of our terror management explanation of consumerism. Finally, we consider what might be done to foster "life-sustaining consumption," divested of the malignant, psychopathological desire for infinite amounts of superfluous stuff that undermines human happiness, fosters grotesquely inequitable and destabilizing distribution of economic resources, and threatens the very existence of the human species by polluting and depleting the natural resources upon which our survival ultimately depends.

TERROR MANAGEMENT THEORY

Terror management theory was originally derived from cultural anthropologist Ernest Becker's efforts (especially in *The Birth and Death of Meaning*, 1971; *The Denial of Death*, 1973; and *Escape from Evil*, 1975) to generate a broad account of the motivational underpinnings of human behavior by integrating and synthesizing insights gleaned from biology, anthropology, psychology, sociology, philosophy, theology, and the humanities. Our analysis of human affairs starts with the relatively noncontroversial Darwinian assumption that all forms of life are biologically oriented toward self-preservation and that there is a wide variety of structural, functional, behavioral, and (for some creatures) psychological means to adapt to specific environmental circumstances so as to sustain the species or evolve into new and more complex life forms. Fish have gills; rose bushes have thorns; squirrels bury acorns and then find them months later; termites eat wood and dung-beetles eat, well, dung. There thus seems to be no limit to the marvelous variety of ways to successfully adhere to the ultimate biological imperative: staying alive.

Humans are also a natural form of life, subject to the same need to adapt to external circumstances in order to survive and reproduce as other creatures. Accordingly, the important question that must be considered is, what is the specific nature of human evolutionary adaptations that render us a unique species? Human beings are not especially formidable from a purely physical perspective as isolated individuals; we are not especially large and our senses (especially olfactory and auditory) are not so keen; we are slow and have weak claws and teeth for meat-eating predators. However, we are highly social, vastly intelligent creatures. These attributes have fostered cooperation and division of labor and led to the invention of tools, agriculture, cooking, houses, and a host of other very useful habits and devices that allowed our ancestral forebears to rapidly multiply from a small band of hominids in a single neighborhood in Africa to the huge populations of Homo sapiens that currently occupy almost every habitable inch of the planet.

Surely one of the important aspects of human intelligence is self-awareness: we are alive and we know that we are alive; and this sense of self allows us to reflect on the past and ponder the future, and in so doing, secure the present. As Kierkegaard (1844/1957) noted, however, knowing one is alive is tremendously uplifting, but we are also perpetually troubled by the concurrent realization that all living things, ourselves included, ultimately die, and that death can occur for reasons that can never be anticipated or controlled. Human beings are thus, by virtue of the awareness of death and their ultimate helplessness before and vulnerability to annihilation, in constant danger of being incapacitated by overwhelming anxiety. We are destined, like ears of corn, to wither and die, if one is lucky enough to have dodged a predator's grasp, an enemy's lunge, or the benignly indifferent battering of a tidal wave or earthquake. As Leopold Bloom said in James Joyce's (1966) *Ulysses*

> Integral parts of the human whole: the necessity of destruction to procure alimentary sustenance: the painful character of the ultimate functions of separate existence, the agonies of birth and death: the monotonous menstruation of simian and (particularly) human females extending from the age of puberty to the menopause: inevitable accidents at sea, in mines and factories: certain very painful maladies and their resultant surgical operations, innate lunacy and congenital criminality, decimating epidemics: catastrophic cataclysms which make terror the basis of human mentality . . . . (p. 697)

Following Otto Rank (1932), Norman Brown (1959), and Ernest Becker (1973), we posit that humans, ingeniously but quite unconsciously, solved their existential dilemma by developing cultural worldviews: commonly held beliefs about reality that serve to reduce the potentially overwhelming terror resulting from the awareness of death. All cultures provide a sense of meaning by offering an account of the origin of the universe, a blueprint for acceptable conduct on earth, and a promise of immortality: symbolically, by creating large monuments and great works of art or science, amassing great fortunes, or having children; and literally, through the various kinds of afterlives that are a central feature of organized religions. These cultural modes of death transcendence allow individuals to feel like they are heroic participants in a world of meaning.

Thus, whereas cultures vary considerably, they share in common the same defensive psychological function: to provide meaning and value and in so doing bestow psychological equanimity in the face of death. All cultural worldviews are ultimately shared fictions, in the sense that none of them is likely to be literally true, and their existence is generally sustained by social consensus. When everyone around us believes the same thing, we can be confident of the veracity of our beliefs.

But, and here's the rub, when we do encounter people with different beliefs, this poses a challenge to our death-denying belief system, which is why people are generally quite uncomfortable around (and hostile toward) those who are different. Additionally, because no symbolic cultural construction can actually overcome the physical reality of death, residual anxiety is unconsciously projected onto such groups of individuals, designating them as scapegoats: all-encompassing repositories of evil, the eradication of which would make earth as it is in heaven. We therefore typically respond to people with different beliefs by berating them, trying to convert them to our system of beliefs, or just killing them and in so doing asserting that "my God (or political-economic system) is better than yours and we'll kick your ass to prove it."

In summary, terror management theory posits that the juxtaposition of the basic biological inclination toward self-preservation common to all living things with the uniquely human awareness of death creates the potential for overwhelming terror that is ameliorated through the construction and maintenance of culture. Culture provides a sense that we live in a stable, orderly, and meaningful universe, and it confers self-esteem through the provision of social roles with associated standards of conduct that allow individuals to view themselves as persons of enduring value in a world of meaning. Consequently, people's actions are directed toward sustaining a dual component cultural anxiety-buffer: faith in their worldviews and a sense that they are valued components of that meaningful reality.

In the empirical assessment of terror management theory, two lines of initial research have tested and supported hypotheses derived from it. First, we demonstrated that self-esteem does indeed serve an anxiety-buffering function in a series of studies where momentarily elevated or (in some studies) dispositionally high self-esteem resulted in lower self-reports of anxiety, physiological arousal, and vulnerability-denying, defensive distortions in response to graphic depictions of death, threat of electrical shock, and after being told that one has personality attributes associated with an early death, respectively (Greenberg et al., 1993; Greenberg et al., 1992).

Second, if a cultural worldview and self-esteem protect people specifically from death-related concerns, then reminders of mortality should lead to the bolstering of these psychological constructs. In support of this general hypothesis, a large body of evidence has shown that momentarily making death salient (*mortality salience*), typically by asking people to think about themselves dying, intensifies people's strivings both to protect and fortify aspects of their worldviews and to bolster their self-esteem. The first and most common finding has been that mortality salience increases positive reactions to similar others or those who share cherished aspects of one's cultural worldview and negative reactions toward those who violate cherished cultural values or are merely different. For example, Greenberg et al. (1990; Study 1) had Christian participants think about death or watch television and then rate two targets who were similarly portrayed except for being either Christian or Jewish. As predicted, although there was no difference between participants' evaluations of the targets in the control condition, mortality salience participants had more favorable reactions to the Christian target and less favorable reactions to the Jewish target. In Study 3, following a mortality salience or control induction, American participants read short essays either highly supportive or highly critical of the American way of life and then reported their impressions of the author. Not surprisingly, participants favored the pro-American author over the anti-American author in the control condition; but this tendency was exaggerated following mortality salience.

Subsequent studies demonstrated behavioral effects of mortality salience. Ochsmann and Mathy (1994) found that German university students sat closer to a German confederate and further away from a Turkish confederate after mortality salience, relative to a control condition; McGregor et al. (1998) showed that mortality salience produced greater physical aggression against someone who did not share one's political orientation; and Greenberg, Simon, Porteus, et al. (1995) demonstrated that participants were more uncomfortable sifting sand through an American flag, or using a crucifix as a hammer, following a mortality salience induction. The general tenor of this and other related work is that mortality salience increases conformity to and defense of the worldview to which the individual subscribes.

More recent research has shown that mortality salience also intensifies self-esteem striving as manifested by such diverse behaviors as psychological distancing from negatively framed groups, individuals, and animals; contributing to worthy charities; engaging in risky behaviors; and increasing investment in romantic relationships and physical appearance (e.g., Goldenberg, Pyszczynski, Greenberg, & Solomon, 2000; Taubman-Ben-Ari, Florian, & Mikulincer, 1999). Additionally, mortality salience effects have been obtained by researchers in eight other countries, using a wide variety of operationalizations of mortality salience, and appear to be unique to thoughts of death, as opposed to other threatening or unpleasant stimuli (see Greenberg, Solomon, & Pyszczynski, 1997). We have recently developed a dual-process model of conscious and unconscious defenses to death (Pyszczynski, Greenberg, & Solomon, 1999) that provides an account of the cognitive processes that underlie reactions to mortality salience, pinpointing heightened accessibility of death-related thoughts outside of consciousness as the cause of these effects.

A TERROR MANAGEMENT ACCOUNT OF CONSPICUOUS CONSUMPTION

How does terror management theory help us to understand humankind's insatiable lust for money and conspicuous consumption of goods and services? For Becker and terror management theory, conspicuous possession and consumption are thinly veiled efforts to assert that one is special and therefore more than just an animal fated to die and decay. Spending eternity in a heavenly afterlife is a quaint and attractive prospect (e.g., Islamic Jihad's Sheik Abdulla Shamni's 1995 [reported by Abu-Nasr, 1995, p. 1A] description of heaven as "a world of castles, flowing rivers, and lush fields" where the blessed "can eat the most delicious food, the most luscious fruits and the tenderist cuts of meat"), but ultimately intangible and empirically uncertain, whereas large piles of gold, enormous mounds of possessions, and lavish consumption are ineluctably real and symbolically indicative of immortal power. The notion that the urge to splurge is fundamentally defensive death denial above and beyond the quite legitimate pursuit of material comfort and aesthetic pleasure is supported by both the historical record and contemporary empirical research.

Historical Record

Money and Possessions in Indigenous Cultures

Psychoanalytic anthropologist Geza Roheim studied the economic behavior of indigenous peoples in New Guinea and Melanesia in the early 1900s to understand the psychological underpinnings of money and avaricious possessiveness. Roheim (1934) found that the primary motive for acquiring money and possessions in virtually all known tribal cultures is ultimately symbolic and ceremonial, in the service of gaining and maintaining prestige, and has little to do with money as a rational medium of exchange of goods and services:

> In the life of the people of Duau whom I know, and also in the lives of other New Guinea and Melanesian people, money . . . plays a conspicuous role. The shell-money in question signifies wealth, but even more than wealth it means social prestige . . . . the great aim in life for everybody in Duau is . . . in piling up and distributing yams. But however 'rich' anybody may be this makes no difference in practical life, it does not mean less work and more pleasure. . . . In societies of this kind wealth

means magic power and magic power means wealth. (p. 401)

The underlying motive for accumulating money is thus to acquire magic power through social prestige.

However, *prestige* means to assume a commanding position in people's minds, and the word *prestige* is derived from words meaning conjuror's tricks, illusions, deceptions, or enchantment. People lust for money to quench their thirst for power, and all power is ultimately bound to issues surrounding sustaining life and forestalling death, ideally permanently. Again following Roheim (1934): "originally people do not desire money because you can buy things for it, but you can buy things for money because people desire it (sic)" (p. 402). Long ago, people began to measure themselves, not by actual achievement, but by garnering prestige (a conjurer's trick, recall) through the ceremonial acquisition of more symbols than one's neighbors:

> The beautiful skins or head-dresses or obsidians displayed at a dance by one rich man excite the interest and envy of visitors of wealth. . . . Such wealthy spectators return home determined to exhibit an even greater value of property the next year. Their effort in turn excites the first man to outdo all his competitors. (A. L. Kroeber, *Handbook of Indians of California*, as cited in Roheim, 1934, p. 402)

Here there is no hint of the rational exchange of goods and services (the typical definition of economic behavior); rather, what we see is the beginnings of a frenzied effort to use deception and illusion to acquire magic power over death through the pursuit of unbridled wealth, a frenzy that continues to this day.

Money and Possessions in Western Civilization

Norman O. Brown (1959) built explicitly on Roheim's work in his examination of the history of money in Western civilization in a chapter entitled "Filthy Lucre" in *Life Against Death*. Brown started by noting that it is very difficult for people today to recognize the true nature of money, because in contemporary societies we make a sharp distinction between the secular and the sacred. Money is now viewed as the rational medium by which we transact our affairs in the material (i.e., secular) world, completely independent of our admittedly nonrational relationship with the spiritual world in the sacred domain. Brown argued that the distinction between secular and sacred is a false and relatively recent one, in that all cultural contrivances are ultimately sacred in nature; all serve the same death-denying function, whether we are aware of it or not.

Money has always been used to buy and sell spiritual absolution (e.g., medieval indulgences) and has always been first and foremost a sacred value, and only secondarily a secular medium of exchange; as Big Daddy knew so well in Tennessee Williams's (1955) *Cat on a Hot Tin Roof*, what we really want to buy with it is everlasting life.

> The human animal is a beast that dies and if he's got money he buys and buys and buys and I think the reason he buys everything he can buy is that in the back of his mind he has the crazy hope that one of his purchases will be life ever-lasting. (p. 73)

Three examples point to this connection between money and the world of the spirit (and of death).

First, gold's value developed partly through its connection to life-giving myths. Becker (1975) observed that "the great economist Keynes noted that the special attraction of gold . . . was due to [its] symbolic identification with the sun . . . " (p. 78) or that which gives life. In Egypt, gold was relatively ignored until it became a popular means of making replicas of a cowrie shell that was "prized as a token of life-giving powers as an amulet to ward off the danger of death and to prolong the existence of the souls that were already dead" (Becker, 1975, p. 77). According to Smith (1929, as quoted in Coblentz, 1965), "the gold models soon became more popular than the original shells, and the reputation for life-giving was then in large measure transferred from the mere form of the amulet to the metal itself" (p. 24).

A second example pertains to the connections between the priesthood and money. The first mints were in temples and churches; the first minters were the priests:

> With the ascendancy of priestcraft it became the priests themselves who monopolized the official trade in sacred charms and in the exchange of favors for gold. The first mints were set up in the temples of the gods, whence our word "money"—from the mint in the temple of Juno Moneta, Juno the admonisher, on the Capitoline hill in Rome. In India the gold fee was the proper one to pay to a god, whose essence was gold. Whence the tradition of the earliest coins being imprinted with the images of the gods, then divine kings, down to presidents in our time. (Becker, 1975, p. 79)

As can be seen, the very roots of the word *money* have ties to the spirit, and thus to death.

A final example concerns the contemporary world's dominant currency, the dollar bill of the United States. Look at the back of a dollar bill. Try to find anything about the use of the dollar as a rational medium of exchange between honest traders, but you cannot. Instead, see the real power behind money: God! *In God We Trust!* Now gaze to the left at the pyramid. There are no pyramids in the United States, so clearly they are not depicted on the dollar as cultural artifacts per se. Why else would there be pyramids on the backs of dollars, except as the ultimate symbol of death-denial and the royal gateway to immortality? Now keep looking up toward the top of the pyramid, broken off and hovering above a bit, apparently levitating, the enlightened (literally) disembodied eyeball. According to Joseph Campbell (1988), this reflects the eye of God opening to us when we reach the top of the pyramid and attain immortality. Even the Latin phrases surrounding the pyramid and eyeball speak to immortality. Loosely translated, the phrase *annuit coeptis* above the floating eyeball means "He favors new undertakings," seemingly giving God's blessing to the nation (and its currency), whereas *novus ordo seclorum* on the banner at the base underlying the pyramid refers to "a new order of the ages," or something that lasts into posterity (B. Fineberg, February 22, 2002, personal communication).

Money: The New Ideology of Immortality

In the past, people's zeal for money and stuff in pursuit of prestige as magic power to ward off death was tempered somewhat by the edicts of the church against the desire for wealth as an end in itself and in support of the proposition that people are responsible for the well-being of those around them. Now that "God is dead," however, in the sense that the Judeo-Christian tradition has waned in power in the last century, the pursuit of money has become the primary immortality ideology for the average American; but now people are unencumbered by a sense of responsibility to the community and unrestricted by moral edicts against massive wealth:

> Money . . . buys bodyguards, bullet-proof glass, and better medical care. Most of all it can be accumulated and passed on, and so radiates its powers even after one's death, giving one a semblance of immortality as he lives in the vicarious enjoyments of his heirs that his money continues to buy, or in the magnificence of the art works that he commissioned, or in the statues of himself and the majesty of his own mausoleum. In short, money is the human mode *par excellence* of coolly denying animal boundness, the determinism of nature. (Becker, 1975, pp. 81–82)

So God isn't dead after all: God has metamorphosized into money and materialism in contemporary society. We may not trust God anymore, but we do trust cash.

In accord with the notion that money, avaricious possession, and conspicuous consumption are essentially aspects of a secular religion—the dominant immortality ideology of the Western world—at a press conference 1 month after the September 11, 2001, terrorist attack on the World Trade Center and the Pentagon, President George W. Bush responded (in part) to the question "is there anything you can say to Americans who feel helpless to protect themselves?" by stating "the American people have got to go about their business. We cannot let the terrorists achieve the objective of frightening our nation to the point where we don't conduct business, where people don't shop" ("Excerpts From the President's Remarks," October 12, 2001, p. B4). Bush reiterated this advice a few days later (reported in Carney & Dickerson, 2001, p. 4): "Well, Mrs. Bush and I want to encourage Americans to go out shopping." Beyond the egregious loss of life, one of the most disturbing aspects of September 11 was the destruction of what were central immortality symbols for most Americans, one economic, the other military. As Becker (1971) observed:

> Modern man is denying his finitude with the same dedication as the ancient Egyptian pharaohs, but now whole masses are playing the game, and with a far richer armamentarium of techniques. The skyscraper buildings . . . the houses with their imposing facades and immaculate lawns—what are these if not the modern equivalent of pyramids: a face to the world that announces: "I am not ephemeral, look what went into me, what represents me, what justifies me." The hushed hope is that someone who can do this will not die. (pp. 149–150)

Empirical Evidence of the Role of Death Denial in Conspicuous Consumption

Could the American Dream actually be just another psychopathological form of death denial raised to the level of civic virtue by cultural ideology? Is there any empirical evidence that bears directly on these claims? Yes. Kasser and Sheldon (2000) asked people to think either about their own death or about listening to music; they then answered questions about their expected financial status 15 years in the future. The results showed inflated fiscal expectations after thinking about death (relative to listening to music), both in terms of overall worth, and especially in the amount participants expected to spend on luxury items such as clothing and entertainment. This suggests that concerns about mortality play a strong, albeit generally unconscious, role in economic aspirations and behavior.

In a second study, Kasser and Sheldon (2000) wondered whether fear of death disposed people to become greedy over-consumers of scarce natural resources. Following either a mortality salience or music control induction, participants engaged in a forest-management simulation. The results were striking. First, people asked to ponder their own mortality reported intending to harvest significantly more of the available acres of forest than their counterparts in the music control condition (62 vs. 49 acres, respectively). Second, mortality salience significantly increased the desire for profit, leading Kasser and Sheldon to conclude: "Interestingly, the results suggested that mortality salience particularly enhanced feelings of greed, or the desire to acquire more than other people" (p. 350). For many in our culture, out-competing others, out-earning them, may be central to feeling of special value. Indeed, in a currency-based culture, how much money you earn and have is an indication of how much you are valued in the culture, and this is spiritual currency as much as, if not more than, it is financial currency. This finding suggests that greedy plundering of natural resources is at least partially engendered by concerns about death.

Another way in which mortality concerns may contribute to consumption is suggested by two studies by Koole and van den Berg (2001) demonstrating that mortality salience increases people's preferences for scenes of cultivated nature over wild nature. Cultivated scenery provides the illusion of order and control over nature and thus may also serve to manage our fears about the realities of existence. By compulsively controlling nature, we create the illusion that we can avoid death. In Becker's (1971) words:

> Life in contemporary society is like an open air lunatic asylum with people cutting and spraying their grass (to deny untidyness, hence lack of order, hence lack of control, hence their death), beating trails to the bank with little books of figures that worry them around the clock (for the same reason) . . . filling shopping carts, emptying shopping carts . . . and all this dedicated activity takes place within a din of noise that tries to defy eternity: motorized lawn mowers, power saws, giant jets, motorized toothbrushes, . . . (p. 150)

In summary, the historical record and empirical research provide convergent support for the proposition that the denial of our mortality is at the root of humankind's feverish pursuit of wealth.

SPIRITS IN A MATERIAL WORLD

Cash is king! If worshipping money and conspicuous consumption have become the dominant American religion of the 21st century, what should we do about it? Clearly, death denial plays a role in our slavish devotion to accumulating infinite amounts of money and stuff, to the detriment of our personal and interpersonal health.

If cash is king, should we perhaps kill the king? This would be premature and unfortunate, because surely economic behavior is not driven solely by death denial. Surely money does indeed serve as a rational and efficient means of exchanging goods and services among people engaged in productive activities. Surely fiscal rewards can be a potent stimulant to creative and productive activities. Surely material and corporeal creatures are avid consumers; it is both physically necessary and aesthetically pleasing. The trick, of course, is how to preserve the life-enhancing aspects of economic behavior while disposing of the unfortunate, destructive, death-denying aspects.

From a theoretical perspective, it is important to recognize that all forms of economic organization are ultimately based on an explicit or implicit understanding of human nature and that both capitalist and communist economies are based on fallacious accounts of human nature. On the Right, champions of free enterprise in unbridled pursuit of capital and unfettered consumption presume that people are completely autonomous and entirely self-interested individuals who enter the world with different talents and that anyone who tries hard enough is likely to succeed. Furthermore, this success is purely the result of individual effort, unencumbered and unassisted by other people and social institutions. The Horatio Alger story of a poor shoe-shine boy becoming rich by hard work and perseverance, and the story of the Marlboro man, the lone cowboy apparently running an entire ranch by himself, are deeply embedded in popular culture and clearly reflect this vision of human nature.

On the Left, communists presume that people are naturally industrious and altruistic, are content with having their material necessities met, and are like lumps of clay molded by their environments. Self-interest is hence an unfortunate byproduct of a dysfunctional economic environment. People are not naturally selfish but become that way through exposure to a specific set of economic arrangements. The goal is thus to foster "equality" by constructing a social order that emphasizes participation in the community and encourages the obliteration of individual differences and self-interested behavior.

However, both the free-market and communist view of human nature are wrong; or, rather, each is only half right. As living creatures, we have individual biological needs that must be actively met to ensure survival; there thus must be an inborn element of self-interest as standard equipment in the human animal: If I'm hungry it doesn't help me to watch my sister eat a hot-dog, regardless of my sincere interest in her welfare. Human beings are also fundamentally social creatures; we are not biologically constructed to function independently, and the same gregariousness we see in our primate precursors exists in us. Thus, we have a biologically based propensity to affiliate with and care for others.

So a proper understanding of human nature recognizes the simultaneous desire to pursue individual self-interest and competitively distinguish ourselves as superior to those around us (to "stick out") and to cooperate with others as members of a broader social order that serves our social interests (to "fit in"). Becker (1973), following Rank (1932), called the simultaneous desire to stick out and to fit in the *twin ontological motives*. (See also Brewer's, 1991, optimal distinctiveness theory for an independent articulation of these motives.) Rank postulated that the fear of death motivates the urge to distinction in pursuit of immortality, as it does the desire to be comfortably embedded in a death-transcending collective. A number of mortality salience studies have supported the role of these two motives in terror management. For example, following a mortality salience or control induction, Simon et al. (1997) told participants (on the basis of recently completed personality assessments) that they were either very similar to or quite different from their fellow students. Participants then completed a social projection measure assessing themselves in terms of their perceived similarity to others. We predicted and found that being told one is very similar to others would instigate a compensatory reaction to differentiate oneself (to "stick out") in response to mortality salience (and relative to control conditions), but that being told one is very different from others would result in an increased desire to "fit in" in response to mortality salience (and relative to control conditions) and thus rating oneself as more similar to others.

Accordingly, social institutions in general, and economic institutions in particular, should be constructed so as to balance harmoniously these needs. Institutions that foster the development of one need, "sticking out" or "fitting in," to the exclusion of, or in opposition to, the other need are doomed to fail because they each amputate half of what we are.

Capitalist economic orders are based on the lopsided assumption that people are solely self-interested, competitive, independent individuals trying to stick out. The result is economic behavior driven by pure greed. The primary goal is the infinite accumulation of a death-denying abstraction: money. Capitalists are more concerned about the "health" of the economy than the health of people or the planet. A healthy economy is one with a low deficit and high gross national product, even if people are miserable and unhealthy and the natural environment is polluted and depleted to the point where it can no longer sustain human life.

Communist economic organization is based on the equally lopsided assumption that people have minimal physical needs and desires that can be directed and regulated by central authorities. By the totalitarian imposition of rigid controls over all aspects of life, individual expression is stifled, motivation is crushed, and innovation is trampled. Decisions are made by a relatively few inept bureaucrats or (even worse) a single monomaniacal leader (e.g., Stalin or Mao), always (at least to date) with disastrous results: stagnant inefficiency and wholesale plundering of natural resources.

CONCLUSION: THE HUMAN MARKETPLACE

So, if Left and Right are both beside the point, how do we get the human factor back into the marketplace? First, we need to expose as psychopathological, and then dispose of, or at least actively strive to minimize, the defensive, death-denying aspects of the money motive in our economic institutions and our economic behavior. Cash is not king; money is not God. You really can't take it with you (although the Egyptian Pharaohs certainly thought they could—little did they know that their stash for the afterlife would later fill museums and rich people's living rooms around the globe), nor (sorry Big Daddy) can money purchase everlasting life. When our desire for money is for the sake of money, we become slaves to the market to the detriment of our psychological well-being. As John Maynard Keynes (1932) observed:

> When the accumulation of wealth is no longer of high social importance, there will be great changes in the code of morals. We shall be able to rid

ourselves of many of the pseudo-moral principles which have hag-ridden us for two hundred years, by which we have exalted some of the most distasteful of human qualities into the position of the highest virtues. We shall be able to afford to dare to assess the money-motive at its true value. The love of money as a possession—as distinguished from the love of money as a means to the enjoyments and realities of life—will be recognized for what it is, a somewhat disgusting morbidity, one of the semi-criminal, semi-pathological propensities which one hands over with a shudder to the specialists in mental disease. (p. 369)

This is not a new idea. In fact, Aristotle held similar views: Consider the following passage from the Encyclopædia Britannica describing his position on these matters:

There is, for example, no sense in producing or acquiring more shoes than can possibly be worn. This is self-evident. With regard to money, however, which has become exchangeable against everything, the illusion arises that it is good to accumulate it without limit. By doing so, man harms both the community and himself because, concentrating on such a narrow aim, he deprives his soul and spirit of larger and more rewarding experiences. ("Aristotle," 2003)

This quote is astonishing in that it highlights both how little things have changed since Ancient Greece and how little Western civilization has learned from Aristotle despite the extensive lip service to his great importance and influence.

In addition to making an effort—thus far futile—to dissuade people from the love of money for its own sake, societies must develop economic institutions, even a culture, that cultivate and facilitate the expression of both the basic tendency for humans to pursue their own self-interest (to "stick out") and the concurrent desire to be a member of a community (to "fit in"). This is in fact what Adam Smith had in mind in his 1776 classic *An Inquiry Into the Nature and Causes of the Wealth of Nations*.

Smith is well-known for his argument that human beings are motivated by passionate self-interest: the unbridled pursuit of basic animal as well as culturally constructed desires. According to Smith, the best economic order is one that maximizes individual freedom so as to allow this basic motive to be satisfied directly. When everyone acts in their own "enlightened" self-interest, they will naturally produce goods and services that are responsive to the needs of the community. This is of course the famous notion of the "invisible hand." If someone makes bicycles and someone else bakes bread, and people need and want bicycles and bread, then it makes sense for one person to make bikes and the other to bake bread. It makes sense too that those who make the best (in terms of quality relative to price) bikes and bread prosper more than those who make poorly designed or shabbily constructed bikes or tasteless bread.

Less well known, however (especially by conservative pundits who have not read his work directly), is Smith's assertion that people are not solely motivated by self-interest; additionally, they are also amenable to reason and imbued with sympathy: a sincere concern for the well-being of others. Accordingly, for Smith (1776/1937), enlightened self-interest can only properly exist (in the sense of being morally justified) when complemented with concern for and sympathy with others. Smith also argued that governments are responsible for ensuring that human sympathies are not dampened by the "mean rapacity" of "monopolizing spirit of merchants and manufacturers," in which case the average citizen "generally becomes as stupid and ignorant as it is possible for a human being to become" (p. 460).

The truly humane marketplace thus requires a delicate balance of "enlightened" self-interest, reason, and sympathy (empathy with and compassion for our fellow human beings).[1] The primary goal of the humane market should be the satisfaction of individual and collective needs and desires as determined by people through the democratic process, rather than by "market forces." A healthy economy would produce maximum satisfaction of genuine needs and desires within a social context that provides value and meaning to as many people as possible. The human marketplace would be limited, not by capital constraints, but by technology and resources (a quantitative measure of human stupidity is the difference between what we are technologically able to accomplish in the world and what we actually choose to do), accompanied by concern for preservation of the physical environment upon which our survival always ultimately depends.

Unfortunately, the United States is perhaps the most imbalanced of all societies because it is so focused on the mythic value of individualism. In most places in the world, even relatively individualistic cultures like Germany and the Netherlands, there is a sense that citizens are part of a family or community and that the needs of all people must be met. Americans may be the only people who widely embrace a "dog eat dog" attitude regarding their own ingroup. A prominent example of this is the resistance to

---

[1] Van Vugt (2001) recently studied consumption of scarce resources as a function of self-interest and community involvement. Van Vugt hypothesized that because people are motivated by self-interest as well as social concerns, they should behave in accordance with whichever motive is activated by external circumstances. In a field study of British households with water meters where some families paid a variable tariff (charges related to use) and others a fixed tariff (charges unrelated to use), he predicted and found that consumption was lower when people were charged for what they used, presumably because self-interest motives are directly engaged under these conditions; however, although consumption was generally higher when charges were unrelated to use, it was only under this condition that this tendency was blunted in households with high community identification (e.g., people who felt strongly attached to their community, felt they had many friends in their community, and felt that their community was a great place to live), presumably because social concerns are more likely to be effective under these conditions. A second study replicated this effect in a simulated natural resource crisis in a laboratory setting. Van Vugt concluded, and we agree, that these findings suggest that effective social interventions should be designed in order to constructively engage both motive systems—self-interest and social identity.

implementing national health insurance, despite the ample resources to do so. Although Americans are undoubtedly more collectivistic than they think they are, a substantial shift toward a communal orientation regarding one another is needed to even approach the sort of optimal balance we have been discussing.

A final pie in the sky possibility is that the human race will grow up before it destroys itself and everything around it. If we did not need to deny our puniness and ultimate mortality, our most destructive and acquisitive propensities would cease to serve any psychological function and, like many dysfunctional habits, might eventually be abandoned. Then perhaps human beings could become consumers of life instead of their lives being consumed by consumption.

REFERENCES

Abu-Nasr, D. (1995, January 30). Devout human bombs die in Allah's name. *Charleston Gazette*, p. 1A.

Aristotle. (2003). Encyclopædia Britannica. Retrieved April 21, 2003, from http://www.britannica.com/eb/article?eu=114501

Becker, E. (1971). *The birth and death of meaning*. New York: Free Press.

Becker, E. (1973). *The denial of death*. New York: Free Press.

Becker, E. (1975). *Escape from evil*. New York: Free Press.

Brewer, M. (1991). The social self: On being the same and different at the same time. *Personality and Social Psychology Bulletin, 17*, 475–482.

Brown, A. (2001, May 10). Please Lord, make me rich. *The London Times*.

Brown, N. O. (1959). *Life against death: The psychoanalytical meaning of history*. Middletown, CT: Wesleyan University Press.

Campbell, J. (1988). *The power of myth* (with Bill Moyers; B. S. Flowers, Ed.). New York: Doubleday.

Carney, J., & Dickerson, J. F. (2001, October 22). A work in progress. *Time*, p. 4.

Coblentz, S. A. (1965). *Avarice: A history*. Washington, DC: Public Affairs Press.

Excerpts from the President's remarks on war on terrorism. (2001, October 12). *New York Times*, p. B4.

Frank, R. H. (1999). *Luxury fever: Why money fails to satisfy in an era of excess*. New York: Free Press.

Goldenberg, J., Pyszczynski, T., Greenberg, J., & Solomon, S. (2000). Fleeing the body: A terror management perspective on the problem of human corporeality. *Personality and Social Psychology Review, 4*, 200–218.

Greenberg, J., Pyszczynski, T., & Solomon, S. (1986). The causes and consequences of a need for self-esteem: A terror management theory. In R. F. Baumeister (Ed.), *Public self and private self* (pp. 189–212). New York: Springer-Verlag.

Greenberg, J., Pyszczynski, T., Solomon, S., Pinel, E., Simon, L., & Jordan, K. (1993). Effects of self-esteem on vulnerability-denying defensive distortions: Further evidence of an anxiety-buffering function of self-esteem. *Journal of Experimental Social Psychology, 29,* 229–251.

Greenberg, J., Pyszczynski, T., Solomon, S., Rosenblatt, A., Veeder, M., Kirkland, S., et al. (1990). Evidence for terror management theory II: The effects of mortality salience on reactions to those who threaten or bolster the cultural worldview. *Journal of Personality and Social Psychology, 58,* 308–318.

Greenberg, J., Simon, L., Porteus, J., Pyszczynski, T., & Solomon, S. (1995). Evidence of a terror management function of cultural icons: The effects of mortality salience on the inappropriate use of cherished cultural symbols. *Personality and Social Psychology Bulletin, 21,* 1221–1228.

Greenberg, J., Solomon, S., & Pyszczynski, T. (1997). Terror management theory of self-esteem and cultural worldviews: Empirical assessments and conceptual refinements. In M. P. Zanna (Ed.), *Advances in experimental social psychology* (Vol. 29, pp. 61–139). Orlando, FL: Academic Press.

Greenberg, J., Solomon, S., Pyszczynski, T., Rosenblatt, A., Burling, J., Lyon, D., et al. (1992). Assessing the terror management analysis of self-esteem: Converging evidence of an anxiety-buffering function. *Journal of Personality and Social Psychology, 63,* 913–922.

Joyce, J. (1966). *Ulysses.* New York: Vintage. (Original work published 1914)

Kasser, T., & Ryan, R. M. (1993). A dark side of the American dream: Correlates of financial success as a central life aspiration. *Journal of Personality and Social Psychology, 65,* 410–422.

Kasser, T., & Sheldon, K. M. (2000). Of wealth and death: Materialism, mortality salience, and consumption behavior. *Psychological Science, 11,* 348–351.

Keynes, J. M. (1932). *Essays in persuasion.* New York: Harcourt Brace.

Kierkegaard, S. (1957). *The concept of dread.* Princeton, NJ: Princeton University Press. (Original work published 1844)

Koole, S., & van den Berg, A. (2001, July). *Lost in the wilderness: Terror management and the experience of nature.* Paper presented at the First International Conference on Experimental Existential Psychology: Finding Meaning in the Human Condition. Free University Amsterdam, Amsterdam, The Netherlands.

McGregor, H., Lieberman, J. D., Greenberg, J., Solomon, S., Arndt, J., Simon, L., et al. (1998). Terror management and aggression: Evidence that mortality salience motivates aggression toward worldview threatening individuals. *Journal of Personality and Social Psychology, 74,* 590–605.

Moreton, C. (1997, December 28). The things that shaped our year. *The Independent* (London), p. 11.

Morris, B. (1986, November 20). This little piggy went to market: Times profile of Ivan Boesky. *The London Times.*

Myers, D. G. (1993). *The pursuit of happiness.* New York: Avon.

Myers, D. G., & Diener, E. (1995). Who is happy? *Psychological Science, 6,* 10–19.

Myers, N. (1997). Consumption: Challenge to sustainable development. *Science, 276,* 53–55.

Ochsmann, R., & Mathy, M. (1994). *Depreciating of and distancing from foreigners: Effects of mortality salience.* Unpublished manuscript, Universitat Mainz, Mainz, Germany.

Pyszczynski, T., Greenberg, J., & Solomon, S. (1999). A dual process model of defense against conscious and unconscious death-related thoughts: An extension of terror management theory. *Psychological Review, 106,* 835–845.

Rank, O. (1932). *Art and artist.* New York: Knopf.

Rise and rise of the super-rich. (1999, July 14). *Guardian,* p. 2.

Roheim, G. (1934). The evolution of culture. *International Journal of Psycho-Analysis, 15,* 387–418.

Roheim, G. (1943). The origin and function of culture. *Monographs of Nervous and Mental Disease, 69.*

Simon, L., Greenberg, J., Arndt, J., Pyszczynski, T., Clement, R., & Solomon, S. (1997). Perceived consensus, uniqueness, and terror management: Compensatory responses to threats to inclusion and distinctiveness following mortality salience. *Personality and Social Psychology Bulletin, 23,* 1055–1065.

Smith, A. (1937). *An inquiry into the nature and causes of the wealth of nations* (E. Cannan, Ed.). New York: Random House. (Original work published 1776)

Solomon, S., Greenberg, J., & Pyszczynski, T. (1991). A terror management theory of social behavior: The psychological functions of self-esteem and cultural worldviews. In M. P. Zanna (Ed.), *Advances in experimental social psychology* (Vol. 24, pp. 91–159). Orlando, FL: Academic Press.

Taubman-Ben-Ari, O., Florian, V., & Mikulincer, M. (1999). The impact of mortality salience on reckless driving: A test of terror management mechanisms. *Journal of Personality and Social Psychology, 76,* 35–45.

Van Vugt, M. (2001). Community identification moderating the impact of financial incentives in a natural social dilemma: Water conservation. *Personality and Social Psychology Bulletin, 27,* 1440–1449.

Veblen, T. (1902). *The theory of the leisure class: An economic study of institutions.* New York: Macmillan.

Williams, T. (1955). *Cat on a hot tin roof.* New York: New Directions.

III

CLINICAL ISSUES

9

ACQUISITIVE DESIRE: ASSESSMENT AND TREATMENT

JEFFREY KOTTLER, MARILYN MONTGOMERY, AND DAVID SHEPARD

A 50-year-old single man came into the therapist's office for a first session. The therapist looked at the man, noticing his shaking hands and downcast eyes. He also couldn't help but observe that he was immaculately dressed in an Armani jacket—easily worth $1,500. The therapist was impressed. It was way more than he could afford, but he felt a twinge of pride that he would even recognize Armani when he saw it.

"Ronald" introduced himself with a rather shaky voice.[1] Every time his hands moved, the therapist could hear the jangling of a gold bracelet attached to a very expensive watch. The therapist took all this in, still surprised to see such an affluent, successful client in this clinic that generally served working-class people who could only afford to pay on a sliding scale.

"I hate to tell you," Ronald began, "but I feel a bit humiliated to be coming to a place like this." He gestured with his arms to take in a sweep of the

Marilyn Montgomery and David Shepard contributed equally to this chapter.

[1]"Ronald" and other case examples in this chapter are composites of clinical cases of the authors. All identifying information has been changed to preserve individual anonymity.

building. "But I just cannot afford to pay for a therapist in private practice right now." Ronald pulled down the sleeve of his cashmere jacket and adjusted the crease on his worsted wool slacks.

The therapist felt a sting but quickly righted himself by making the clinical observation that the client was devaluing him. Already a diagnosis was beginning to form—the symptoms, the expensive jacket and watch, the negative transference—all pointed to a narcissistic man suffering from an agitated depression, probably caused by the loss of some external support that shored up a fundamentally weak sense of self-worth.

The man's story confirmed the therapist's speculations. Ronald had grown up with few material pleasures; his father was a mediocre physical education teacher, forcing the family to move from town to town as his alcoholism continually got him fired. His mother was a sour, bitter woman, preferring to complain about her husband's ineffectualness rather than leave the marriage. Ronald's description of his childhood was succinct: "I hated it." Determined to transcend his unhappy beginnings, Ronald had become a successful real estate broker, ultimately selling houses to the wealthiest clientele in the community. As the local housing market boomed, Ronald had luxuriated in the trappings of success. Ronald's eyes lit up as he told how his house was once photographed for *Architectural Digest* and as he described his collection of vintage Cadillacs. The therapeutic alliance was solidified once the therapist slipped in the fact that he, like Ronald, knew the value of a 1978 El Dorado.

Ronald then related how everything had collapsed. The housing market had gone bad and his spouse had left him. He had lost his house and all but one of his cars. The worst of it, Ronald told the therapist, was his reaction to all of this—the sense of impending doom, the inability to stop his hands from shaking, and the feeling of humiliation so intense that he became afraid to socialize with any of his friends.

The therapist was aware of his uncharitable feeling of satisfaction that Ronald probably now had less net worth than he did. And for all his devaluing of therapy and the humiliation of being at a mental health clinic, Ronald needed him. Feeling confident and a little bit powerful, the therapist devised and proceeded with his treatment plan: (a) address the anxiety through cognitive–behavioral interventions, (b) explore the childhood roots of Ronald's low self-worth, and (c) support him in taking steps to reduce his social isolation. Within a few months, Ronald's mood improved significantly and his agitation abated. He returned to his normal activities.

"You're a wonderful counselor," Ronald told the therapist enthusiastically, "and you've helped me really understand myself." On that happy note, therapy ended.

About a month later, the therapist received a desperate call from Ronald. "Everything was going great. Couldn't be better. I even bought another El Dorado. It's a car you'd love, too. But then the IRS caught up with me. I don't want to tell you how much I owe. And I'm being sued. I did some things that I shouldn't have done, but I needed the money. I owe a lot. I'm in big trouble. I want to see you, but I have to tell you . . . . I'm basically broke."

What stunned the therapist the most was the realization that he had never thought to ask Ronald concrete questions about how much debt he owed or whether he could pay his taxes. The therapist had done a thorough job assessing Ronald's mental status, but he had completely ignored his financial status. No wonder Ronald was agitated and depressed! His compulsive acquisition habits had brought him to the brink of bankruptcy and the IRS was breathing down his neck. The therapist had failed Ronald in some important ways, even though he believed he was doing solid therapy and using interventions grounded in theory and research data.

The therapy had been a "Band-aid" and had ultimately failed for a number of reasons. First, by focusing on Ronald's psychological distress and its probable familial derivations, the therapist neglected the true root of the client's problems: his desire to acquire status and expensive belongings so much so that his financial, and therefore emotional, health was imperiled. Second, the therapist's countertransference issues around acquisitive desire (AD) had blocked him from engaging in a conversation with Ronald about the personal costs of his compulsion to purchase status-enhancing luxuries. Because the therapist had not resolved his own shame about working in a low-fee clinic, he avoided the pain of talking about the things Ronald had that he himself could not afford. The therapist envied his client too much. Also, the therapist liked the fact that Ronald saw him as someone able to appreciate the finer things, and he did not want to interfere with their communal basking in the glow of knowing the value of an Armani jacket or a vintage car.

Ronald's case is an illustration of a psychological disorder that may be termed *acquisitive desire* (AD; Kottler, 1999). Like substance-abuse and eating disorders, problems of AD represent a multifaceted cluster of enduring cognitive, behavioral, and social factors that are linked with other symptoms such as anxiety, depression, and impulsivity. Although AD is not strictly a discrete condition that manifests itself in a single way, AD disorders have in common an intense desire to acquire, possess, or hoard objects. We see AD as an overarching construct that may include features such as compulsive shopping, hoarding, greed, purchasing or collecting objects, and the neurotic pursuit of possessions. A final symptom of AD is the common phenomenon of clients regarding their therapist as a personal possession.

ACQUISITIVE DESIRE IN THE LIVES OF CLIENTS AND THEIR THERAPISTS

Because AD often appears with symptoms of other disorders, therapists may treat the other symptoms (e.g., Ronald's depression and narcissism) without connecting the symptoms to the underlying, long-term hold that AD has in the lives of clients. Assessment and diagnosis of AD problems are often complicated because of the different processes and meanings involved in the various so-called ADs. For some people, AD is "self-medication" for depression or anxiety; for others, it is a symbol of success or status; it can also be a manifestation of obsessive–compulsive disorder. When the therapist is not aware of the ways that symptoms can be indications of a deeper AD, the treatment may not be as successful as it could be.

Another factor to consider is that we therapists live in the same material world as our clients. We are exposed to the same advertising, the same attractive shops in our local malls, and the same alluring cars in our neighbors' driveways. We feel the same pressures to be successful and to own the same symbols of this success. For some of us, it may be an expensive car, jacket, or watch; for others, it may be a particular university diploma or office address. In academia, many of us may "collect" acquisitions such as grants or publications in prestigious journals. We feel the same needs to compete with our colleagues, the same desire for symbols of success. We therapists thus have our own issues with acquisition, and these can impair our ability to interpret the meaning and consequences of AD in the lives of our clients.

The purpose of this chapter is to provide clinicians with a roadmap for recognizing and treating all types of AD, using clinical examples from our own practices. We also address countertransference issues therapists face because of their own ADs.

RESEARCH ON AD DISORDERS

What motivates people to consume? Is this a universal (and normal) psychological drive? If so, why do some people cross the line between a healthy desire to be materially comfortable and an unhealthy preoccupation or compulsion to acquire? What processes or states are associated with AD getting out of hand? Are the various manifestations of AD distinct from one another in ways that might have implications for treatment?

Recognizing Acquisition-Related Disorders

During the Great Depression (another time when the material world was strongly in focus), some writers for a British medical journal sought to understand the psychological processes underlying desires for property and motivations for possessiveness (Ginsberg, Isaacs, Marshall, & Suttie, 1935). Their explanations for why people consume included the following, summarizing the psychological thinking of the time: (a) Acquisition is a way of assuaging social anxiety; (b) acquisition represents a desire for security and status gained by having more than one's neighbors; (c) acquisitive tendencies result when self-assertive tendencies are weak; and (d) the desire for an object rarely represents a desire for the object itself, but rather is a symbolic triangulation between the object, the person desiring it, and a hoped-for effect on another person.

Despite this auspicious presentation of a number of hypotheses that could have provided the springboard for further study, psychological attention to AD waned to virtually nothing until fairly recently. Perhaps this is because the decades of affluence that ensued (the 1950s, 1960s, 1980s, and 1990s) convinced psychologists that chasing after possessions was so common as to be unremarkable goal-directed behavior (Csikszentmihalyi, 1999, 2000). Congruent with this thinking, an area of psychology termed *consumer psychology* has grown over the last decade, investigating various aspects of people's purchasing behaviors and experiences. From this body of work comes the idea that people purchase many objects out of a measurable "need for uniqueness"—a kind of counter-conformity motivation that varies in strength across individuals (Tian & McKenzie, 2001). These studies offer insights into how people shop for, and why they value, their prized possessions, but generally do not draw attention to the dysfunctional aspects of the desire to consume and acquire. Indeed, research on the various dysfunctional forms of AD, and its treatment, is sparse (though see chap. 10, this volume).

Impulse Control

Many forms of AD, and certainly compulsive buying, appear to be closely related to *impulse-control disorders*. People with impulse-control disorders display three characteristics: (a) they cannot resist an impulse to do something, even though they think it may be harmful to themselves or others; (b) they experience a rising sense of tension (often described as "restlessness," "anxiety," or "pressure") that becomes unbearable as they contemplate the deed; and (c) they experience a strong sense of relief, satisfaction, or gratification as they give in and commit the act. The aftermath may or may not include remorse, guilt, and regret (Maxmen & Ward, 1995). Often, people with an impulse-control disorder have (or have family histories of) mood disorders and substance-abuse disorders (McElroy, Hudson, Harrison, Keck, & Aizley, 1992). Kleptomania is an impulse-control disorder with some features in common with AD, but it is distinct in that it involves the theft of things that are meaningless and without value to the thief after they are acquired.

The aspects of AD that appear to be related to impulse control are not clearly distinguishable from some compulsive, AD-related disorders. For example, Faber and colleagues have developed a program of research on identifying (but not treating) compulsive buying (see chap. 10, this volume).

They sought to identify the attitudes and behaviors (O'Guinn & Faber, 1989) as well as demographic profiles and psychiatric co-morbidities (Christenson, Faber, de Zwaan, & Raymond, 1994) of the compulsive buyer, and they developed a clinical screener for compulsive buying (Faber & O'Guinn, 1992). The typical compulsive buyer, according to this research, is a midlife female who began compulsive buying in late adolescence and whose buying usually results in adverse psychosocial consequences. When compared to matched controls, compulsive buyers have a higher lifetime prevalence of anxiety, substance use, and eating disorders, and they are more depressed, anxious, and compulsive. Additionally, 96% of their compulsive buyers described buying behaviors that resembled an impulse-control disorder (Christenson et al., 1994).

Compulsive gambling is another example of an acquisition-related impulse-control disorder. Whereas compulsive buyers are typically women, male compulsive gamblers outnumber women 2 to 1 (Volberg & Steadman, 1988). Compulsive gambling conjures up images of a haggard desperado unable to leave a smoke-filled casino, but the *Diagnostic and Statistical Manual of Mental Disorders* (4th ed.; *DSM–IV–TR*; American Psychiatric Association, 2000) criteria also capture the socially acceptable gambling of the wheelers and dealers who get involved in business scams, as seen in the following case:

> He had been in for a few weeks with his wife for couples therapy, and it was one of those cases that never seems to get off the ground. They presented as an attractive, well-groomed couple—the kind you might envy—with the usual communication troubles about money and stepchildren and perhaps some sub-clinical levels of anxiety and depression. After a few weeks, they "no showed" and never came back or returned follow-up phone calls. About a year later, his picture was on the front page of the newspaper; the story headline read, "Money at the core of lifestyle that led to jail, charge of attempted murder." The story depicted the shock of all who knew him as a kind and wonderful man, an active parent in the PTA who, beneath the surface, was caught in a web of financial dealings and property acquisitions that had gradually become more and more illegal. "It was greed," confessed one of his business partners of their fast-and-loose business dealings, "we all went in on greed." The authorities got involved when the man and his wife got into a more vehement argument than usual and he knocked her unconscious. "They argued over money," reported the detective assigned to the case.

This case illustrates how compulsions and impulse-control problems can exist concurrently. In addition to a compulsive acquisition style reminiscent of compulsive gambling, several failures of impulse control are evident, including the physical aggression that came to characterize the couple's conflicts. The differential etiology and phenomenology of poor impulse control and impulse-driven compulsions directed toward acquisition are, as yet, poorly understood.

Obsessive Compulsions

AD sometimes manifests itself as an *anxiety-related compulsion*. Many compulsive buyers (67%) describe a phenomenology of buying that also closely resembles obsessive–compulsive disorder (Christenson et al., 1994). Obsessive–compulsive behavior differs from impulse-control disorders in that with compulsions, the actual act is ego-dystonic and the person does not get relief by following through with the urge to acquire. These individuals know that their behavior is inappropriate, but they feel helpless to stop it. Compulsive hoarding is the disorder that best fits this category. Compulsive hoarders, unlike avid collectors, have trouble discarding objects that they recognize as worthless, such as old newspapers or mail (Frost & Hartl, 1996). They recognize that their cluttered living spaces interfere with their lives and often their social goals, but they feel helpless to alter their acquisitive patterns. Recent research has revealed that compulsive hoarders often experience depression and anxiety, and they experience social and familial impairment, much more so than with other anxiety or obsessive–compulsive disorders (Frost & Hartl, 1996).

Existential Identity Problems

The "existential crisis" that seems to characterize some clients with AD probably best fits the *DSM–IV–TR* category of *identity problem*, which falls under the unceremonious distinction of "other conditions that may be a focus of clinical attention" (American Psychiatric Association, 2000, p. 731). Affluent, consumer-oriented societies such as ours insist that people distinguish themselves with self-made identities (Erikson, 1956/1980). Optimally, young people emerge into adulthood with a sense of personal identity that includes "a sense of psychosocial well-being" and "a feeling of being at home in one's body, a sense of 'knowing where one is going,' and an inner assuredness of anticipated recognition from those who count" (Erikson, 1956/1980, pp. 127–128). However, when society is diverse, diffuse, and rapidly changing, it is easier for some "emergent adults" to sort out the coming-of-age question of "who am I" with an answer of "I am what I own" (Arnett, 2000). Currently, there are many social influences that discourage traditional, thoughtful, or moral approaches to answering the existential questions of life and instead encourage quick-fix, postmodern, material answers (Côté, 2000). Under these circumstances, wrote Josselson (1994):

> identity then tends to be phrased not in terms of what the individual will stand for, be faithful to, or try to become or generate in the world, but instead what the individual will purchase. For such young people, the burning issues are those of consumption: for example, which are the best stereo speakers? (p. 23)

By midlife, most adults find that these kinds of answers to life's questions have begun to wear very thin. However, individuals who have spent their early adulthood "shopping for identity" may not have developed inner resources for discovering and constructing a life that represents a commitment to the core values of one's self.

Narcissism and Greed

A final type of disorder associated with AD is narcissistic personality disorder. Newspaper tabloids revel in publishing splashy stories about the bank president who was discovered to have a gold-plated toilet installed in his private chambers, paid for with bilked investors' funds, or about the school superintendent who was discovered to require a leased island condo for "business meetings." Sensational and far-fetched as these stories may seem, they are about real individuals whose neurotic greed has gotten so far out of hand that they get caught. When forced to seek help, they are usually diagnosed with a narcissistic personality disorder, which is characterized by self-aggrandizement paired with extreme reactivity to failure (Rodewalt & Morf, 1998).

People with narcissistic personalities often develop lifestyles of grandiosity. Material culture offers many opportunities for people to express grandiosity and to solicit admiration through the use of possessions. Many highly successful people display personality traits that could seem narcissistic. However, narcissistic personality disorder is indicated only when competitive acquisition of the biggest and best house, car, office, suit, laptop, or boat is accompanied by excessive pride, disdain for others, and by an insistence on admiring attention. When preoccupation with success becomes inflexible and maladaptive and causes impairment—in other words, when the individual crosses the line between living with an impressive, sweeping style and living exploitatively—then AD-related narcissism is considered a psychological disorder (American Psychiatric Association, 2000).

PRELIMINARY ASSESSMENT AND DIAGNOSIS

Because American culture tends to deny problems related to ADs, clinicians tend to misidentify AD problems and misconstrue the role they play in other disorders (e.g., mood disorders). Clinicians who want to be effective in this area must make a conscious decision to assess clients' psychosocial well-being in the area of acquisition and possessions.

Before asking any specific questions, the therapist can listen for acquisition-related themes as clients describe the circumstances that brought them to therapy. For example, clients with impulse-related acquisitive disorders often come to therapy because they are overwhelmed with problems in many areas of life such as work, career, and family, similar to clients with substance abuse. Clients with anxiety-related acquisitive disorders such as compulsive hoarding or collecting usually reveal other impairments in social and familial areas of life. Clients with narcissistic greed may reveal an exploitive or manipulative style, as well as jealousy and competitiveness, without even realizing the social inappropriateness of their boastfulness. Clients with a narcissistic sense of entitlement may speak with disdain for others, use score-keeping metaphors, mention social isolation, reveal a concern with impression management, or talk about their lack of satisfaction despite their success. Any of these patterns suggest working hypotheses for a therapist to explore in more depth after an initial assessment is made and rapport has been established (Kottler, 1999).

Even when an AD disorder is not immediately suspected, it is helpful to ask routine, concrete questions about money and possessions in the initial clinical assessment. It is also useful to inquire about clients' cognitions, behaviors, and affect related to possessions and to follow up with concrete questions about clients' vague allusions to problems with money or possessions. Because clients, like therapists, experience shame and ambivalence about their possession-related behavior, they may initially cloak acquisition problems by talking about their other concerns.

In one case where the client presented with typical "midlife crisis" issues, the therapist extensively discussed with the client the life goals he regretted not reaching and his hopes and plans to begin bettering himself. It was only when the client and therapist stood up to conclude the intake session that the former said, "Oh, by the way, sometimes I have a hard time getting rid of things, and that's probably affecting why I'm having trouble selling the house." The therapist laughed sympathetically, "Sure, a lot of us have that problem." "No, I mean I *really* have trouble letting go, like letting the water out the bathtub. You never know when you might need it, you know?"

The therapist realized that she had missed something big. To avoid similar clinical faux pas, we suggest therapists ask their clients specific questions, such as the following: What are some of your prized possessions; when and how did you acquire them; how do you go about finding things that you might want to buy; how do you feel when you are able to buy something you've wanted for a long time; what do you do with possessions you no longer need; who owes you money; to whom do you owe money?

Honest answers to these questions depend on the initial rapport established, and many clients require a more firmly established therapeutic alliance before disclosing their deepest concerns about acquisition and possessions. Nevertheless, the answers to these questions in the intake and the manner in which the client reacts to these questions may suggest possible problems and areas for future exploration.

After the therapist suspects that AD in one of its forms is operating in the client's life, the second step is to determine the degree to which this is true and how entrenched the problem is in the person's symptomatology and life context. A few additional questions can be used to determine the degree of a client's emotional attachment to his or her possessions (Belk, 1992). These might include the following: do you have strong feelings about [object or acquisition activity]; can something else be substituted for [the object or acquisition activity]; could you sell the object for its fair market value or quit the acquisition activity?

The therapist may want to note what happens when negotiating the fee and requesting payment for the session. A sudden excuse such as "Oh! I forgot my checkbook! Gosh, can I pay you next week?" or a sheepish request for you to hold the check a few days before cashing it is probably more than a coincidence and may offer a good bridge into discussing specifics about a clients' financial debt structure in the next meeting. Long-time therapeutic wisdom indicates that what happens in the session is a reflection of the client's life in the "real world," and the business of paying for sessions is no exception.

It is important for therapists to recognize that the desire to acquire, in and of itself, is not a disorder or evidence of some emotional problem; indeed, the process of shopping and collecting can be satisfying and meaningful without being a compulsion. Likewise, there is an undeniable pleasure in owning objects, for their intrinsic beauty or utilitarian value, or as a reflection of one's identity and accomplishments. The decision about whether AD is a problem must depend on the same criteria that therapists use to assess the mental health impact of any behavior (Kottler, 1999): It diminishes quality of life; it interferes with reaching important goals; it acts as a distraction from close personal relationships or as a substitute for intimacy; it results in other negative consequences, either overt or subtle; it is excessive and out of balance with other life priorities; there is diminished impulse control; and owning or pursuing this object or these objects creates significant suffering.

TREATMENT REGIMEN

After thorough and comprehensive assessment procedures are undertaken to identify issues related to AD, the next step is to plan a treatment program that addresses the multifaceted and multidimensional nature of these problems. Kottler and Stevens (1999) have developed a general treatment plan for most forms of AD disorders. The plan is flexible and can be adapted to deal with the specific features of the AD problem, be it anxiety, compulsion, narcissism, or neurotic greed. The following sections outline the steps that we find helpful in the treatment of AD. After the therapist and client have established a firm collaborative therapeutic relationship, the steps can be followed in any order that suits the individual case.

Establish a Solid Therapeutic Relationship

Regardless of the therapist's theoretical orientation, the treatment of AD begins with developing a strong working alliance. Because issues surrounding AD can be threatening to the client's core identity, it is important to find a therapeutic stance that enhances the comfort level of the client and engages him or her in the treatment process. For example, with highly successful and wealthy clients, the therapist may want to adopt a businesslike, consultant-type relationship because it is a collaborative, credible style familiar to these clients.

> Frank had formed an investment banking company in the mid-1990s, had sold his company before the market nose-dived, and now found himself with more money than he could spend in a lifetime. Reaching 40, he still wanted the one thing that had eluded him—a lasting intimate relationship, leading to marriage and children. In the first session, Frank was quite specific about what he wanted out of therapy: "I know my problem," he asserted in a calm, confident voice. "I have a fear of abandonment, resulting from my mother's going back to work when I was two. So I abandon women before they abandon me. I have to break this pattern. But since I've figured this much out already, I'm thinking we can have this solved in a couple of weeks, right?"
>
> The therapist felt the urge to say something like, "Well, from my experience, this kind of problem may take longer than a few weeks," but she also knew that challenging Frank's need to be in control might drive him from therapy. Instead, she praised Frank for his insightful self-analysis, took out a notebook, and worked out with him a sequential treatment plan, as though they were creating a strategic plan for starting a business. As they went through each step of the therapeutic process, Frank could immediately see, on paper, that treatment might require at least several months, and he was comfortable with the plan. He also appreciated the therapist's willingness to grapple with his deeper issues early in treatment. "It felt like we were rolling up our sleeves and getting down to business."

Understand the Cultural Context of the Behavior

It is important to explore with the client the socialization processes that influence the role of acquisitions in the client's life. Clients begin to hear messages about the value of acquisitions from early childhood, and advertising, peer pressures, family traditions, and cultural–ethnic beliefs reinforce these messages (see chap. 2, this volume). Helping clients understand how these messages impact their ADs can help them to see these desires as learned values that can therefore be unlearned.

> Katherine grew up in Britain, to parents with an aristocratic lineage but, secretly, cash-poor. Her parents devoted their lives to maintaining the façade of wealth and remaining accepted in exclusive society circles.

Katherine internalized the value that the appearance of wealth was critical to self-worth. As an adult, Katherine continually bought haute couture dresses well beyond her financial means. In therapy, she explored her family's long tradition of connecting outward appearance with internal dignity and ultimately recognized that she did not need to uphold this destructive family legacy.

Explore Unfinished Business

Regardless of theoretical orientation, it may be necessary to explore "unfinished business" with the client, including traumas, deprivations, and other childhood wounds. Acquisitions may be a means of self-soothing or a substitution for love and attention not received in earlier life. Muensterberger (1994) suggested that many collectors have suffered emotional or physical trauma in early life; the objects they collect provide a solace for the lingering pain from these experiences or a vehicle to help cope with unfulfilled needs and longings.

Attachment issues are also implicated in AD. Riddy (2000) conducted a qualitative study of 27 British self-reported addictive shoppers. She found that about half reported major trauma during childhood that involved a disruption of the mother–child bond, such as the mother leaving home, suffering from depression, or being hospitalized for extended periods.

Fiona Murray is a self-described shopping addict who eloquently wrote about how a legacy of family emotional deprivations influenced her adult addictive behavior (Murray, 2000). Murray's grandmother died when her mother was born, and "It was inevitable that my mother, without the nurture and connectedness with her mother, was emotionally unavailable to me" (p. 222). As she grew up, Murray's mother repeated the pattern of leaving home for several days at a time, and upon returning, would give her daughter presents:

> My mother seemed to be saying, "I love you. Forgive me." . . . Throughout my adult life I would seek reparation for myself in the form of alcohol or shopping whenever I felt hurt, isolated or abandoned. I also understand why I once felt compelled to buy others presents when I felt that I had displeased or hurt them. I was looking for absolution in the same way that my mother had once sought it from me. . . . I experienced the euphoria of shopping at the early age of eight or nine for it represented one of the few occasions where I was the recipient of some meaningful female attention, even if it was only the sales assistant fussing over me. (p. 223)

Explore the Family System

The notion that the family may inadvertently "enable" the behavior of one of its members in order to maintain system homeostasis is useful in treating the shopping or collecting addict. Riddy (2000) described a hypothetical example of a "feedback loop" wherein a husband and wife support each other's addictive behaviors. An alcoholic husband, rather than facing his own problem, scapegoats his wife. She turns to shopping as an escape from the husband's blame, distancing herself further from the family, which causes the children to misbehave. The husband responds by drinking more and putting more blame on his wife, who, in turn, increases her shopping. An actual example can be illustrated by a case from our clinical work.

> Susan and Roger came for couples counseling in order to break their cycle of fighting. In the session, Susan nastily denigrated Roger's acquisitive behaviors and attacked his "shallow materialism," which she claimed to abhor. Susan was starting a business and feared that Roger's need for "toys" like big-screen TVs and high-end sound systems placed impossible demands on her to succeed. Roger argued that she was making him so miserable that he had to have "the best of everything" in order to feel better about his life. At one point he exclaimed, "You say you hate what I buy, but you sure seem to enjoy watching that TV!" As the therapy progressed, it became clear that Susan was unconsciously supporting Roger's purchasing habits despite her constant attacks. Her barrage of criticisms enabled her to have impressive things without feeling personally responsible for their excessive spending. When the therapist helped Susan to see the part she was playing in the system, she stopped attacking Roger, who, in turn, stopped spending more than they could afford.

Unearth the Cognitive Patterns and Narratives Related to the Behavior

For some clients, using cognitive and narrative therapy interventions can expose underlying dysfunctional beliefs as well as external messages that influence the client's ADs. For example, one woman was told by her parents when she was a little girl that her birth was an unwanted "accident." She developed the core belief, "I am worthless" and interpreted most of the negative experiences in her life as confirmation of this. As an adult, she became an obsessive collector of expensive antiques in a futile struggle to bolster her self-esteem. The therapist helped the client see how buying valuable antiques served to counteract her maladaptive assumption that she had no value as a person.

Find Leverage to Secure a Commitment to Change

Because some AD problems are functionally similar to addictions, techniques used in treating addictive disorders can be borrowed and applied to these problems. Exploring with clients the consequences and functional uses of symptoms can increase their motivation for change. Miller and Rollnick (1991) have described an interactive process that is effective for helping clients with tenacious addictive disorders to explore both their desire for change and their ambivalence about making changes. Specifically, they advocate the use of questions to invite clients to describe the origins and course of problem development and their broader life circumstances. By listening nonjudgmentally and highlighting both the positive and negative aspects of the client's problem, a therapist can elicit self-motivational statements from clients. The therapist can affirm, reinforce, and reflect back to clients their self-statements that function as arguments for change, such as problem recognition, expressions of concern, intentions to change, and expressions of optimism. Follow-up questions directed to clients can help to secure a commitment to change and subsequently to direct the focus to short- and long-term goals. These strategies, used skillfully by the therapist, often immediately increase client motivation to change (Miller & Rollnick, 1991; Rollnick, 1998).

> Suzanne's compulsive shopping habit engaged her emotionally like nothing else in her life did. She was overweight and lonely, and longed for companionship that she could rarely find. Despite daily resolutions to attend exercise class and meet people at community activities, Suzanne found herself in the mall after work, seeking solace by impulsively buying hot fudge sundaes and small trinkets for herself and her home. Although she felt better when doing these things, and when bringing home and unwrapping her new purchases, by the next morning she felt guilty, weak, and determined not to give in to herself again. Suzanne's therapist used questions to highlight the decisional balance that Suzanne weighed out every day, and gently persisted until Suzanne could articulate for herself how her self-indulgent shopping was working against her larger hopes and dreams for herself.

Deal With Guilt and Shame Issues

We have discovered that when clients do alter their acquisitive patterns, residual feelings of shame and guilt often surface. Recent research lends some support to our clinical experiences. In Riddy's (2000) study, all but three of the 27 addictive shoppers interviewed described feelings of self-disgust, guilt, and depression shortly after making a purchase. In Elliott's (2000) qualitative study, using a sample of 50 British addictive shoppers, all the participants reported feelings of guilt and remorse after the shopping experience, including a desire to keep their purchases a secret from others. Additionally, we have found that some clients experience shame and guilt when they become aware of how their behaviors may have adversely affected their intimate partners and families.

Fill the Void That May Be Left

For some clients, the pursuit of material goals can provide a sense of purpose and focus to their lives. Stopping the acquisitive behaviors can remove the sense of direction around which they have organized their daily existence (see chap. 6, this volume.) For others, buying can be a distraction from existential guilt, the painful awareness of not living up to one's potential. Therefore, the therapist may want to find ways to help clients fill the void that will be left when the buying patterns stop; otherwise, clients may resort to previous acquisitive patterns to ward off emerging feelings of internal disorganization and meaninglessness. Ideally, the period when clients begin to face this void can be an opportunity to explore with them issues of personal meaning and values around which a more existentially satisfying life can be constructed. The therapist may also want to use this stage of treatment to explore the possibility of living a voluntarily simple lifestyle, perhaps based on spiritual rather than materialistic values.

> Andres came to therapy because of a depression he attributed to his failure as a novelist. The therapist soon discovered that Andres easily spent 8 hours a day buying and selling Beatles paraphernalia on an Internet auction site. His closets were overflowing with album covers and John Lennon dolls. The therapist assumed that if she could get Andres to stop his collecting addiction, he would immediately channel his energies into his writing career. Shamed by her interpretation of his collecting as a defense against taking responsibility for his writing ambitions, Andres sold off his entire collection within a week. Without the shopping distraction, or some other means of organizing his daily life, Andres sat immobilized at his computer, experiencing in full-force the terror that he lacked the talent to write. Andres's depression worsened until the therapist realized that Andres needed some other sense of purpose while they addressed the underlying meanings of his writer's block. She suggested that Andres spend no more than an hour a day at his computer and that he instead focus the bulk of his time on cleaning out his garage and transforming it into a home-office. With this new structure to his daily life, Andres's mood brightened and he regained the ego strength necessary to examine in therapy his underlying fears.

Explore Fears of Failure and Intimacy

Our experience suggests that the fear of failure and the concern about intimacy frequently underlie self-destructive acquisitive behaviors. The case of Andres is an example of a client who avoided the shame of failure by engaging in nonstop collecting. Indeed, Andres's success at bargaining on e-Bay enabled him to cope with his otherwise intolerable feelings of inadequacy as a professional writer. Another client, married to an emotionally detached computer engineer, bought shoes to assuage her feelings of emptiness in a relationship devoid of genuine intimacy.

When core issues are addressed and resolved, buying or collecting patterns do not necessarily come to a complete halt. Rather, the nature of the acquisitive behavior shifts from being compulsion or impulse driven to being a pleasurable, choice-based activity and a pursuit that no longer impairs important areas of functioning.

Envision a Different Future

A critical treatment step is to explore what the client's life will look like when acquisitive behaviors are changed. The object of such an exercise is to help clients feel empowered enough to feel that they have choices about how they act in the future.

> Anne was a compulsive shopper who was also neglecting to pay off her considerable school loans for college. Her situation had reached the point where she was receiving a weekly threatening letter demanding that she pay her debts or have her wages garnished. She went to work each day wracked by the fear that her employer would inevitably discover her addiction and fire her. Sadly, she responded to her ensuing stress by shopping even more. Anne's therapist suggested they do a guided visualization in which she imagined receiving a letter from the loan agency with a large "0" in the balance column. Anne then saw herself working productively at her job, secure in the knowledge that she would be able to keep all of her earnings. The visualization concluded with Anne walking into her favorite store, perusing an aisle of goods she could afford, and buying a single item with an ensuing feeling of pride.

Structure Ongoing Support

Part of a comprehensive treatment approach is to check to see what forms of affiliation may have been neglected as the client's problems with AD become more acute and what kinds of support systems are in place to help the client maintain the treatment goals of individual therapy. If necessary, the therapist may work on re-connecting the client with family, friends, or other forms of affiliation. As with other addictions, if the client's social networks reinforced his or her self-destructive behaviors, the therapist should help the client separate from these groups and develop more healthy means of support. For some clients, 12-Step programs may be helpful. For others, the demand that they stop all addictive behaviors may be an intolerable pressure in our consumer-oriented, materialistic world. We have found that referring clients to their community's Consumer Credit Counseling Service may help them get their financial lives in order, although this cannot address the underlying disorder.

THERAPEUTIC COUNTERTRANSFERENCE WITH ACQUISITIVE DESIRE

A number of countertransference issues arise when working with AD. Perhaps the most common is envy. As therapists, we may believe that we have somehow transcended ADs and that we adhere to the more enlightened values we would like to teach to our clients. However, most of us are fooling ourselves. We want success, approval, wealth, and comfort as much as most upwardly mobile middle-class Americans.

Consequently, feelings of envy and jealousy are natural, perhaps inevitable, when we work with wealthy clients. We may even find ourselves resenting our wealthy clients, belittling them in our minds as shallow and superficial. By resenting them we may be denying our distaste for the parts of ourselves that wish we could live like our wealthy clients do.

One way we may defend against our feelings of envy is to reinforce our wealthy clients' mistaken assumptions that we are as wealthy as they are. Because our wealthy clients are paying us high fees, they may assume that we have the kind of incomes they do, not realizing that no therapist gets rich from private practice alone. Many therapists can recall incidents when they indulged in a little passive impression management about their wealth. One therapist recalled a session where a wealthy client told her he had seen her driving a BMW, like his. "I did not disabuse him of the notion, telling myself I did not want to impede exploration of his fantasies or the development of a positive transference. But these were rationalizations of the fact that I *wanted* him to think I owned a BMW." Another therapist recalled this story: "A client told of her vacation plans. It just so happened that she and her boyfriend were choosing between two very swanky resorts at the same time my husband and I had just booked reservations at one of those places. I self-disclosed that I had stayed at one of her choices—clearly, to make myself look like I was on her financial and worldly level." Yet another therapist confessed, "I find myself thinking, 'It's a good thing I have an office in a high-rent part of town, so my wealthy clients will think I'm as financially successful as they are.'" She justified her expensive leather couch as a business expense, but admitted that there was something gratifying in being perceived, even mistakenly, as "one of them." By creating impressions but not bringing up "money talk" as part of the therapeutic agenda, therapists may be complicit in creating an unhelpful setting where they pretend to be above mundane financial considerations, even though such considerations may be crucial to the case.

In fact, any conversation about money or possessions can stir up unpleasant feelings for the therapist. If we feel we have not put enough money away for retirement, it stings when a client tells us that she will retire at age 45. If we are fighting with our spouse about how much to spend on a new house or car, we may feel guilty when offering advice to a couple struggling with their own financial issues. If our caseload is dropping, it does not feel very good to listen to clients talk about their success. To the degree that we measure our self-worth according to our financial achievements, working with wealthy or successful clients is bound to stir up feelings of shame and inadequacy. We believe that, just as therapists are trained to think about issues of gender, race, and so on and how their stance on these variables influences their therapy, similar training is necessary to address the therapists' awareness of their own issues concerning money, social class, and materialism.

Personal Values and Nonjudgmental Acceptance

As much as we have been trained to remain nonjudgmental of our clients, holding this stance can be particularly difficult with clients whose ADs seem obviously self-destructive or destructive to others. We may feel the urge to exhort our clients to "stop buying things you cannot afford!" Alternatively, values we hold dear, such as working hard to earn what we get in life or seeing all people as equal, may present us with special challenges when clients are clearly enjoying advantages that they did not work for or when they communicate an air of superiority. One therapist was working with a single woman who was determined to have a child through insemination. She hated the fact that all of her friends were married and having babies and she was not. The therapist, who had strong values about appropriate circumstances for bringing a child into this world, was horrified that the client's reason for having a child—to keep up with her friends—was so superficial. Aware of her strong judgmental reaction, the therapist feared that she would reveal her anger if she explored the issue with the client. Unable to work through this countertransference, the therapist avoided confronting the client about this issue altogether.

When the Therapist Is a Possession

Another common countertransference issue is dealing with the client who treats their therapist as a "possession." We all have had clients who talk about us as "their therapist." One psychologist described his experience this way:

> You know, they [wealthy clients] try hard not to do this, but you sometimes get the feeling that to them, you're really just one of "the help," similar to other service professionals that clean the pool or manage their legal affairs or cater their parties.

Clients who treat us as one more thing they have acquired can provoke a variety of responses. We may feel an initial boost to our self-esteem that later turns to resentment. We may also feel used and exploited. A therapist described her reaction to a client who told her, "I'd like to refer people I know to you, but I want you all for myself." She immediately thought of how much more money she might be making if she changed the client's attitude. She attempted to engage in an objective exploration of the issue, but the results were disastrous. Her irritation with the client came through, and he was deeply wounded, setting back months of effort in building a working alliance.

CONCLUSION

As self-reflective practitioners we are in a unique position to aid our clients with acquisitive disorders because we contend with the same acquisitive pressures they do, and some of us have found healthy ways of coping with them. Treatment of AD can only be effective when we respect the intensity of these pressures on both our clients and ourselves. Thus, it is just as important to design an effective treatment plan for our clients as it is to acknowledge the normalcy and prevalence of our own ADs. When we pull out of our driveways in the morning, we may find ourselves noticing how our house compares with our neighbors. We may experience pangs of longing when we see a luxury car passing us on the highway. When we enter our offices each morning, we may wonder if we'd feel happier with our work if we replaced that well-worn couch with an expensive leather one. Becoming aware of our desires and evaluating the degree to which they impair or improve our lives is the critical first step if we are to help our clients cope with the same pressures. One of the oldest pieces of wisdom in our profession, going all the way back to Freud, is certainly relevant here: Discovering our desires and ultimately accepting them without judgment is the precondition —perhaps, even the source—of our power to heal.

REFERENCES

American Psychiatric Association. (2000). *Diagnostic and statistical manual of mental disorders* (4th ed.; text revision). Washington, DC: Author.

Arnett, J. (2000). Emergent adulthood: A theory of development from the late teens through the twenties. *American Psychologist, 55,* 469–480.

Belk, R. W. (1992). Attachment to possessions. *Human Behavior and Environment: Advances in Theory and Research, 12,* 37–62.

Christenson, G. A., Faber, R. J., de Zwaan, M., & Raymond, N. C. (1994). Compulsive buying: Descriptive characteristics and psychiatric co-morbidity. *Journal of Clinical Psychiatry, 55,* 5–11.

Côté, J. (2000). *Arrested adulthood: The changing nature of maturity and identity.* New York: New York University Press.

Csikszentmihalyi, M. (1999). If we are so rich, why aren't we happy? *American Psychologist, 54,* 821–827.

Csikszentmihalyi, M. (2000). The costs and benefits of consuming. *Journal of Consumer Research, 27,* 267–272.

Elliott, R. (2000). Addictive shopping as a form of family communication. In A. Baker (Ed.), *Serious shopping: Psychotherapy and consumerism* (pp. 154–182). London: Free Association Books.

Erikson, E. (1980). *Identity and the life cycle.* New York: Norton. (Original work published 1956)

Faber, R. J., & O'Guinn, T. C. (1992). A clinical screener for compulsive buying. *Journal of Consumer Research, 19,* 459–469.

Frost, R. O., & Hartl, T. L. (1996). A cognitive–behavioral model of compulsive hoarding. *Behaviour Research and Therapy, 34,* 341–350.

Ginsberg, M., Isaacs, S., Marshall, T. H., & Suttie, I. D. (1935). A symposium on property and possessiveness. *British Journal of Medical Psychology, 15,* 51–83.

Josselson, R. (1994). The theory of identity development and the question of intervention. In S. Archer (Ed.), *Interventions for adolescent identity development* (pp. 12–25). Thousand Oaks, CA: Sage.

Kottler, J. A. (1999). *Exploring and treating acquisitive desire: Living in the material world.* Thousand Oaks, CA: Sage.

Kottler, J. A., & Stevens, H. (1999). Interventions. In J. A. Kottler (Ed.), *Exploring and treating acquisitive desire: Living in the material world* (pp. 103–111). Thousand Oaks, CA: Sage.

Maxmen, J. S., & Ward, N. G. (1995). *Essential psychopathology and its treatment* (2nd ed.). New York: Norton.

McElroy, S. L., Hudson, J. L., Harrison, G. P., Keck, P. E., Jr., & Aizley, H. G. (1992). The *DSM–III–R* impulse-control disorders not elsewhere classified: Clinical characteristics and relationship to other psychiatric disorders. *American Journal of Psychiatry, 149,* 318–327.

Miller, W. R., & Rollnick, S. (1991). *Motivational interviewing: Preparing people to change addictive behavior.* New York: Guilford Press.

Muensterberger, W. (1994). *Collecting: An unruly passion.* San Diego, CA: Harcourt Brace & Company.

Murray, F. (2000). Shame on credit. In A. Baker (Ed.), *Serious shopping: Psychotherapy and consumerism* (pp. 221–241). London: Free Association Books.

O'Guinn, T. C., & Faber, R. J. (1989). Compulsive buying: A phenomenological exploration. *Journal of Consumer Research, 16,* 147–157.

Riddy, P. (2000). Addictive shopping as a form of family communication. In A. Baker (Ed.), *Serious shopping: Psychotherapy and consumerism* (pp. 154–182). London: Free Association Books.

Rodewalt, F., & Morf, C. C. (1998). On self-aggrandizement and anger: A temporal analysis of narcissism and affective reactions to success and failure. *Journal of Personality and Social Psychology, 74,* 672–685.

Rollnick, S. (1998). Readiness, importance, and confidence: Critical conditions of change in treatment. In W. R. Miller & N. Heather (Eds.), *Treating addictive behaviors* (2nd ed., pp. 49–60). New York: Plenum.

Tian, K. T., & McKenzie, K. (2001). The long-term predictive validity of the consumers' Need for Uniqueness Scale. *Journal of Consumer Psychology, 10,* 171–193.

Volberg, A., & Steadman, H. J. (1988). Refining prevalence estimates of pathological gambling. *American Journal of Psychiatry, 148,* 652–657.

10

SELF-CONTROL AND COMPULSIVE BUYING

RONALD J. FABER

In May 2001, a 47-year-old Chicago woman who embezzled nearly $250,000 from her former employer appeared in U.S. District Court for sentencing. Her defense attorney had argued that she should not go to jail because her actions were beyond her control. He claimed that the embezzling was the direct result of her need to continue engaging in buying binges and that these were a form of self-medication in response to depression. In a ruling that surprised many, Judge Matthew Kennelly accepted this argument and declined to sentence her to jail (O'Conner, 2001; Moore, 2001). For the first time, a legal authority had recognized compulsive buying as a legitimate illness and as a legal defense.

This ruling set off a great deal of debate in the media. Many felt outrage that the defendant "got off." Yet, although the judge's sentence did not involve jail time, it did include repaying the money, a $30,000 fine, 6 months of weekend home confinement, 6 weeks in a work release center, and 5 years probation (Moore, 2001). More important, he required the woman to continue the psychiatric counseling she was receiving and forbade her to acquire any new credit cards. In arriving at this sentence, Judge Kennelly chose to view compulsive buying as an illness, rather than to assume that it was a willful act that required punishment. This ruling also highlights the importance of understanding the role self-control plays in this disorder.

Certainly not all people (or even most) who overspend are true compulsive buyers. However, for some people this is a legitimate problem that has much in common with other problematic behaviors such as alcoholism, drug addiction, kleptomania, and eating disorders. It is, therefore, important that we understand this behavior and its etiology and begin to effectively treat those who suffer from it.

The purpose of this chapter is to demonstrate the importance of self-control in understanding compulsive buying. I begin with a discussion of what compulsive buying is and a brief historic overview of research in this area. Although there are several components to defining compulsive buying, two of the central elements are that individuals experience an inability to control this behavior and that it ultimately leads to negative consequences. Partly for these reasons, I argue that compulsive buying should be classified as an impulse control disorder in future editions of the American Psychiatric Association's *Diagnostic and Statistical Manual of Mental Disorders*. To explain why people engage in behaviors such as compulsive buying that lead to harmful consequences, I discuss escape theory (Baumeister, 1991). Key elements of this theory not only match some of the characteristics identified in research on compulsive buying, but also provide an explanation for why compulsive buyers are unable to control their behavior. To enrich readers' understanding of compulsive buying and to help demonstrate how compulsive buying relates to the specific concepts being discussed, I use quotes from compulsive buyers who my colleagues and I have interviewed over the years (see Faber, 2000a, 2000b; Faber & O'Guinn, 1988; O'Guinn & Faber, 1989).

DEFINING THE PROBLEM

Several definitions of compulsive buying have been proposed (see Exhibit 10.1). These definitions have some things in common as well as a couple of differences. One key difference among these definitions is that some researchers see the disorder as involving both shopping and buying (Edwards, 1992; Goldsmith & McElroy, 2000), whereas others see it as involving only purchasing (Black, 2000; O'Guinn & Faber, 1989). Either characterization may be possible, but the disorder seems to be more closely tied to the act of purchasing (Faber, 2000b).

More important than the differences are the commonalities appearing in the definitions in Exhibit 10.1: The behavior occurs repetitively or frequently, it is excessive, and it has negative consequences. Some compulsive buyers report shopping almost every day and feeling anxious on days they do not go shopping (O'Guinn & Faber, 1989). Others are more episodic. For

EXHIBIT 10.1
Selected Definitions of Compulsive Buying

A. Goldsmith and McElroy (2000) define *compulsive buying* as follows:
1. Maladaptive preoccupation with buying or shopping, or maladaptive buying or shopping impulses or behavior, as indicated by at least one of the following:
    (a) Frequent preoccupation with buying or impulse to buy that is/are experienced as irresistible, intrusive, and/or senseless.
    (b) Frequent buying of more than can be afforded, frequent buying of items that are not needed or shopping for longer periods of time than intended.
2. The buying preoccupations, impulses or behaviors cause marked distress, are time consuming, significantly interfere with social or occupational functioning, or result in financial problems (e.g., indebtedness or bankruptcy).
3. The excessive buying or shopping behavior does not occur exclusively during periods of hypomania or mania. (p. 218)

B. O'Guinn and Faber (1989) define it as follows:

chronic, repetitive purchasing that occurs as a response to negative events or feelings. The alleviation of these negative feelings is the primary motivation for engaging in the behavior. Buying should provide the individual with short-term positive rewards, but result in long-term negative consequences. (p. 149)

C. Black (2000) refers to it as

a behavioral syndrome characterized by excessive and inappropriate impairment in one or more life domains. (p. 191)

D. Edwards (1992) called it
a chronic, abnormal form of shopping and spending characterized in the extreme by an overpowering, uncontrollable, and repetitive urge to buy. (p. 54)

---

these individuals, buying becomes a repetitive, almost automatic, response to a specific set of feelings or circumstances. On average, it appears that compulsive buyers report experiencing this urge two to three times per week, although reports of the frequency of binge buying range from once a month to several times a day (Christenson et al., 1994; Schlosser, Black, Repertinger, & Freet, 1994).

Evidence of this disorder can be seen in the number of shopping trips, the time spent shopping or buying, the total amount spent on purchases, and the amount of debt amassed. Some compulsive buyers report purchasing multiple quantities of an item, such as eight T-shirts or three raincoats at one time (Christenson et al., 1994; O'Guinn & Faber, 1989). Although compulsive buying has been found to be unrelated to a person's actual level of income (Faber, O'Guinn, & Krych, 1987; Scherhorn, Reisch, & Raab, 1990), it ultimately leads people to incur large debts. Studies have found that, on average, almost 50% of compulsive buyers' take-home pay goes toward the payment of nonmortgage related debt, compared with a little over 20% for other consumers (Christenson et al., 1994; O'Guinn & Faber, 1989).

Other negative consequences can range from dissatisfaction with the amount of time spent buying to major family disputes and divorce; stealing, embezzling, and writing bad checks; and even suicide attempts (Christenson et al., 1994; Faber et al., 1987; O'Guinn & Faber, 1989). It is typically not until these serious consequences emerge that compulsive buyers actually admit that they have a problem.

Several researchers have found that compulsive buyers report experiencing strong and uncontrollable urges to buy (Christenson et al., 1994; DeSarbo & Edwards, 1996; O'Guinn & Faber, 1989). Many compulsive buyers experience this as a mounting tension that can only be relieved through purchasing (Christenson et al., 1994; McElroy, Keck, Pope, Smith, & Strakowski, 1994). In extreme forms, some compulsive buyers have reported experiencing dissociative states in which they engage in behaviors without being aware of it or they experience their actions as if watching someone else (Boundy, 2000; Christenson et al., 1994).

Part of the reason that compulsive buying is not yet taken as seriously as other disorders may be that it is not currently included in the *DSM–IV–TR* (American Psychiatric Association, 2000). That there is still much debate over how to best categorize compulsive buying may be harming its chances for inclusion. Some researchers believe that compulsive buying should be classified as a form of an obsessive–compulsive disorder (OCD), whereas others feel it should be categorized as an impulse-control disorder (Christenson et al., 1994; Faber 2000a) or an affective-spectrum disorder (McElroy et al., 1994). Goldsmith and McElroy (2000) provided a good discussion of these arguments and the differences between the various classifications.

Another, and perhaps more important, reason for the absence of compulsive buying as a category in *DSM–IV–TR* may be that most of the literature about this disorder is relatively recent. The bulk of published work on compulsive buying has appeared only in the last 15 years. However, earlier accounts of compulsive buying do exist in the psychiatric literature.

A Historical Account of Compulsive Buying

Many people assume that compulsive buying is a recent phenomenon. In fact, this problem existed and was recognized in psychiatric textbooks almost a century ago. Emil Kraepelin (1915) first discussed buying mania (*oniomania*) in his listing of psychiatric impulse disorders. He described this as impulsively driven buying leading to a senseless amount of debt. He also noted that this problem occurred primarily among women.

Bleuler (1924) elaborated on this disorder, stressing that people suffering from it were unable to control their actions or even to recognize the senseless nature of their purchasing. He stated "that not withstanding a good school intelligence, the patients are absolutely incapable to think differently [sic], and to conceive the senseless consequences of their act, and the possibilities of not doing it" (Bleuler, 1924, p. 540). Bleuler and Kraepelin listed this condition as one of a number of reactive impulse disorders or monomanias. Also included in this category were pyromania, kleptomania, and extreme (morbid) collecting.

Although this disorder has been around for some time, there was hardly any mention of it in either the popular press or the academic literature until the mid-1980s. At that time, spurred in part by the formation of some self-help groups by people experiencing the problem, accounts occasionally began to appear in magazines and newspapers (Holmstrom, 1985; Mundis, 1986). A few articles also began to appear in the academic literature in several disciplines including psychotherapy (Krueger, 1988), addiction (Glatt & Cook, 1987), and consumer behavior (Faber et al., 1987; O'Guinn & Faber, 1989).

The growing amount of attention given to compulsive buying during the past 15 years has led many people to perceive it as a modern disorder rooted in recent cultural changes. Some point to the rise of credit cards as a cause of this disorder (Boundy, 2000). Others have related it to the rise in consumer culture (Cushman, 1990; Elliott, 1994). Still others maintain that the breakup of the family structure and the loss of a sense of community in modern life have reduced people's ability to establish a clear identity. As a result, people have begun to use consumption as an alternative way to express and create their identity (Langman, 1992; Shields, 1992).

Unfortunately, however, no epidemiological surveys exist to document the prevalence of compulsive buying. Thus, it is unclear whether this problem has been truly growing in recent years or whether it has just received more media and professional attention. This may well be analogous to the situation with anorexia. Although many experts have claimed anorexia and eating disorders are becoming much more common, the only well-controlled study that actually reanalyzed medical records in a community over time suggests that this may not be true (Lucas, Beard, O'Fallon, & Kurland, 1988). Greater awareness of a problem may lead to more diagnoses because of this awareness, but it does not necessarily indicate that the problem is growing.

Compulsive Buying as an Impulse-Control Disorder

Kraepelin (1915) and Bleuler (1924) viewed compulsive buying as an impulse-control disorder. This can be seen both by their descriptions of it and by the fact that they listed it with other disorders such as pyromania and kleptomania that are now classified as impulse-control disorders. The DSM–IV states that the essential feature of impulse-control disorder is "the failure to resist an impulse, drive, or temptation to perform an act that is harmful to the person or to others" (American Psychiatric Association, 1994, p. 663).

Most people with these disorders feel a growing tension or arousal prior to committing the act. The behavior provides an immediate, short-term feeling of gratification or pleasure, but there is often a great deal of self-reproach or guilt following the behavior.

Impulse control is a key factor in a number of listed disorders, including substance abuse and mood disorders. The *DSM–IV* also contains a classification for other impulse problems under the heading of Impulse-Control Disorders Not Elsewhere Classified. In this category six problem behaviors are listed, including Kleptomania, Pathological Gambling, and Impulse-Control Disorder Not Otherwise Specified (NOS; a catchall category for other impulse-related disorders). It seems highly likely that compulsive buying should be listed here as well. However, the most recent edition of the *DSM–IV–TR* (American Psychiatric Association, 2000) does not mention it anywhere.

It is interesting that there appears to be a wide gender gap in the incidence of the specific Impulse-Control Disorders NOS. For example, intermittent explosive disorder, pyromania, and pathological gambling are much more common in males than females, whereas kleptomania and trichotillomania are far more common in women (American Psychiatric Association, 1994). The gender differences are generally around two thirds versus one third. Compulsive buying is also found to have a gender imbalance. Studies have found that as many as 85% to 90% of all compulsive buyers are women (Elliott, 1994; Faber, 2000a). A number of explanations may be offered for these gender differences, but the most important is likely to be a socialization difference. Historically, in most Western cultures, engaging in activities such as gambling or aggression have been more socially acceptable for men. Women, on the other hand, are more likely than men to do the buying and are taught at a young age that this is an enjoyable activity. Both genders are more likely to develop problems in areas in which they have more frequent experiences and receive greater social rewards.

Researchers investigating several different forms of impulse-related disorders have found that people with one disorder often have either a personal or a family history of other related disorders (Mitchell, 1990). For example, an overlap has been found between people suffering from bulimia and kleptomania (Norton, Crisp, & Bhat, 1985) and between bulimia, alcoholism, and drug abuse (Williamson, 1990). Relationships have also frequently been found between compulsive buying and many of these more defined forms of impulse-control disorders, including alcoholism and substance abuse (Glatt & Cook, 1987; Schlosser et al., 1994); bulimia (Faber, Christenson, de Zwaan, & Mitchell, 1995; Krueger, 1988); mood and affect disorders (Christenson et al., 1994; McElroy et al., 1994); and the Impulse-Control Disorders NOS (Christenson et al., 1994; Schlosser et al., 1994).

Descriptions and accounts of compulsive buying also seem to match all of the characteristics of impulse-control disorders discussed in the *DSM–IV*. Compulsive buyers report that they experience an uncontrollable or irresistible urge to buy (Christenson et al., 1994; Faber et al., 1987; Schlosser et al., 1994). These irresistible urges are associated with approximately half of all purchasing experiences for compulsive buyers (Christenson et al., 1994). Compulsive buyers experience these urges for an average of a little over 1 hour per day. Most buyers state that they try to resist but that their attempts are generally unsuccessful (Christenson et al., 1994).

Ultimately, excessive buying leads to harmful consequences for the individual and perhaps others. These include the inability to pay debts, financial or legal problems, and marital family or social difficulties such as serious fights with one's spouse or divorce (Christenson et al., 1994; O'Guinn & Faber, 1989). The inability to control this behavior even in the face of serious consequences could be seen in the comments of two compulsive buyers cited by O'Guinn and Faber (1989, p. 155):

> Buyer A: I didn't have one person in the world I could talk to. I don't drink. I don't smoke. I don't do dope. But I can't stop. I can't control it. I said I can't go on like this. . . . My husband hates me. My kids hate me. I've destroyed everything. I was ashamed and I just wanted to die.

> Buyer B: I would always have to borrow between paychecks. I could not make it between paychecks. Payday comes and I'd pay all my bills, but then I'd piss the rest away, and I'd need to borrow money to eat, and I would cry and cry and cry. And everyone would say, "Well just make a budget." Get serious. That's like telling an alcoholic not to go to the liquor store. It's not that simple.

Taken as a whole, these findings seem to argue persuasively for the inclusion of compulsive buying in the *DSM* as another form of impulse-control disorder.

MOTIVATIONS BEHIND COMPULSIVE BUYING

Although compulsive buyers experience their problem as uncontrollable, many people assume that these people simply lack willpower. This disparity may arise from the mistaken belief that impulsive and compulsive buying are the same things. Impulse buying has been characterized as a contest between desire and willpower (Hoch & Loewenstein, 1991). In situations in which desire is greater than willpower, people make purchases.

Some researchers writing about compulsive buying share this viewpoint. For example, Nataraajan and Goff (1991) suggested that all buyer behaviors can be categorized by two key factors: buying motive and control over buying. They define *buying motive* as the degree of desire or urge to buy. Placing people along a continuum for each factor and then dichotomizing and crossing these factors yields a fourfold typology. *Compulsive buyers* are those people classified as being low in control and high on the buying motive.

However, an important distinction exists between the concepts of compulsive buying and impulse buying. *Impulse buying* generally refers to a reaction to external stimuli that is experienced as an immediate desire for a specific item. In contrast, research examining compulsive buying has found that a desire for the items purchased is often absent. If compulsive buyers have a desire for anything, it is the act of buying (and its accompanying gratifications), not a desire to own specific goods. Several studies report that compulsive buyers often speak of hiding their purchases and not using or even looking at them after they were bought (Faber et al., 1987; O'Guinn & Faber, 1989; Scherhorn et al., 1990).

More direct examinations of the desire for goods have compared compulsive buyers with more general samples using Belk's (1985) Materialism Scale (Edwards, 1992; O'Guinn & Faber, 1989; Scherhorn et al., 1990). These studies have found that there was no difference between the two groups in their level of possessiveness. Differences were more likely to occur instead on the interpersonal dimensions of materialism such as envy and nongenerosity. When a related measure assessing object attachment (i.e., how much desire for an object was the motivation for purchasing) was used, general consumers were actually found to score higher than compulsive buyers (O'Guinn & Faber, 1989).

The lack of special attachment to the specific item purchased can also be seen in interviews with compulsive buyers. A male compulsive buyer, when asked about this issue, stated, "I really think it's the spending. It's not that I want it, because sometimes, I'll just buy it and I'll think, 'Ugh, another sweatshirt.'" The fact that buying is done without much conscious thought may also help to explain why the item is not important to compulsive buyers. This was apparent from the comments of another informant who said, "I couldn't tell you what I bought or where I bought it. It was like I was on automatic."

What motivates compulsive buying if it is not the items purchased? Researchers have proposed that buying may serve a number of different functions for compulsive buyers (Faber, 2000b). Chief among these appears to be that buying provides a mood regulation function (Faber & Christenson, 1996).

A comparison of compulsive buyers with a matched control sample asked people to indicate how often they experienced a number of different mood states both before and during buying episodes (Faber & Christenson, 1996). The compulsive buyers indicated that they experienced almost all of the mood states more often than the comparison group. This was true for moods felt both prior to and during shopping. However, the biggest differences were that compulsive buyers felt negative mood states more often than the comparison group prior to shopping and positive mood states more often while shopping. Respondents were also asked whether buying changed their mood. Only about one fourth of the comparison sample stated that purchasing changed their mood. However, almost all of the compulsive buyers (95.8%) indicated that buying did change their mood. Furthermore, among those who indicated their mood state changed as a result of buying, compulsive buyers were more likely than the comparison sample to say that this change was in a positive direction.

Although the apparent importance of mood manipulation has been noted in the compulsive buying literature, it does not clearly indicate why this should be an important factor in the development of this disorder. However, recent theory and research on eating disorders have pointed to some interesting notions of why these behaviors occur and how control and disinhibition play a role in them (Heatherton & Baumeister, 1991; Joiner, Heatherton, Rudd, & Schmidt, 1997). Work on eating disorders may have particularly important implications for understanding compulsive buying. Previous research has shown a direct link between these two problem behaviors, such that people with one disorder are more likely also to have symptoms or diagnoses of the other (Barth, 2000; Faber et al., 1995; McElroy et al., 1994).

ESCAPE THEORY AND COMPULSIVE BUYING

A key to understanding compulsive buying is the recognition that the behavior, by definition, is self-destructive. Numerous studies have discussed the negative consequences of overspending. Why then, would someone engage in such self-destructive actions?

One review of the literature on self-defeating behaviors has suggested that people are not prone to harming themselves (Baumeister & Scher, 1988). Instead, such actions are viewed as resulting either from poor strategies that do not work as intended or from a conscious choice to take some risk to avoid more harmful losses. This latter hypothesis has led to the development of escape theory as an explanation for why some people engage in self-destructive behaviors (Baumeister, 1991).

Escape theory proposes that self-awareness can be very painful for some people (Baumeister, 1991; Duval & Wicklund, 1972). To avoid the occurrence of negative self-awareness, people attempt to narrow their attention to a single element in their environment. By focusing on just the immediate present and the sights and sounds within it, people are able to block out more painful thoughts about themselves. Such cognitive narrowing prevents consideration of long-term implications of an action, as well as of cause and effect thinking.

Researchers have pointed to escape theory to explain why people may become bulimic (Heatherton & Baumeister, 1991; Heatherton & Vohs, 1998). They suggest that binge eating serves as an activity that blocks out more painful thoughts about the self. While engaging in the activity of binge eating, cognitive narrowing prevents consideration of its long-term implications.

Escape theory maintains that the need to avoid self-awareness often starts with having exceptionally high standards or expectations of oneself

(Duval & Wicklund, 1972). As a result, the individual is bound, at least occasionally, not to meet these extreme expectations. This creates feelings of failure, which ultimately result in lower self-esteem, as well as anxiety and depression (Heatherton & Baumeister, 1991; Heatherton & Vohs, 1998; Higgins, 1987). These feelings may be extremely painful. To escape them and to avoid self-awareness, the person focuses on an immediate, concrete, low-level task. This cognitive narrowing creates disinhibition and prevents consideration of the longer term consequences of the action (Heatherton & Baumeister, 1991; Heatherton & Vohs, 1998). Another consequence of cognitive narrowing is the failure to recognize the implausibility of beliefs, thus allowing noncritical, irrational thoughts to emerge that produce magical or fanciful thinking (Heatherton & Baumeister, 1991). Evidence for the adverse self-awareness and cognitive narrowing predicted by escape theory can be seen in studies of compulsive buyers.

Self-Awareness in Compulsive Buyers

The notion that compulsive buyers hold high standards is apparent in their tendency to be perfectionists (DeSarbo & Edwards, 1996; Faber, 2000a; O'Guinn & Faber, 1989). They often report that they tried hard to please their parents during childhood but generally felt as if they failed (Faber & O'Guinn, 1988). Sometimes this need for perfectionism appears to be an expectation that had been placed on them by their parents. For example, one woman we interviewed stated, "I was trying to show my parents, 'Yes, you do have to worry about me. I am not perfect.'" More often, however, the need to be perfect seems to have been internalized by the compulsive buyer, as indicated in the story of another informant:

> Because you are the oldest you're supposed to be the good little person. I was always trying to win their [parents] approval but couldn't. You know you could have stood on your head and turned blue and it wouldn't matter. I got straight As and all kinds of honors and it never mattered.

Anger at the fact that they tried to be perfect while the same was not expected of others is also a common theme among compulsive buyers. One woman told of her parents giving her sister clothes just so she would stay in school, whereas she herself got nothing for being a top student. Another compulsive buyer stated:

> My sister has never grown up. She's 36 years old and my father is still supporting her. They live very close by. They babysit her children all the time. They never did that for me. They give her things. They never did that for me. So my sister was given everything. Both of them [sisters] were given help and my brother too. And I was given nothing.

The inability to please their parents and the failure to receive recognition for their hard effort leads many compulsive buyers to develop very low self-esteem. Low self-esteem among compulsive buyers has been reported in numerous studies (Elliott, 1994; O'Guinn & Faber, 1989; Scherhorn et al., 1990). These studies have typically found significantly lower self-esteem scores among the compulsive buyers than for consumers in general. The degree to which compulsive buyers suffer from poor self-esteem can also be seen in many of the interviews my colleagues and I have conducted. For example, a 30-year-old male stated, "I always refer to myself as being very shallow and superficial. I don't feel there's much more behind me than what you see."

Low self-esteem is particularly apparent when compulsive buyers compare themselves with their siblings. For example, one informant stated, "I had acne, braces and glasses and she [sister] was gorgeous." Two others stated:

> Buyer C: Right now my brothers are both millionaires. My father's a millionaire. I was not poor, but I was not very rich.

> Buyer D: I have a brother who is now a dentist, who is everything Mother and Dad ever wanted without question. He was bright and he was very engaging and he is very well to do and all of that. And then there is [informant's name] and my mother did my schoolwork ever since I was in fifth grade. She did all of my schoolwork, even my college papers. It's not much to be proud of.

It seems clear from the quotes above that compulsive buyers can be characterized as having high levels of adverse self-awareness. Ultimately, such awareness is likely to lead to depression and anxiety (Higgins, 1987). Research has shown that compulsive buyers have higher than average levels of depression (McElroy et al., 1994; Schlosser et al., 1994) and anxiety (Christenson et al., 1994; Scherhorn et al., 1990). Compulsive buyers also score significantly higher than matched control participants on a measure of stress reaction that assesses the frequency and intensity of negative emotional states under everyday life conditions (Faber, Peterson, & Christenson, 1994). Not only do compulsive buyers experience these negative feelings more often, but the depth of their feelings may also be more extreme. Studies report that between 25% and 50% of compulsive buyers have a clinical history of major depressive disorder (Christenson et al., 1994; McElroy et al., 1994; Schlosser et al., 1994). This may account for the success that has been reported in treating compulsive buying with antidepressant drugs such as fluvoxamine (Goldsmith & McElroy, 2000).

Negative Self-Feelings in Compulsive Buyers

Escape theory predicts that to avoid unpleasant feelings brought about by negative self-awareness, people engage in actions that produce cognitive narrowing. Compulsive buying appears to be one such activity. On the basis of this theory, we would expect that disinhibition to buying would be greatest immediately following experiences of negative self-awareness. Compulsive buyers often report such a pattern.

One study asked compulsive buyers to complete the following sentence fragment, "When I don't feel good about myself, I am likely to . . . " (Faber et al., 1987). Using the same sentence fragment with a noncompulsive buying sample, Belk (1985) reported the most common responses to be "act depressed," "try to feel better," and "withdraw from others." He made no mention of any responses related to buying or shopping. Among compulsive buyers, however, "spend money/shop" was tied with "sleep/withdraw" as the most commonly mentioned responses. Thus, it would seem that for compulsive buyers, avoidance behaviors in general and binge buying more specifically become primary responses to negative feelings.

An even stronger indication of the degree to which buying may represent a means of coping with negative feelings comes from another sentence completion fragment used in both studies. This item asked people to complete the sentence, "I am most likely to buy myself something when . . . ". Belk (1985) reported that about 20% of his respondents mentioned some type of emotion (either negative or positive). Among compulsive buyers, however, almost three quarters finished the sentence by including some mention of a negative emotion such as "I'm depressed," or "I feel bad about myself" (Faber et al., 1987).

Other researchers have also found that compulsive buying may be a reaction to negative mood states (Christenson et al., 1994; O'Guinn & Faber, 1989; Scherhorn et al., 1990). Elliott (1994) developed a mood repair scale to determine the degree to which shopping alleviated depressive mood states. He found that this measure was highly correlated with compulsive buying.

A different approach to examining what triggers compulsive buying episodes was used by Faber, Ristvedt, Mackenzie, and Christenson (1996). They asked compulsive buyers to indicate from a list of over 400 items which situations were associated with a worsening of their compulsive buying problems. The specific items on the list had been suggested as possible cues that might influence the behaviors of either compulsive buyers or people with other types of impulse-control disorders. Twenty-three items were selected by at least one third of the sample. It is interesting that items like advertising were not selected. Instead, two primary factors emerged. The first represented shopping-related stimuli (e.g., malls, stores, having money, credit cards). The second factor is best characterized as negative emotions. Included here was feeling fat, overweight, bored, stressed, depressed, angry, hurt, or irritable. Thus, it seems that negative emotional states serve as a trigger for many compulsive buying episodes.

Whereas negative mood states often precede buying for compulsive buyers, such individuals frequently describe the actual act of buying in extremely positive terms. Compulsive buyers use terms like *intoxicated* and *powerful* to describe their buying experience (Elliott, 1994; Faber et al., 1987). These extreme emotional states may represent a form of cognitive narrowing in which one is so preoccupied with the emotional feeling that cognitive considerations of future problems are completely removed from consideration. This may explain why some of these informants have stated that the only time they escape from negative feelings is when they are shopping (Elliott, 1994; Friese & Koenig, 1993).

Cognitive Narrowing in Compulsive Buyers

The intense level of cognitive narrowing that can accompany compulsive buying episodes is reflected in the fact that many compulsive buyers do not want to be interrupted or distracted while engaging in this behavior. For this reason, some people report that they view salespeople as an unwanted intrusion in their shopping. Most prefer to go shopping by themselves rather than with others (Elliott, 1994; Schlosser et al., 1994). Companion shoppers are seen as a distraction and a drag on the level of intensity and arousal buyers can achieve (Prus, 1993). Having others along may prevent compulsive buyers from completely losing themselves in the experience and from blocking out their aversive thoughts. The desire to block out other thoughts may lead some compulsive buyers to purchase things on the Internet or through on-line auction sites such as e-Bay. Research examining Internet use has reported some people experience "flow states" while on-line, enabling them to achieve extreme concentration and block out all competing distractions and thoughts (Hoffman & Novak, 1996).

The extreme level of cognitive narrowing that can be achieved through buying is reflected in the adjectives used by compulsive buyers to describe their purchasing experiences. These include terms such as *feeling high*, *getting a rush*, *being alive*, and *elated* (Faber & Christenson, 1996; Faber et al., 1987; Scherhorn et al., 1990). This is perhaps best captured in a quote from an informant describing a specific buying episode she recalled:

> It was almost like my heart was palpitating, I couldn't wait to get in to see what was there. It was such a sensation. In the store, the lights, the people; they were playing Christmas music. I was hyperventilating and my hands were starting to sweat, and all of a sudden I was touching sweaters and the whole of it was just beckoning to me.

The tendency to become immersed in such self-involving experiences has been referred to as *absorption*. Compulsive buyers have been found to score higher on a measure of absorption than a matched control group (Faber et al., 1994). Compulsive buyers frequently mention how much they notice stimuli such as colors, textures, sounds, and smells while shopping (Schlosser et al., 1994). During such experiences, thoughts of negative self-awareness are likely to be pushed aside and any inhibitions or self-control that would emanate from this self-awareness are equally likely to be absent.

Compulsive Buying and Irrational Beliefs

According to escape theory, cognitive narrowing is also likely to make people more predisposed to irrational or magical thinking. Among bulimic individuals, this is seen in fantasies of how changing one's body will help to solve all of one's problems (Polivy & Herman, 1983). Similar fantasies are common among compulsive buyers. Many report that during buying episodes they imagine themselves as being more powerful or admired. For some people this feeling comes from the ability to charge purchases on a credit card. For example, one compulsive buyer stated, "I got this great high. It was like you couldn't have given me more of a rush just for the power of having that card." For others, fantasies and irrational thoughts that accompany buying emerge from their self-perceptions of being more fashionable, more admired or being part of an exclusive and desirable group (Krueger, 2000; Scherhorn et al., 1990). In many cases buying seems to provide a feeling of grandiosity. Some research has found that compulsive buyers are more prone to fantasizing than other consumers (Elliott, 1994; O'Guinn & Faber, 1989).

This ability to fantasize and to engage in magical thinking may allow compulsive buyers to avoid the reality of not being able to afford their purchases. Two informants described typical thought processes that they went through while buying. One reported: "I'm thinking, 'Gee, wouldn't it be nice to really be able to do this, to really be able to afford this,' knowing all along full well I couldn't possibly." The other said:

> The attention I got in there was incredible. She waited on me very nicely, making sure it would fit and if it didn't they would do this and that; and I guess I enjoyed being on the other end of that. I had no idea how I was going to pay for it. I never do.

The disinhibition and irrational beliefs that occur when people engage in cognitive narrowing reduce or eliminate their ability to control their actions. This is why it is reasonable to consider this problem a psychiatric one rather than one that should be punished through the legal system.

CONCLUSION: AREAS FOR NEEDED RESEARCH

The role of control, or the inability to exert control, seems to be a central element in compulsive buying. It is what distinguishes compulsive buyers from others who enjoy buying or shopping. The inability to control the behavior is not due to a lack of willpower but rather is more in line with disinhibition that occurs as a result of cognitive narrowing. A greater understanding of this process is necessary for understanding and treating compulsive buying.

Escape theory holds much promise for explaining some of the key characteristics of compulsive buyers. The concept of cognitive narrowing may help to account for the high level of absorption compulsive buyers report and the intensity of their buying experience. Cognitive narrowing also has been linked to the production of irrational thoughts that may disinhibit rational considerations and lead one to view one's self differently. This may help to explain why compulsive buyers have a higher propensity to fantasize. Finally, escape theory suggests that certain kinds of behavior are used to avoid aversive self-awareness. This explains why compulsive-buying episodes might be triggered by feelings of negative self-worth.

Our understanding of escape theory may also benefit from borrowing ideas from research in compulsive buying. Escape theory is rooted in a specific psychological orientation. However, previous work on compulsive buying and other disorders suggests that they are best explained by a biopsychosocial model (Donovan, 1988, Faber, 2000a). This model implies that problem behaviors are a result of multiple factors, including biological, sociological, and psychological precursors. Biological factors may explain why some people use escape whereas others adopt alternative coping strategies. In addition, changes in brain chemistry brought on through escape behaviors and cognitive narrowing may help to explain why short-term positive mood states occur. Sociological factors may also be helpful in explaining why people use different behaviors to escape. Expanding escape theory to include biological (e.g., neurochemical and genetic) and sociological (e.g., childhood socialization and cultural) elements may be a productive area for future research.

Recent research in escape theory also suggests that multiple variables work in combination to create various disorders (Joiner et al., 1997; Vohs, Bardone, Joiner, Abramson, & Heatherton, 1999). For example, Vohs et al. found that bulimic symptoms may result from a specific three-way interaction between perfectionism, body dissatisfaction, and self-esteem. The combination of high perfectionism, low self-esteem, and high body dissatisfaction sets up the aversive self-awareness that can trigger a need for escape and ultimately predicts bulimic symptoms (Vohs et al., 1999). Future work with compulsive buyers that examines similar complex interrelationships appears promising.

A final critical area for future work with compulsive buying involves the development of sufficient documentation so that this disorder may be officially included in the DSM. Many informants have reported the inability to find help for this disorder even among therapists. As one informant noted:

> I mean if you tell me I have cancer; okay, what do we do about it? If you've got a name for it there is something you can do with it. But when you're just running crazy by this thing that's driving you to do these things but you don't know why, you really can't stop. And that's bad.

A *DSM* classification may help therapists recognize, label, and treat this disorder (see also chap. 9, this volume). This also increases the chances that insurance companies will pay for treatment and improves the likelihood that people will seek out and find relief. In other words, *DSM* recognition is an essential step for moving compulsive buying from the realm of jokes and derision into the light of understanding, compassion, and treatment.

REFERENCES

American Psychiatric Association. (1994). *Diagnostic and statistical manual of mental disorders* (4th ed.). Washington, DC: Author.

American Psychiatric Association. (2000). *Diagnostic and statistical manual of mental disorders* (4th ed.; text revision). Washington, DC: Author.

Barth, F. D. (2000). When eating and shopping are companion disorders. In A. L. Benson (Ed.), *I shop, therefore I am: Compulsive buying and the search for self* (pp. 268–287). Northvale, NJ: Aronson.

Baumeister, R. F. (1991). The self against itself: Escape or defeat? In R. C. Curtis (Ed.), *The rational self: Theoretical convergence in psychoanalysis and social psychology* (pp. 238–256). New York: Guilford.

Baumeister, R. F., & Scher, S. J. (1988). Self-defeating behavior patterns among normal individuals: Review and analysis of common self-destructive tendencies. *Psychological Bulletin, 104,* 3–22.

Belk, R. W. (1985). Materialism: Trait aspects of living in the material world. *Journal of Consumer Research, 12,* 265–280.

Black, D. W. (2000). Assessment of compulsive buying. In A. L. Benson (Ed.), *I shop, therefore I am: Compulsive buying and the search for self* (pp. 191–216). Northvale, NJ: Aronson.

Bleuler, E. (1924). *Textbook of psychiatry.* New York: Macmillan.

Boundy, D. (2000). When money is the drug. In A. L. Benson (Ed.), *I shop, therefore I am: Compulsive buying and the search for self* (pp. 3–26). Northvale, NJ: Aronson.

Christenson, G. A., Faber, R. J., de Zwaan, M., Raymond, N., Specker, S., Eckert, M. D., et al. (1994). Compulsive buying: Descriptive characteristics and psychiatric comorbidity. *Journal of Clinical Psychiatry, 55,* 5–11.

Cushman, P. (1990). Why the self is empty. *American Psychologist, 45,* 599–611.

DeSarbo, W. S., & Edwards, E. A. (1996). Typologies of compulsive buying behavior: A constrained clusterwise regression approach. *Journal of Consumer Psychology, 5,* 231–262.

Donovan, D. M. (1988). Assessment of addictive behaviors: Implications of an emerging biopsychosocial model. In D. M. Donovan & G. A. Marlatt (Eds.), *Assessment of addiction behaviors* (pp. 3–48). New York: Guilford.

Duval, S., & Wicklund, R. A. (1972). *A theory of objective self-awareness*. San Diego, CA: Academic Press.

Edwards, E. A. (1992). The measurement and modeling of compulsive buying behavior. *Dissertation Abstracts International, 53*(11–A), UM 9308304.

Elliott, R. (1994). Addictive consumption: Function and fragmentation in postmodernity. *Journal of Consumer Policy, 17*, 159–179.

Faber, R. J. (2000a). A systematic investigation into compulsive buying. In A. L. Benson (Ed.), *I shop, therefore I am: Compulsive buying and the search for self* (pp. 27–54). Northvale, NJ: Aronson.

Faber, R. J. (2000b). The urge to buy: A uses and gratifications perspective. In S. Ratneshwar, D. G. Mick, & C. Huffman (Eds.), *The why of consumption: Contemporary perspectives on consumer motives, goals, and desires* (pp. 177–196). London: Routledge.

Faber, R. J., & Christenson, G. A. (1996). In the mood to buy: Differences in the mood states experienced by compulsive buyers and other consumers. *Psychology and Marketing, 13*, 803–820.

Faber, R. J., Christenson, G. A., de Zwaan, M., & Mitchell, J. E. (1995). Two forms of compulsive consumption: Comorbidity of compulsive buying and binge eating. *Journal of Consumer Research, 22*, 296–304.

Faber, R. J., & O'Guinn, T. C. (1988). Dysfunctional consumer socialization: A search for the roots of compulsive buying. In P. Vanden Abeele (Ed.), *Psychology in micro and macro economics* (Vol. 1, pp. 1–15). Leuven, Belgium: International Association for Research in Economic Psychology.

Faber, R. J., O'Guinn, T. C., & Krych, R. (1987). Compulsive consumption. In M. Wallendorf & P. Anderson (Eds.), *Advances in consumer research* (pp. 132–135). Provo, UT: Association for Consumer Research.

Faber, R. J., Peterson, C., & Christenson, G. A. (1994, August). *Characteristics of compulsive buyers: An examination of stress reaction and absorption*. Paper presented at the 104th Annual Convention of the American Psychological Association, Los Angeles.

Faber, R. J., Ristvedt, S. L., Mackenzie, T. B., & Christenson, G. A. (1996, October). *Cues that trigger compulsive buying*. Paper presented at the 24th annual meeting of the Association for Consumer Research Conference, Tuscon, AZ.

Friese, S., & Koenig, H. (1993). Shopping for trouble. *Advancing the Consumer Interest, 5*, 24–29.

Glatt, M. M., & Cook, C. C. (1987). Pathological spending as a form of psychological dependence. *British Journal of Addiction, 82*, 1257–1258.

Goldsmith, T., & McElroy, S. L. (2000). Compulsive buying: Associated disorders and drug treatment. In A. L. Benson (Ed.), *I shop, therefore I am: Compulsive buying and the search for self* (pp. 217–242). Northvale, NJ: Aronson.

Heatherton, T. F., & Baumeister, R. F. (1991). Binge eating as escape from self-awareness. *Psychological Bulletin, 110*, 86–108.

Heatherton, T. F., & Vohs, K. D. (1998). Why is it so difficult to inhibit behavior? *Psychological Inquiry, 9,* 212–215.

Higgins, E. T. (1987). Self-discrepancy: A theory relating self to affect. *Psychological Review, 94,* 319–340.

Hoch, S. J., & Loewenstein, G. F. (1991). Time inconsistent preferences and consumer self-control. *Journal of Consumer Research, 18,* 492–507.

Hoffman, D. L., & Novak, T. P. (1996). Marketing in hypermedia computer-mediated environments: Conceptual foundations. *Journal of Marketing, 60,* 50–68.

Holmstrom, D. (1985, October 15). Controlling compulsive spending. *American Way, 18,* 67–69.

Joiner, T. E., Heatherton, T. F., Rudd, M. D., & Schmidt, N. (1997). Perfectionism, perceived weight status, and bulimic symptoms: Two studies testing a diathesis-stress model. *Journal of Abnormal Psychology, 106,* 145–153.

Kraepelin, E. (1915). *Psychiatrie* (8th ed.). Leipzig: Verlag Von Johann Ambrosius Barth.

Krueger, D. (1988). On compulsive shopping and spending: A psychodynamic inquiry. *American Journal of Psychotherapy, 42,* 574–585.

Krueger, D. (2000). The use of money as an action symptom. In A. L. Benson (Ed.), *I shop, therefore I am: Compulsive buying and the search for self* (pp. 288–310). Northvale, NJ: Aronson Press.

Langman, L. (1992). Neon cages: Shopping for subjectivity. In R. Shields (Ed.), *Lifestyle shopping: The subject of consumption* (pp. 40–82). London: Routledge.

Lucas, A. R., Beard, C. M., O'Fallon, W. M., & Kurland, L. T. (1988). Anorexia nervosa in Rochester, Minnesota: A 45-year study. *Mayo Clinic Proceedings, 63,* 433–442.

McElroy, S. L., Keck, P. E., Jr., Pope, H. J., Jr., Smith, J. M., & Strakowski, S. M. (1994) Compulsive buying: A report of 20 cases. *Journal of Clinical Psychiatry, 55,* 242–248.

Mitchell, J. E. (1990). *Bulimia nervosa.* Minneapolis: University of Minnesota Press.

Moore, B. (2001, July 6). Out of the mall and into court: The "shopaholic defense"; Successful "retail therapy" argument is a wake-up call for a consumer-driven culture. *Los Angeles Times,* p. E-1.

Mundis, J. (1986, January 5). A way back from deep debt. *New York Times Magazine,* pp. 22–26.

Nataraajan, R., & Goff, B. G. (1991). Compulsive buying: Toward a reconceptualization. *Journal of Social Behavior and Personality, 6,* 307–328.

Norton, K. R., Crisp, A. H., & Bhat, A. V. (1985). Why do some anorexics steal? Personal, social and illness factors. *Journal of Psychiatric Research, 19,* 385–390.

O'Conner (2001, May 24). Judge buys shopaholic defense in embezzling. *Chicago Tribune,* p. 1.

O'Guinn, T. C., & Faber, R. J. (1989). Compulsive buying: A phenomenological exploration. *Journal of Consumer Research, 16,* 147–157.

Polivy, J., & Herman, C. P. (1983). *Breaking the diet habit: The natural weight alternative*. New York: Basic Books.

Prus, R. (1993). Shopping with companions: Images, influences and interpersonal dilemmas. *Qualitative Sociology, 16*, 87–110.

Scherhorn, G., Reisch, L. A., & Raab, G. (1990). Addictive buying in West Germany: An empirical study. *Journal of Consumer Policy, 13*, 355–387.

Schlosser, S., Black, D. W., Repertinger, S., & Freet, D. (1994). Compulsive buying: Demography, phenomenology, and comorbidity in 46 subjects. *General Hospital Psychiatry, 16*, 205–212.

Shields, R. (1992). The individual consumption cultures and the fate of the community. In R. Shields (Ed.), *Lifestyle shopping: The subject of consumption* (pp. 99–113). London: Routledge.

Vohs, K. D., Bardone, A. M., Joiner, T. E., Abramson, L. Y., & Heatherton, T. F. (1999). Perfectionism, perceived weight status, and self-esteem interact to predict bulimic symptoms: A model of bulimic symptom development. *Journal of Abnormal Psychology, 108*, 695–700.

Williamson, D. A. (1990). *Assessment of eating disorders: Obesity, anorexia and bulimia nervosa*. New York: Pergamon.

11

MONEY, MEANING, AND IDENTITY: COMING TO TERMS WITH BEING WEALTHY

STEPHEN GOLDBART, DENNIS T. JAFFE, AND JOAN DIFURIA

John is a 43-year-old software entrepreneur whose startup company produced stock options worth $45 million.[1] He took his options and left the company, spending a year buying everything he had always dreamed about: a vacation home in the Caribbean, a sailboat, a larger family home, and every electronic toy he wanted. However, financial success and the freedom to do whatever he wanted did not turn out to be a bed of roses. He observed:

> Having money has turned out to be more emotionally complicated than I could have ever imagined. . . . I feel uncomfortable with some of the comments and reactions I'm getting from people. . . . I should be happy, but deep inside I feel something is missing. Now that I have the option to spend my time any way I choose, I'm no longer sure of what I really want to do. I used to tell myself I would do all sorts of things, "if only I

---

[1]All of the cases reported in this chapter come from the clinical practices of the authors. Names and identifying information have been changed to protect the individuals involved.

had the money." I've bought all the toys I've wanted. Now I have to face the truth: I really don't know what's important to me.

Sylvia, a successful 47-year-old advertising executive whose unexpectedly large inheritance increased her life choices but caused a downturn in her relationships, said:

I'm excited about the freedom and opportunities that my inheritance affords me but I'm afraid to show my excitement because I might turn off my friends . . . even my closest friends to whom I can usually speak freely about everything from my work life to my sex life. Now I fear that my recent purchases and travels will only trigger envy and jealousy. . . . I even feel constricted with my husband. He's excited, but we both wonder whether this money will affect the power balance in our relationship. I never thought that the benefits of wealth would be so troublesome!

The last decade of the 20th century saw an unprecedented growth of wealth in the United States. Even with the economic downturn of the new millennium, people like John and Sylvia, minted with financial independence at a young age, are facing enviable life choices. Included in the rising tide of new wealth are a growing number of people, most of them baby-boomers in their 50s, who are coming into sizable inheritances, selling their businesses, or just harvesting the results of their good work and good fortune, giving them room to consider other options. In each case, they have more wealth than they ever imagined; in many cases, it has had unintended consequences in their lives, both positive and negative.

They are finding that money may lead them to confront difficult and challenging questions such as these: "What can I do to feel productive?" "How much money is enough?" "How much of my assets do I want to spend on things for myself?" "Do I dedicate time and money to philanthropy?" "How can I raise my children to appreciate the value of work and money?"

Having arrived at an unprecedented crossroads, this fortunate cohort and their heirs are forced to come to terms, sometimes for the first time, with their attitudes toward money, and many are struggling with its impact on their life. Eight years ago, we started seeing more individuals with these issues in our practice at the Money, Meaning & Choices Institute in the San Francisco Bay area (www.mmcinstitute.com). We coined the term *sudden wealth syndrome* to describe the emotional challenges and identity issues that ensue from coming into money. Many people have come to us suspecting that, with their primary focus on work and financial gain, they have lost their moorings somewhere along the way. Unlike those who come from "old money," many of our clients have not grown up with wealth and therefore are not well-equipped to deal with both its challenges and opportunities. The experience of sudden wealth includes anxiety and overconfidence as well as guilt and depression, as people come to terms with their good fortune.

In this chapter, we explore how the acquisition and experience of money varies in accordance with the core psychological attitudes and beliefs that comprise what we call *wealth identity*. We present a developmental model of wealth identity and of the dynamics of establishing a balanced relationship with wealth and money in one's life, share case vignettes to illustrate the meaning and potential applications of the model, and conclude with some of the implications of the model for helping people come to terms with their privilege and decide how to use their wealth for socially responsible, and personally fulfilling, outcomes.

Although we focus on an affluent group that represents less than 1% of the U.S. population, we do not want to neglect or minimize the issue of wealth distribution. Our concern here, however, is with the choices that this select group makes about using their wealth. It is our hope that, in light of this special focus, people of privilege will make choices that include a substantial commitment to social issues.

MONEY AS A CHALLENGE TO PERSONAL IDENTITY

The psychological challenges of having and inheriting money are amplified by social and cultural beliefs about wealth. In a society where big money is touted as the cure to life's problems, it is hard to readily recognize or have much sympathy for those who suffer from a windfall. Most people only dream of having such problems. However, those who do come into money also confront the limitations of most people's view of the American Dream, which is, "If I had all the money in the world, I would be happy and fulfilled." Contrary to conventional wisdom, recent studies on the relationship between wealth and well-being suggest that money, at least for those living in economically developed nations, does not buy happiness. As Csikszentmihalyi (1999) reported, the relationship between material success and a sense of well-being is complex and ambiguous; the wealthy are no more likely than their economically disadvantaged counterparts to report that they are in fact, happy. These findings are further supported by Myers (2000), who suggested that the American Dream has become "life, liberty, and the purchase of happiness" but that even the very rich are only "slightly happier than the average American" (p. 59). Myers went on to note that the number of people reporting themselves "very happy" has slightly declined between 1957 and 1998 and that the divorce rate doubled and teen suicide tripled. He noted: "we are twice as rich and no happier" (p. 61). These findings are consistent with our clinical experience. Whereas money provides for sustenance and enables a multitude of choices otherwise unavailable, it also poses profound new, and often difficult, challenges to identity and purpose in life. Simply put, wealth in and of itself does not answer deeply held questions of personal meaning and fulfillment.

Herein lies the problem: Since the 1980s, the driving force in American culture has been financial gain, overshadowing other criteria for having a successful life, such as family cohesiveness, intimacy, aesthetics, and the pursuit of wisdom. There is nothing wrong with people making money, but maintaining balance and perspective is critical. At this historical moment, however, too many people have mixed up personal and psychological well-being with financial well-being. Not surprisingly, the real value of consumption as a form of psychological gain can be as confusing as the real meaning and purpose of wealth itself.

Philosopher Jacob Needleman (1991) explored the moral and psychological dilemmas that money poses for people. If you don't have it, he observed, its pursuit can dominate your life. When people get enough to make a real difference, many mixed feelings emerge. There are two ways our society values the pursuit of money: on one hand, it is touted as the most important task, while on the other hand it is viewed as evil. Needleman suggested that balance occurs when one simply has money without emotional conflict. One uses it to pursue one's values, one's life goals, and meaning. However, he also suggested that the path to this is rocky and difficult, even for those who find themselves with substantial wealth.

Money alone is not the issue. Social status and recognition come with wealth, leading to feelings of power and entitlement, but also to feelings of entrapment and isolation. Society has a highly mixed attitude toward wealth. Admiration toward those who have achieved financial success is mixed with jealousy and resentment, particularly when the wealth-holder is viewed as a person who has not earned it or does not deserve it. We now recognize how acquiring and inheriting money has a marked impact on people's core identity, on the beliefs and values that map how wealth-holders see themselves and on how others see and treat them.

To a degree, the longer one has to grow accustomed to the challenges and opportunities of wealth, the more likely one would have the chance to master its difficulties. So sudden wealth may have a greater psychological shock value than being born into wealth or obtaining an expected inheritance. However, many people who come from "old money" do not necessarily fare better than those who have recently earned or inherited it. Remember Dudley Moore in the movie *Arthur*, the story of a young man whose family money undermined his motivation and sense of responsibility. Several accounts by heirs themselves have described the psychological wounding they experienced. For example, O'Neill (1997) offered a personal account of growing up in the "gilded ghetto" of wealth and told many stories, including her own, of living in isolation, alcoholism, and other forms of abuse that she felt are common among the wealthy in society. Blouin, Gibson, and Kiersted (1995) and Schervish, Coutsoukis, and Lewis (1994) both offered a series of accounts of people who attribute experiences ranging from feeling abandoned by caregivers, isolation from society, guilt about having money, aimless and unable to commit to life work, and other painful wounds directly to the fact that they grew up wealthy. Sedgwick (1985) presented a particularly sensitive account of his own and other heirs' response to inheritance:

> For all rich kids, the act of inheritance is entirely passive. Yet this sometimes makes the guilt more severe, and more permanent. True criminals, at least, have something to confess. They can receive forgiveness; they can reform; they can put their sins behind them. But rich kids start to feel that they are the sin themselves, and every crime that was committed out of greed now hangs on their heads. They see the inequity that lies about them, or read about it in their money mail, and they think they are responsible for it. Because they are on top, they must be squashing those on the bottom. This is the true embarrassment of riches. . . . To clear themselves they often feel . . . an unspecified and diffuse need to do penance, to suffer in some way as to square things with the almighty dollar. (pp. 106–107)

We find that wealth poses a psychological challenge to a person's core beliefs and psychological resources. At first it is experienced, not surprisingly, as an extraordinary gift. However, this gift may mean altering patterns and ways of living that are familiar and comfortable. This simple but very powerful idea has been supported by contemporary thinking about psychological development. Colarusso and Nemiroff (1979), researchers on adult development, provided a useful approach. They proposed that psychological development is a continuous process from birth to death. In childhood and adolescence we *create* a sense of self. During adulthood, we *evolve* and *refine* this sense of self. Our core images of ourselves, the beliefs and emotionally charged ideas that make up who we are, are very important to our psychological stability. When life events are congruent with these early beliefs we feel grounded and safe. Continuity does not imply goodness or badness of feeling, but satisfying the psyche's love of predictability and consistency.

When life events are discontinuous with one's core images and beliefs, one is challenged to either evolve one's sense of self or to act in ways to resolve the disparity between past and present. In summary, people must "change or regress." Life today presents people with many discontinuous events—unexpected death of a spouse, loss of job, career difficulties and failures, and business downturns. When facing such discontinuities, one must make shifts or alterations in identity to come to terms with the new realities. Identity is less subject to change during the money earning–wealth accumulation phase of life, as people are so focused on their job or company that they do not have time to step back and wonder who they are. Yet when the newly affluent stop working, they confront the challenges of an inner transition, as described in the stories of John and Sylvia with which this chapter began.

In the process of becoming wealthy, people often leave their old world and culture. As with survivor guilt, they may feel guilty about their fortune, wondering why they have been luckier than others less fortunate. Consequently, they may be left feeling uncomfortable in both their old and their new environments.

So not unlike other major turning points in psychological development, coming into money may herald a series of life challenges and transitions. At best, understanding the place of money in a person's life can be the beginning of a new life stage that offers more choices but still poses issues of meaning, personal empowerment, and social responsibility. After sifting through the impact of money on self-esteem, personal relationships, work, and community, people are better able to embark on new ventures with an invigorated set of priorities. With clarity of values, people can define exactly the kind of lifestyle they want. By aligning life and legacy plans with a family consensus on core values, people's time and money resources are more likely to be used in a satisfying and fulfilling way. Clarity of values combined with a solid sense of identity enables people effectively to steward their wealth, making choices in service of a life filled with meaning and pleasurable purpose. The responsibility of wealth is finding the right direction for the multitude of choices available and balancing needs to take care of oneself, one's family, and one's social legacy.

How do people reach clarity of values and find surefootedness in their experience of wealth? Our clinical experience with people of new wealth has helped us understand the transition into wealth as a rite of passage into a new identity and life stage. People grow into their money following a maturation process that we call the *developmental stages of wealth identity*. This model describes the journey to wealth as a set of developmental opportunities and tasks. It can be used in the same fashion as other popular models of adult development such as Gail Sheehy's (1984) *Passages* or Erik Erikson's (1980) stages of life development. Our ideas, which grow from contemporary psychoanalytic object-relations theory and self psychology (Goldbart, 2001), explore the effect of coming into wealth on one's life. Progress toward a positive and stable identity as a wealthy person is affected by several elements of prior personal development and social context, which we review below.

Personality–Character Style

Stability and coherence of identity certainly help people weather any significant psychological challenge, including wealth. Those people who have a history of instability of self structure, who have weak ego strength, and who have a rigid all-or-nothing defensive organization (e.g., found in individuals with borderline and narcissistic personalities) have greater difficulties mastering the developmental tasks of wealth identity.

Life Stage

The presence of money must become integrated into one's personal journey through various core life developmental tasks. During young adulthood, the issues of personal growth are made more complex by the temptations that come with having money. In middle adulthood, the ways in which identity is defined through work or professional achievement are important factors. Moreover, identity is affected by whether one has earned the money or inherited it and how much time and planning one has had to prepare for it.

Family System

Parents, siblings, and other important people are models of money-related behavior and beliefs. Generally speaking, people have an easier time if they come from families that demonstrated clarity of money values and beliefs, two-way communication about money matters, and effective means to resolve money-related conflicts than if their families were confused or uncertain about money values or viewed money as a taboo subject or a source of difficulty and conflict. People benefit from having a stable, cohesive, and supportive family as they grapple with the developmental tasks of wealth identity.

Cultural and Religious Beliefs

As with family style, culture and religion play important roles in the development of wealth identity. Culture and religion provide many, if not most, of the people on this globe with an organized set of beliefs about money. Some cultures have a prescribed way of understanding the role of money in life, providing a useful, if not overly rigid, structure for handling the emotional challenges of wealth. Cultural beliefs like "money is the root of all evil" can play into a client's pre-existing anxiety or guilt, increasing the likelihood of self-defeating behaviors or stalling progress through the four stages of identity development.

DEVELOPMENTAL STAGES OF WEALTH IDENTITY

The point at which one receives a substantial amount of wealth, becomes aware of having it, or gains control over it is a significant milestone in one's life. Like all powerful events, however, the event only signals the start of a process of internal response to the new status. This section presents the Money, Meaning & Choices Institute model of the stages that people experience in coming to terms with themselves as wealthy and highlights the challenges and opportunities that occur along the way. We identify four developmental stages of wealth identity: (a) honeymoon, (b) wealth acceptance, (c) identity consolidation, and (d) achieving balance. These four stages map a person's progression from the early experience of coming into wealth to the development of a mature wealth identity that brings together optimal lifestyle time management, an empowered sense of wealth stewardship, and a legacy plan.

This model can be a useful diagnostic tool to help therapists and their clients assess where they are on the journey of wealth identity development. The model can also help answer questions as to why some people are more vulnerable to psychological problems associated with having and inheriting money. Simply put, money-related psychological issues very well may be the consequence of the ability to master and complete these four stages of wealth identity development. Knowing where a client stands and what tasks they are grappling with enables therapists to better understand, empathize with, and facilitate a client's maturation.

Stage I: Honeymoon

This stage marks the psychological awakening to wealth, when a person stops and begins to consider what it means to be wealthy. Its psychology shares characteristics with what Mahler, Pine, and Bergman (1975) described as the height of normal narcissism, the 1-year-old child's feeling of being both the center of the world and having a love affair with the world. People in this stage experience an incredible sense of elation and power, viewing the "world as their oyster." Anything and everything seem possible. With sudden wealth, there is an adrenaline-raising blend of excitement and disbelief, as well as feelings of being blessed, lucky, and all-powerful.

In many ways it is like the honeymoon phase of a love relationship. Feeling powerful and invulnerable, many people go on a spending spree, buying the things and pleasure pursuits that they have always wanted. Purchasing power becomes synonymous with psychological power and egocentric joy. For those who pursue this phase with an almost manic-like energy, "I buy therefore I am" seems to be their philosophical guideline. For those who had insufficient loving attention from their parents when they were young, this stage is an opportunity to fill the psychological emptiness with the things and people that money can buy.

The stage comes to an end when people recognize the limits of their egocentrism but are able to spend without guilt or in ways that are not ultimately self-destructive. They buy things that have meaning and they buy things that are for fun. Sally, for example, reported:

> During the first year or so of being truly wealthy I was on a "spending high." I bought everything I wanted and everything I really didn't need.

Then I settled down: Now I'm free to enjoy my wealth, but I also detest waste. I've found my balance point for spending without guilt.

There is a continuum of difficulties during this stage. At one extreme lies narcissistic overengagement with wealth and at the other stands schizoid-paranoid engagement with wealth. The first speaks to those who become overengaged with their egocentric self-interests and overidentified with their wealth. For them, "party time [is] all the time." These are people who display unrealistic money practices and are unaware of the impact that money might have on self and others. During the high-flying days of the 1990s we worked with many young, instant, "dotcom" millionaires who saw themselves as invulnerable, who spent wildly and did not diversify their portfolios. Many of them ended up in the "sudden loss of wealth" sector, their journey being characterized by "hubris turning into humility." The more they over-idealized themselves as wealthy, the harder it was for them to readjust to the return to their old status. Not all people stuck in this stage were wild consumers. Some kept their consumption in check but distanced themselves from others by maintaining a narcissistic self-image: an attitude of "I'm holier than thou—better than you—because I'm rich."

Opposite difficulties are experienced by people who are markedly inhibited in their capacity to experience the pleasures and power of their wealth. In a schizoidlike style, their fears, feelings of shame and guilt, and excessive anxiety block their ability to experience this stage. In the worst of cases we see people who are so paranoid about the physical and emotional risks associated with their wealth that they buy a lifestyle that is autistic in character. They hide themselves from others, refusing to communicate about their money concerns with even the closest of intimates. Think here of Howard Hughes, a man impaired and imprisoned by his own wealth. Over time he became more anxious and suspicious, living in a fortress that protected him from the world.

Stage II: Wealth Acceptance

If Stage I is associated with the psychology of being a 1-year-old, Stage II reflects the toddler stage of psychological development. At this age, children begin to realize the limits of their egocentricity. They also confront the disquieting reality that mom and dad are both good and bad, nurturing and limit-setting, available and unavailable. The developmental challenge is the achievement of *integration*, the capacity to bear mixed feelings about self and others and to bring together the powerful narcissistic view of the self with the reality of vulnerability and limits in self, others, and society.

During this phase the experience of wealth is characterized by emotional complexity and contradictions. There is increased awareness of the variety of ways in which wealth has made life more interesting and rich and also more complicated and difficult.

There is a fall from the grace of narcissistic self-involvement of Stage I. The impact of money on self-image, self-esteem, and relationships with family and friends is felt. Successful resolution of this phase means accepting the emotional complexities of wealth and in so doing, mobilizing the capacity for integration. This can be seen in the person's capacity to find "the middle ground" between the opportunities and obstacles of wealth.

Some problems do not go away and others can arise. Coming into this stage, the person struggles with challenges such as feeling overwhelmed by complex emotions. Furthermore, the belief that money is the key to everything sometimes results in self-defeating choices, anxiety, or depression, as well as in difficulties dealing with partners, family, and friends.

People who are overwhelmed by the challenges of wealth to self and relationships are often unable to move from the honeymoon phase to the level of acceptance. Such people behave as if money is the key to all of life's entitlements and find they are sorely mistaken.

For example, one woman reported that she had difficulty engaging in an intimate postdivorce relationship because she could not handle having more money than the man she loved. Another man believed he could buy both friendship and his way out of emotional conflicts with his wife. Both of these people found that money, far from being a solution, only made their original challenges with intimacy and self-worth more complex.

Money and people's ambivalence about having it often make choices fraught with angst. One female heir felt it would not be fair for her to take a job as it would take food out of the mouths of those who needed to work. She therefore worked for foundations without pay but then undervalued herself for not earning money. With her financial advisor, she felt so overwhelmed by her mixed feelings about her money that she would listen and take notes, but make no choices. She lived an ultra-frugal life, experiencing great difficulty in moving from an apartment to a small house that she could easily afford. She just could not allow herself to feel good about her wealth.

Feelings about wealth may be projected outward. One client of a financial advisor wanted more tax write-offs. When the advisor told him that he could afford to buy a bigger house and a second home, the client felt offended, believing that his advisor envied him, and stopped returning the advisor's phone calls. He fled the relationship because of his own inner inability to come to terms with his new wealth.

Stage III: Identity Consolidation

During this stage money-related changes begin to be integrated into a new, evolved sense of self-identity. People are able to find middle ground on the continuum of identity consolidation: between over-identification with wealth ("I am my money—it defines my identity") at one end and under-identification with wealth ("I am not my money—I will deny the impact it has on me") at the other end. By facing these struggles, they begin to resolve them and integrate them into a complex whole.

They consciously sort through, develop, and select past and present money-related attitudes, beliefs, and principles. They define their own values around relationships, giving, and lifestyle, and they attain a personal comfort zone with their wealth. Not feeling forced in any direction by having money, they are now able to choose on the basis of their values, needs, and desires. They re-evaluate the efficacy of past and childhood money values and beliefs. Over time, their choices are internalized into an expanded self-definition. Successful resolution of this phase results in a person who is both comfortable with and an effective steward of wealth.

Some of the difficulties that can arise in this stage include the following: (a) feeling stuck in a money-related identity crisis of meaning and purpose; (b) finding it difficult to make peace between past and present money beliefs and values; and (c) being caught between past and present, unable to fully enjoy life and feel empowered.

At this stage people ask themselves, "Now that I accept the fact that I am rich, who am I to be?" The conflicts and challenges of earlier phases are now perceived as reflecting conflicts between past and present money-related beliefs and values. Some past money beliefs and values may no longer seem relevant. Yet many people have difficulties making peace between past and present money values and end up feeling guilty or not entitled to the new identity that wealth offers. Some people come to this stage haunted by the past in ways that disrupt or impede the present. Others remain caught between past and present in a purgatory of having money and not letting themselves fully enjoy it or letting it fully empower them. For example, one heir had a "hidden life" where she worked part time as a writer and artist. She dressed down and lived frugally, not wanting to be seen even by progressive philanthropy groups as "a person of money."

Stage IV: Achieving Balance—Time, Stewardship, and Legacy

By the end of Stage III, wealth becomes a solid part of one's identity. In Stage IV the person achieves full responsibility for the wealth through the initiation of a life plan where money is seen as a resource to fulfill personal needs, goals, and values. One is able to see that one can implement any set of values with money: One can spend and enjoy it, invest it, or give it away. Clarity of money values, consciously determined while mastering Stage III developmental tasks, provides direction for making choices about how one will make both short- and long-term time and energy investments. In summary, the person comes to terms with having money, determines the values and principles to guide his or her financial behavior, and designs a plan for what to do with it and how to use it.

So the essence of this last stage is planning and implementing money and lifestyle priorities that reflect identity consolidation, stewardship, and legacy goals. This stage has two components: (a) the creation of a plan for how one's life choices—in domains of self, relationships, productive activity, and community—reflect one's newly crystallized core money values[2]; and (b) the creation of an organized strategy for the implementation of this plan, with the collaboration of significant others (e.g., partner, family, friends, colleagues).

Without a plan, even a person with a strong sense of identity can be like a well-made ship without a map or direction. There may be forays into one domain of life without sufficient consideration of needs in other domains. We may see a lack of balance in time management that takes the form of insufficient planning for the impact of change on significant others and that may result in distracting, time-consuming conflicts, such as when a married partner acts independently or unilaterally without regard for the impact of a lifestyle change on the spouse.

Those who want to "do well" with their money, but feel overwhelmed by choices and options, can at this stage overcome inertia and the many demands from the social world by defining their own personal strategic philanthropy mission and plan. Their feelings and concerns about having wealth can now fuel a process of defining a legacy plan that is aligned with their values and beliefs. The person comes to terms with his or her choices by making a commitment to sharing with the community. Another feature of this stage is the commitment to a passionate interest that can grow with age.

For example, Randall took over leadership of a family foundation started by his grandfather that had a charter to fulfill certain of his family's values. He made the decision to move his family from a wealthy suburb in Northern California back to the Midwestern small town where his grandfather had made his fortune in order to lead the foundation's efforts to build the economy and education of this small town. His children have, in turn, become active in the foundation's activities in the community. Similarly, a Chinese family defined its legacy by setting up a family foundation in which significant amounts of money went back to China to build infrastructure in their homeland. The younger generation, however, was born in the United States and wanted to give foundation money to causes in this country that are more reflective of its own concerns. The family is respectfully engaged in deciding such issues in their family meetings.

---

[2]Money, Meaning & Choices Institute has developed a five-step Wealth and Life Planning System that people can use as a framework for mastering the developmental tasks of this stage.

ELEMENTS OF POSITIVE WEALTH IDENTITY

A second perspective on the development of wealth identity comes from looking at the specific areas where money affects one's life. We define five areas that relate to a person's sense of meaning and emotional connection to money. Each of the five areas concerns an important element of the psychological relationship to the saving, spending, and sharing of wealth. To develop a positive wealth identity, people must resolve conflicts and overcome their vulnerabilities in each one.

Self-Esteem and Personal Security

Folklore aside, money alone does not lead people to feel better about themselves or more personally secure. In fact, money may lead people to feel a great deal of anxiety. A sense of personal value, self-respect, and personal identity should be based on more than one's wealth. Unless people feel inner strength, the fear of losing their money may lead them to feel continually vulnerable, despite their wealth. A person must develop a coherent foundation of self-esteem and personal security not primarily dependent on his or her net worth. Even when coming into significant money, a person may continue to feel vulnerable and insecure. People who are stuck in Stage I or II of wealth identity may find that wealth plays a dominant role in their self-esteem and may overvalue their self-worth by the size of their assets. Conversely, they may have a sense of not deserving the money, accompanied by feelings of guilt and shame.

A solid core of self-esteem comprises a multitude of factors, including the capacity to love and be loved, to be recognized by and connected to family and community, and to be successful and productive. Certainly the achievement of financial independence, a symbol of success in our society, can enhance self-esteem. Earned wealth, being the result of successful achievement, can be an important building block of authentic self-esteem. However, money and work success alone may not provide adequate, stable self-esteem.

Jack, a handsome, competitive, 35-year-old Silicon Valley businessman, married with young children, took his small software company public. He awakened one morning to discover that he no longer had to work. Instead of feeling elated, he felt shocked and anxious about what to do with himself. He tried spending more time with his kids; he went sailing and took vacations, but ended up yearning to go back to the office. Like many who have committed their hearts and souls to their high-tech dreams, meaning and purpose in life was found at work. There he felt at his best. Although he claimed that his relationship with his wife and kids was all-important to him, in fact he had spent precious little time with them. Jack lived his passions at the office and passed the time at home. He claimed to be bored and under-stimulated at home, but underneath this defensive veneer Jack felt uneasy, unsure of himself, and uncomfortable with the unpredictability and emotionality of ordinary family life.

At work, Jack was in charge and felt powerful; at home Jack was bumbling and impotent. Being at home reminded him of his "nerdy" years as a teenager, before he found his power and self-esteem in the computer industry. Family life was filled with memories of feeling inadequate, of being the last one picked for sport teams, and of not fitting into the in-crowd at school. It did not help matters that he had a more socially adept brother who was all he was not and was everything his father had ever wanted in a son. Jack lucked out, however: His teenage obsession with things high-tech paid off big, simultaneously (and artificially) raising the stock of his self-esteem. His father, a career salesperson who never made it to management, now admired his success; Jack had won the sibling rivalry for his father's attention.

However, like the stock of many startups, Jack's self-esteem was precariously balanced. Now faced with the benefits of financial freedom and a wife demanding that he become a full partner in the family, Jack needed to come to terms with the emotional business of his past and his defensive over-investment in work achievement so that he could be free to appreciate the pleasure and value of spending time with his family.

The impact of wealth on self-esteem can be even more problematic for inheritors than it is for earners of wealth. Inheritors may suffer far more from shame, doubt, and guilt than their counterparts among wealth earners. The luck of the bloodline does not automatically make for an increase in self-esteem or self-worth.

The struggle to develop a sense of self-esteem for wealthy heirs is recounted in scores of stories (e.g., Blouin et al., 1995; O'Neill, 1997; Sedgwick, 1985). Heirs often experience a difficult and multi-year struggle that lasts well into adulthood as they seek to find a sense of purpose and vitality and to overcome feelings of guilt, worthlessness, and depression.

Lifestyle

Lifestyle pertains to how people get pleasure from using their money, that is, the way they spend and the nature of their life. Positive identity is seen in those who feel genuine pleasure and satisfaction from spending their money and who spend in ways that are not ultimately compulsive or self-destructive. They buy things that are meaningful and they buy things for fun. Having mastered the developmental challenges of Stage III, they practice a value-based spending, balancing saving and sharing of money with spending. They enjoy spending without excess shame or guilt.

People can feel out of control in this area along two extremes. People sometimes over-spend and spend impulsively, resulting in ephemeral pleasure, a sense of waste, and potential negative financial consequences. Or, on the other side of the spectrum, people sometimes radically underspend and feel inhibited by a sense of nonentitlement and feelings of shame and guilt.

Money can be a resource or a temptation to addiction and compulsive spending. Consider stories of people winning the lottery or inheriting and quickly spending it away. One might expect that they were not truly in control of their wealth and in the end it did not add to their lives.

Others spend their money to ameliorate psychological problems within themselves or in relationship to others. Sam, a 38-year-old high-tech executive, is 2 years away from his goal of $8 million to retire. He works 12 hours a day, 6 days per week, as he has since he graduated from college. His wife and children feel they hardly know him, except for the summer holidays. Sam tries to make up for his absence by creating the perfect family vacation, taking his family to exotic places and hiring all the help he can get, including chauffeurs, cooks, and other personal assistants to meet all of their needs. Each year Sam planned a more extravagant family holiday: from the Bahamas, to Bora Bora, and then onward to a private Fijian island. He made sure that the staff at their destinations was ready to fulfill all of their desires. If his wife wanted a personal trainer, she got one; if his son wanted his own windsurfing coach for the week, no problem. However, Sam couldn't understand how unappreciative his family seemed to be. His 14-year-old son said it all: "Dad, without a doubt, you plan super vacations. But I don't really like them. You don't really know what I like, what I want. I don't really want to go on these vacations anymore."

In a money and meaning consultation session, Sam acknowledged his obsession with the perfect holiday as a kind of compensation for his absence from family life most of the year. He learned that he ran his vacations in the same fashion he ran his business. Sam was tired of the pressure, the number of e-mails and meetings, and the need to insure quarterly growth at almost any human cost. He knew this was a crazy way to live but feared changing the leadership style and culture of his very successful company. Indeed, even with all of his resources, he felt powerless to stand up for himself in service of a more balanced lifestyle. His only solution: "Look, in a few years, I'll cash out."

In fact, people like Sam often do not cash out. They become addicted to the cycle of intense work, big money, status, and consumption. They simply do not have an alternative. Their lives are a heady flow of adrenaline and narcissism, of sheer effort matched with intelligence and commitment leading to big spending. For people like Sam, it is a high payoff version of "workaholism" that offers big money and position, with the trade-off being diminishing self-care, psychological maturity, and family harmony. In the subculture of the New Rich, large amounts of cash inflows are matched by equally large outflows of consumption as an important symbol of success, overshadowing other aspects of adult psychological development. One's sense of self as a complete and responsible mature person is reduced to one's financial value, which creates a confusion between emotional well-being and financial well-being. In other words, one let the fraction define the whole.

Trust in Relationships

A person's willingness to trust others in a personal relationship is affected by wealth. The presence of money can make it hard to trust others, even as it attracts them. Wealthy people must learn how to select and trust special other people or they often feel that money undermines the nature of relationships. People can always wonder if someone likes them for their money or for who they are. A mature person finds ways to distinguish the personal friends who are genuine. When a person finds his or her personal comfort zone in handling the impact of money on personal relationships, he or she is able to trust other people and deal with money issues without poisoning or undermining relationships. Vulnerability arises when intimacy, trust, and stability are over-determined or undermined by money matters. Conflicts over money can contaminate relationships with loved ones, causing money-driven hardships and heartaches.

The arrival of a life-changing amount of money can be either a great blessing or a curse for a marriage. Opportunities abound, but choices about money can divide as rapidly as unite a relationship. Consider Ken and Helen Jones, who after 35 years of work and raising three children had the good fortune of a combination stock windfall and inheritance. Overnight they went from being middle-class Americans to having a portfolio worth $50 million. It was all great until they tried to agree on how to spend their time and money. He bought a second house, a vineyard, and a sailboat. She felt the need to help children and families, so started a foundation. Helen hated his materialism; Ken hated her "holier than thou" view of the world. Unable to find a constructive way of talking out their differences, they each retreated into separate ventures and ended up divorcing.

Vulnerability can also be seen in people with exaggerated fears about being "taken advantage of" by others. Some people have irrational fears of contact with others of differing economic classes. Fears about how others may respond to money issues can result in secrecy or at its extreme, the "Howard Hughes syndrome" of privacy with a paranoid edge.

Emily, a 43-year-old social worker, found herself the unexpected heir of $5 million that her parents had secretly squirreled away. They never talked to Emily, their only child, about money, except to say that they were "comfortable." Instead of feeling elated by her newfound fortune, Emily found herself feeling anxious about its impact on her life. Ultimately her feelings of guilt (her parents lived modestly and rarely took vacations) and concern about the potential envy of others (was it her imagination that her best friend was almost resentful rather than grateful that she had picked up the dinner tabs lately?) led her to continue her parents' secretive attitude toward money.

Instead of money providing more choices and freedom, Emily felt deeply disturbed, inhibited, and constricted by it. She needed to hide her money and was unable to use it to enhance her life.

Stewardship

Stewards see themselves as safeguarding a resource for the benefit of future beneficiaries. In mastering the developmental challenges of Stage IV, they view wealth as a multidimensional resource that is preserved and shared for the benefit of both current and future generations. Healthy individuals want to look around and consider what can be done for other people and for the future. Stewardship is reflected in having a "future sense" of money decisions, wanting to leave a meaningful legacy, and being thoughtful about the impact of distributions to future generations. Stewards plan for how wealth can make a difference in their own lives, as well as in the larger community. Success in this area is reflected in having a plan for the distribution of wealth and in leaving a value-based legacy for future generations.

We feel that people who view their wealth as primarily for their own use, who do not have or want a legacy plan, and who are not concerned about the future use of their money distributions are living in denial of the world beyond their personal sphere. They see wealth as a private resource for personal use and enjoyment, and they feel no further responsibility. Wealth does not, and should not, make someone a saint. Spending is not a sin. However, the presence of significant money can lead people to consider issues beyond themselves, such as how it can affect heirs and the community.

Sandra, a 48-year-old entrepreneur who had strong feelings about her future legacy, had this to say:

> In our business we make sure that our employees know we value their hard work, but that we see their families as their top priority. We provide incentives for our employees to volunteer in their local communities as well. Where we live, housing is very expensive and the public schools are in poor condition. The cost of living is such that many parents have to work more than one job just to make ends meet. The real needs of my community are affordable housing, good public schools and jobs that pay better wages to working people . . . I want to be remembered as someone who took action to bring about lasting changes in my community. I want to know that my children will be able to live happily and safely here or wherever they choose to live.

Other wealthy people see their legacy as being primarily to society and give less to their children. Financier Warren Buffett has made it clear that he will leave his children enough to be comfortable, but most of his wealth will go to a foundation. Gary, a 52-year-old recently retired venture capitalist, is concerned about what money will do to his children, and he adopted an attitude that his heirs should be self-reliant:

My financial success is the direct result of endless hours of hard work and commitment. I strongly believe that self-esteem can only be earned. I don't plan to leave my kids anything more than is enough to complete their college education. I plan to give the majority of my earnings to the University business school that inspired my career. I believe that giving people money doesn't fix their lives, it ruins their lives, making it impossible for them to find their passion and place in our society.

A common pattern is for the next generation of heirs to inherit some money, but more important, to learn that their self-worth and life work lie in philanthropy. The Rockefeller family, after the founding fortune accumulated by John D. Rockefeller, has carefully cultivated careers of philanthropy and social activism in several generations of heirs. Other families of more modest means set up a family foundation and achieve purpose and meaning in their lives by using their time and energy to make a difference in society. This life focus can help heirs overcome any conflict they may feel about coming into money.

If one's life is no longer defined by having to make money, then the question becomes: What does one do to define who one is and what one stands for? As described in Stage IV, defining one's legacy and the meaning of one's wealth is a key step toward a full definition as a person of wealth.

Financial Awareness

This factor indicates the degree to which people are aware of money matters: how much they have, how it is invested, and how it is spent and shared. Not knowing about money is a way of denying it or not being responsible for taking care of it. Just as a person takes care of a prized possession, so people should take care of their money to insure their future. Such behavior indicates a solid hold on one's finances, characterized by the feeling of truly "owning one's money." Although details of wealth management may be delegated to a team of professionals, a mature wealth-holder is keenly aware and in charge of saving, spending, and sharing money. Delegating some aspects is fine, but a person who is fully in charge of money matters must be "in the know" about the spending, saving, and sharing of his or her wealth. Lack of awareness is seen in people who have difficulty claiming ownership of their wealth, or, even worse, avoid or deny responsibility for it altogether. They may behave as if the wealth is really not their own or is magically taken care of by others. These are the wealthy people who are prey to all sorts of schemes that relieve them of their money.

Many heirs and people who achieve sudden success are not really prepared to handle their money, because they have not been taught to do so. However, they need to inform themselves and begin a learning process. The existence of trusts and family financial advisors sometimes makes them feel dependent and reinforces a childlike lack of awareness and oversight. This childlike dependency often leaves them feeling incomplete, undeveloped, and vulnerable. Sometimes after a setback or huge loss they take the reins. At other times they struggle to control their money against well-meaning but misguided financial advisors. Success here does not mean making all choices on their own or rejecting professional advice. Rather it means being informed about what is happening and taking part in major financial decisions.

Not infrequently we see contradictions between a person's money awareness at work compared to their personal wealth. For example, Sandy, a 38-year-old CFO of a high-tech firm in Silicon Valley, spends much of her day dealing with money matters, a role in which she has gained much professional and financial recognition. When asked about her personal money management, however, she becomes anxious and indecisive. She often feels confused and uncertain after hearing the advice of the three financial advisors she employs to manage her vast assets. When it comes to her personal money matters, in her words, "I act as if I'm stupid, unsure of myself, or as if it doesn't really belong to me, although I know it does!"

Inheritors also often suffer from difficulties with money awareness. Heirs are given money without necessarily being given the skills to manage their wealth. Some heirs feel disconnected from their money, as if it still belongs to the family member who made the distribution. One variation on this theme is the so-called "trust babies," those whose inheritance becomes an obstacle to growing up. Yet others feel guilty or ashamed about their "bloodline good fortune," hiding their wealth from others, as well as themselves. Maxine, a 45-year-old who worked part-time as a substitute teacher and art consultant, had lived off a trust her whole life. She had little idea of her net worth and avoided thinking about her money, fearing that if she focused on it, she would "break out in hives." She continued to use her parents' financial advisor, never questioning any of his decisions. When her financial statements arrived in the mail, she opened and filed them without reading them. Even talking about her money with her brother, a trusted ally and friend, made her feel anxious and distracted.

COUNSELING AND CONSULTATION

We have seen people pursue different paths to help them progress in their own development. First, and probably most available, there are workshops, groups, and support networks that are sponsored by investment banks, financial service groups, and philanthropy networks where people can discover what to do to preserve their money and how they can use their money as a vehicle for personal development, family unity, and social change. Such networks offer several things. They offer the support of people who are struggling with similar issues and a safe and confidential environment in which to explore these issues. They also offer clear outlets where heirs can learn about issues from money management to philanthropy without feeling burdened by the pain and difficult choices that are put upon them by those in need.

Second, various types of personal and family counseling and coaching can help one discover a basis for making choices, develop understanding of one's mixed feelings, and chart a course for the future. At Money, Meaning & Choices Institute we have developed a Wealth and Life Planning System that provides a step-by-step strategy for helping clients to surface money-related emotional issues; define core values; and determine lifestyle, philanthropic, and legacy plans. We facilitate maturation of wealth identity and also encourage money dialogue as an opportunity for family unity: Family members have a chance to stop the action of daily life, take genuine stock of where they are today, and create value-based action plans.

A third option is to meet as a family. We find that families are coming together to explore the issues of wealth in their lives and to talk about the choices facing their children and heirs. The family can gather informally, at the family home or at a meal, or they can have a more formal gathering where they talk about specific approaches to money, be it investing, spending, or giving. We find that meeting as a family to discuss values, how money can be shared and used, and what is important to each member is an effective way for coming to terms with wealth (Jaffe, Goldbart, & DiFuria, 2003).

CONCLUSION: TAKING RESPONSIBILITY AND ACTION FOR HAVING WEALTH

We have looked at how individuals who experience sudden earned or inherited wealth must go through a process of self-discovery and personal development. As they progress through developmental stages and master the core issues associated with each stage, people come to terms with their wealth and integrate it into their lives. Some people proceed easily on their own through these developmental stages and tasks, encountering few obstacles or concerns. Others find support in family, friends, or in networks for heirs or philanthropists who are working on similar issues. Other people consult professionals like ourselves when they find themselves with unexpected or unwanted feelings or with difficult struggles related to aspects of their wealth.

At the beginning of this chapter we suggested that the world does not make this an easy task. We live in a society that overvalues money and promotes the belief that money removes all cares and problems. Our society also holds ambivalent feelings of envy and resentment that are projected onto wealthy people, further complicating their developmental journey. Some people have to contend with exaggerated feelings of guilt at having money and the pressure of responsibility to do something with it. Often, such feelings cause the affluent to remove themselves from the company of all but other people of the same financial status. Although it may be pleasant living in "the gilded ghetto" (O'Neill, 1997), it is by no means a solution. If one is not comfortable or is unable to make one's way through all areas of the community, and to develop close relationships with people representing a diversity of social classes and experiences, one's life is diminished. The challenge of "achieving balance" in the final stage of wealth identity is finding a place for oneself *in the world* that maximizes wealth as a resource for self, family, and society.

We find that people who become wealthy must be aware that they have a journey ahead of them. They need to be aware that they will be invaded by a mass of difficult feelings and that their wealth will at first seem like a handicap to overcome or a burden disguised as a blessing. People around them may behave strangely, and they will have to make choices about gray matters that previously were cut-and-dried. What does one do if there no longer is a need to earn a living? What should one do if one has more money than is needed to live a rich and full life? Achieving a positive wealth identity means redefining one's inner psychological map and answering a question that most Americans only dream of having the opportunity to answer: What is the real meaning and purpose of my wealth . . . for myself, my family, and my community?

REFERENCES

Blouin, B., Gibson, K., & Kiersted, M. (Eds.). (1995). *The legacy of inherited wealth.* Blacksburg, VA: Trio.

Colarusso, C. A., & Nemiroff, R. A. (1979). Some observations and hypotheses about the psychoanalytic theory of adult development. *International Journal of Psychoanalysis, 60,* 59–71.

Csikszentmihalyi, M. (1999). If we are so rich, why aren't we happy? *American Psychologist, 54,* 821–827.

Erikson, E. (1980). *Identity and the life cycle.* New York: W. W. Norton.

Goldbart, S. (2001). *Mapping the terrain of the heart: Passion, tenderness, and the capacity to love.* New York: Jason Aronson.

Jaffe, D., Goldbart, S., & DiFuria, J. (2003). Family meetings that work. In H. L. Schneider (Ed.), *Wealthy and wise* (pp. 80–93). New York: Wiley.

Mahler, M., Pine, F., & Bergman, A. (1975). *The psychological birth of the human infant.* New York: Basic Books.

Myers, D. G. (2000). The funds, friends, and faith of happy people. *American Psychologist, 55,* 56–67.

Needleman, J. (1991). *Money and the meaning of life*. New York: Doubleday.

O'Neill, J. (1997). *The gilded ghetto: The psychology of affluence*. Milwaukee, WI: The Affluenza Project.

Schervish, P., Coutsoukis, P., & Lewis, E. (Eds.). (1994). *The gospels of wealth*. Westport, CT: Praeger.

Sedgwick, J. (1985). *Rich kids*. New York: Morrow.

Sheehy, G. (1984). *Passages: Predictable crises of adult life*. New York: Bantam.

IV

THE INFLUENCE OF COMMERCIALISM ON CHILD DEVELOPMENT

12

THE COMMERCIALIZATION OF CHILDHOOD: UNDERSTANDING THE PROBLEM AND FINDING SOLUTIONS

DIANE E. LEVIN AND SUSAN LINN

Children have long been a target for advertisers, but since the 1980s they have been subjected to an escalating and unprecedented onslaught of corporate marketing. The proliferation of electronic media, the deregulation of children's television, and a booming economy have all contributed to the transformation of children into a consumer group. Children aged 2 to 14 years now influence purchases of about $500 billion annually (Packaged Facts, 2000). These days, kids are big business.

The amount of money spent on marketing to children doubled during the 1990s—currently about $12 billion a year (Rice, 2001)—as corporations compete for *share of mind* and *life-time brand loyalty*. In 2000, Burger King spent $80 million on children's advertising (Cebrzynski & Zuber, 2001). The year before, Quaker Oats spent $15 million on a 5-month campaign just to reinvigorate sales of the sugared cereal Cap'n Crunch (Thompson, 1999).

The authors contributed equally to this chapter.

For children, being a target of a multitude of marketing campaigns translates into a bombardment of advertising from the moment they wake up until they go to sleep. The average child now sees 40,000 commercials annually on television alone (Kunkel, 2001). However, marketing to children goes far beyond advertisements on television. Corporate giants like McDonald's and Disney use their power, sophisticated technology, extensive research, and the expertise of child psychologists to create advertising strategies aimed at children. Media phenomena such as *Spider-Man* and *Pokémon* are marketed through seamless links between TV and movie characters, computer games, Web sites, toys, food, clothing, accessories, and more.

How have children become such an important consumer group? Why are children so vulnerable to marketing, and how do marketers exploit this vulnerability? What price do children pay for this exploitation? Is marketing to children ethical, and should psychologists be involved in this practice? What if anything should be done to protect children? These are the questions we attempt to answer in this chapter.

THE EVOLUTION OF CHILDREN AS A TARGET MARKET: FROM DEREGULATION TO VIRAL MARKETING

Electronic media have transformed how children spend their time, and the commercialization of childhood can only be understood in that context. Children in the United States between ages 2 and 18 spend almost 40 hours per week with electronic media, including television, computers, videos, movies, and the radio. The average child now spends more time in front of a screen than doing anything else but sleeping (Roberts, Foehr, Rideout, & Brodie, 1999).

In the United States, electronic media have long been the driving force in marketing to children. This has not been the case everywhere. In the early days of television, most other industrialized countries made policy decisions that kept children's television educational and protected children from advertising (Carlsson & Von Feilitzen, 1998). Today, such policies are still in effect in several countries. For example, Sweden and Norway prohibit television advertising that directly targets children below 12 years of age. In Canada, the Province of Quebec prohibits television advertising directed at children below the age of 13. Greece bans television advertising of toys to children between 7:00 a.m. and 10:00 p.m. (Valkenburg, 2000).

In contrast, children in the United States have no such protection. U.S. policy decisions have always reflected the view that television was for entertainment purposes, not education, and therefore should be run as a business that pays for itself through advertising. From the start, advertising to children on television has been a commonplace and accepted practice in the United States (Minow & Lamay, 1995).

In the 1970s the Federal Trade Commission (FTC) gained the authority to regulate deceptive and unfair advertising, including advertising to children (Kunkel, 2001). In addition, the Federal Communications Commission (FCC) regulated children's television and placed a limit on the number of advertising minutes per hour (Engelhardt, 1986). Under these early regulations, developing and marketing products (such as toys) and TV programs together was prohibited (i.e., the program-length commercial). These policies helped to hold back the flood of advertising to children.

In 1980 Congress took away the FTC's power to regulate unfair or deceptive advertising, and in 1984 the floodgates opened wide when the FCC deregulated children's television, ending the ban on program-length commercials (Kunkel, 2001). Programs such as *Masters of the Universe* were used to market whole lines of toys. This technique for marketing products to children was highly effective; by 1987, 60% of children's toys were linked to media (Cross, 2000).

Although violent content has always been a part of the commercialized media culture, it became one of the most lucrative approaches used for marketing to children after deregulation. Most of the highly realistic toys and other products that were developed after deregulation were linked to violent TV programs (Carlsson-Paige & Levin, 1990). Each new, "successful" violent program was more violent than the one that preceded it. The *Teenage Mutant Ninja Turtles* TV show in the late 1980s had an average of 50 acts of violence per episode, whereas in the early 1990s, episodes of the *Mighty Morphin Power Rangers* averaged 100 acts of violence (Lisosky, 1995). Within 1 year of deregulation, 9 of the 10 best selling toys had TV shows, 7 of which had violent themes.

Deregulation of children's television fueled marketing to children through other media as well. For instance, in 1990, the *Teenage Mutant Ninja Turtles* movie (based on the television series) had the second-highest ticket sales in movie history on the first weekend of its release. More than 300 licensed products that were linked to the movie arrived on toy shelves in time for the movie's opening (Hammer & Miller, 1990). In 1994, the *Power Rangers* reached an industry pinnacle with worldwide sales surpassing $1 billion as marketing of violence to children through the media increasingly became a worldwide phenomenon.

Today, blockbuster movies with PG-13 or R ratings, such as the movie series *Jurassic Park*, *Men in Black,* and *Spider-Man*, sell millions of dollars worth of toys recommended for children aged 4 or 5. There are also the highly lucrative link-ups with the video game market, which are not counted in toy sales figures but which are becoming substitutes for toys at younger and younger ages.

New and increasingly sophisticated strategies for marketing to children have continued to develop. Media cross-advertising has become the norm. TV programs, movies, and video games are often generated from one concept or feature the same characters; each serves as an advertisement for the other, as well as for all the products linked to them. Now Internet Web sites have also been added to the equation (McChesney, 1999).

In addition to cross-marketing, movies and television programs also rely on product placement, that is, companies pay to have their products serve as props, scenery, or even plotlines within a program. The popular 2001 Miramax film *Spy Kids*, for instance, actually included a McDonald's meal, in addition to cross-marketing in the form of toys and food products. Meanwhile, on TV programs such as the tween[1] hit, *Dawson's Creek*, jewelry and clothing worn by popular characters are for sale on the show's Web site.

One of the most successful examples of cross-marketing in recent years is the Pokémon phenomenon (Linn, 2000). Pokémon is not just a trading-card game, but also a popular TV cartoon, a series of Nintendo games, a movie, a line of stuffed animals, a Radio City Music Hall extravaganza, a line of Halloween costumes, and products for thematic birthday parties including a set of cake decorations. A *USA Today* story (Content, 1999) reported that Pokémon expected to sell $6 billion worth of licensed products worldwide in 1999, when the craze was at its peak.

A particularly worrisome example of cross-marketing in recent years is the marriage between toy companies and the food industry. Mattel now produces a Barbie "McDonald's Fun Time" play set. The box, adorned with the enticement, "Lots of yummy food," contains miniature French fries, Big Macs, and other high calorie delights, including a Sprite soft drink machine. Hasbro offers a McDonald's Play-Doh set with molds for burgers and buns, as well as machines for churning out shakes and soft-serve ice cream.

In some marketing efforts, the "toys" actually *are* food. The Hasbro M&M Mini Candy Copter comes with a replaceable canister filled with M&Ms. Spin Pops, linked to media hits such as *Spider-Man*, *Powerpuff Girls*, and *Batman*, are lollipops that fit into a battery-operated spinning handle.

With the advent of *Teletubbies*, for the first time, even babies became fair targets for advertising through television (Linn & Poussaint, 1999). This PBS children's television program, imported from the BBC in 1998, was the first television program directed at 12-month-olds. It unleashed a flood of video and computer programs for babies and toddlers, as well as cardboard books for babies designed to look just like packages of food, such as Fruit Loops, Oreos, Sun-Maid Raisins, and Cheerios. Now there are whole lines of media-linked toy lines for infants and toddlers (Levin & Rosenquest, 2001).

In recent years, new strategies for reaching children have been added to the mix to permeate even further into children's lives. There are now magazines aimed at children that carry advertisements for adult products; for instance, minivan ads appear in *Sports Illustrated for Kids*. Databases of child

---

[1]*Tweens* is the advertising industry's designation for preteens as a marketing demographic.

customers are being built from information gathered through the Internet and from electronic toy registries at stores like Toys R Us (National Institute on Media and the Family, 2002). As school budgets become increasingly strained and the cost of educational material rises, schools often make up for the shortfall by accepting both direct and indirect advertising from corporations (Consumers Union, 1998). For instance, schools receive $750 million annually from companies selling snack or processed foods (Egan, 2002).

When children approach adolescence, they are targets of a recently developed practice, called *word-of-mouth* or *"viral" marketing* (Siegel, Coffey, & Livingston, 2002). This approach relies on sending marketers out into a community to identify the most popular children. These kids are given free products to distribute; in this way, the product is identified as "cool" and becomes attractive to the less popular children who also want to be "cool." Companies also hand out free CDs or other products and "seed" Internet chat rooms to tout the glories of a particular product in a seemingly spontaneous fashion.

CHILD DEVELOPMENT: WHY CHILDREN ARE VULNERABLE AND HOW MARKETERS EXPLOIT THEM

Theories of children's social, emotional, and cognitive development are routinely used in the field of consumer psychology to map out in great detail and with great sophistication how children of different ages respond to advertising (Friestad & Wright, 1994; John, 1999). Such work is invaluable to marketers who target children. An understanding of child development is also central to grasping the profound impact marketing can have on childhood because it helps to explain why children are so vulnerable to manipulation by marketers and how marketing techniques exploit those vulnerabilities.

Cognitive–developmental theorists such as Jean Piaget (1952) have emphasized that children do not interpret experience the way adults do. The younger children are, the more they tend to focus on the dramatic and concrete aspects of how things look, rather than on what they hear, and the less they look beneath the surface at motivations, intentions, and abstract ideas. They do not make logical causal connections between events and instead focus on one idea at a time, not the relationships between them. Because of this, when young children see advertising or product-based programs, they focus on the most graphic, concrete aspects of what they see and do not put the product they see in a meaningful context. Preschool children have a hard time distinguishing between programs and commercials (Atkin, 1982). Before the age of about 8, they have trouble understanding the persuasive intent of advertising and are unable to understand the intentions that underlie commercials (John, 1999; Kunkel, 2001). For instance, they are unlikely to realize that the people in the ad are smiling and appear to be having fun because they are actors who are paid to smile so that a toy may appeal to a viewer, not necessarily because the product makes them happy.

Children age 8 and younger are especially vulnerable to the exploitative techniques used by marketers because their ability to reason logically and abstractly is not fully developed. For instance, when young children see an advertisement they tend to believe what they see (Kunkel, 2001). They do not question whether the product can really do what they see it doing on the screen or whether the commercial is relying on special effects. If a product is different in an exciting-looking way from what they already own, children are often lured into wanting it. When products do not bring happiness or perform as the ad promises, children can be left feeling disappointed without fully understanding why (Carlsson-Paige & Levin, 1990). Verbal warnings, such as "batteries are not included," are unlikely to register in children who are engaged by powerful visual images (Hoffner, Cantor, & Thorson, 1989). In addition, they have a hard time factoring in the cost of a product; for instance, they may think that money comes from a machine at a bank without understanding how their parents earn the money (Carlsson-Paige & Levin, 1990). The powerful messages from the salient images of an advertisement can be more compelling than parents' arguments against either the tactics of the ad or the nature of the product, potentially undermining parental authority and increasing stress on parent–child relationships.

The work of Erik Erikson (1963) on psychosocial development provides another lens for understanding children's special vulnerability to marketing. Erikson described children as passing through a series of stages as they develop relationships with the social world. For instance, he described how young children need to develop a sense of trust, that is, a deep belief that they are safe and can rely on others to meet their needs in predictable ways. As children develop trust, they learn to believe or trust what they see and hear. In the absence of having highly logical skills to reason otherwise, children are especially vulnerable to trusting what they see and are told in advertisements. For example, parents frequently tell us about their children's disappointment and anger when products do not live up to advertised promises.

According to Erikson, children also need to develop a sense of autonomy, that is, a belief in themselves as capable beings, separate from their parents. In the marketing world, however, Erikson's construct of "autonomy" gets simplified into "control." Children's need for "control" is used to justify marketing products that parents may not like, which foments family stress. For instance, in a discussion of Kraft Lunchables, one marketer commented, "Parents do not fully approve—they would rather their child ate a more traditional lunch—but this adds to the brand's appeal among children because it reinforces their need to feel in control" (Neville, 2001, p. 17).

Concern about how marketing can exploit children's developmental vulnerabilities, as well as its potential to do harm, led the American Academy of Pediatrics (1995) to conclude that "advertising directed toward children is inherently deceptive and exploits children under age 8 years of age" (p. 295). In Europe, similar concerns caused Sweden to push for limits on children's advertising within the European Union, which many other European Union members are now considering individually (Mitchener, 2001).

Although these organizations and nations have been working to protect children, the marketing industry continues to exploit children by using the cognitive and psychosocial differences between children and adults to transform children into a special "market segment." With help from psychologists (Kanner, 2000), they use theories of child development to create marketing strategies specifically designed for the children's market. In fact, the works of Piaget and Erikson are cited in such treatises as *What Kids Buy and Why: The Psychology of Marketing to Kids* (Acuff & Reiher, 1997).

The concept that children are different from adults and develop over time has had a profound influence on how marketers approach advertising to the "kid market." The CEO of a firm specializing in youth marketing summed it up this way: "Only a decade ago, advertisers lumped all kids into one broad category. Now they realize age segmentation is essential. After all, a 12-year-old is 50% older than a kid who is 8" (Rice, 2001, p. S1).

However, the marketing world's version of child development can be distorted. For instance, in recent years, the industry has embraced the notion that children are "getting older younger" (Cohen & Cahill, 2000, p. 271). Executives argue that today's children are smarter and more sophisticated than their counterparts a decade or so ago and are therefore less likely to be manipulated by commercials. For instance, a former CEO of Mattel justified current marketing practices by saying in *Business Week*, "I have a high regard for the intelligence of kids" (Leonhard & Kerwin, 1997, p. 62). In fact, statements like this confuse intelligence with development. No matter how intelligent 5-year-olds may be, they still cannot fully grasp persuasive intent, thus leaving them extremely vulnerable to manipulative advertising.

Advertising executives also confuse the trappings of sophistication with maturation. In response to concerns about children's vulnerability to marketing, an advertising executive replied, "It's a point of fact that today's child is more savvy than ever before about what it's like to live in a commercial society . . . [A]nd what parents are telling us is that kids are requesting brands and are brand-aware almost as soon as their verbal skills set in" (Hood, 2000, p. 15).

That babies and toddlers request or recognize brands does not reflect marketing "savvy" and the capacity to decode and resist advertising messages. It does suggest, however, that very young children are highly susceptible to marketing, a fact that is borne out by academic research (Borzekowski & Robinson, 2001). The rationale that children are more "intelligent" and "sophisticated" is faulty, yet it is often used as justification for escalating the barrage of child-targeted marketing.

The marketing industry's embrace of the notion that children leapfrog through development at breakneck speed is simplistic, potentially harmful, and self-serving. For instance, there is evidence that girls are entering puberty at an earlier age (Kaplowitz, Slora, Wasserman, Pedlow, & Herman-Giddens, 2001). There is also evidence that they are beginning to abuse drugs, alcohol, and tobacco at younger ages (Jacobs, Joffe, Knight, Kulig, & Rogers, 2001; Nelson et al., 2001). However, we have found no evidence that children's emotional development is keeping pace with their bodies or their behavior. What are their psychological and emotional experiences of the physical and behavioral trappings of maturation? How does a 7-year-old understand the plastic sexuality of Britney Spears? How do 10-year-olds cope with pressure to dress and act in sexually provocative ways? According to the toy industry, proof of children's sophistication lies in statistics showing that children are leaving traditional toys behind at younger ages, trading them in for video games and pop culture icons. The industry's solution to this "problem" has been to market dolls that are representations of pop culture. That may solve their sales problems, as media-based toys are a gold mine both for toy and media companies. However, we do not know the impact that dolls based on sexy pop stars may have on the emotional and social development of young girls. Nor can we discount the likelihood that targeting children with marketing campaigns for more "sophisticated" toys contributes to their apparent disinterest in the more traditional playthings that better serve development (Levin, 1998).

Contrasting the care and respect with which Erikson and Piaget wrote about children with the ways their work is used to exploit children raises important issues. In the next sections, we discuss some of the growing evidence that intensive marketing harms children and explore the ethical questions that arise from these problems.

THE COSTS OF MARKETING TO CHILDREN

Marketing can be connected with many problems associated with contemporary childhood. Life-threatening behaviors including consumption of alcohol and tobacco have long been linked to marketing (Sargent et al., 1997; Wyllie, Zhang, & Casswell, 1998), as has extreme dieting among adolescent girls (Kilbourne, 1999; chap. 14, this volume). In recent years, a growing body of evidence has also linked marketing to other life-threatening phenomena such as youth violence and the escalation of childhood obesity.

Marketing Violence

The marketing of violence to children has been the subject of U.S. Senate Committee on Commerce, Science, and Transportation meetings

(U.S. Senate, 1999). In 2000, a major study by the FTC (2000) concluded that marketing violence to children and youth is a common entertainment industry practice. Even R-rated movies, intended for audiences age 17 and older, are marketed to younger children. In addition, there has been a steady escalation in the levels of violence allowed for movies given the G, PG, and PG-13 ratings (Kennedy, 2002).

The negative impact of the violence marketed to children has been the focus of increasing concern. There is a rapidly growing body of research that shows how the violence children see in the media is harming them and contributing to the high levels of youth violence in society. In July 2000, six major medical and mental health organizations issued a joint statement about the harmful effects of viewing media violence (American Academy of Pediatrics, 2000). After reviewing more than 1,000 studies conducted over 30 years, they concluded that the evidence points overwhelmingly to a causal connection between media violence and aggressive behavior in some children, as well as increases in aggressive attitudes, values, and behavior. Moreover, they concluded that prolonged viewing of media violence can lead to emotional desensitization toward violence in real life.

Violence is a learned behavior, and aggressive behavior at age 8 is predictive of levels of aggression in adulthood (Eron & Slaby, 1994). Young children are especially vulnerable to the impact of entertainment violence (American Academy of Pediatrics, 2000). They are easily seduced into paying attention to the dramatic images and actions that violence on the screen provides. They also have a hard time sorting out fantasy from reality; they believe what they see and do not make clear distinctions between real life and what is on the screen. Young children also have difficulty figuring out the cause and effect of the actions they see. They repeatedly get messages from the media that violence is fun and exciting and that no one gets hurt. Children incorporate these messages about violence into their play and their behavior, trying them out, and using them as building blocks for social, emotional, and intellectual development. Violence can seem like a normal and expected aspect of life. Telling children that the entertainment violence is "pretend" or even "bad" usually takes a back seat to the excitement and power that it seems to provide (Levin, 1998).

The negative impact of media violence is amplified by all of the marketing that accompanies programs, especially the violent media-linked toys that affect children's play. Creative play is essential to children's development and learning (Christie, 1998; Jarrell, 1998). Children use play to figure things out, to learn how to solve problems, and to experience the sense of internal power and control that problem solving and mastery can bring. Rather than allowing children to create their own play, violent media-linked toys can channel them into using their play to imitate the violent scripts they see in the media. This kind of imitation leaves children focused on violence as a way to feel powerful and solve problems (Levin, 1996).

Marketing Junk Food

Twenty-five percent of American children are overweight or at risk for obesity (Troiano & Flegal, 1998). That means that they are at risk for heart disease, stroke, and other weight-related health problems. Recent years have seen an increased number of children diagnosed with Type II diabetes, which is usually found in adults. Several studies link obesity with excessive television viewing (Crespo et al., 2001; Dennison, Erb, & Jenkins, 2002; Gortmaker et al., 1996). The problem, however, is not just that kids are sedentary couch potatoes; while they are watching television, they are inundated with food advertisements. For example, in one 6-hour period, we observed 40 food commercials on Nickelodeon, the popular children's television station.

Controversy over advertising candy, snacks, and sugar cereals on television is not new. The advocacy group Action for Children's Television took on that battle in the 1970s. Today, however, despite the 1990 Children's Television Act which limits advertising time (but not what is advertised) during children's programming, food commercials account for most of the advertising during children's peak viewing hours (Taras & Gage, 1995). On Saturday mornings, children see one food commercial about every 5 minutes (Horgan, Choate, & Brownell, 2001), and most of these ads are for foods high in fat, sugar, and calories (Kotz & Story, 1994). Children's requests for products, including food, are linked to television advertising (Jeffrey, McLellarn, & Fox, 1982; Taras, Sallis, Patterson, Nader, & Nelson, 1989). In fact, one 30-second food commercial can affect the brand choices of children as young as age 2, and repeated exposure has more impact (Borzekowski & Robinson, 2001).

Over the past decade, techniques for marketing unhealthy food to children have become increasingly sophisticated and insidious. The *New York Times* reported that $750 million is spent annually selling snacks, processed foods, and sodas in schools (Egan, 2002). Fast food and snack food corporations have child-oriented Web sites replete with games, contests, and movie promotions. As we are writing this chapter, a visit to the Web site Hersheys.com, for instance, links to *Spider-Man*. BurgerKing.com links right to *Men in Black* as well as to Nickelodeon. McDonalds.com links to the Disney film, *Country Bears*.

Visit any supermarket and you will find shelves filled with links between the media industry and food manufacturers. Characters from the hit Nickelodeon TV program *Rugrats* have graced packages of Kraft Macaroni & Cheese as well as Farley's Fruit Rolls, a Good Humor Ice Cream Sandwich (peanut butter & jelly-flavored), and Comic Book Bubble Gum (with comics printed on the gum itself; view & chew) by Amurol. And that's just one program! Such tie-ins are designed to lure children into selecting food on the basis of favorite movie or TV characters. They are also designed to keep children continually reminded of products. As one marketing expert says, corporations are "trying to establish a situation where kids are exposed to their brand in as many different places as possible throughout the course of the day or the week, or almost anywhere they turn in the course of their daily rituals" (Kjos, 2002, p. 1).

THE ETHICS OF MARKETING TO CHILDREN

By conceptualizing childhood as a market segment, corporations focus on making profits, often at the expense of what is best for children. We have already discussed the problems associated with marketing violent media and junk food to children. However, another kind of problem can be found in the commercial messages themselves, regardless of what product is being marketed, and in the ethics of a corporate culture that sanctions and even encourages the exploitation of children's social and developmental vulnerabilities. For instance, many commercials are designed to take advantage of a need to belong and to associate the acquisition of products with happiness, fun, making friends, or being "cool." The head of one advertising agency explained:

> Advertising at its best is making people feel that without their product, you're a loser. . . . Kids are very sensitive to that. If you tell them to buy something, they are resistant. But if you tell them that they'll be a dork if they don't, you've got their attention. You open up emotional vulnerabilities, and it's very easy to do with kids because they're the most emotionally vulnerable. (Harris, 1989, p. 1)

The marketing industry's lack of concern for children's well-being is reflected plainly in the annual Golden Marble Awards, where the industry honors the best advertising and promotional campaigns directed at children. These awards, similar to the Emmy awards or the Oscars, are given solely on the basis of artistic merit and do not take into account the products being advertised or the impact of the ads on children's health or well-being.

The Golden Marble Awards have been presented each year since 1998 at a conference called Advertising and Promoting to Kids. Over the past several years, there has been a proliferation of such conferences that focus solely on children as a consumer group. Conferences like Advertising and Promoting to Kids, Kid Power Food and Beverage Marketing, Kid Power Latin America, and Tween Power present state-of-the-art knowledge about marketing to children. Marketing executives attend sessions where they can "Hear from ethnic marketing experts on how to reach Hispanic, African American and Asian American kids" and "Discover the latest research on reaching kids and tweens at different stages in their lives" (Advertising and Promoting to Kids, 2002, p. 1).

The 2002 Kid Power Food and Beverage Marketing annual conference materials promised attendees information about "successful kid-targeted strategies" for the food, beverage, and restaurant industries at workshops such as "Creating 'Gotta Have It'," "Excitement in the Beverage Aisle–Taking Disney's Magic to the Grocery Store," and "From Supermarkets to Soccer Fields: Kids Wants, Moms Behaviors [sic]." Nowhere in the conference brochure (Kid Power Food and Beverage Marketing, 2002) is any reference made to how children's lives might be affected by the products being marketed or the techniques being used to market them.

The information presented at conferences like these is based on extensive research with children and families. In 1999, the advertising agency Saatchi and Saatchi employed psychologists and anthropologists to visit the homes of 200 children across the United States to produce what was described as an "exhaustive" study whose sole purpose was to help corporations market to children more effectively (Selling to Kids, 1999).

Unlike academic research, most corporate research on marketing to children is proprietary and the results are either kept secret or sold to corporate clients for a great deal of money. However, through publicity announcements and industry newsletters, some information is available about the nature of these studies. Perhaps the most egregious study is one on nagging, conducted in 1998 by Western Media International in conjunction with Lieberman Research Worldwide. Based on interviews with 150 mothers of children age 3 to 8 who kept logs of various nags, "The Fine Art of Whining: Why Nagging Is a Kid's Best Friend" (Business Wire, 1998) identifies which kinds of parents are most likely to give in to nagging. Not surprisingly, divorced parents or those with teenagers or younger children top the list. The study also enumerates the purchases attributed to nagging—4 out of 10 trips to "placed entertainment establishments like the Discovery Zone and Chuck E. Cheese"; 1 out of every 3 trips to a fast-food restaurant; and 3 out of every 10 home video sales.

Evoking the "nag factor" or "pester power" is a common marketing strategy for marketers who target children without regard for how the practice affects parent–child relationships. In October 2001, an executive for Heinz had this to say about the launch of their campaign to sell multi-hued ketchup, "All our advertising is targeted to kids. . . .You want that nag factor so that seven-year-old Sarah is nagging mom in the grocery store to buy Funky Purple [ketchup]. We're not sure mom would reach out for it on her own" (Eig, 2001, p. B1).

THE ROLE OF PSYCHOLOGISTS IN MARKETING TO CHILDREN

Companies that market to children routinely hire child psychologists who play a central role in the marketing campaigns (Rice, 2001). Is this consistent with the ethics of psychologists? The Ethical Standards of the American Psychological Association state that psychologists should "apply and make public their knowledge of psychology in order to contribute to human welfare" (American Psychological Association, 1992). Yet psychologists who help companies market successfully to children routinely use principles and practices of child psychology—from developmental theory to diagnostic techniques—for the sole purpose of increasing profits. As we have seen, the results for children include feelings of distrust, conflicts with parents, violence, obesity, and other problems.

Advertising agencies such as Saatchi and Saatchi, and corporations such as Nabisco (Cuthbert, 1999), rely on psychologists to gather and interpret data about children. Psychologists conduct focus groups, consult on specific campaigns, and use projective tests to help corporations improve their sales pitches to children. In fact, marketing agencies are as relentless in their quest for knowledge about children as is any academic institution, and they are certainly better funded. It is ironic that most of the research being done on children is in the corporate world. As one marketing expert stated, "We've probably done more recent original research on kids, life stages and recognition of brands than anybody" (Hood, 2000, p. 15). What is missing in reports of data collected for market research are the questions that should be central to all psychological research conducted with children: "Am I using this information to make children's lives better?" and "How will this application of child psychology benefit children?" Whatever their private concerns might be, it seems that no one in the advertising industry publicly questions whether children benefit from marketing messages that play to their vulnerabilities.

Obviously, anyone is free to read books about psychology or to take courses in child development. However, because knowledge of how children change and develop over time is used (or misused) in the world of marketing to exploit children's vulnerabilities, shouldn't we question the ethics of trained psychologists who, presumably for a substantial fee, pass on their expertise to help executives become more effective at exploiting children for profit (Kanner, 2000)?

WHAT SHOULD BE DONE?

The advertising industry's use of psychology as a tool to manipulate children should provide special incentive for psychologists to take a stand against child-targeted marketing. Anyone who cares about children has cause for serious concern. In addition to the threat it poses to their physical and mental health, marketing undermines children's social and spiritual well-being. For instance, the behavior and values inculcated by marketing messages, such as impulse buying, unthinking brand loyalty, and a "me first" mentality, are antithetical to values such as critical thinking and cooperation that are essential to democracy. Moreover, the message central to almost all marketing campaigns—that a particular product can bring us happiness—is contrary to the teaching of all mainstream religions (Belk, 1983).

In recent years parents, healthcare professionals, and educators have all expressed concern that children's immersion in commercial culture is harming them (American Academy of Pediatrics, 1995; Donahue, 1998; Molnar, 1996), but stemming the tide of corporate marketing aimed at children is not going to be easy. Capitalism is such a part of American society that many people dismiss child-targeted marketing as just another means for corporations to turn a profit. In that sense, children can be viewed as similar to other populations, such as minorities, workers, and women, who have been subject to commercial exploitation in this country. By viewing children this way, it becomes clear that the history of other social struggles contains an important lesson (see chap. 4, this volume). One family, one teacher, one psychologist, or one advocacy group alone will have difficulty combating a $12 billion industry.

The need for systemic change certainly does not relieve parents or professionals of individual responsibility to the children in our charge. We cannot help children cope with the impact of marketing until we come to terms with its impact on us; we must monitor our own vulnerabilities to consumerism, as well as our responses to advertising.

We can help children become informed consumers by engaging them in ongoing dialogues about consumerism and marketing. In addition to working with them at home, we can advocate for media literacy to be taught at home and in schools (DeGaetano & Bander, 1996; Levin, 1998). However, it is important to note that, to date, we have found no evidence that helping children decode marketing actually has an impact on purchasing behavior.

To the extent possible, we can set limits on children's access to electronic media and help them critically process the advertising and commercial pressures to which they are still exposed. We can pay closer attention to the circumstances under which children watch television and use other media—where, when, how much they watch, and with whom. For instance, children are often alone when they watch TV; no adult is there to help them process marketing messages. One relatively easy step parents can take to limit and monitor viewing is to keep television out of their child's bedroom. Yet 32% of children ages 2 to 7 have televisions in their rooms, as do 65% of children ages 8 to 18 (Roberts et al., 1999).

At the same time, too much of the burden for counteracting the negative impact of commercialization on children is falling on parents whose efforts are continually undermined by the sheer quantity of marketing to which children are subjected. We believe that society should help parents in their efforts to raise healthy children, not undermine them. We also believe that multifaceted efforts from academia, advocacy groups, the advertising industry, and the government are needed to stem the tide of child-targeted corporate marketing:

More research. Most of the academic research on the impact of marketing to children was conducted before 1980, and very little research has examined how the rapid escalation of marketing to children is affecting them. Our colleagues who conduct research point to a lack of funding as the primary reason for this dearth of information. The federal government and private foundations should allocate funding for research into the psychosocial and health consequences of marketing to children, as well as into media literacy or other strategies for counteracting the harmful effects.

Raise awareness. Public awareness should be raised about the impact of marketing on children and about measures that can be taken to reduce the exploitation of children by advertisers and marketers. For example, public education campaigns could be developed to inform parents about how advertising and marketing practices can harm children, as well as how to limit the negative impact. Along with the 3Rs, consumer literacy programs should be developed and implemented in schools to help children cope with the minefields created by commercialization.

Industry guidelines. Corporations and the advertising industry should share in the burden of creating a healthy environment for children. The industry does have a regulatory bureau, the Children's Advertising Review Unit (CARU), which is operated by the Better Business Bureau. The guidelines for advertising address many of the concerns we raise in this chapter. However, several circumstances render CARU ineffective. First, compliance with the guidelines is voluntary. Second, the organization is extremely small, making it virtually impossible for it to monitor all, or even a large portion of, advertising that targets children. The industry should develop guidelines that take into account the best interest of children—along with profits—and consider psychological safety as well as physical safety when developing and marketing products to children.

Consulting psychologists. As long as marketing to children is legal, it will be legal for psychologists to work on marketing campaigns. However, we believe that psychology, as a profession, should take a strong stand against psychologists who use their knowledge to help companies exploit children for profit. We also believe that market research with children should be subject to the same regulations as academic research. That is, to protect the rights of participants in research, protocols should be evaluated by human subject review committees and participants should have the right of informed consent. On a positive note, psychologists can play an important role in furthering parents' and teachers' understanding about the impact of marketing on children and in developing effective techniques to counteract commercial culture.

Regulation. Given that the advertising industry is not effectively regulating itself, we should consider the possibility of more government regulation. The United States regulates marketing less than most other industrialized democracies (Mikkelsen, 2001). However, there is precedent for protecting children from society's ills, including child labor laws and regulations for marketing tobacco. We could regulate corporate marketing to children either by age (e.g., limiting marketing to children under age 8) or by product category (e.g., violence or fast food). The first step should be a federal investigation of corporate marketing practices that target children, similar to the FTC's investigation of marketing violent media.

Short of a ban on marketing to children, the FCC's role in protecting children from media marketing should be strengthened. Congress passed new FCC regulations governing children's television in 1990 that reinstated limits on advertising minutes per hour during children's TV. However, they did not reinstate the ban on program-length commercials (Minow & Lamay, 1995), and they should do so. The FCC and the FTC should also mandate consistent age-based ratings of TV programs, movies, video games, and toys. In addition, Congress should restore to the FTC the powers taken away in 1980 that enabled the FTC to create regulations that protect children from exploitation and abuse by advertisers.

CONCLUSION

Marketing to children has become so pervasive, and its impact so far reaching, that children's lives are commercialized from birth. Growing evidence documents marketing's negative effects on children's physical, psychological, and social well-being. We believe that the best way to counteract these hazards is through a societywide commitment to combat the commercialization of childhood. Such a commitment to take a stand on what is best for children is reflected in child labor laws, child pornography laws, and mandatory schooling, as well as recent laws about tobacco advertising. We believe that now is the time for everyone who cares about children or has influence over their lives to work together toward reducing commercialism and thus creating an environment that promotes healthy development.

REFERENCES

Acuff, D. S. (with Reiher, R. H.). (1997). *What kids buy and why: The psychology of marketing to kids*. New York: Free Press.

Advertising and Promoting to Kids. (2002). Retrieved August 28, 2002, from http://www.kidscreen.com/apk/2002

American Academy of Pediatrics. (1995). Position statement: Children, adolescents, and advertising. *Pediatrics, 95*(2), 295–297.

American Academy of Pediatrics. (2000, July 26). *Joint statement on the impact of entertainment violence on children*. Washington, DC: Congressional Public Health Summit.

American Psychological Association. (1992). Ethical principles of psychologists and code of conduct. Retrieved June 27, 2003 from www.apa.org/ethics/code1992.html

Atkin, C. K. (1982). Television advertising and socialization to consumer roles. In D. Pearl (Ed.), *Television and behavior: Ten years of scientific progress and implications for the eighties* (pp. 191–200). Rockland, MD: National Institute of Mental Health.

Belk, R. W. (1983). Worldly possessions: Issues and criticisms. In R. P. Bagozzi & A. M. Tybout (Eds.), *Advances in consumer research* (Vol. 10, pp. 514–519). Ann Arbor, MI: Association for Consumer Research.

Borzekowski, D. L. G., & Robinson, T. (2001). The 30-second effect: An experiment revealing the impact of television commercials on food preferences of preschoolers. *Journal of the American Diabetic Association, 101*(1), 42–46.

Business wire. (1998). The fine art of whining: Why nagging is a kid's best friend. Retrieved August 1998 from http://80-web.lexis-nexis.com

Carlsson, U., & Von Feilitzen, C. (1998). *Children and media violence: Yearbook for the UNESCO International Clearinghouse on Children and Violence on the Screen.* Gotenborg, Sweden: UNESCO International Clearinghouse on Children and Violence on the Screen.

Carlsson-Paige, N., & Levin, D. E. (1990). *Who's calling the shots? How to respond effectively to children's fascination with war play and war toys.* Gabriola Island, British Columbia: New Society.

Cebrzynski, G., & Zuber, A. (2001, February 5). Burger behemoths shake up menu mix, marketing tactics. *Nation's Restaurant News*, p. 1.

Christie, J. (1998). Play: A medium for literacy development. In D. Fromberg & D. Bergen (Eds.), *Play from birth to twelve and beyond* (pp. 50–55). New York: Garland.

Cohen, M., & Cahill, E. (2000). Getting older younger: Developmental differences in children and the challenges of developmental compression. *International Journal of Advertising and Marketing to Children, December 1999/January 2000,* 271–278.

Consumers Union. (1998). *Captive kids: A report on commercial pressures on kids at school.* Retrieved August 8, 2002 from www.consumersunion.org

Content, T. (1999, November 10). Pokémon poised to stomp Elmo, Furby. *USA Today*, pp. 1b–2b.

Crespo C. J., Smit, E., Troiano, R., Bartlett, S. J., Macera, C. A., & Andersen, R E. (2001). Television watching, energy intake, and obesity in U.S. children: Results from the third national health and nutrition examination survey, 1988–1994. *Archives of Pediatric and Adolescent Medicine, 155,* 360–365.

Cross, G. (2000). *An all-consuming century: Why commercialism won in modern America.* New York: Columbia University Press.

Cuthbert, W. (1999, April 26). Fantasy, control key to youth promos. *Strategy*, p. 25.

DeGaetano, G., & Bander, K. (1996). *Screen smarts: Raising media literate kids.* Boston: Houghton Mifflin.

Dennison, B. A., Erb, T. A., & Jenkins, P. L. (2002). Television viewing and television in bedroom associated with overweight risk among low-income preschool children. *Pediatrics, 109,* 1028–1035.

Donahue, D. (1998, October 1). Struggling to raise good kids in toxic times: Is innocence evaporating in an open-door society? *USA Today,* pp. 1–2D.

Egan, T. (2002, May 20). In bid to improve nutrition, schools expel soda and chips. *New York Times,* pp. A1, 18.

Eig, J. (2001, October 24). Edible entertainment: Food companies grab kids by fancifully packaging products as toys, games. *The Wall Street Journal,* p. B1.

Engelhardt, T. (1986). Saturday morning fever: The hard sell takeover of kids' TV. *Mother Jones, 11*(6), 38–48, 54.

Erikson, E. (1963). *Childhood and society* (2nd ed.). New York: W.W. Norton.

Eron, L., & Slaby, R. (1994). Introduction. In L. Eron, J. Gentry, & P. Schlegel (Eds.), *Reason for hope: A psychological perspective on youth and violence.* Washington, DC: American Psychological Association.

Federal Trade Commission. (2000). *Marketing violent entertainment to children: A review of self-regulation and industry practices in the motion picture, music recording and electronic game industries.* Washington, DC: Author.

Friestad, M., & Wright, P. (1994, June). The persuasion knowledge model: How people cope with persuasion attempts. *Journal of Consumer Research, 21,* 1–31.

Gortmaker, S. L., Must, A., Sobol, A. M., Peterson, K., Colditz, G. A., & Dietz, W. H. (1996). Television viewing as a cause of increasing obesity among children in the United States, 1986–1990. *Archives of Pediatric Adolescent Medicine, 150,* 356–362.

Hammer, J., & Miller, A. (1990, April 20). Ninja Turtle power: Add a record-grossing movie to the toy industry's latest craze. *Newsweek,* 60–61.

Harris, R. (1989, November 12). Children who dress for excess: Today's youngsters have become fixated with fashion. The right look isn't enough—it also has to be expensive. *Los Angeles Times,* p. 1.

Hoffner, C., Cantor, J., & Thorson, E. (1989). Children's responses to conflicting auditory and visual features of a televised narrative. *Human Communication Research, 16,* 256–278.

Hood, D. (2000, November). Is advertising to kids wrong? Marketers respond. *Kidscreen,* pp. 15–18.

Horgan, K. B., Choate, M., & Brownell, K. (2001). Television food advertising: Targeting children in a toxic environment. In D. G. Singer & J. L. Singer (Eds.), *Handbook of children and the media* (pp. 447–462). Thousand Oaks, CA: Sage.

Jacobs, E. A., Joffe, A., Knight, J. R., Kulig, J., & Rogers, P. D. (2001). Alcohol use and abuse: A pediatric concern. *Pediatrics, 108,* 185–189.

Jarrell, R. (1998). Play and its influence on the development of young children's mathematical thinking. In D. Fromberg & D. Bergen (Eds.), *Play from birth to twelve and beyond* (pp. 69–76). New York: Garland.

Jeffrey, D. B., McLellarn, R. W., & Fox, D. T. (1982). The development of children's eating habits: The role of television commercials. *Health Education Quarterly, 9*(2/3), 174–189.

John, D. R. (1999). Consumer socialization of children: A retrospective look at twenty-five years of research. *Journal of Consumer Research, 26*(3), 183–213.

Kanner, A. D. (2000, February). Stuffing our kids: Should psychologists help advertisers manipulate children? *California Psychologist,* 24–25.

Kaplowitz, P. B., Slora, E. J., Wasserman, R. C., Pedlow, S. E., & Herman-Giddens, M. E. (2001). Earlier onset of puberty in girls: Relation to increased body mass index and race. *Pediatrics, 108,* 347–353.

Kennedy, L. (2002, June 30). The rating game: With the latest summer flicks full of violence and sex, critics say Hollywood is pushing the envelope too far in making films for kids. *The Boston Sunday Globe,* pp. N13, N17.

Kid Power Food and Beverage Marketing. (2002). *Fourth Annual Conference Brochure.* Little Falls, NJ: Kid Power Exchange.

Kilbourne, J. (1999). *Deadly persuasion.* New York: Free Press.

Kjos, T. (2002, April 15). Marketers compete fiercely for spending on kids. *Arizona Daily Star,* p. 1.

Kotz, K., & Story, M. (1994). Food advertisements during children's Saturday morning television programming: Are they consistent with dietary recommendations? *Journal of the American Dietetic Association, 94,* 1296–1300.

Kunkel, D. (2001). Children and television advertising. In D. G. Singer & J. L. Singer (Eds.), *The handbook of children and media* (pp. 375–393). Thousand Oaks, CA: Sage.

Leonhard, D., & Kerwin, K. (1997, June 30). Is Madison Avenue taking "Get 'em while they're young" too far? *Business Week,* 62.

Levin, D. E. (1996). Endangered play, endangered development. In A. Phillips (Ed.), *Playing for keeps* (pp. 73–88, 169–171). St. Paul, MN: Red Leaf.

Levin, D. E. (1998). *Remote control childhood? Combating the hazards of media culture.* Washington, DC: National Association for the Education of Young Children.

Levin, D. E., & Rosenquest, B. (2001). The increasing role of electronic toys in the lives of infants and toddlers. *Contemporary Issues in Early Childhood, 2,* 242–247.

Linn, S. (2000). Sellouts. *The American Prospect, 11*(22), 17–20.

Linn, S., & Poussaint, A. F. (1999, May/June). The real trouble with Teletubbies. *American Prospect,* pp. 18–25.

Lisosky, M. (1995, March). *Battling standards worldwide — "Mighty Morphin Power Rangers" fight for their lives.* Paper presented at the World Summit for Children and Television, Melbourne, Australia.

McChesney, R. W. (1999). *Rich media; poor democracy: Communication politics in dubious times.* New York: New Press.

Mikkelsen, L. (2001). *Restricting television advertising to children.* Oakland, CA: Prevention Institute.

Minow, N. N., & Lamay, C. L. (1995). *Abandoned in the wasteland: Children, television, and the first amendment.* New York: Hill and Wang.

Mitchener, B. (2001, May 29). Sweden pushes its ban on children's ads. *Wall Street Journal,* p. B13.

Molnar, A. (1996). *Giving kids the business: The commercialization of America's schools.* Boulder, CO: Westview Press.

National Institute on Media and the Family. (2002). *Fact sheets: Children and advertising.* Minneapolis: Author. Retrieved September 9, 2002, from http://www.mediaandthefamily.org

Nelson, P. R., Brown, J. M., Brown, W. D., Koops, B. L., McInerny, T. K., Meurer, J. R., et al. (2001). Improving substance abuse prevention, assessment, and treatment financing for children and adolescents. *Pediatrics, 108,* 1025–1029.

Neville, L. (2001, November 2). Kids' brands must exercise pest control. *Brand Strategy,* p. 17.

Packaged Facts. (2000, March). *The kids' market.* New York: MarketResearch.com.

Piaget, J. (1952). *The origins of intelligence in the child.* New York: International University Press.

Rice, F. (2001, February 12). Superstars of spending; Marketers clamor for kids. *Advertising Age,* p. S1.

Roberts, D. F., Foehr, U. G., Rideout, V. J., & Brodie, M. (1999). *Kids and media at the new millennium.* Menlo Park, CA: The Henry J. Kaiser Family Foundation.

Sargent, J. D., Dalton, M. A., Beach, M., Bernhardt, A., Pullin, D., & Stevens, M. (1997). Cigarette promotional items in public schools. *Archives of Pediatrics and Adolescent Medicine, 151*(12), 1189–1196.

Selling to Kids. (1999). Market research ages 6 and up: Savvy Gen Y-ers: Challenge, involve them. *Selling to Kids,* 4.

Siegel, D. L., Coffey, T. J., & Livingston, G. (2002). *The great tween buying machine: Marketing to today's tweens.* Ithaca, NY: Paramount Market.

Taras, H. L., & Gage, M. (1995). Advertised foods on children's television. *Archives of Pediatric Adolescent Medicine, 149,* 649–652.

Taras, H. L., Sallis, J. F., Patterson, T. L., Nader, P. R., & Nelson, J. A. (1989). Television's influence on children's diet and physical activity. *Journal of Developmental and Behavioral Pediatrics, 10*(4), 176–180.

Thompson, S. (1999, November 22). Cap'n goes AWOL/as sales flatten; Quaker redirects cereal brand's marketing. *Advertising Age,* p. 8.

Troiano, R. P., & Flegal, K. M. (1998). Overweight children and adolescents: Description, epidemiology, and demographics. *Pediatrics, 101,* 497–504.

U.S. Senate Committee on Commerce, Science, and Transportation (106th Congress). (1999, May 4). Youth violence. *Congressional Daily Record Daily Digest,* D477.

Valkenburg, P. (2000). Media and youth consumerism. *Journal of Adolescent Health, 27*(2S), 52–56.

Wyllie, A., Zhang, J. F., & Casswell, S. (1998). Responses to televised alcohol advertisements associated with drinking behaviour of 10-17-year-olds. *Addiction, 93*(3), 361–371.

13

COMMERCIALISM'S INFLUENCE ON BLACK YOUTH: THE CASE OF DRESS-RELATED CHALLENGES

VELMA D. LAPOINT AND PRISCILLA J. HAMBRICK-DIXON

Over the past decade child development researchers, policy makers, practitioners, families, and the general public have become increasingly concerned about the impact of the culture of consumption on children's development. This concern has been engendered by the intense and pervasive marketing practices of corporations and industries. As part of the proceedings of a conference on corporate and industry influences on child development, we (Hambrick-Dixon & LaPoint, 1999) coined the term *commercialism influences* to refer to the impact of the confluence of practices by corporations and industries in producing, manufacturing, advertising, and selling products and services to child and adolescent consumers (Commercial Alert 2001). We further identified the sources of these corporate and industry products and services as including (a) the food industry (e.g., fast foods, snack foods); (b) polluting industries; (c) the drug, alcohol, and firearm industries; (d) media industries (e.g., music, images, television, radio, video games, Internet); and (e) the fashion industry (e.g., dress, hair, cosmetics).

Research, scholarly reports, and advocacy related to the impact of commercialism influences on child development show opposing interests and agendas, with some professionals viewing these influences on children with concern, and others viewing them as opportunities. For example, on the one hand, several recent national conferences and publications, including research and federal reports, have documented concern and alarm about potential and actual commercialism influences on child development (Chandler & Heinzerling, 1999; Clay, 2000; Commercial Alert, 2001; Federal Trade Commission [FTC], 2000; Holloman, LaPoint, Alleyne, Palmer, & Sanders-Phillips, 1998; Institute for American Values [IAV], 2001; LaPoint & Alleyne, 1998; Molnar, 2001; Singer & Singer, 2000; Stop the Commercial Exploitation of Children [SCEC], Strasburger & Wilson, 2002; U.S. General Accounting Office [GAO], 2000; Work Group on Commercialism and Youth, Families, and Communities [Work Group], 2001). On the other hand, professional trade associations have convened annual conferences on and presented awards for "effective" strategies to market to children (IAV, 2001; SCEC, 2001). In addition, several publications have described how to market products to children in light of the continuing mega-growth in profits from young consumers (Cohen & Cahill, 1999/2000; Del Vecchio, 1997; McNeal, 1999; Teenage Research Unlimited, 2001). These marketing practices to children include using the skills of behavioral science professionals (e.g., anthropologists, psychologists, and sociologists) to conduct marketing research with children and youth (e.g., focus groups, ethnography, interviews, and questionnaires) and hiring adolescent data collectors (Cohen & Cahill, 1999/2000; Klein, 1999; Osborne, 2002; Thompson, 1999).

One might wonder whether the concern about the impact of commercialism influences on children's development is only a "White, middle-class issue" and a movement with little relevance to the lives of poor children or ethnic minority group children (Commercial Alert, 2001; Hambrick-Dixon & LaPoint, 1999; LaPoint, 1999; LaPoint & Alleyne, 1998, 2001). More specifically, are commercialism influences more relevant to children whose families can afford to overindulge their children and pay for youth products and services? Exposure to these products and services may present challenges to families with challenges, such as children internalizing materialistic values (De Graff, Wann, & Naylor, 2001; Institute for American Values, 2001; Kindlon, 2001; chap. 2, this volume). However, poor children and ethnic minority group children of color are also very likely to be affected by commercialism influences, and these influences may be further exacerbated by poverty and racism (Hambrick-Dixon & LaPoint, 1999; Holloman et al., 1998; LaPoint & Alleyne, 1998).

Although much speculation exists about the relationship between race, socioeconomic status, and the impact of commercialism influences on children's development, few studies have systematically examined these relationships. First, few studies are available on how children, regardless of race and social class, are socialized into the consumer role and how they cope with exposure to marketing pressures (Chandler & Heinzerling, 1999; Holloman et al., 1998; LaPoint, 1999; LaPoint & Alleyne, 1998). Second, ethnic minority group children of color are generally omitted, minimized, or presented pejoratively in published research on the topic of children in the marketplace (Chandler & Heinzerling, 1999; Holloman et al., 1998; LaPoint & Alleyne, 1998). This reflects the state of research on ethnic minority group children generally (Fisher, Jackson, & Villarruel, 1998; McAdoo, 2002).

This chapter is concerned with the potential adverse effects of commercialism influences in children's lives, but particularly in the lives of Black children and youth. We examine Black youth in terms of a specific source of commercialism influences, the fashion industry, and one area in which these influences have been identified, dress-related challenges. Although fashion, dress, and other terms (e.g., clothing, appearance) are typically used interchangeably, we use the term *dress* to refer to (a) a process that modifies and supplements the body to address physical needs and meet cultural expectations about how people should look; and (b) a product where a multitude of items, resulting from human creativity and technology, can be applied to the body (Eicher, Evenson, & Lutz, 2000; Roach-Higgins, Eicher, & Johnson, 1995). Some examples of youth dress include products and related services such as clothing, make-up, hairstyles, nail styles, body piercing, tooth-capping, and tattooing.

We selected dress-related challenges because a growing body of literature is available on the impact of commercialism influences on youth dress socialization. Some of this literature indicates that Black youth are presented with unique dress-related challenges, given the existence of certain marketing practices such as the use of Black cultural expressions, celebrities, and models to propagate materialistic messages. Furthermore, some Black youth, especially those who are low-income, are either the victims or perpetrators of assaults and murder during the thefts of popular, brand-named, celebrity-endorsed, or designer dress items (Holloman et al., 1998; LaPoint & Alleyne, 2001). Thus, our primary objectives in this chapter are to describe (a) aspects of general youth consumer marketing, with a focus on dress, in the context of the culture of consumption; (b) dress-related socialization and challenges unique to Black youth; and (c) research, policy, practice, and advocacy implications of commercialism influences on dress-related challenges to Black youth, their families, and communities.

THE YOUTH CONSUMER MARKET

From a sociocultural perspective, American society has been studied as a culture of consumption. Principles such as "you are what you own" and "you are what you wear" seem to dominate the lives of Americans across ethnic, social class, gender, and age boundaries (De Graff et al., 2001; Jacobson & Mazur, 1995; Schor, 1998). In addition, many youth, who often imitate adults, appear to be preoccupied or obsessed with having expensive, designer, brand-labeled, or celebrity-endorsed dress. They have apparently accepted cultural values and messages of society that equate material possessions with beauty, character, competence, power, and success (Garbarino, 1995; Holloman et al., 1998; IAV, 2001; LaPoint & Alleyne, 1998; Nader, 1997).

Since the mid-1950s, children have been studied as consumers and considered to be a potential lucrative market (Chandler & Heinzerling, 1999; McNeal, 1999). In recent years, research on young consumers has focused primarily on the effects of specific goods and services on children's development, such as television programming, commercials, and the illegal use of products such as alcohol and tobacco (Chandler & Heinzerling, 1999). However, few empirical studies of dress and youth behavior exist, especially dress-related challenges to youth (Chandler & Heinzerling, 1999; LaPoint & Alleyne, 1998, 2001).

As the youth market continues to generate billions of dollars in revenues, marketing to children continues to intensify and proliferate, resulting in youth buying and consuming more, including dress products and services (LaPoint & Alleyne, 1998, 2001; SCEC, 2001). Although the size of the children's market has been variously estimated, there is difficulty in interpreting these estimates, given data-gathering techniques and sources. For example, data are aggregated across child age groups and across a myriad of products. Further, corporate research is often geared and biased toward marketers and is thus private and inaccessible to most social scientists and the public.

Given the challenges in estimating youth spending on dress generally, and by Black youth specifically, we can provide one example of profits generated by targeting Black youth for dress. The Tommy Hilfiger corporation began by primarily marketing preppy wear associated with the leisure class (Klein, 1999). The designer and corporate mogul realized that poor and working class Black youth were attracted to his dress line because of their "status-giving" qualities. By marketing to Black youth, Hilfiger corporate sales went from $53 million in 1991 to $847 million in 1998, in part because middle-class White, Asian, and Latino youth, who mimic Black style in everything from dress, lingo, and music, also bought this dress (Klein, 1999). According to other commentators who track marketing to Black youth, trends in the accelerated growth of sales for dress products also exist for Adidas, Nike, and other leading apparel corporations (Chapelle, 1998; Hughes, 2002; Klein, 1999).

As a particular source of commercialism influences, the fashion industry capitalizes on the developmental status and needs of youth when marketing dress. Studies have demonstrated that adolescents, as a distinct societal group, are more likely to dress in ways that show individuality at the same time that conformity and membership in particular groups are highlighted (Eicher, Baizerman, & Michelman, 1995; Holloman et al., 1998; Johnson & Lennon, 1999; Simpson, Douglas, & Schimmel, 1998). Adolescents tend to like persons whom they perceive as looking similar to them and dislike those whom they perceive as looking different. Similarly, in their quest to be accepted by their peers, many adolescents dress in particular ways that identify them as members of a particular group. At the same time that they are trying to fit in with their peers, however, many adolescents experiment frequently with changing their appearance and may look strange or ridiculous to the adults from whom they are trying to differentiate themselves (Creekmore, 1980; Eicher et al., 1995; Ford & Drake, 1982; Simpson et al., 1998; Stone, 1995).

According to Chandler and Heinzerling (1999), marketers supply and promote products and services, including dress, as a means of satisfying youth needs. However, the imposition of continuous and unrelenting marketing is primarily to satisfy the corporate need for profit. Thus, the consumer needs of youth, like adults, are exaggerated and artificially created by both the American and global culture of consumption (De Graff et al., 2001; Hambrick-Dixon & LaPoint, 1999; IAV, 2001; Jacobson & Mazur, 1995; Klein, 1999; LaPoint & Alleyne, 1998; SCEC, 1991).

The culture of consumption presents youth with a host of dress-related challenges. According to Holloman et al. (1998), youth may (a) develop distorted values, attitudes, and behavior toward the self and others as they become obsessed with acquiring and wearing dress items; (b) engage in competitive, antisocial, and illegal behavior to obtain certain dress items through theft, acts that may be accompanied by assaults and murder; (c) wear particular dress that may be judged to be disruptive, inappropriate, unhealthy, and even fatal under certain procedures such as tattooing, body piercing, and tooth capping; and (d) place undue pressure on parents, families, and others to obtain or purchase certain dress products and services. A growing body of research and information about these dress-related challenges among youth is available (Chandler & Heinzerling, 1999; Holloman et al., 1998; LaPoint & Alleyne, 1998, 2001).

DRESS-RELATED CHALLENGES UNIQUE TO BLACK YOUTH

Dress issues pose developmental and socialization challenges to all youth, but Black youth generally face a unique set of experiences. These experiences include (a) being exposed to media with materialistic messages using Black cultural expressions and Black models and celebrities; (b) being devalued by society because of their Black identity; (c) growing up in low-income circumstances; and (d) being the subject of negative systemic actions and biased reporting by varying institutional personnel and the media (Chapelle, 1998; Holloman et al., 1998; Klein, 1999; LaPoint & Alleyne, 1998).

Although we discuss these experiences throughout the rest of the chapter as though they are common to all Black youth, we acknowledge that variations exist among Black youth and their families in areas such as national origin, social class, geographical region, language, faith-based beliefs, and child-rearing (Fisher et al., 1998; McAdoo, 2002; Taylor, 1995, 2002). Thus, variations can also exist in Black dress socialization and dress-related challenges. For example, some parents, family members, and other adults, including those in Black communities, socialize children using dress practices from a variety of sources that may more effectively resist and counter commercialism influences. These families may (a) use their own dress-related knowledge, attitudes, and practices; (b) select various school types (e.g., parochial, private, general public, public charter, or magnet) that may use dress codes and uniforms; or (c) select or interact with faith-based communities that have varying dress standards and practices (Holloman et al., 1998; LaPoint & Alleyne, 2001). It is important, therefore, to note that not all Black youth have the same experiences in dress socialization and dress-related challenges.

Media Exposure and Marketing

Like other youth, Black youth are exposed to media with materialistic messages that market youth products and services in venues such as television, videos, movies, and magazines. However, targeted marketing to Black youth presents special challenges in terms of the quantity and content of their exposure to materialistic messages. We present some research and reports on the amount of materialistic messages that Black youth are exposed to from television, as well as the content of these materialistic messages. The content of these materialistic messages involves marketers generally "packaging" and "selling back" facets of Black cultural expressions. This same process is done with Black models and celebrities, as ways to attract and get Black youth to purchase dress and other products and services.

Huston and Wright (1998) reviewed research on mass media and children's development. This research implies that Black youth are exposed to more marketing. For example, research indicates that Black youth, regardless of social class, tend to watch more television than their White counterparts. One reason for this is that television is a form of low cost entertainment and Blacks, who are disproportionately poor, have fewer entertainment options (Huston & Wright, 1998). We know that television, both cable and commercial, is largely financed by corporate products in commercials. Thus, Black youth are more likely to be exposed to more advertising, especially for youth products and services, in comparison to other children.

Marketing strategies that use cultural expressions and Black models and celebrities are based on research indicating that individuals are most likely to imitate models who are similar to the viewers (Huston & Wright, 1998; Lee & Browne, 1995). Marketers have become adept in knowing how to "package and re-sell" the cultural expressions of Black youth (Chapelle, 1998; Holloman et al., 1998; Hughes, 2002; Klein, 1999; LaPoint & Alleyne, 1998, 2001). Academic research shows that Black youth tend to wear bold designs, bright colors, and other styles, reflecting their African and Black cultural heritages, expressions, and styles (Eicher, 1995; Eicher et al., 2000; Foster, 1997; Holloman et al., 1998; O'Neal, 1999; Wares, 1990). Social scientists maintain that despite the destructive impact of slavery, many Black people in the United States and the Diaspora, including youth, retain many African cultural expressions in areas such as worldview, family life, psychology, spirituality and religion, dance, and music (Boykin & Ellison, 1995; Hill, 1997; McAdoo, 2002; Taylor, 1995, 2002). This includes cultural expressions of dress, as previously indicated. Thus, Black youth's dress may differ from those of White European American middle-class youth, who are often considered to be the social norm (Holloman et al., 1998). Yet, fashion trends show that these two groups are increasingly wearing each others' "prototypical" dress—where, for example, some White, middle-class youth wear Black hip-hop dress (e.g., low-hung baggy pants, oversized shirts) and some Black youth wear college prep dress (e.g., polo shirts, oxford shoes), albeit with hip-hop modifications (Chapelle, 1998; Kakutani, 1997).

Marketing dress to youth involves creating and packaging "cool" styles. According to Klein (1999), "cool" has characterized various aspects of Black cultural heritage and expressions such as dress, music, language, and dance. Examples of "cool" music types among Black youth are urban soul, reggae, rhythm and blues (R&B), and hip-hop. The marketing of Black youth "cool" seeks to have middle-class, White youth and others adopt the "cool look" in dress styles set by Black youth; this marketing also seeks to have Black youth adopt the appearance of being wealthy, often in today's popular hip-hop style, with expensive brand-named, designer, or celebrity-endorsed dress (Klein, 1999; LaPoint & Alleyne, 1998, 2001).

"Cool" dress styles among Black youth, considered a pacesetter among all youth, are marketable and profitable (Chapelle, 1998; Holloman et al., 1998; Hughes, 2002; Klein, 1999; LaPoint & Alleyne, 1998). Prior to the 1980s, corporate marketers had not really viewed the Black youth market as profitable for dress and other products and services. However, with the advent of marketing hip-hop culture, marketers began to recognize multimillion dollar profits and began using multidimensional marketing strategies where dress, videos, movies, music, and other products could all be linked, packaged, and sold at one time

(Chapelle, 1998; Hughes, 2002; Klein, 1999). For example, although music videos are one type of product, dress and other products such as food, beverages, music, violence, and sexuality can be marketed to youth within music videos.

The practice of marketing Black cultural expressions to all youth, and Black youth specifically, has received attention not only from academics (Holloman et al., 1998; LaPoint & Alleyne, 1998, 2001) but also from journalists (Chapelle, 1998; Hughes, 2002; Klein, 1999). For example, Klein described the marketing strategies of major corporate entities such as Nike, Adidas, and Tommy Hilfiger in regards to sneakers, athletic wear, and other apparel. She also described ethnographic marketing strategies such as marketers traveling to impoverished Black communities to interview Black youth about their reaction to products such as expensive sneakers. According to Klein, marketers from Nike even coined the term *bro-ing* for this type of interview. (It appears as if the word is derived from the word, *brother*, a term of endearment among Black youth and adults). These marketing strategies may be viewed as exploitative of poor Black youth, as there are typically differences in age, social class, and race between corporate marketer and consumer (Chapelle, 1998; Klein, 1999). One example of a common item, used by some Black youth, that has become profitable is the *do-rag*, that is headgear used generally to set and keep hair in place, prior to dressing to go out (LaPoint & Alleyne, 1998). Although used for decades, the headgear evolved from several sources including a discarded female stocking (i.e., lower leg and foot section) that was cut and made into a stocking cap. It was an essentially inexpensive, recycled, or free item. The headgear then became marketed as a polyester piece of cloth that could be tied around the head, with some modifications (e.g., longer fabric in the back), selling for about $2–4, depending on the retail outlet. Some Black youth began wearing it, typically with casual wear, outside the home, to the dismay of many Black adults. From there, the headgear seemed to have evolved into an elastic-banded cap, marketed in a multitude of colors with a brand or designer name label, and sold for upwards of $8–20 (LaPoint & Alleyne, 1998, 2001).

Marketers have clearly found that dress targeted to Black youth, especially expensive sneakers, athletic wear, and casual attire, could reap huge profits if Black models and celebrities such as rap singers and athletes endorsed products (Chapelle, 1998; Holloman et al., 1998; Hughes, 2002; Klein, 1999). One study indicated that Black adolescents' decisions to purchase expensive sneakers were influenced by Black celebrity endorsements, especially in commercials on cable television versus commercial television (Lee & Browne, 1995). Several reports also indicate that marketers "package" the images of Black celebrities so that their images can be "co-branded" with a given product such as sneakers. The celebrities' images, together with the product, can be resold to Black youth in product endorsement commercials (Hughes, 2002; Klein, 1999; LaPoint & Alleyne, 2001; Naughton, 1992). The "packaging and re-selling" of Black models and celebrities has been the focus of several reports that highlight debate and controversy about the roles and responsibilities of Black celebrities in marketing dress and other products to Black youth. Some of the issues include (a) convincing corporate executives that certain celebrities, "despite being Black" (i.e., non-White), could be "packaged and sold" for product endorsements; (b) endorsing products that contribute to the actual or potential harm that may result from dress-related challenges such as youth committing dress-related crimes; and (c) determining whether celebrities or corporations have ethical responsibilities or financial liabilities to compensate individuals or communities for dress-related challenges (Chapelle, 1998; Goldman & Papson, 1998; Holloman et al., 1998; LaPoint & Alleyne, 2001; Naughton, 1992; Telander, 1995). Although similar issues may exist regarding the use of celebrities in general, because fewer Black celebrities are used, it may be that they have greater influence on Black youth, with the effect that these youth buy more of the endorsed products (Chapelle, 1998; Klein, 1999).

Low Socioeconomic Status

Black youth represent 15% of the child population, yet they are disproportionately poor, with one third living in poverty and many experiencing a host of inadequacies in areas such as education, employment, medical care, and housing (McLoyd & Lozoff, 2001; Taylor, 1995). Although Black youth consumers are similar in many ways to other American youth, their disproportionate poverty seems to influence dress, especially among adolescents (Holloman et al., 1998; LaPoint & Alleyne, 2001). Many low-income Black youth may want to project perceived middle- or upper-class wealth, status, and power by wearing high-priced designer and celebrity-endorsed dress. Of course, Black youth are not alone in imitating adults, as children of all racial and ethnic groups do the same (Holloman et al., 1998; LaPoint & Alleyne, 1998, 2001).

Some low-income Black youth may not have the means to afford expensive dress. These youth may resort to several options: (a) exerting pressure on parents and family members for money or for the items themselves; (b) working part-time, if in school, to make their own purchases; and (c) engaging in theft and drug dealing (Boyd-Franklin & Franklin, 2000; Holloman et al., 1998; LaPoint & Alleyne, 1998, 2001). As previously discussed, violence, including assault and even murder, sometimes occurs during thefts of dress items or money to obtain such items

(Brunswick & Rier, 1995; Holloman et al., 1998; LaPoint & Alleyne, 1998, 2001; Nobles & Goddard, 1989). Thus, dress-related crime reported among Black youth may be attributed to systemic structural challenges, as well as vulnerabilities to marketing practices (Holloman et al., 1998; LaPoint & Alleyne, 2001; Telander, 1995).

Negative Systemic Actions and Biased Reporting

The marketing of dress to Black youth obviously works. As trendsetters for youth dress, they represent a multibillion-dollar market for the fashion industry. Although Black youth, from a marketing perspective, represent a profitable success, there is an ironic flip side: Their consumption of dress and other products also "targets" them for negative actions and biased reporting by some institutional personnel (e.g., school administrators, teachers, police, retail salespersons) and the media. That is, many Black youth find themselves in a double bind, in which, by purchasing the very dress products that ensure that they are "cool," they end up being criticized and targeted by other youth, the police, media reporters, and marketers seeking future profits (Alleyne & LaPoint, 2001).

Consider media reports of dress-related challenges. Although media reporters describe dress-related crimes such as the theft of expensive sneakers and jackets, such incidents are often reported as sound bites. When reporters describe events in an abbreviated manner, the context is often omitted or minimized, particularly the complexity of many Black youth being exposed to targeted marketing in the midst of poverty. This can lead to sensationalism, oversimplification, and misunderstanding of dress-related challenges (Alleyne & LaPoint, 2001; Holloman et al., 1998). Such de-contextualization leads observers to view youth involved in dress-related crimes as totally responsible, essentially "blaming the victims" for the incidents. When dress-related challenges become de-contextualized, some Black youth, especially males, may be stereotyped or profiled by police or other authorities as potential criminals because of their dress, which often includes baggy pants, athletic suits, and expensive sneakers (Alleyne & LaPoint, 2001; Boyd-Franklin & Franklin, 2000; Holloman et al., 1998). We should also note that although some biased reporting may occur, some media reports have presented broader information on how commercial enterprises have targeted and exploited Black youth as a profitable market for expensive dress (Alleyne & LaPoint, 2001; Holloman et al., 1998).

Black youth may also be negatively assessed by researchers, media, and the public because of the types of products they purchase and consume. In an ethnographic study of Black youth consumerism, Chin (2001) found that 10-year-old, low-income Black children generally purchase same types of products (e.g., action figure toys, sneakers) as do middle-class White youth. However, because the youth are both Black and poor, their purchases are often viewed with bias. Researchers, media representatives, and the public assume that Black youth should have consumption priorities that focus on what are perceived to be "necessary" items, not popular youth-oriented items. Chin asserted that being distainful of poor Black youth consuming like other youth is ethnocentric.

A third example of how Blacks are re-victimized through their purchase of marketed dress is that they often become the victims and perpetrators of crimes related to dress. That is, sometimes Black youth who have obtained the dress specified as "cool" become targets of theft and violence by other Black youth who want to be cool, too. Although there are broader contextual factors that also play into these offenses, and the assailants themselves must bear some responsibility, the role of marketing cannot be ignored. Tragic consequences may occur for both the youth victims (e.g., disability, death) and the assailants (e.g., adjudication, incarceration). Also, these consequences take their toll on families and communities (Holloman et al., 1998; LaPoint & Alleyne, 2001; Telander, 1995).

Finally, Black youth are often "re-targeted" by marketers. Black youth are, as we have seen, initially targeted by marketers in order to make and increase profits over time. However, as the standards of cool dress are established by Black youth, with other youth generally following, Black youth are later re-targeted for more marketing and for more profits (LaPoint & Alleyne, 2001). For example, marketing strategies to poor Black youth seem to have become intensified, as marketers go into impoverished communities and directly interact with Black youth to sample their attitudes and feelings about various dress products (Klein, 1999). Although this newer "in vivo" ethnographic marketing strategy is increasingly used, it is exploitive, because poor Black youth are not reaping any benefits from the marketing of their culture.

IMPLICATIONS FOR RESEARCH, POLICY, PRACTICE, AND ADVOCACY

The previous review of literature, from sociocultural and Black cultural perspectives, provides insight into the dress-related challenges faced by Black youth, their families, and communities. It can be argued that commercialism influences, within a culture of consumption, interface with the contextual and cultural experiences of Black youth in the area of dress and dress-related challenges. Black youth are placed at risk for potential adverse conditions of commercialism influences given materialistic messages that use their cultural expressions and Black models and celebrities in marketing dress. Potential risks to many Black youth are further compounded by conditions of poverty that engulf their lives. Racism and ethnocentrism devalue Black youth identity generally and are reflected in some biased media reports on dress-related challenges. Thus, Black youth face dress-related challenges that evolve when some of their cultural expressions, role models, and celebrities are "packaged" and "resold" back to them. Moreover, they face a double bind, in which, by purchasing the very dress products that ensure that they are "cool," they end up being targeted by other youth in thefts, as well as by the police, media reporters, and marketers seeking future profits.

We reviewed literature in the areas of marketing to youth in the context of a culture of consumption and dress-related socialization and challenges unique to Black youth. The literature shows that Black youth, like American youth in general, are influenced by rampant commercialism influences. This trend is likely to continue to affect youth, their families, and communities in the future. Given the nature of dress-related challenges that may potentially adversely affect all youth, and Black youth specifically, this review of literature has several implications for research, policy, practice, and advocacy.

Studies need to be conducted by social scientists who are interested in promoting child development, not by marketers, to understand Black youth dress, the marketplace, and other socialization settings. Such research would provide information about Black youth as consumers so that their welfare and the general welfare of all children can be enhanced (Chandler & Heinzerling, 1999; Holloman et al., 1998; LaPoint & Alleyne, 2001). Moreover, the development of sociocultural and ecological frameworks for research on Black youth in the marketplace could elucidate the broader context of commercialism influences. Although some dress-related challenges to youth, families, and communities have been identified, few studies have systematically examined how families and other socialization agents, among Blacks in particular, socialize children around dress and provide a system of support to reduce and prevent dress-related challenges (LaPoint & Alleyne, 1998, 2001). For example, what proactive child-rearing practices do Black parents and families use to assist children in coping with dress-related commercialism influences? What types of school policies and practices promote positive outcomes related to dress socialization among youth in schools? What variations exist in children's understanding of and resiliency to commercialism influences (e.g., developmental status, nature of exposure to commercialism influences)? What is the role of culturally based strategies (e.g., communalism, spirituality) in mitigating potentially adverse commercialism influences (LaPoint & Alleyne, 1998, 2001)?

Some studies on Black youth as consumers indicate that marketing may have adverse effects such as pressures to make unneeded dress purchases and to be loyal to certain brands (LaPoint & Alleyne, 1998, 2001). Other findings highlight the need for the development, implementation, and evaluation of consumer education programs for youth and their families in schools and other community settings to mitigate the potential adverse effects of commercialism influences in children's lives (Chandler & Heinzerling, 1999; LaPoint & Alleyne, 1998, 2001). Such programs should use culturally responsive outreach (e.g., inclusive partnerships with community-based representatives) and education strategies and materials that incorporate the diverse experiences of Black constituents (e.g., social class, ethnicity, gender) and learning styles such as auditory, visual, and tactile (LaPoint & Alleyne, 2001).

Although it is important to obtain data on Black children as a group, it is also important to address the diversity among these children in terms of developmental status, social class, national origin, and gender to determine how these relate to commercialism influences. At the same time, studies are needed on the effects of these influences on children's development to inform policies and interventions for youth (LaPoint & Alleyne, 2001). Such research may help to reduce stereotypes about a specific group of children who may, for various reasons, show the effects of exposure to commercialism influences in ways that differ from samples that are typically White, middle- and upper-class. There is also a need for reliable and culturally valid instruments and multiple data collection sources and strategies that can provide an accurate picture of commercialism influences on all children, in general, and ethnic minority group children, in particular.

Many Blacks, and others, who advocate on behalf of diverse populations have been involved in policy and program development relating to commercialism influences at local, state, and federal levels (Commercial Alert, 2001; IAV, 2001; SCEC, 2001; Work Group, 2001). However, information may be lacking because some Blacks, across income groups, may be (a) uninformed or misinformed about issues of commercialism influences, (b) insufficiently organized for advocacy, (c) reluctant to criticize other members of Black communities, and (d) compromised by competing priorities wherein they are aware of potentially adverse commercialism influences, yet still promote commercialist activities for financial gain (Chapelle, 1998; Hambrick-Dixon & LaPoint, 1999; Holloman et al., 1998; LaPoint & Alleyne, 1998, 2001). For example, some Blacks may be unaware of the dress-related challenges to Black youth described in this chapter as well as health, psychological, and educational challenges due to industries such as food (Caution, 1984), music (Ferguson, 2001), and others (Commercial Alert, 2001). All of this has the effect of creating and reinforcing various social problems related to commercialism influences among youth and their families.

Given these circumstances, those who may be aware of the impact of commercialism influences on youth may shift the responsibility for promoting and mitigating these influences to Blacks themselves or the broader system. These issues are reflected in the debates about using Black models and celebrities in marketing specific products and services. In addition, many newly owned Black corporations may view marketing youth dress products to Black youth as lucrative economic opportunities, not as factors contributing to dress-related challenges (Chapelle, 1998; Hughes, 2002; LaPoint & Alleyne, 1998, 2001). Finally, whereas advocacy organizations seek to protect youth from potentially adverse commercialism influences, there is a need to ensure that they have effective and culturally accurate programming and outreach for Black youth, families, and communities. They should attempt to establish linkages with existing Black and other advocacy organizations that have a similar mission, namely, to mitigate the potential adverse effects of commercialism influences. Despite federal policy activities (e.g., investigative reports, congressional briefings) addressing the potential adverse impact of such influences on children's development, leading advocates have raised questions about how effective federal policies are and will be in protecting children from the types of adverse marketing practices cited in reports by the FTC and GAO (Commercial Alert, 2001; IAV, 2001; Ruskin, 1999; SCEC, 2001). While championing the federal government's role in this area, advocates indicate that competing priorities exist at the national level. For example, on the one hand, many behavioral scientists conduct research and develop strategies on how marketers can more effectively influence children to purchase and consume more products and services, and there are powerful corporate lobbyists who promote commercial interests and seek to minimize protective initiatives for children and their families (Commercial Alert, 2001; Hambrick-Dixon & LaPoint, 1999; IAV, 2001; LaPoint & Alleyne, 1998, 2001; SCEC, 2001). On the other hand, some behavioral scientists conduct research on the potential adverse impact of commercialism influences on children and develop strategies to mitigate it.

CONCLUSION

Several implications for research, policy, program, and advocacy have been proposed regarding commercialism influences on Black youth, families, and communities. Although there are some commonalities regarding influences relating to dress and dress-related challenges for all youth, families, and communities, there are unique issues that face Blacks. A variety of research, policy, program, and advocacy intervention strategies can effectively promote the optimal development and functioning of all youth, families, and communities and mitigate the adverse effects of commercialism influences, including dress-related challenges.

REFERENCES

Alleyne, S., & LaPoint, V. (2001). [Content analysis of popular press literature on dress and dress-related challenges]. Unpublished raw data.

Boyd-Franklin, N., & Franklin, A. J. (with P. Toussaint). (2000). *Boys into men: Raising our African American teenage sons.* New York: Plume.

Boykin, A. W., & Ellison, C. E. (1995). The multiple ecologies of Black youth socialization: An Afrographic analysis. In R. Taylor (Ed.), *African-American youth: Their social and economic status in the United States* (pp. 93–128). Westport, CT: Praeger.

Brunswick, A. F., & Rier, D. A. (1995). Structural strain: Drug use among African-American youth. In R. Taylor (Ed.), *African-American youth: Their social and economic status in the United States* (pp. 225–246). Westport, CT: Praeger.

Caution, G. (1984). The effects of TV advertisements on Black children. *The Psychiatric Forum, 12,* 72–81.

Chandler, T. N., & Heinzerling, B. M. (1999). *Children and adolescents in the market place: Twenty-five years of academic research.* Ann Arbor, MI: Pierian.

Chapelle, T. (1998, January). Slaves of fashion: Black culture sells. *Emerge, 9,* 42–48.

Chin, E. (2001). *Purchasing power: Black kids and American consumer culture.* Minneapolis: University of Minnesota Press.

Clay, R. A. (2000). Advertising to children: Is it ethical? *American Psychological Association Monitor on Psychology, 31,* 52–53.

Cohen, M., & Cahill, E. (1999/2000). Getting older younger: Developmental differences in children and the challenge of developmental compression. *Advertising and Marketing to Children, 4,* 271–278.

Commercial Alert. (2001). *Study Group and Invitational Scholar's Forum on Corporate and Industry Influences on Children's Development.* Retrieved June 15, 2001, from http://www.commercialalert.org.

Creekmore, A. M. (1980). Clothing and personal attractiveness of adolescents related to conformity, clothing mode, peer acceptance, and leadership potential. *Home Economics Research Journal, 8,* 203–215.

De Graff, J., Wann, D., & Naylor, T. H. (2001). *Affluenza: The all-consuming epidemic.* New York: Berrett-Korehler.

Del Vecchio, G. (1997). *Creating ever-cool: A marketer's guide to a kid's heart.* New York: Pelican.

Eicher, J. B. (Ed.). (1995). *Dress and ethnicity.* New York: Berg.

Eicher, J. B., Baizerman, S., & Michelman, J. (1995). Adolescent dress. In M. E. Roach-Higgins, J. B. Eicher, & K. K. P. Johnson (Eds.), *Dress and identity* (pp. 121–128). New York: Fairchild.

Eicher, J. B., Evenson, S. L., & Lutz, H. A. (2000). *The visible self: Global perspectives on dress, clothing, and society.* New York: Fairchild.

Federal Trade Commission. (2000). *Marketing violent entertainment to children: A review of self-regulation and industry practices in the motion picture, music recording, and electronic game industries: A report to the Federal Trade Commission.* Retrieved March 5, 2000, from http://www.ftc.gov/opa/2000/09/index.htm

Ferguson, R. F. (2001). Test-score trends along racial lines, 1971 to 1996: Popular culture and community academic standards. In N. J. Smelser, W. J. Wilson, & F. Mitchell (Eds.), *America becoming: Racial trends and their consequences* (pp. 348–390). Washington, DC: National Academy Press.

Fisher, C. B., Jackson, J. F., & Villarruel, F. A. (1998). The study of African American and Latin American children and youth. In W. Damon (Series Ed.) & R. M. Lerner (Vol. Ed.), *Handbook of child psychology: Vol. 1. Theoretical perspectives* (5th ed., pp. 1145–1207). New York: Wiley.

Ford, I. M., & Drake, M. F. (1982). Attitudes toward clothing, body, and self: A comparison of two groups. *Home Economics Research Journal, 11,* 187–196.

Foster, H. B. (1997). *New rainments of self: African American clothing in the antebellum south.* New York: Berg.

Garbarino, J. (1995). *Raising children in a socially toxic environment.* San Francisco: Jossey-Bass.

Goldman, R., & Papson, S. (1998). *Nike culture: The sign of the swoosh.* Thousand Oaks, CA: Sage.

Hambrick-Dixon, P. J., & LaPoint, V. (1999, October). *A model of corporate and industry influences on children's development.* Paper presented at the meeting of the Study Group and Invitational Scholars' Forum: Corporate and Industry Influences on Children's Development, Washington, DC.

Hill, R. (1997). *The strengths of African American families: Twenty-five years later.* Lanham, MD: University Press of America.

Holloman, L. O., LaPoint, V., Alleyne, S. I., Palmer, R. J., & Sanders-Phillips, K. S. (1998). Dress-related behavioral problems and violence in the public school setting: Prevention, intervention, and policy: A holistic approach. *Journal of Negro Education, 65,* 267–281.

Hughes, A. (2002, May). Hip-hop economy. *Black Enterprise, 32,* 70–75.

Huston, A. C., & Wright, J. C. (1998). Mass media and children's development. In W. Damon (Series Ed.) & I. E. Sigel & K. A. Renninger (Vol. Eds.), *Handbook of child psychology: Vol. 4. Child psychology in practice* (5th ed., pp. 999–1058). New York: Wiley.

Institute for American Values. (2001). *Watch out for children: A mothers' statement to advertisers.* New York: Institute for American Values. Retrieved September 5, 2001, from http://www.rebelmothers.org.

Jacobson, M. F. , & Mazur, L. A. (1995). *Marketing madness: A survival guide for a consumer society.* Minneapolis, MN: Westview.

Johnson, K. K. P., & Lennon, S. J. (Eds.). (1999). *Appearance and power.* New York: Berg.

Kakutani, M. (1997, February 16). Common threads. *The New York Times Magazine*, p. 18.

Kindlon, D. (2001). *Too much of a good thing: Raising children of character in an indulgent age*. New York: Hyperion.

Klein, N. (1999). *No logo: Taking aim at the brand bullies*. New York: Picador.

LaPoint, V. (1999, October). *Youth dress-related challenges: The role of youth, families, schools, and communities*. Paper presented at the meeting of The Study Group and Invitational Scholars' Forum: Corporate and Industry Influences on Children's Development, Washington, DC.

LaPoint, V., & Alleyne, S. I. (1998). [Youth dress and behavior]. Unpublished raw data.

LaPoint, V., & Alleyne, S. I. (2001). *The ecology of youth dress and dress-related challenges*. Unpublished manuscript, Howard University.

Lee, E. B., & Browne, L. A. (1995). Effects of television advertising on African American teenagers. *Journal of Black Studies, 25*, 523–536.

Lopiano-Misdom, J., & De Luca, J. (1997). *Street trends: How today's alternative youth cultures are creating tomorrow's mainstream markets*. New York: HarperCollins.

McAdoo, H. P. (Ed.). (2002). *Black children: Their social, educational, and parental environments* (pp. 13–26). Thousand Oaks, CA: Sage.

McLoyd, V. C., & Lozoff, B. (2001). Racial and ethnic trends in children's and adolescents' behavior and development. In N. J. Smelser, W. J. Wilson, & F. Mitchell (Eds.), *America becoming: Racial trends and their consequences* (pp. 311–350). Washington, DC: National Academy Press.

McNeal, J. U. (1999). *The kids market: Myths and realities*. Ithaca, NY: Paramount.

Molnar, A. (2001). *Giving kids the business: The commercialization of America's schools*. New York: Perseus.

Nader, R. (1997). *Children first: A parent's guide to corporate predators*. Washington, DC: Public Citizen.

Naughton, J. (1992, February 9). Marketing Michael: The making of a commercial superstar. *The Washington Post Magazine*, pp. 11–30.

Nobles, W. W., & Goddard, L. L. (1989). Drugs in the African American community: A clear and present danger. In J. Dwart (Ed.), *State of Black America, 1989* (pp. 161–181). Washington, DC: National Urban League.

O'Neal, G. S. (1999). The power of style: On rejection of the accepted. In K. K. P. Johnson & S. J. Lennon (Eds.), *Appearance and power* (pp. 127–139). New York: Berg.

Osborne, L. (2002, January 13). Consuming rituals of the suburban tribe. *The New York Times Magazine*, pp. 28–31.

Roach-Higgins, M. E., Eicher, J. B., & Johnson, K. K. P. (Eds.). (1995). *Dress and identity*. New York: Fairchild.

Ruskin, G. (1999, October). *Commercialism in American society: Implications for children*. Paper presented at the meeting of the Study Group and Invitational Scholars' Forum: Corporate and Industry Influences on Children's Development, Washington, DC.

Schor, J. B. (1998). *The overspent American: Why we want what we don't need*. New York: HarperPerennial.

Simpson, L., Douglas, S., & Schimmel, J. (1998). Tween consumers: Catalog clothing purchase behavior. *Adolescence, 33,* 637–644.

Singer, D. G., & Singer, J. L. (Eds.) (2000). *Handbook of children and the media*. Thousand Oaks, CA: Sage.

Stone, G. P. (1995). Appearance and the self. In M. E. Roach-Higgins, J. B. Eicher, & K. K. P. Johnson (Eds.), *Dress and identity* (pp. 19–39). New York: Fairchild.

Stop the Commercial Exploitation of Children. (2001). Retrieved December 10, 2001, from http://www.commercialexploitation.com

Strasburger, V. C., & Wilson, B. J. (with J. B. Funk, E. Donnerstein, & B. McCannon). (2002). *Children, adolescents, and the media*. Thousand Oaks, CA: Sage.

Taylor, R. L. (Ed.). (1995). *African American youth: Their social and economic status in the United States*. Westport, CT: Praeger.

Taylor, R. L. (Ed.). (2002). *Minority families in the United States: A multicultural perspective* (3rd ed.). Upper Saddle River, NJ: Prentice Hall.

Teenage Research Unlimited. (2001). *Teens spend $155 billion in 2000*. Retrieved December 10, 2001, from http://www.teenresearch.com/Prview.cfm?edit_id=75

Telander, R. (1995). Senseless. In M. E. Roach-Higgins, J. B. Eicher, & K. K. P. Johnson (Eds.), *Dress and identity* (pp. 427–435). New York: Fairchild.

Thompson, B. (1999, October 24). The selling of the clickerati: Kids commerce. *The Washington Post Magazine*, pp. 11–14, 25–29, 32.

U.S. General Accounting Office. (2000). *Commercial activities in schools* (Report No. GAO/HEHS-00-156). Washington, DC: Author.

Wares, L. (1990). African dress. In B. M. Starke, L. O. Holloman, & B. K. Nordquist (Eds.), *African American dress and adornment: A cultural perspective* (pp. 86–102). Dubuque, IA: Kendall Hunt.

Work Group on Commercialism and Youth, Families, and Communities: Implications for Research, Policy, Practice, and Advocacy. (2001). Retrieved December 10, 2001, from http://www.commercialexploitation.com

14

"THE MORE YOU SUBTRACT, THE MORE YOU ADD": CUTTING GIRLS DOWN TO SIZE

JEAN KILBOURNE

Most of us believe that advertising has no influence on us. This is what advertisers want us to believe. If that were true, however, why would companies spend more than $200 billion a year on advertising (Coen, 1999)? The average American is exposed to more than 3,000 ads every day and will spend 3 years of his or her life watching television (Jacobson & Mazur, 1995). Advertising makes up about 70% of our newspapers (Twitchell, 1996) and 40% of our mail (McCarthy, 1990). Advertising is our environment. We swim in it as fish swim in water. As Sut Jhally (1998) said, "To not be influenced by advertising would be to live outside of culture. No human being lives outside of culture." We may not pay attention to very many of these ads, but we are powerfully influenced, mostly on an unconscious level, by the experience of being immersed in an advertising, market-driven culture, in which all of our institutions, from political to religious to educational, are increasingly for sale.

Although some people, especially advertisers, continue to argue that advertising simply reflects society (Sullum, 1997), advertising does a great deal more than simply reflect cultural attitudes and values. Far from being a passive mirror of society, it is an effective and pervasive medium of influence and persuasion, and its influence is cumulative, often subtle and primarily unconscious (see chap. 7, this volume). Advertising performs much the same function in industrial society as myth performed in ancient and primitive societies: It is both a creator and perpetuator of the dominant attitudes, values, and ideology of the culture, as well as the social norms and myths by which most people live. At the very least, advertising helps to create a climate in which certain attitudes and values flourish and others are not reflected at all.

There has never been a propaganda effort to match that of modern advertising (Jhally, 1998). More thought, more effort, and more money go into advertising now than have gone into any other campaign to change social consciousness. The story that advertising tells is that the way to be happy, to find satisfaction, and to be free politically is through the consumption of material objects. Moreover, the major motivating force for social change throughout the world today is this belief that happiness comes from the market.

Advertising is an increasingly ubiquitous force in our lives, and it sells much more than products. We delude ourselves when we say that we are not influenced by advertising, and we trivialize and ignore its growing significance at our peril.

ADVERTISING AND ADOLESCENTS

At no time are we more vulnerable to the seductive power of advertising than during adolescence. Adolescents are relatively new and inexperienced consumers and, as such, prime targets. They are in the process of learning their values and roles and of developing their self-concepts. Most teenagers are sensitive to peer pressure and find it difficult to resist or even to question the dominant cultural messages perpetuated and reinforced by the media. Mass communication has made possible a kind of national peer pressure that erodes private and individual values and standards, as well as community values and standards. As Margaret Mead (1977) once said, today our children are not brought up by parents; they are brought up by the mass media.

Advertisers are aware of their power and do not hesitate to take advantage of the insecurities and anxieties of young people, usually in the guise of offering solutions. A cigarette provides a symbol of independence. Designer jeans or sneakers convey status. The right perfume or beer resolves doubts about femininity or masculinity. Most young people are vulnerable to these messages. Adolescence is a time of doubt and insecurity for most young people, but a particular kind of insecurity afflicts adolescent girls.

Adolescence as a Time of Crisis for Girls

As most of us know so well by now, when a girl enters adolescence, she faces a series of losses—loss of self-confidence, loss of a sense of efficacy and ambition, and the loss of her "voice," the sense of being a unique and powerful self that she had in childhood. Girls who were active, confident, and feisty at the ages of 8 and 9 and 10 often become hesitant, insecure, and self-doubting by 11. Their self-esteem plummets. As Carol Gilligan (1982), Mary Pipher (1994), and other social critics and psychologists (e.g., Sadker & Sadker, 1994) have pointed out in recent years, adolescent girls in America are afflicted with a range of problems, including low self-esteem, eating disorders, binge drinking, date rape and other dating violence, teen pregnancy, and cigarette use. Teenage women today are engaging in far riskier health behavior in greater numbers than any prior generation (Roan, 1993).

According to a 1998 status report by a consortium of universities and research centers, girls have closed the gap with boys in math performance and are coming close in science (Vobejda & Perlstein, 1998). However, they are also now smoking, drinking, and using drugs as often as boys their own age. Although girls are not nearly as violent as boys, they are committing more crimes than ever before and are far more often physically attacking each other.

It is important to understand that these problems go far beyond individual psychological development and pathology. Even girls who are raised in loving homes by supportive parents grow up in a toxic cultural environment, at risk for self-mutilation, eating disorders, and addictions. The culture, both reflected and reinforced by advertising, urges girls to adopt a false self, to bury alive their real selves, to become *feminine*, which means to be nice and kind and sweet, to compete with other girls for the attention of boys, and to value romantic relationships with boys above all else. Girls are put into a terrible double bind. They are supposed to repress their power, their anger, and their exuberance and be simply "nice," although they also eventually must compete with men in the business world and be successful. They must be overtly sexy and attractive but essentially passive and virginal. It is not surprising that most girls experience adolescence as painful and confusing, especially if they are unconscious of these conflicting demands (Gilligan, 1982; Pipher, 1994).

It is impossible to speak accurately of girls as a monolithic group. The socialization that emphasizes passivity and compliance does not apply to many Black and Jewish girls, who are often encouraged to be assertive and outspoken (Thompson, 1994). Working-class girls are usually not expected to be stars in the business world. Far from protecting these girls from eating disorders and other problems, these differences more often mean that the problems remain hidden or undiagnosed and that the girls are even less likely to get help (Steiner-Adair & Purcell, 1996). Eating problems affect girls from

Black, Asian, Native American, Hispanic, and Latino families and from every socioeconomic background. The racism and classism that these girls experience exacerbate their problems. Sexism is by no means the only trauma they face.

Targeting Girls

Girls try to make sense of the contradictory expectations of themselves in a culture dominated by advertising. Advertising is one of the most potent messengers in a culture that can be toxic for girls' self-esteem. Indeed if we look only at advertising images, this would be a bleak world for girls and women. Girls are a favorite target of advertisers because they are new consumers, are beginning to have significant disposable income, and are developing brand loyalty that might last a lifetime. Teenage girls spend more than $4 billion annually on cosmetics alone (J. D. Brown, Greenberg, & Buerkel-Rothfuss, 1993).

Seventeen, a magazine aimed at girls about 12 to 15, sells these girls directly to advertisers in an ad in *Advertising Age* (the major publication of the advertising industry) that says, "She's the one you want. She's the one we've got." The copy continues, "She pursues beauty and fashion at every turn" and concludes with, "It's more than a magazine. It's her life." In another similar ad, *Seventeen* refers to itself as a girl's "Bible." Many girls read magazines like this and take the advice seriously. Regardless of the intent of the advertisers, what are the messages that girls are getting? What are they told?

ADVERTISERS' IMAGE OF IDEAL BEAUTY

Primarily girls are told by advertisers that what is most important about them is their perfume, their clothing, their bodies, and their beauty. Their "essence" is their underwear. "He says the first thing he noticed about you is your great personality," says an ad featuring a very young woman in tight jeans. The copy continues, "He lies." Even very little girls are offered makeup and toys like Special Night Barbie, which shows them how to dress up for a night out. Girls of all ages get the message that they must be flawlessly beautiful and, above all these days, they must be thin.

Even more destructively, they get the message that this is possible and that, with enough effort and self-sacrifice, they can achieve this ideal. Thus many girls spend enormous amounts of time and energy attempting to achieve something that is not only trivial but also completely unattainable. The glossy images of flawlessly beautiful and extremely thin women that surround us would not have the impact they do if we did not live in a culture that encourages women to believe that they can and should remake their bodies into perfect commodities. These images play into the American belief of transformation and ever-new possibilities, no longer through hard work but through the purchase of the right products. This belief is by no means universal. People in many other cultures may admire a particular body shape without seeking to emulate it.

The Impact of the Ideal Image of Beauty

Women are especially vulnerable because our bodies have been objectified and commodified for so long. Young women are the most vulnerable, especially those who have experienced early deprivation, sexual abuse, family violence, or other trauma (Smith, Fairburn, & Cowen, 1999; Thompson, 1994). Cultivating a thinner body offers some hope of control and success to a young woman with a poor self-image, overwhelming personal problems, and no easy solutions.

Although troubled young women are especially vulnerable, these messages affect all girls. Researchers at Brigham and Women's Hospital in Boston found that the more frequently girls read magazines, the more likely they were to diet and to feel that magazines influence their ideal body shape (Field et al., 1999). Nearly half reported wanting to lose weight because of a magazine picture, even though only 29% were actually overweight. Studies at Stanford University and the University of Massachusetts found that about 70% of college women say they feel worse about their own looks after reading women's magazines (Richins, 1991; Then, 1992). Another study of young men and women found that a preoccupation with one's appearance takes a toll on mental health (Fredrickson, Roberts, Noll, Quinn, & Twenge, 1998). Women scored much higher than men on what the researchers called "self-objectification." This tendency to view one's body from the outside in—regarding physical attractiveness, sex appeal, measurements, and weight as more central to one's physical identity than health, strength, energy level, coordination, or fitness—has many harmful effects, including diminished mental performance, increased feelings of shame and anxiety, depression, sexual dysfunction, and the development of eating disorders.

These images of women seem to affect men most strikingly by influencing how they judge the real women in their lives. Strasburger (1989) found that male college students who viewed just one episode of *Charlie's Angels*, the hit television show of the 1970s that featured three beautiful women, were harsher in their evaluations of the attractiveness of potential dates than were male students who had not seen the show. In a second study, male college students shown centerfolds from *Playboy* and *Penthouse* were more likely to find their own girlfriends less sexually attractive.

The Obsession With Thinness

Adolescent girls are especially vulnerable to the obsession with thinness for many reasons. One is the ominous peer pressure on young people.

Adolescence is a time of self-consciousness and terror of shame and humiliation. Boys are shamed for being too small, too "weak," too soft, or too sensitive; girls are shamed for being too sexual, too loud, too boisterous, too big (in any sense of the word), or having too hearty an appetite. Many young women have told me that their boyfriends wanted them to lose weight. One said that her boyfriend had threatened to leave her if she didn't lose 5 pounds. "Why don't you leave him," I asked, "and lose 160?"

The situation is very different for men. The double standard is reflected in an advertisement for a low-fat pizza: "He eats a brownie . . . you eat a rice cake. He eats a juicy burger . . . you eat a low fat entree. He eats pizza . . . you eat pizza. Finally, life is fair." Although some men develop eating problems, the predominant cultural message remains that a hearty appetite and a large size is desirable in a man, but not so in a woman.

Normal physiological changes during adolescence result in increased body fat for women. If these normal changes are considered undesirable by the culture (and by parents and peers), this can lead to chronic anxiety and concern about weight control in young women. A 10-year-old girl wrote to New Moon, a feminist magazine for girls, "I was at the beach and was in my bathing suit. I have kind of fat legs, and my uncle told me I had fat legs in front of all my cousins and my cousins' friends. I was so embarrassed, I went up to my room and shut the door. When I went downstairs again, everyone started teasing me" (H. Henderson, personal communication, March 22, 1999).

The obsession starts early. Some studies have found that from 40 to 80% of 4th-grade girls are dieting (Stein, 1986). Today at least one third of 12- to 13-year-old girls are actively trying to lose weight by dieting, vomiting, using laxatives, or taking diet pills (Rodriguez, 1998). One survey found that 63% of high school girls were on diets, compared with only 16% of boys (Rothblum, 1994). A survey in Massachusetts found that the single largest group of high school students considering or attempting suicide are girls who feel they are overweight (Overlan, 1996). Imagine—girls made to feel so terrible about themselves that they would rather be dead than fat. This would not be happening if it were not for our last "socially acceptable" prejudice—weightism (Steiner-Adair & Purcell, 1996). Fat children are ostracized and ridiculed from the moment they enter school, and fat adults, women in particular, are subjected to public contempt and scorn. This strikes terror into the hearts of all women, many of whom, unfortunately, identify with the oppressor and become vicious to themselves and to each other.

No wonder it is hard to find a woman, especially a young woman, in America today who has a truly healthy attitude toward her body and toward food. Just as the disease of alcoholism is the extreme end of a continuum that includes a wide range of alcohol use and abuse, so are bulimia and anorexia the extreme results of an obsession with eating and weight control that grips many young women with serious and potentially very dangerous results.

Although eating problems are often thought to result from vanity, the truth is that they, like other addictions and compulsive behaviors, usually have deeper roots,not only genetic predisposition and biochemical vulnerabilities,but also other factors such as sexism, racism, weightism, and childhood sexual abuse (Hsu, 1990; Jonas, 1989; Krahn, 1991; Smith et al., 1999; Thompson, 1994).

Advertising clearly does not cause eating problems any more than it causes alcoholism. Anorexia in particular is a disease with a complicated etiology, and media images probably do not play a major role. However, these images certainly contribute to the body-hatred so many young women feel and to some of the resulting eating problems, which range from bulimia to compulsive overeating to simply being obsessed with controlling one's appetite. Advertising does promote abusive and abnormal attitudes about eating, drinking, and thinness. It thus provides fertile soil for these obsessions to take root in and creates a climate of denial in which these diseases flourish.

The influence of the media is strikingly illustrated in a recent study (Becker & Burwell, 1999) that found a sharp rise in eating disorders among young women in Fiji soon after the introduction of television to the culture. Before television was available, there was little talk of dieting in Fiji. "You've gained weight" was a traditional compliment and "going thin" the sign of a problem. In 1995 television came to the island. Within 3 years, the number of teenagers at risk for eating disorders more than doubled: 74% of the teens in the study said they felt "too big or too fat" and 62% said they had dieted in the past month. This does not prove a direct causal link between television and eating disorders; Fiji is a culture in transition in many ways. However, it seems more than coincidental that the Fijian girls who were heavy viewers of television were 50% more likely to describe themselves as fat and 30% more likely to diet than those girls who watched television less frequently. As Ellen Goodman (1999) wrote, "The big success story of our entertainment industry is our ability to export insecurity: We can make any woman anywhere feel perfectly rotten about her shape" (p. A23).

FEAR OF FEMALE POWER

Not everything is intentional on the part of advertisers. Some advertising is intended to arouse anxiety and affect women's self-esteem. However, some simply reflects the unconscious attitudes and beliefs of the individual advertisers, as well as what Carl Jung referred to as the "collective unconscious." Advertisers are members of the culture, too, and have been as thoroughly conditioned as anyone else. The magazines and the ads deliberately create and intensify anxiety about weight because it is so profitable to do so. On a deeper level, however, they reflect cultural concerns and conflicts about women's power (Faludi, 1991; Kilbourne, 1986). Real freedom for women would change the very basis of our male-dominated society. It is not surprising that many men (and women, to be sure) fear this.

This fear is reflected in an ad that ran in several women's and teen's magazines in 1997 with the headline, "The more you subtract, the more you add." Surprisingly, it is an ad for clothing, not for a diet product. Overtly, it is a statement about minimalism in fashion. However, the fact that the girl in the ad is very young and very thin reinforces another message, a message that an adolescent girl constantly gets from advertising and throughout the popular culture: the message that she should diminish herself, that she should be less than she is.

On the most obvious and familiar level, this refers to her body. However, the loss, the subtraction, the cutting down to size also refers, albeit indirectly, to her sense of her self, her sexuality, her need for authentic connection, and her longing for power and freedom. I certainly do not think that the creators of this particular ad had all this in mind. They are simply selling expensive clothing in an unoriginal way, by using a very young and very thin woman and an unfortunate tagline. It would not be important at all were there not so many other ads that reinforce this message and did it not coincide with a cultural crisis taking place now for adolescent girls.

"We cut Judy down to size," says an ad for a health club. "Soon, you'll both be taking up less space," says an ad for a collapsible treadmill, referring both to the product and the young woman exercising on it. The obsession with thinness is most deeply about cutting girls and women down to size. It is only a symbol, albeit a very powerful and destructive one, of tremendous fear of female power (Faludi, 1991; Kilbourne, 1986). Powerful women are seen by many people (women as well as men) as inherently destructive and dangerous. Some argue that it is men's awareness of just how powerful women can be that has created the attempts to keep women small. Indeed, thinness as an ideal has always accompanied periods of greater freedom for women: As soon as women got the vote, boyish flapper bodies came into vogue. No wonder there is such pressure on young women today to be thin, to shrink, to be like little girls, not to take up too much space, literally or figuratively.

Dieting as a Route to Power and Control

At the same time that there is relentless pressure on women to be small, there is also pressure on them to succeed, to achieve, to "have it all." Women can be successful as long as they stay "feminine" (i.e., powerless enough not to be truly threatening). One way to do this is to present an image of fragility, to look like a waif. This demonstrates that one is both in control and still very "feminine." One of the many double binds tormenting young women today is the need to be both sophisticated and accomplished, yet also delicate and childlike. Again, this applies mostly to middle- and upper-class White women.

The changing roles and greater opportunities for women promised by the women's movement have been trivialized and reduced to the private search for the slimmest body. In one commercial, three skinny young women dance and sing about the "taste of freedom." They are feeling free because they can now eat bread, thanks to a low-calorie version. You can never be too thin, girls are told. This mass delusion sells a lot of products. It also causes enormous suffering, involving girls in quests for power and control based on their beauty and the products they own, while deflecting attention and energy from that which might really empower them.

The quest for independence can be a problem too if it leads girls to deny the importance of and need for interpersonal relationships. Girls and young women today are encouraged by the culture to achieve a very "masculine" kind of autonomy and independence, one that excludes interdependence, mutuality, and connection with others. Catherine Steiner-Adair (1986) suggested that perhaps eating disorders emerge at adolescence because it is at this point that "females experience themselves to be at a crossroads in their lives where they must shift from a relational approach to life to an autonomous one, a shift that can represent an intolerable loss when independence is associated with isolation" (p. 107). In this sense, she viewed eating disorders as political statements, a kind of hunger strike: "Girls with eating disorders have a heightened, albeit confused, grasp of the dangerous imbalance of the culture's values, which they cannot articulate in the face of the culture's abject denial of their adolescent intuitive truth, so they tell their story with their bodies" (p. 110).

Silencing Girls

Most of us know by now about the damage done to girls by the tyranny of the ideal image, weightism, and the obsession with thinness. Girls also get other messages that "cut them down to size" more subtly. In ad after ad girls are urged to be "barely there"—beautiful but silent. Girls clearly are not just influenced by images of other girls; they are even more powerfully attuned to images of women, because they learn from these images what is expected of them, what they are to become. They see these images again and again in the magazines they read, even those magazines designed for teenagers, and in the commercials they watch.

"Make a statement without saying a word," says an ad for perfume. Indeed this is one of the primary messages of the culture to adolescent girls. "The silence of a look can reveal more than words," says another perfume ad, this one featuring a woman lying on her back. In another ad, a young woman's turtleneck is pulled over her mouth. An ad for a movie soundtrack features a chilling image of a young woman with her lips sewn together.

It is not only the girls themselves who see these images. Their parents and teachers and doctors see them and they influence their sense of how girls should be. A 1997 study done at the University of Michigan found that, beginning in preschool, girls are told to be quiet much more often than are boys (Martin, 1998). Although boys were much noisier than girls, the girls were told to speak softly or to use a "nicer" voice about three times more often. Girls were encouraged to be quiet, small, and physically constrained. The researcher concluded that one of the consequences of this socialization is that girls grow into women afraid to speak up for themselves or to use their voices to protect themselves from a variety of dangers (Martin, 1998).

A television commercial features a very young woman, shot in black and white but with colored contact lenses. She never speaks but she touches her face and her hair as a female voiceover says, "Your eyes don't just see, they also speak. . . . Your eyes can say a lot, but they don't have to shout. They can speak softly. Let your eyes be heard . . . without making a sound." The commercial ends with the young woman putting her finger in her mouth.

"Score high on nonverbal skills," says a clothing ad featuring a young African American woman, whereas an ad for mascara tells young women to "make up your own language." An Italian ad features a very thin young woman in an elegant coat sitting on a window seat. The copy says, "This woman is silent. This coat talks." Girls, seeing these images of women, are encouraged to be silent, mysterious, not to talk too much or too loudly. In so many different ways, they are told "the more you subtract, the more you add."

Body Language in Advertisements

Many ads feature girls and young women in very passive poses, limp, doll-like, sometimes acting like little girls, playing with dolls and wearing bows in their hair. One ad uses a pacifier to sell lipstick and another the image of a baby to sell BabyDoll Blush Highlight. As Erving Goffman (1978) pointed out in *Gender Advertisements*, we learn a great deal about the disparate power of male and female individuals simply through the body language and poses of advertising. Women, especially young women, are generally subservient to men in ads, both in size and position.

A double-paged spread for Calvin Klein's clothing for kids conveys a world of information about the relative power of boys and girls. One of the boys seems to be in the act of speaking, expressing himself, whereas the girl has her hand over her mouth. Boys are generally shown in ads as active and rambunctious, whereas girls are more often passive and focused on their appearance. The exception to the rule involves African American children, male and female, who are often shown in advertising as passive observers of their White playmates (Seiter, 1993).

Girls are often shown as playful clowns in ads, perpetuating the attitude that girls and women are childish and cannot be taken seriously, whereas even very young men are generally portrayed as secure, powerful and serious.

People in control of their lives stand upright, alert and ready to meet the world. In contrast, female individuals often appear off-balance, insecure, and weak. Often women's body parts are bent, conveying unpreparedness, submissiveness, and appeasement. Women exhibit what Goffman (1978) called *licensed withdrawal*, the appearance of being psychologically removed, disoriented, defenseless, or spaced out.

Female individuals touch people and things delicately and caressingly, whereas male individuals grip, clench, and grasp. Girls and women cover their faces with their hair or hands, conveying shame or embarrassment, and no matter what happens, they keep on smiling. "Just smiling the bothers away," as one ad says. This ad is particularly disturbing because the model is a young African American woman, a member of a group that has long been encouraged to just keep smiling, no matter what. She's even wearing a kerchief, like Aunt Jemima. The cultural fear of angry women is intensified dramatically when the women are African American (Nelson, 1997).

MASS MEDIA AS SEX EDUCATION

As girls come of age sexually, the culture gives them impossibly contradictory messages. As the *Seventeen* ad says, "She wants to be outrageous. And accepted." Advertising slogans such as "Because innocence is sexier than you think," "Purity, yes. Innocence, never," and "Nothing so sensual was ever so innocent" place them in a double bind. Somehow girls are supposed to be both innocent and seductive, virginal and experienced, all at the same time. As they quickly learn, this is tricky.

Women have long been divided into virgins and whores. What is new is that girls are now supposed to embody both within themselves. This is symbolic of the central contradiction of the culture—women must work hard and produce and achieve success and yet, at the same time, they are encouraged to live impulsively, spend a lot of money, and be constantly and immediately gratified. This tension is reflected in women's attitudes toward many things, including sex and eating. Girls are promised fulfillment both through being thin and through eating rich foods, just as they are promised fulfillment through being innocent and virginal and through wild and impulsive sex.

Girls and boys are surrounded by messages urging them to be sexually active. Teachers report a steady escalation of sex talk among children, starting in preschool, as our children are prematurely exposed to a barrage of sexual information and misinformation through advertising, television shows, music, and films (Meltz, 1997). "You can learn more about anatomy after school," says an ad for jeans featuring a very young couple pressed against each other. This ad manages to trivialize sex, relationships, and education all in one sentence.

The consequences of all this sexual pressure on children are frightening. The average age of first sexual intercourse is about 16 for girls and 15 for boys (J. D. Brown et al., 1993). Far more disturbing are the statistics that 7 in 10 girls who had sex before the age of 14, and 6 in 10 of those who had sex before the age of 15, report having sex involuntarily (Kaiser Family Foundation, 1996). One of every 10 girls under the age of 20 becomes pregnant in the United States each year, more than in any other industrialized country in the world (J. D. Brown et al., 1993): twice as high as in England and Wales, France, and Canada, and nine times as high as in the Netherlands and Japan (Kaiser Family Foundation, 1996). As many as one in six sexually active adolescents has a sexually transmitted disease (J. D. Brown et al., 1993).

Advertising and the media clearly are not solely to blame for these appalling statistics, but they are the leading source of sex education in the nation and they create a climate that encourages a very cavalier attitude toward sex. The typical teenage viewer who watches an average of 3 to 5 hours of television a day sees a minimum of 2,000 sexual acts per year on television alone (J. D. Brown et al., 1993). There is also abundant depiction of sexual activity in music videos, books, videos, cartoons, video games, and song lyrics aimed at teenagers, almost all of it portraying sexual behavior as consequence-free and much of it exploiting women's bodies and glamorizing sexual violence. Magazines targeting girls and young women are filled with ads and articles on how to be beautiful and sexy and appealing to boys—all in the service of advertisers, who sell their wares on almost every page. "How Smart Girls Flirt," "Sex to Write Home About," "15 Ways Sex Makes You Prettier," and "Are You Good in Bed?" are some of the cover stories for a teen magazine called *Jane*, which, though marketed to 20-something women, is nonetheless quite popular with teenagers.

At the same time, there is rarely any accurate information about sex (the networks still refuse to run condom ads) and certainly never any emphasis on relationships or intimacy. (There is hardly time in 30 seconds for the sexual encounter, let alone any development of character!) Citizens have to fight to get sex education into schools, and the government refuses to fund any program that does not insist on abstinence as the only choice suitable for young people (how quickly people forget their own adolescence). Most of the sex education that young people do get teaches them that sex can hurt or kill them but not that it can bring pleasure, joy, and connection (Bernstein, 1995). How are they to learn to say "Yes!" in a loving and responsible way?

It is difficult to do the kind of research that would prove the effects of the media on sexual attitudes and behavior because of the perceived sensitivity of sex as a topic and because of the difficulty in finding a comparison group. However, the few existing studies consistently point to a relationship between exposure to sexual content and sexual beliefs, attitudes, and behavior. J. D. Brown and Steele (1995) have found a correlation between watching higher doses of "sexy" television and early initiation of sexual intercourse, and studies of adolescents have found that heavy television viewing is predictive of negative attitudes toward virginity. In general, key communication theories and years of research on other kinds of communications effects, such as the effect of violent images, suggest that people are indeed affected by the ubiquitous, graphic, and consequence-free depictions of sexual behavior that surround us in all forms of the mass media.

Jane Brown and her colleagues concluded from their years of research that the mass media are important sex educators for American teenagers. Other potential educators, such as parents, schools, and churches, are doing an inadequate job and, even if that were to change dramatically, the media would remain compelling teachers. Brown faulted media portrayals for avoiding the "three C's"—commitment, contraceptives, and consequences—and concluded, "it is little wonder that adolescents find the sexual world a difficult and often confusing place and that they engage in early and unprotected sexual intercourse with multiple partners" (J. D. Brown et al., 1993, p. 523).

The emphasis for girls and women is always on being desirable, not on experiencing desire. Girls who want to be sexually active instead of simply being the objects of male desire are given only one model to follow, that of exploitive male sexuality. It seems that advertisers cannot conceive of a kind of power that is not manipulative and exploitive or a way that women can be actively sexual without being like traditional men.

Women who are "powerful" in advertising are uncommitted. They treat men like sex objects: "If I want a man to see my bra, I take him home," says an androgynous young woman. They are elusive and distant: "She's the first woman who refused to take your phone calls," says one ad, as if it were a good thing to be rude and inconsiderate. Why should any of us, male or female, be interested in someone who will not take our phone calls, who either cares so little for us or is so manipulative?

Mostly, however, girls are not supposed to have sexual agency. They are supposed to be passive, swept away, overpowered. "See where it takes you," says a perfume ad featuring a couple passionately embracing. "Unleash your fantasies," says another. This contributes to the strange and damaging concept of the "good girl" as the one who is swept away, unprepared for sex, versus the "bad girl" as the one who plans for sex, uses contraception, and is generally responsible. A young woman can manage to have sex and yet in some sense maintain her virginity by being "out of control," drunk, or deep in denial about the entire experience.

No wonder most teenage pregnancies occur when one or both parties is drunk (Reed, 1991). Alcohol and other mind-altering drugs permit sexual activity at the same time that they allow denial. One is almost literally not there. The next day one has an excuse: I was drunk, I was swept away, I did not choose this experience.

REBELLION AND RESISTANCE

Adolescent girls are told that they have to give up much of what they know about relationships and intimacy if they want to attract men. Most tragically, they are told they have to give up each other. The truth is that one of the most powerful antidotes to destructive cultural messages is close and supportive female friendships. Unfortunately, girls are often encouraged by the culture to sacrifice their relationships with one another and to enter into hostile competition for the attention of boys and men. "What the bitch who's about to steal your man wears," says one ad. Many ads feature women fighting or glaring at each other.

Some girls do resist and rebel. Some are encouraged (by someone, perhaps a loving parent or a supportive teacher) to see the cultural contradictions clearly and to break free in a healthy and positive way. Others rebel in ways that damage themselves. A young woman seems to have only two choices: She can bury her sexual self, be a "good girl," give in to what L. M. Brown and Gilligan (1992) called "the tyranny of nice and kind" (p. 53)— and numb the pain by overeating or starving or cutting herself or drinking heavily. Or she can become a rebel, flout her sexuality, seduce inappropriate partners, smoke, drink flamboyantly, and use other drugs. Both of these responses are self-destructive, but they begin as an attempt to survive, not to self-destruct.

Many girls become women who split themselves in two and do both— have a double life, a secret life—a good girl in public, out of control in private. A feminist in public, involved in an abusive relationship or lost in sado-masochistic fantasies in private. A lawyer by day, a barfly by night. Raiding the refrigerator or drinking themselves into a stupor alone in their kitchens at night, after the children are in bed and the laundry is done. Doing well in school, but smoking in order to have a sexier, cooler image. Being sexual only when drunk.

Few healthy alternatives are available for girls who want to truly rebel against restrictive gender roles and stereotypes. The recent emphasis on Girl Power has led to some real advances for girls and young women, especially in the arenas of music and sports, but it is as often coopted and trivialized. Magazines like *New Moon, Hues,* and *Teen Voices* offer a real alternative to the glitzy, boy-crazy, appearance-obsessed teen magazines on the newstands, but they have to struggle for funds because they take no advertising. There are some good zines and Web sites for girls on the Internet, but there are also countless sites that degrade and endanger them. And Barbie continues to rake in $2 billion a year (Goldsmith, 1999). Barbie's makers have succumbed to pressure somewhat and have remade her with a thicker waist, smaller breasts, and slimmer hips. (As a result, according to Anthony Cortese [1999], she has already lost her waitressing job at Hooters and her boyfriend Ken has told her that he wants to start seeing other dolls.)

Girls who want to escape the stereotypes are viewed with glee by advertisers, who rush to offer them, as always, power through products. The emphasis in the ads is always on their sexuality, which is exploited to sell them makeup and clothes and shoes. A trio of extremely thin African American women brandish hair appliances and products as if they were weapons—and the brand is 911. A cosmetics company has a line of products called "Bad Gal." In one ad, eyeliner is shown in cartoon version as a girl, who is holding a dog saying, "grrrr . . . ," surely a reference to "grrrrls," a symbol these days of "girl power." Unfortunately, girl power doesn't mean much if girls do not have the tools to achieve it. Without reproductive freedom and freedom from violence, girl power is nothing but a marketing slogan.

So, for all the attention paid to girls in recent years, what girls are offered mostly by the popular culture is a superficial toughness, an "attitude," exemplified by smoking, drinking, and engaging in casual sex, all behaviors which harm themselves. In 1990, Virginia Slims offered girls a T shirt that said, "Sugar and spice and everything nice? Get real." In 1997, Winston used the same theme in an ad featuring a tough young woman shooting pool and saying, "I'm not all sugar & spice. And neither are my smokes." As if the alternative to the feminine stereotype was sarcasm and toughness, and as if smoking was somehow an expression of one's authentic self ("get real"). In the year 2000, Virginia Slims used the slogan "Find your voice," as if addiction were a route to self-expression.

Readers and viewers of these ads clearly do not take them literally. We do take them in, however—another grain of sand in a slowly accumulating and vast sandpile. If we entirely enter the world of ads, and imagine them to be real for a moment, we find that the sandpile has completely closed us in, and there's only one escape route: buy something. "Hey girls, you've got the power of control" says an ad for . . . hairspray. "The possibilities are endless" (clothing). "Never lose control" (hairspray again). "You never had this much control when you were on your own" (hair gel). "Inner strength" (vitamins). "Only Victoria's Secret could make control so sensual" (girdles). "Stronger longer" (shampoo). The empowerment, the enlightenment, is as impossible to get through products as is anything else—love, security, romance, passion. On one level, we know this. On another, we keep buying and hoping—and buying.

Other ads go further and offer products as a way to rebel, to be a real individual. "Live outside the lines," says a clothing ad featuring a young woman walking out of a men's room. This kind of rebellion is not going to rock the world. Not surprisingly, the young woman is very thin and conventionally pretty. Another pretty young woman sells a brand of jeans called "Revolt." "Don't just change . . . revolt," says the copy, but the young woman is passive, slight, her eyes averted.

"Nude with attitude" features an African American woman in a powerful pose, completely undercut by the brevity of her dress and the focus on her long legs. Her "attitude" is nothing to fear—she's just another sex object. Good thing, given the fear many people have of powerful African American women (Nelson, 1997).

Some ads do feature women who seem really angry and rebellious, but the final message always is the same. "Today, I indulge my dark side," says an ad featuring a fierce young woman tearing at what seems to be a net. "Got a problem with that?" The slogan is "be extraordinary not ordinary." The product that promises to free this girl from the net that imprisons her? Black nail polish.

Nail polish. Such a trivial solution to such an enormous dilemma. But such triviality and superficiality is common in advertising. How could it be otherwise? The solution to any problem always has to be a product. Change (transformation) is thus inevitably shallow and moronic, rather than meaningful and transcendent. These days self-improvement seems to have more to do with calories than with character, with abdomens rather than absolutes, with nail polish than with ethics.

It has not always been so. Joan Jacobs Brumberg (1997) described this vividly in *The Body Project: An Intimate History of American Girls*:

> When girls in the nineteenth century thought about ways to improve themselves, they almost always focused on their internal character and how it was reflected in outward behavior. In 1892, the personal agenda of an adolescent diarist read: "Resolved, not to talk about myself or feelings. To think before speaking. To work seriously. . . . To be dignified. Interest myself more in others."
>
> A century later, in the 1990s, American girls think very differently. In a New Year's resolution written in 1982, a girl wrote: "I will try to make myself better in every way I possibly can with the help of my budget and baby-sitting money. I will lose weight, get new lenses, already got new haircut, good makeup, new clothes and accessories." (p. xxi)

Not that girls didn't have plenty of problems in the 19th century. Surely by now we should have come much further. This relentless trivialization of a girl's hopes and dreams, her expectations for herself, cuts to the quick of her soul. Just as she is entering womanhood, eager to spread her wings, to become more sexual, more empowered, and more independent, the culture moves in to cut her down to size.

CONCLUSION

What can we do about all of this? The first thing we must do is to get past the cultural belief, promoted so heavily by advertising, that there is a quick fix, an instant solution to every problem—and that one should not even discuss a problem unless one has a solution firmly in mind. There is no quick fix for the problems discussed in this chapter (or indeed this book), no panacea, but there are many things we can and must do. We must recognize the interrelationships of problems such as addictions, eating disorders, the increasing commercialization of the culture, sexual abuse, the exploitation of children by advertisers, and the objectification of women and girls. We cannot solve these problems by treating them as separate issues. They are all public health problems and must be treated as such.

A sea change in public health in recent years has shifted the focus from the individual to the environment. We are learning that many, if not all, of our problems can be reduced by changing the environment. We must create environments where healthy choices are easier to make. Public health experts generally refer to this approach as a "systems" approach, which recognizes that dynamic interactions occur, not only between the individual and the environment, but also among various levels of the environment (Mosher, 1997). The individual is viewed as part of a complex social, physical, and political web—family, school, community, workplace, state, and so on (see chaps. 4 & 12).

Therapists must take the cultural environment into consideration, too. Just as they cannot successfully treat lesbians or gay men or people of color without taking homophobia and racism into account, they cannot treat anyone without taking sexism into account. It is also important in this culture to consider the impact of commercialism on many of the issues brought up in therapy (e.g., eating disorders, addiction, and sexual abuse; see also chap. 9, this volume).

Another important aspect of breaking through the climate of denial is to teach media literacy in our schools, starting in kindergarten. We all need to be educated to become critical viewers of the media. As parents, we can help our children to become media literate, both by fighting for media literacy programs in our schools and by talking with our children about the media, using "teachable moments" to ask questions ("What exactly is that beer commercial selling?") and raise consciousness. Many organizations, ranging from the New Mexico Media Literacy Project to the American Academy of Pediatrics, have programs for parents, schools, and communities. These organizations, as well as public health and other organizations, are listed on the resource list on my Web site (www.jeankilbourne.com).

Whether we are girls, women, boys, or men, all of us need real connection in our private lives and in our public policy, not the illusion of connection provided by advertising. As parents, the most important thing we can do for our children is to connect deeply and honestly with them. A 2-year study of more than 12,000 adolescents found that the best predictor of health and the strongest deterrent to high-risk behavior in teens was a strong connection with at least one adult, at home or at school. This finding held up regardless of family structure, income, race, education, amount of time spent together, where or with whom the child lives, or whether one or both parents work (Dooley & Fedele, 1999). The message is clear: Good relationships create the resilience that prevents dangerous, acting-out behaviors in our children.

We also need to work politically to create the kind of culture that makes it easier to have successful relationships with our children. Sylvia Ann Hewlett and Cornel West (1998), who have formed a parenting movement called the National Parenting Association, have argued that "at the root of the assault on families is the triumph of a marketing culture which promotes hedonistic, narcissistic, and individualistic ways of being in the world. These ways of being make it harder for anyone to support or to honor non-market activity, of which parenting is a primary example" (p. 29). We must recognize that many children do not have the possibility of a strong connection with a parent, so we must make sure they get these connections elsewhere. We must support youth centers, good schools, mentoring programs, and programs to identify children of addicts and other children at risk. Many organizations, both national and local, are devoted to helping girls thrive despite a toxic cultural environment. These include Girls, Inc. (based in New York), Dads & Daughters (Duluth, Minnesota), the New Moon Foundation (Duluth, Minnesota), GenAustin (Austin, Texas), and the Daughters/Sisters Project (Seattle, Washington).

There is no quick fix, but there is a great deal we can and must do. I once heard a parable about a wise old woman who lived in a village. A boy in the village decided to trick her. He trapped a small bird and told his friends that he would take it to the woman and ask her if it were dead or alive. "If she says it is dead, I will release it," he said, "and if she says it is alive, I will crush it to death." The children went to the old woman and the boy said, "I have a bird in my hands. Is it dead or alive?" The old woman looked at him and replied, "It is in your hands."

REFERENCES

Becker, A. E., & Burwell, R. A. (1999, May). *Acculturation and disordered eating in Fiji.* Poster presented at the annual meeting of the American Psychiatric Association, Washington, DC.

Bernstein, N. (1995, January/February). Learning to love. *Mother Jones*, pp. 45–49, 54.

Brown, J. D., Greenberg, B. S., & Buerkel-Rothfuss, N. L. (1993). Mass media, sex and sexuality. In V. C. Strasburger & G. A. Comstock (Eds.), *Adolescent medicine: Adolescents and the media* (pp. 511–525). Philadephia: Hanley & Belfus.

Brown, J. D., & Steele, J. R. (1995, June 21). *Sex and the mass media.* A report prepared for the Henry J. Kaiser Family Foundation.

Brown, L. M., & Gilligan, C. (1992). *Meeting at the crossroads: Women's psychology and girls' development.* New York: Ballantine Books.

Brumberg, J. J. (1997). *The body project: An intimate history of American girls.* New York: Random House.

Coen, R. J. (1999). *Spending spree. The advertising century* [Special issue]. *Advertising Age, 126,* 136.

Cortese, A. (1999). *Provocateur: Women and minorities in advertising.* Lanham, MD: Rowman & Littlefield.

Dooley, C., & Fedele, N. (1999). A response to the Columbine tragedy. *Connections (Jean Baker Miller Training Institute)*, 2.

Faludi, S. (1991). *Backlash.* New York: Crown.

Field, A. E., Cheung, L., Wolf, A. M., Herzog, D. B., Gortmaker, S. L., & Colditz, G. A. (1999). Exposure to the mass media and weight concerns among girls. *Pediatrics, 103*, 36–41.

Fredrickson, B. L., Roberts, T. A., Noll, S. M., Quinn, D. M., & Twenge, J. M. (1998). That swimsuit becomes you: Sex differences in self-objectification, restrained eating, and math performance. *Journal of Personality and Social Psychology, 75*, 269–284.

Gilligan, C. (1982). *In a different voice.* Cambridge, MA: Harvard University Press.

Goffman, E. (1978). *Gender advertisements.* Cambridge, MA: Harvard University Press.

Goldsmith, J. (1999, February 10). A $2 billion doll celebrates her 40th without a wrinkle. *Boston Globe*, p. D3.

Goodman, E. (1999, May 27). The culture of thin bites Fiji teens. *Boston Globe*, A23.

Hewlett, S. A., & West, C. (1998). *The war against parents.* New York: Houghton Mifflin.

Hsu, L. K. (1990). *Eating disorders.* New York: Guilford Press.

Jacobson, M. F., & Mazur, L. A. (1995). *Marketing madness: A survival guide for a consumer society.* Boulder, CO: Westview Press.

Jhally, S. (Producer/Director). (1998). *Advertising and the end of the world* [Motion picture]. Northampton, MA: Media Education Foundation.

Jonas, J. M. (1989). Eating disorders and alcohol and other drug abuse. Is there an association? *Alcohol Health & Research World, 13*, 267–271.

Kaiser Family Foundation, Alan Guttmacher Institute, & the National Press Foundation. (1996, June 24). *Emerging issues in reproductive health (fact sheet).*

Kilbourne, J. (1986). The child as sex object: Images of children in the media. In M. Nelson & K. Clark (Eds.), *The educator's guide to preventing child sexual abuse* (pp. 40–46). Santa Cruz, CA: Network Publications.

Krahn, D. D. (1991). Relationship of eating disorders and substance abuse. *Journal of Substance Abuse, 3*, 239–253.

Martin, K. A. (1998). Becoming a gendered body: Practices of preschools. *American Sociological Review, 63*, 494–511.

McCarthy, C. (1990, November 11). In thingdom, laying waste our powers. *The Washington Post*, p. F3.

Mead, M. (1977). Untitled speech given at Richdale Community College, Richdale, TX.

Meltz, B. (1997, November 13). Decoding preschoolers' sexualized behavior. *Boston Globe*, pp. F1, F4.

Mosher, J. F. (1997). The emergence of an alcohol policy reform agenda in the United States: A Don Cahalan legacy. *Drugs and Society, 11*, 74–91.

Nelson, J. (1997, July/August). Accepting rage. *Ms.*, pp. 92–95.

Overlan, L. (1996, July 2). "Overweight" girls at risk. *Newton Tab*, p. 15.

Pipher, M. (1994). *Reviving Ophelia: Saving the selves of adolescent girls*. New York: G.P. Putnam's.

Reed, B. G. (1991). Linkages: Battering, sexual assault, incest, child sexual abuse, teen pregnancy, dropping out of school and the alcohol and drug connection. In P. Roth (Ed.), *Alcohol and drugs are women's issues* (pp. 130–149). Metuchen, NJ: Scarecrow Press.

Richins, M. L. (1991). Social comparison and idealized images of advertising. *Journal of Consumer Research, 18*, 71–83.

Roan, S. (1993, June 8). Painting a bleak picture for teen girls. *Los Angeles Times*, p. 28.

Rodriguez, C. (1998, November 27). Even in middle school, girls are thinking thin. *Boston Globe*, pp. B1, B9.

Rothblum, E. D. (1994). "I'll die for the revolution but don't ask me not to diet": Feminism and the continuing stigmatization of obesity. In P. Fallon, M. A. Katzman, & S. C. Wooley (Eds.), *Feminist perspectives on eating disorders* (pp. 53–76). New York: Guilford Press.

Sadker, M., & Sadker, D. (1994). *Failing at fairness: How our schools cheat girls*. New York: Simon & Schuster.

Seiter, E. (1993). *Sold separately: Children and parents in consumer culture*. Winchester, MA: Unwin Hyman.

Smith, K. A., Fairburn, C. G., & Cowen, P. J. (1999). Symptomatic relapse in bulimia nervosa following acute tryptophan depletion. *Journal of the American Medical Association, 56*, 171–176.

Stein, J. (1986, October 29). Why girls as young as 9 fear fat and go on diets to lose weight. *Los Angeles Times*, pp. 1, 10.

Steiner-Adair, C. (1986). The body politic: Normal female adolescent development and the development of eating disorders. *Journal of the American Academy of Psychoanalysis, 14*, 95–114.

Steiner-Adair, C., & Purcell, A. (1996). Approaches to mainstreaming eating disorders prevention. *Eating Disorders, 4*, 294–309.

Strasburger, V. C. (1989). Adolescent sexuality and the media. *Pediatric Clinics of North America, 36*, 747–773.

Sullum, J. (1997, May 23). Victims of everything. *New York Times*, p. A31.

Then, D. (1992, August). *Women's magazines: Messages they convey about looks, men and careers*. Paper presented at the 100th Annual Convention of the American Psychological Association, Washington, DC.

Thompson, B. W. (1994). *A hunger so wide and so deep*. Minneapolis: University of Minnesota Press.

Twitchell, J. B. (1996). *Adcult USA: The triumph of advertising in American culture*. New York: Columbia University Press.

Vobejda, B., & Perlstein, L. (1998, June 17). Girls closing gap with boys, but not always for the best. *Boston Globe*, p. A3.

AUTHOR INDEX

Numbers in italics refer to listings in the reference section.

SUBJECT INDEX

three-way causation of, 183
See also Eating disorders
Burger King, children's advertising by, 213
Bush, George W., 137
Business leaders, transcendent goals of, 94
Buying, compulsive. *See* Compulsive buying
Buying motive, 174

Cable shopping channels, 111
See also Internet buying
Campaign finance, and tax laws, 80
Campbell, Joseph, 136–137
Capital, psychological, 95–96
Capitalist economic system
and advertising, 17–18
consumption needed by, 3, 12
and family structure, 18
and human nature, 139, 141
and isolated sense of autonomy, 114
See also Corporate culture;
Corporations; at Marketing
Carbon dioxide
atmospheric concentration of, 71
and deforestation, 72
Cartesian view of mind, 96
Caspian Sea oil, 72
Cat on a Hot Tin Roof (Williams), 135
Charlie's Angels (television show), 255
Child development
advertising effect on, 57
and commercialism influences, 233–235
and culture of consumption, 233
and marketing to children, 217–220
Children, marketing to. *See* Marketing to
children
Children's Advertising Review Unit
(CARU), 227
Children's Television Act (1990), 222
Chödrön, Pema, 109, 117
Chouinard, Yvon, 94
Christianity, vs. Roman Empire, 104
Classical conditioning, in advertising, 112,
114
Clean water, 73–74
Clients, wealthy, 165, 189–209
Climate change, from overconsumption, 71
Clinical practice
and materialistic value orientation,
23–24
payment in, 158
See also Psychologists; Therapists

Clinical psychology, commercial encroach-
ment on, 60
Cognitive approach, to consumption
behavior, 81–82
Cognitive–behavioral therapy, as short-term,
60
Cognitive narrowing
in compulsive buyers, 180–181, 182
research needed on, 182–183
Cognitive patterns, in acquisitive desire,
161
Cognitive perspectives, and materialistic
value orientation, 22–23
Colleges. *See* Education, higher
Commercial encroachment, 58
See also Corporate culture
Commercial gaze, 57–58
Commercialism influences, 233–235, 267
and Black youth, 243–246
(*See also* Dress-related challenges
to Black youth)
and needed research, 244
and youth fashion industry, 236–237
See also Marketing to children
Commitment to changing acquisitive
desire, 161–162
Commodification, 58
of clinical psychology, 60
of higher education, 58–60
of university classes, 60
of public services, 61
of women's bodies, 254
Communist economic organization, on
human nature, 140, 141
Community, and consumer mentality, 118
Comparative advantage, 51
Compassionate action, and consumerism,
118
Competence
as basic need, 14
and materialistic value orientation, 20
Competition
and feeling of special value, 138
globalists' belief in, 52
Compulsive buying (shopping), 154, 162,
164, 170–172
biopsychosocial model of, 183
in embezzlement court trial, 169–170
and escape theory, 170, 177–182, 183
history of, 172–173
as impulse control disorder, 170, 172,
173–175

and irrational beliefs, 182
literature on, 172
motivations behind, 175–177
question of increase in, 173
research needed on, 182–184
selected definitions of, 171
Compulsive gambling, 154
Compulsive hoarding, 155
Compulsive shopping. *See* Compulsive buying
Conditioning, in advertising, 112–113, 114
Connectedness with others
and mindfulness, 117–118
need for, 267
See also Relationships
Consciousness
and mindfulness vs. mindlessness, 110
(*See also* Mindfulness)
and transcendent goals, 93–94
Conspicuous consumption 70, 128
and terror management, 128, 134–139
Consumer behavior
automaticity in, 107, 108, 110
and compulsive buyer, 176
and mindfulness, 115–117, 121
as filling experiential vacuum, 101–102
and mindfulness, 121
of poor Black youth, 243
Consumer choices
nonconscious, 110–113
See also Product choices
Consumer Credit Counseling Service, 164
Consumer culture. *See* Culture of consumption
Consumerism
and capitalist economy, 3
and corporations, 49–50
educational interventions on, 119–120
and happiness, 83
and mindfulness, 107–108, 109, 115–118
nascent development of study of, 6
and need for fulfillment, 113–115
and mindfulness, 108, 109, 117–118
nonconscious choices in, 110–113
and psychology, 7, 49
research on, 121
teaching children about, 226, 227
Consumer psychology, 153
and child development, 6, 217
Consumption
and acquisitive desire, 152
(*See also* Acquisitive desire)
by all living things, 127

Arendt on danger of, 103, 104
conspicuous, 70, 128, 134–139
current dominance of, 11
culture of, 3–4, 12
(*See also* Culture of consumption)
vs. flow, 103
greedy extravagance in, 128–129
as human preoccupation, 127–128
industrialized world's increase in, 70
life-sustaining, 130
motivations behind, 113
and profit, 3
psychological value of, 192
and psychology, 70, 76, 82–83
absence of in psychological study,
4–5
behavioral approaches, 79–80
cognitive approach, 81–82
neo-analytic (depth) approaches,
76–78
social psychological approaches,
80–81
and self-interest vs. community identification, 143n
See also Consumerism; Materialism;
Materialistic value orientation
Consumption tax, 80
Contingency management, 79
Contingent worth, 102
"Control," and advertising for children, 218
Coping mechanisms, materialist, 102
Corporate culture
and advertising, 56–58
(*See also* Advertising)
alternatives to, 62
in clinical psychology, 60
and freedom, 50, 61–62
greed sanctioned by, 62–63
and higher education, 58–60
institutionalized, 61–62
internalized, 62
and marketing to children, 223, 226
(*See also* Marketing to children)
in poor cultures, 54
work and family affected by, 55–56
Corporations
and consumerism, 49–50
power and influence of, 50
Cortese, Anthony, 264
Counterculture of 1960s, 81
Countertransference, in acquisitive-desire
cases, 151, 164–166

widespread presence of, 253–254
See also Bulimia
Ecological self, 78
Economic behavior, life-enhancing vs. death-denying aspects of, 139
Economic deprivation, and materialism, 15
Economic development, and happiness, 45–46
Economic globalization, 51
See also Globalization
Economic growth, cultural belief in, 24
Economic organization
and humane marketplace, 141–144
and views of human nature, 139–141
Economics, environmental factors as province of, 4
Ecotherapy, 78
Education, higher
commercial encroachment on, 58–60
globalization of considered by WTO, 51
and resource costs, 77
Education, use of grades in, 24
Educational interventions, 118–120, 121
Egyptian pharaohs, as denying death, 138, 141
Electronic media
and marketing to children, 214
See also Media; Television
Emily (case example), 204–205
Emotional distancing, from environmental problems, 77
Emotional Intelligence (Goleman), 118n
Empathy, and materialistic values, 20
Enabling, of addictive behaviors, 160–161
Engendered Lives (Kaschak), 57
Enjoyment
failure to find, 117–118
as flow, 99–100
vs. materialism 103–104
vs. pleasure, 97–98
substitutes for, 99
See also Happiness; Subjective well-being
Entitlement, narcissistic sense of, 157
Environment (cultural)
advertising as, 251
need to change, 267
Environmental concerns
and Arendt on consumption, 103, 104
climate change, 72
deforestation, 72
distancing from, 77
and globalization, 52
and human behavior, 76
and information presentation, 82

loss of soil and agricultural land, 74–75
and materialistic value orientation, 22
and mindfulness, 116
and psychologists' role, 24
and voluntary simplicity movement, 81, 104
water, 73–74
and world's consumption level, 130
Environmental factors (psychological), and mainstream psychology, 4
Envy
toward acquisitive-desire clients, 164–165
toward wealthy people, 208
Erikson, Erik, 194, 218, 219, 220
Escape from Evil (Becker), 130
Escape theory, 177
and compulsive buying, 170, 177–182, 183
Ethics
and Black celebrities, 241
of marketing to children, 4, 223–224, 225
Ethnographic marketing strategies, 240, 243
Ethyl Corporation, 53
Eudaimonia, 19–20
See also Happiness; Quality of experience or life; Subjective well-being; Well-being of clients
European Union
and limits on children's advertising, 219
Maastricht Agreement of, 52
Evangelical Christians, and greed as Godly, 129
Evolution
and materialism, 16, 31
and transcendent goals, 93–94
Existential identity problems, 155–156
Existential insecurity, 30
Existential thought, 13
Existential vacuum, 101
Experience(s)
life as, 92
material, 92, 100–101
Experiential sampling method, 98
teenagers' reports, 101
See also Mood surveys
Exposure, in advertising, 111–112
Exxon-Valdez oil spill, 82

of higher education, 51
as possible sharing of noncommercial treasures, 63
Global warming, 71, 72, 77
Goals
material, 93
transcendent, 93–95
God, as metamorphosized into money, 137
Goffman, Erving, 260, 261
Gold, value of, 136
Golden Marble Awards, 223
Goldstein, Joseph, 115
Goodman, Ellen, 257
Good Work project, 91
Greed
in American consumption, 128–129
vs. generosity, 62–63
and mortality salience, 138
narcissistic, 157
prevalence of, 129
seen as Godly, 129
See also Conspicuous consumption; Overconsumption
"Green labels," 82
Greenwald, Gerald, 96
Guilt
in acquisitive desire, 162
over wealth, 193, 197, 202, 207, 208–209

Halfway, Ore., name changed by, 58
Happiness
and consumerism, 83
and energy consumption, 103
and market, 252
and material well-being, 24, 102–103
pursuit of, 104
and socioeconomic level, 102
and winning lottery, 102
and wealth, 129, 191
See also Quality of experience or life; Subjective well-being; Well-being of clients
Hazardous waste, 73
Health insurance, national, 143
Heirs, wealthy, 192–193, 202, 206, 207
See also Wealth identity
Hewlett, Sylvia Ann, 268
Higher education. *See* Education, higher
Hip-hop culture, marketing of, 239–240
HMOs, 60
Hochschild, Arlie, 55, 56

Hollingworth, H. L., 5
Homes in U.S., increased size of, 70
Horatio Alger story 139–140
Hues magazine, 264
Hughes, Howard, 197, 204
Humanistic theories, 13
and materialistic value orientation, 22
Human marketplace, 141–144
Human nature, self-interest and cooperation in, 139–141

Iceland, hydrogen-based economy for, 75
Identity
advertising effect on, 57
of newly affluent, 193
Identity problem, 155–156
Ideology of immortality, 137–138
Implicit Association Task (IAT), 33–34, 35
Impulse buying, 175–176
Impulse-control disorder, 153–154
compulsive buying as, 170, 172, 173–175
Indigenous cultures, money and possessions in, 134
Individualism
false sense of, 113
mythic value of, 143
Industrialization, and destructive behavior, 70–71, 77
Industrialized world
need for fulfillment in, 107
overconsumption in, 70, 80
Industrial revolution, and isolated sense of autonomy, 114
Inequality, in distribution of world's wealth, 129–130
Information processing, peripheral, 116
Inner emptiness, and consumerism, 114
Insecurity
as clinical issue, 23
and materialistic value orientation, 13, 14–16
and behavioral or cognitive perspective, 23
and concreteness of materialistic goals, 30
and messages about acquisitiveness, 17–18
Insecurity, job, 56
Insight (mindfulness) meditation, 108–109
Institutionalized corporate culture, 61–62

First (results due to measurement), 29–30, 31–35
Second (materialistic goals more distant), 30, 35–39
Third (unhappy people become materialistic), 30, 39–40
Fourth (unhappiness from thinking materialistically), 30, 41–42
Fifth (incompatibility of materialistic with other goals), 31, 42–44
Sixth (materialistic goals less enjoyable to pursue), 31, 44–45
research needed on, 46
measurement of, 29
and modern consumerism, 49
as open-ended motive, 39
research on discouraged, 5
vs. transcendent goals, 93–95
Materialistic value orientation (MVO), 13
clinical examination of, 23–24
as filling experiential vacuum, 101–102
inculcation of, 13
through exposure to materialistic models or values, 16–17
and insecurity, 13, 14–16, 23, 30
and insecurity combined with exposure to materialistic values 17–18
and psychological theories, 22–23
psychology as counteracting, 24
and subjective well-being, 19–20, 29
and autonomy, 21
and competence, 20
and relatedness, 20–21
and welfare of society, 21–22
See also Consumerism; Consumption; Culture of consumption; Shopping
Material Values Survey, 29, 43
Material well-being, and happiness, 24, 102–103
Maxine (case example), 207
McLuhan, Marshall, 101
Mead, Margaret, 252
Media
children brought up by (Mead), 252
consumerist messages from, 12, 16
corporate ownership of, 50
and dress-related challenges to Black youth, 238–241, 242
and income disparities, 18
and marketing to children (electronic media), 214

monitoring children's use of, 226
as sex education, 261–263
violence for children in, 221
See also Advertising; Television
Media literacy, need to teach to children, 226, 267
Meditation, mindfulness (insight), 108–109
Melanesia, money and possessions in, 134–135
Men in Black (movie), 215, 222
Mental health impact, criteria for, 158
Mergers and acquisitions, 56
Methanex, 53
Mighty Morphin Power Rangers, 215
Mind, hoarding and expending impulses of, 96–97
Mindfulness, 78, 108–109
Chödrön on, 117
and consumerism, 107–108, 109, 115–118
educational interventions for, 118–120
empirical agenda for training in, 120–121
enhancing of, 120
and need for fulfillment, 108, 109, 117–118
Mindfulness Based Stress Reduction (MBSR), 120
Mindfulness meditation, 108–109
Mindlessness, 110–111
and consumption, 111
MMT (gas additive), 53
Modeling, materialistic value orientation developed through, 13
Models, materialist, 16–17
and insecurity, 17–18
Money
as fetishist object, 35
vs. personal element, 113
and priesthood, 136
in tribal cultures, 134–135
in Western civilization, 135–137
See also Wealth; Wealth identity
Money, Meaning & Choices Institute, 190, 195, 200n, 208
Money-motive, Keynes on, 142
Mood states, 30
Mood surveys, 34, 43, 44, 176
Mortality, human awareness of, 128
Mortality salience, 30, 132–133
and desires to stick out and fit in, 140
and greedy overconsumption, 138–139
and materialistic values, 39

Racism
    commercialism influences exacerbated
        by, 234
    compared with present attitudes
        toward corporate culture, 62
    eating disorders from, 257
Randall (case example), 200
Rank, Otto, 131, 140
Rebellion and resistance, by adolescent
        girls, 264–266
Recycled paper, 73
Relatedness
    as basic need, 14
    and materialistic value orientation, 20
Relationships
    among adolescent girls, 264
    family, 268
    happiness from, 83
    materialistic acquisition as conflicting
        with, 42, 43–44, 46
    need for, 267–268
    and sex in media, 262
    trust in (wealth identity), 204–205
    and women's quest for independence,
        259
Religion
    and advertising's promise of happiness,
        226
    and individual followers, 12
    transcendent goals of, 93
    and wealth identity, 195
Research
    on acquisitive-desire disorders,
        152–154
    and commercial encroachment on
        universities, 59–60
    on consumerism or capitalism discour-
        aged, 5
    on marketing to children, 227
    need for, 6
        on Black youth as consumers, 244,
        245
        on compulsive buying, 182–183
        on consumerism, 121
        on materialism and SWB, 46
        on mindfulness training, 120–121
Rock concerts, commercial encroachment
        on, 58
Rockefeller family, 206
Roheim, Geza, 134
Roman Empire, and Christianity, 104

Ronald (case example), 149–151
Rugrats (TV program), 222

Saatchi and Saatchi, 225
Sahlins, Marshall, 93
Sally (case example), 196–197
Sam (case example), 203
Sandra (case example), 205
Sandy (case example), 207
Satisfaction With Life Scale (SWLS), 32,
        38, 43
Schools, corporate advertising in, 217
Scott, Walter Dill, 5
Seattle meeting of WTO (1999), 51
Security, in wealth identity, 201–202
Self
    continual development of, 193
    ecological, 78
    as empty (Cushman), 113–114
Self-awareness, 131
    negative (aversive), 177, 178
        in compulsive buyers, 178–179, 183
Self-control, and compulsive buying, 170
Self-esteem
    anxiety-buffering function of, 132
    of compulsive buyers, 179
    and materialistic value orientation,
        19, 20
    and socioeconomic level, 102
    in wealth identity, 201–202
Self-esteem striving, and mortality salience,
        133
Self-image, and thinner body, 255
Self-interest
    on capitalist view, 139
    in communist view, 140
    in human marketplace, 143
    and Smith on human nature, 142–143
Self-medication
    acquisitive desire as, 152
    compulsive buying as, 169
Self-reports, 33
SEL (socio-emotional learning) movement,
        118, 118n, 121
September 11 terrorist attacks
    economic effects of, 69
    shopping as response to, 102, 137
    symbols destroyed in, 137–138
Seventeen magazine, 254, 261
Sex differences. See Gender differences

Sex education, media as, 261–263
Sexism
    compared with present attitudes
        toward corporate culture, 62
    eating disorders from, 257
    institutionalized, 61
Shame, in acquisitive desire, 162
Shamni, Sheik Abdulla, 134
Sheehy, Gail, 194
Shell Oil, 75
Shopping
    compulsive, 162, 164
        (*See also* Compulsive buying)
    as filling experiential vacuum,
        101–102
    as response to terrorism, 137
Shopping addiction, Fiona Murray's
        account of, 160
Silence, as encouraged for women,
        259–260
Simmel, Georg, 113
Simplicity movement, 81, 104
Skinner, B. F., 79
Smith, Adam, 142–143
Social capital, 96
Social comparison
    and materialism, 17, 18, 20
    and overconsumption, 80–81
Socialization, materialistic value orienta-
        tion developed through, 13
Social models, and materialistic value ori-
        entation, 13
Social policy and social criticism, psychol-
        ogy's ambivalent attitude
        toward, 5
Social psychological approaches, to con-
        sumption behavior, 80–81
Social relationships
    and happiness, 31
    See also Relationshps
Societal welfare. *See* Welfare of society
Socioeconomic status
    of Black youth consumers, 241–242
    See also Poverty
Socio-emotional learning (SEL) move-
        ment, 118, 118n, 121
Sociology, environmental factors as
        province of, 4
Soil, loss of, 74–75
Spider-Man (movie), 214, 215, 216, 222
Spy Kids (movie), 216

Steiner-Adair, Catherine, 259
Stereotypes, from advertising, 57
Stewardship, in wealth identity, 199–200,
        205–206
Stimulus control management, 79
Stress, corporate sources of, 56
Strong, E. K., Jr., 5
Structural Adjustment Programs (SAPs),
        54
Structure, as replacement for acquisitive
        desire, 163
Students
    corporate perspective of, 59
    and counterculture, 81
    materialistic goals distant for, 35–38
Subjective well-being (SWB)
    and economic development, 45–46
    and materialism (materialistic value
        orientation), 19–20, 29
        and autonomy, 21
        and competence, 20
        and relatedness, 20–21
    materialism-SWB relationship
        hypotheses
        First (results due to measurement),
            29–30, 31–35
        Second (materialistic goals more
            distant), 30, 35–39
        Third (unhappy people become
            materialistic), 30, 39–40
        Fourth (unhappiness from thinking
            materialistically), 30, 41–42
        Fifth (incompatibility of materialistic
            with other goals), 31, 42–44
        Sixth (materialistic goals less
            enjoyable to pursue), 31, 44–45
        research needed on, 46
    in wealthier vs. poorer nations,
        114–115
    See also Happiness; Quality of experi-
        ence or life; Well-being of clients
"Sudden loss of wealth" sector, 197
Sudden wealth syndrome, 190
Support system, for acquisitive-desire prob-
        lems, 164
Susan and Roger (case example), 161
Sustainability, 76
    and approaches to overconsumption,
        76–82
    need for, 70
    reduced spending conductive to, 69

and world indicators of unsustainable consumption, 70–71, 75–76
and clean water, 73–74
climate change and pollution, 71–72
deforestation, 72–73
loss of soil and agricultural land, 74–75
Suzanne (case example), 162
SWB. *See* Subjective well-being
SWLS (Satisfaction With Life Scale), 32, 38, 43
Sylvia (case example), 190

Tax, consumption 80
Teaching presence, 119
Technology, for conservation of resources, 104
Technology transfer, from universities to commercial sector, 59
Teenage Mutant Ninja Turtles (TV show and film), 215
Teenagers. *See* Adolescents
Teen Voices, 264
Teletubbies, 216
Television
advertisements on, 16
(*See also* Advertising)
and Black youth, 238
and Fiji eating disorders, 257
impossible materialistic ideals from, 30
marketing to children on, 215–216
number of children's commercials, 214
monitoring children's use of, 226
and obesity in children, 222
as sex education, 262–263
See also Media
Television watching
children's time spent in, 214
and materialism, 17
passivity of, 101
Templeton Foundation, 91
Terkel, Studs, 98
Terror, purchasing as response to, 102
Terrorist attacks of September 11. *See* September 11 terrorist attacks
Terror management theory, 130–134
and conspicuous consumption, 128, 134–139
and desires to stick out and fit in, 140
and mortality salience, 30

"That's-Not-All technique, 115–116
Theory of life, 92
Therapeutic countertransference. *See* Countertransference
Therapeutic relationship, in acquisitive-desire treatment, 159
Therapists
acquisition desires in lives of, 152, 167
and countertransference toward acquisitive-desire clients, 164–166
as possessions, 166
See also Clinical practice; Psychologists
Thinness
adolescent girls' obsession with, 255–257, 258
and fear of female power, 258
Time Bind (Hochschild), 55
Tobacco lawsuits settlements, as analogy, 75
Tommy Hilfiger corporation, 236, 240
Trade agreements, international, 52, 53, 54
Tragedy of the commons, 79
Transcendent goals, 93–95
"Trust babies," 207
Trust in relationships
children's development of, 218
in wealth identity, 204–205
Tween Power conference, 223
Tweens, 216, 216n
12-Step programs, for acquisitive-desire problems, 164
Twin ontological motives, 140

Ulysses (Joyce), 131
Uniqueness, need for, 153
Universities. *See* Education, higher
Unsustainable consumption, world indicators of, 70–71, 75–76
and clean water, 73–74
climate change and pollution, 71–72
deforestation, 72–73
loss of soil and agricultural land, 74–75
See also Sustainability
Urbanization, and destructive behavior, 77
U.S. Forest Service, and viewsheds, 82
U.S. Government, and nuclear waste information, 77

Values
    intrinsic, 23–24
    materialist, 16
Van Vugt, M., 143n
Viewsheds, 82
Violence
    in child marketing, 220–221
    in children's TV, 215
Vipassana meditation practice, 108
Viral marketing, 217
Void, from elimination of acquisitive
        desire, 162–163
Voluntary simplicity movement, 81, 104
See also Simplicity movement

Waldorf schools, 119
Water, clean, 73–74
Watson, John B., 5
Wealth
    as distant goal, 35
    distribution of, 129–130, 191
    growth of in U.S., 190
    and happiness, 191
    questions and difficulties from acquisi-
        tion of, 190, 191–194, 208–209
Wealth identity, 191
    case examples of
        Chinese family, 200
        Emily, 204–205
        Gary, 205–206
        Jack, 201–202
        John, 189–190
        Ken and Helen Jones, 204
        Maxine, 207
        Randall, 200
        Sally, 196–197
        Sam, 203
        Sandra, 205
        Sandy, 207
        Sylvia, 190
    counseling and consultation for,
        207–208
    developmental stages of, 194–196
        First (Honeymoon), 196–197
        Second (Wealth Acceptance),
            197–198
        Third (Identity Consolidation),
            198–199
        Fourth (Achieving Balance),
            199–200, 209
    positive elements in, 201

financial awareness, 206–207
    lifestyle, 202–204
    self-esteem and personal security,
        201–202
    stewardship, 205–206
    trust in relationships, 204–205
    See also Conspicuous consumption
Wealth and Life Planning System, 200n, 208
Wealth of Nations, The (Smith), 142
Wealthy clients, envy and jealousy toward,
        165
Web sites for girls, 264
    See also Internet
Weightism, 256, 257
Welfare of society, 21–22
Well-being of clients
    and basic value orientation, 23–24
    See also Happiness; Quality of experi-
        ence or life; Subjective well-being
West, Cornel, 268
Western civilization, money and posses-
        sions in, 135–137
What Kids Buy and Why: The Psychology
        of Marketing to Kids (Acuff and
        Reiher), 219
Williams, Don, 94
Williams, Tennessee, 135
Wilson, E. O., 78
Women's power, fear of, 257–261
Word-of-mouth marketing, 217
Work, and corporate culture, 55–56
Workers, greedy exploitation of, 129
Working alliance, and resentment toward
        client (example), 166
World Bank, 52, 54
World Scientists' Warning to Humanity, 75
World Trade Organization (WTO), 52, 53
    and globalization of higher education,
        51
Worldview(s)
    cultural
        and mortality salience, 133
        as terror management, 131–132
    culture of consumption as, 12–13

Youth
    as consumer market, 235–237
    counterculture students of 1960s, 81
    See also Adolescents; Black youth;
        Girls, adolescent; Marketing to
        children

ABOUT THE EDITORS

Tim Kasser, PhD, graduated from Vanderbilt University, summa cum laude with honors in psychology, and later received his PhD in psychology from the University of Rochester, Rochester, New York. In 1995 he accepted a position at Knox College in Galesburg, Illinois, where he is currently an associate professor of psychology. He has authored over 35 scientific articles and book chapters on materialism, values, and goals, among other topics. His first book, *The High Price of Materialism*, was published in 2002. Tim lives with his wife, two sons, and assorted animals in the Western Illinois countryside.

Allen D. Kanner, PhD, received his undergraduate and graduate psychology degrees from the University of California, Berkeley, and was a postdoctoral fellow in clinical child psychology at McLean Hospital, Harvard Medical School. Early in his career he developed both the adult and the children's Hassles and Uplifts Scales and was on staff at Children's Hospital at Stanford University. In the last decade, he has helped establish the field of ecopsychology, within which he has focused on consumerism, ecofeminism, society's narcissistic relationship with nature, and extinction. Until recently, he was an associate faculty member at the Wright Institute and now teaches at the Saybrook Graduate School and Research Center. He is in private practice in Berkeley and Sebastopol, California and is coeditor of *Ecopsychology: Restoring the Earth, Healing the Mind*. Allen lives with his partner, Mary Gomes, PhD, in Sebastopol, California.